If you wish to contact the author: email ispurr@yahoo.co.uk

Introduction

Through reading this book you will become funnier, and I mean that in a nice way, Funny—ha ha! and not Funny peculiar. This increased funniness will come as a result of learning the many secrets of being humorous, which I've discovered through reading what comedians say about their craft, studying what researchers have found, and coming up with my own ideas.

Your jokes will become juicier, your twitters wittier, and your banter, better. Not only that, your humour will fail less. They'll be fewer groans and moans from your nearest and dearest. What's not to like?

The funnier you become, the more likely it is that people will like you more and seek out your company. Funniness greases the wheels of human interaction. We need it everywhere. Most obviously, great humour is vital in the dating game, but not just there, job ads often specify humour as a useful attribute. To get on at work you need good humour. Good friendship and happy families usually depend on shared humour.

This book is for anyone who has a reasonable sense of humour but would like to improve it. It is based on the belief that humour is a skill that can be developed. A skill is a practised ability, so the book contains plenty of activities aimed at the initiation and development of your humour skills.

Fundamentally, humour is surprise...surprise...surprise. A punch-line is a surprise. A practical joke is a surprise. Slapstick is a surprise. A joker, then, has the surprising ability to see something ordinary, turn the tables, and produce a prized result. This ability can be learnt.

Good humour is not just surprise. It's about appropriate surprise. That's why most of us don't tell dirty jokes to our parents, or put cling film on their toilets. It's just not appropriate, but of course, we may well tell dodgy jokes to our friends, and generally take the piss--different folks need different jokes.

This book explains the many methods that can be used to produce funny surprises. The easiest way is just to copy a successful joke and modify it, what I call a cue joke, but you can be much more original, and make use of the creative techniques that have been developed by psychologists and business gurus. These creative techniques are explained early on, and related to the improvement of chat-up lines in the first instance.

Jokes and their creation are part of this book, but only a part. In real life we don't go around telling each other pre-prepared jokes much, rather, we do spur of the moment stuff. As Kate Fox says:

'In English conversation, there is always an undercurrent of humour. We can barely manage to say 'hello' or comment on the weather without somehow contriving to make a bit of a joke out of it, and most English conversations will involve at least some degree of banter, teasing, irony, understatement, self-denigration, mockery or just silliness.'

So, all those areas are covered, and there's more besides. In particular, groups and the way their humour works, come under fairly close scrutiny. I concentrate on the groups we come across at work, because that's where most of our humour takes place.

Contents

Part 1: Creativity, and your sense of humour

In this first part of the book I start by looking at chat-up lines. It soon becomes obvious that they are pretty grim affairs, which are rather insulting to the person being chatted-up. Few are funny, most are corny, and many are very sexual, which, for the most part, women do not want to hear.

So, the search is on for how to improve the chat-up line. To do this I move on to look at creativity and the invention of difference. After considering the nature of creativity, I look at the various techniques that are used to help people become more creative. Ideas like brain-storming and lateral thinking are explained, as well as some techniques borrowed from industry, which are used to develop new products.

Then, before applying these techniques to chat-up lines, I look quite closely at what the audience wants from a chat-up line. Women do want humour, but want it to be original and not out of a package. What they really want is a chance to assess the character of the chatter-upperer.

Now that the audience is understood (well, sort of), I use the creativity techniques, already explained, to develop new chat-up lines. The hope is that any young men reading this book can use these techniques to develop their own lines. For the women reading this book, why don't you develop some chat-up lines of your own? Or, develop some effective ripostes to repel the unwanted. For those of you who are un-young, there is always hope.

This leads on to a consideration of male and female humour and how it differs. The chat-up line sections raise the issue of this difference, and this section confirms, essentially, that male humour is destructive whilst female humour is constructive.

This first part concludes with a look at how our personality is reflected in the humour we like and use. If you are more outward going, you probably like Michael McIntyre and his positive, affiliative humour, whilst if you're more aggressive in nature, the negativity of Frankie Boyle is much more likely to turn you on.

If you want people to like and trust you, you should use positive humour as you pose no threat, build rapport, amuse, and support others. If you stick to the negative stuff, people will be suspicious, wary, and might well reckon that there is a troubled mind beneath.

Chat-up lines   *'Do you come here often?'*

Let's start with something which should be funny, but often isn't: the chat-up line. There are:

- The corny:

'I bet your last name is Jacobs...because you're a real cracker.'

'Baby you remind me of a parking ticket. You've got fine written all over you.'

'Are you Swedish? Cuz you're the Sweedish girl in the room.'

'If I told you that you had a beautiful body, would you hold it against me?'

- The crude:

'There are 206 bones in the human body. Would you like another one?'

'Wanna play Titanic?' 'Yeah' 'When I say iceberg, you go down.'

'I'm like quick drying cement. After I've been laid it doesn't take long for me to get hard.'

- The tricky:

'I'm invisible, can you see me?' 'Yes' 'How about tomorrow night?'

'Let's shag.' 'No' 'I think there has been some misunderstanding. What do you think I said?' 'Let's shag.' 'OK.'

- The word plays:

'Hi, I'm dyslexic, cook my sock'

'Hi, I'm a dyslexic Mexican. Grab your taco, you've pulled.'

- The witty:

'Do you mind if I end this sentence in a proposition.'

- The insulting:

'Normally I'm not into bestiality, but I'll make an exception in your case.'

'Don't worry, I go more for personality than looks.'

'I've had quite a lot to drink and you're beginning to look pretty good.'

- The romantic:

'Do you have a map? Because I keep getting lost in your eyes.

'I'm not drunk, I'm just intoxicated by you.'

- The boastful:

'Are you religious?' 'Yes' 'Good, because I'm the answer to your prayers.'

'Two words...' Eight inches.'

'I'm a great shag. Ask that girl over there.'

- The self-disparaging:

'Come back to mine and I'll give you the best five seconds of your life.'

'You know, it's not the length of the vector that counts. It's how you apply the force.'

- The disgusting:

'If you were a bogey I'd pick you.'

'I'm an astronaut and my next mission is to explore Uranus.'

- The chat-up line mocker:

'I advise you to surrender immediately, or I'll have to use a pick up line.'

'Hi, I suffer from amnesia. Do I come here often?'

- The poetic:

'Roses are red

Pickles are green

I like your legs,

And what's in between!'

- The vengeful:

'Do you wanna come dance with the big bad wolf?'   'No'   'That's okay, the other two pigs said no as well.'

'Excuse me would you like to dance?'   'No'   'Maybe you didn't hear me...I said you look really fat in those pants.'

- The riposte:

'So, what do you do for a living?'

'I'm a female impersonator.'

'I know how to please a woman.'
'Then please leave me alone.'

'Wanna hear a joke about my cock? Never mind, it's too long.'

'Wanna hear a joke about my pussy? Oh wait, you'll never get it.'

- The beauty appraiser:

'You're so beautiful you made me forget my pick-up line.'

'I have a joke that will make you the hottest babe that's ever walked the planet. Oh wait, I see you've already heard it.'

There are thousands of chat-up lines. They obviously come in all shapes and sizes. I had a closer look at 370 of them, taken from the internet, and found that 40% contained some sexual element, whilst 17% praised the beauty/hotness of the target.
If we look more closely at the humour which is used, we find quite a range. The sound pun is the most popular, as it is contained in about 13% of the chat-up lines.
Some examples:
'If I had a garden I'd put your two lips and my two lips together.'
'If you were a chicken you'd be impeccable.'
'Hey baby, there's a party in my pants, and urine...vited.'
Yes, pretty corny.

Punch lines based on idioms crop up now and again:

'Hey that dress looks nice. Can I talk you out of it?'

'The word of the day is 'legs'. Let's go back to my place and spread the word.'

'How do you get a fat bird into bed?' 'Piece of cake'

'You smell like trash, may I take you out?'

The one-liner, unrelated to the situation is very rare. I guess this one qualifies:

'I have a dirty weekend planned. Do you know what I'm going to do? Three loads of laundry.'

Riddles are pretty unusual, which is surprising as they can be fun and they do get attention. Here are a couple that stand out:

'What's the difference between a boner and a Lamborghini?' 'I don't know, what is the difference between a boner and a Lamborghini?' 'I don't have a Lamborghini right now.'

'What did the hurricane say to the coconut palm tree?' 'I don't know' 'Hold on to your nuts, this is no ordinary blow job.'

There are a few which have a practical element, but are not practical jokes as there is no real victim who is made to look foolish:

'You know what material this is? (Grab your shirt) Boyfriend material'
Crush some ice... Now that the ice is broken, what's your name?
Take a screw out of your pocket, put it in front of a girl and say, 'hey look at that, wanna screw?'
Lick finger and wipe on the girl's/guy's shirt, 'Right, let's get you out of those wet clothes.'

Knock-knock jokes are virtually non-existent. I did find this pathetic attempt, 'Knock Knock' 'Who's there?' 'Me wondering why you're not naked.'

The poetic form is invariably a play on 'Roses are red, etc., but there are other types, e.g. 'I will give you a nickel to tickle my pickle.' The limerick never seems to be used.
The roses are red poems usually muck about after the first line, but not necessarily.
'Roses are red, violets are blue. How would you like it, if I came home with you?'
Usually these poems are sexual in nature:
'Roses are red, orchids are black. I like you best, when you're flat on your back.'
'Roses are black, violets are red. What's it gonna take, to get you in bed?'

Reflection
Clearly, there are many types of chat-up line. Some are funny but mostly they are contrived, corny, crude and cheerless. There must be something better than this!!
Our job then is to invent some new, amusing chat-up lines, which respect the other person.
To do this, we need to understand what is involved in inventing new jokes. So, the next section is about creativity and the techniques that are used in order to be creative, then, after we have found out what a woman and a man actually want to hear in a chat-up line, we will start inventing new chat-up lines.

Creativity and humour

Jonathan Lynn, co-writer of *Yes Prime Minister*:

"*The question that all writers are asked is 'Where do you get your ideas from?' and usually there's no real answer. Some get ideas from the newspapers. I do. I also get them from gazing out of the window at nothing with a totally blank mind (This comes easily to me and is how I spend much of my day). Sometimes I get them when I'm out walking, or when driving. But where do they come from? I think they come from programming your brain in advance, by setting it a problem and then leaving your subconscious to mull over it without your supervision.*" (Lynn, 2011)

In this section we will be looking at creativity as this is fundamental to the production of humour. The nature of creativity will be examined as will the techniques that are used to aid creativity. These techniques will be used to produce improved and original chat-up lines.

Creative thinking, according to Alvino, is:

'*a novel way of seeing or doing things that is characterized by four components-fluency (generating many ideas), flexibility (shifting perspectives easily), originality (conceiving of something new), and elaboration (building on others ideas)*' (McCorkle et al., 2007).

Of course, it would be great to have all four elements in one person, but people may tend to prefer to be either original innovators or elaborating adapters. They may also be better at fluency than really breakthrough originators.

Graham Chapman, of *Monty Python* fame, seems to have been a real breakthrough humour originator. Here's how Jonathan Lynn describes Chapman's working relationship with John Cleese:

"*Hanging out, I watched a couple of Cleese-Chapman working sessions, which were extraordinary. John would sit at his typewriter painstakingly writing and questioning every tiny detail down to the punctuation, while Graham, who usually arrived hungover an hour or so late, would lie on the floor, read Playboy and occasionally bark at the ceiling. I asked John whether he thought it was fair that he did all the work. 'Yes', he said, 'because about once every two days Graham comes up with an idea that is so funny that it makes it all worth it.'*" (Lynn, 2011)

Original joke making, for most people, is 1% inspiration, and 99% perspiration. That is, the apparently sudden creation of an original joke depends on a lot of prior research and, indeed, failure. As an exasperated Eddie Braden, scriptwriter to Morecambe and Wise ironically put it, when he sent the two comics 40 sheets of blank paper, '*Fill these in-It's easy.*' (Sellers & Hogg, 2011)

A basic model of the creative process is: preparation, incubation, illumination, and verification. Or, more simply, in the humour case: *aaaaaaaaaaaah---ah—aha—ha ha.*

Preparation is the *aaaaaaaaaaaaah* stage, for example, slogging through existing jokes in order to find what they cover and what they avoid. Possible ideas present themselves and are often rejected as not being funny, or not being funny enough. Research is carried out into promising areas. Comedians often scour the newspapers at this stage. As the creativity guru, Paul Torrance puts it,*'...the more one knows, the better the chances of producing something creative.'* (Shaughnessy, 1998)

It's SISO, not NINO (Something In, Something Out; Nothing In, Nothing Out).

Incubation is the stage where you don't consciously think about a problem, and the unconscious mind takes over. Unconscious thought enables the brain to make connections between the masses of information lurking in the brain's memory vaults (Yang et al., 2012). You just *ah.*

Illumination is the *aha* moment when insight occurs--- Eureka! A brainwave washes up a joke. Judd Apatow considers that, *'The moment you think of a joke is the best moment.'* Edward de Bono (1990) observes that, *'It is interesting that the reaction to an insight solution is often laughter even when there is nothing funny about the solution itself.'*

Verification is seeing whether other people think the idea is funny *ha ha*, rather than funny *peculiar*. So, new jokes have to be tried out on others to see if they work. Professional comedians often do this by going on tour and testing their new material, dropping what doesn't work.

Now, you might be saying to yourself, *'This is all very well but I'm not very creative and I don't think I'd be very good at inventing new jokes.'* It's true that some people are more creative than others, but all of us have the potential to be creative. In particular, women may see joke creation as more of a male preserve, however, although the research evidence is contradictory and inconclusive, the studies which show girls and women are more creative outnumber those which find boys and men are more creative (Hill & Rogers, 2012).

Personality type has quite a bearing on creativity. If you are neurotic, extravert and/or open you are more likely to be creative. If you are agreeable and/or conscientious you are less likely to be creative (Batey et al. 2010). (These five factors have a particular meaning to psychologists. Neurotic means nervous rather than confident. Extravert means outgoing and not reserved. Open means curious and not cautious. Agreeable means friendly, not unkind, and conscientious means organised rather than easy going.)

Let's look a little closer at the creative process, and the techniques which have been developed to aid creativity.

The incubation period is the interesting one as far as creativity is concerned. Here, the conscious, logical mind has been switched off and the unconscious takes over consideration of the problem. Whereas the conscious mind focuses, neglecting less obvious and less accessible information, the unconscious focuses less and makes more associations with remote stuff lodged in the cobwebs of the dusty corridors of the museum of the mind. There is a move from what is known as convergent to divergent thinking (Dijksterhuis & Meurs, 2006).

The implication of this is that if we want to be creative, and produce more original humour we should allow the unconscious to take over, by deliberately doing something else, or just going to sleep. Of course, it also helps to be, naturally, a divergent rather than a convergent thinker, like Holden Caulfield, the hero in *The Catcher in the Rye* (Salinger, 2010). As Holden said:

'I don't know. The trouble with me is, I like it when somebody digresses. It's more interesting as well...I guess I don't like it when somebody sticks to the point all the time...The boys that got the best marks in Oral Expression were the ones that stuck to the point all the time...'

There have been studies of convergent and divergent thinkers. The classic is an American one by Getzels & Jackson (1963) who considered the relation between IQ and creativity. They observed that high IQ is not necessarily related to high creativity, and that the highly creative may not do well on IQ tests. Conventional IQ tests require one correct answer, not a number of novel answers. This suits the convergent rather than the divergent thinker.

Both high creative and high IQ students were asked by Getzels & Jackson to complete a story based on a picture of a businessman sitting in an aeroplane. The high IQ students tended to produce conventional responses, e.g. he was going home to his wonderful family. The high creatives tended to produce more original and funny responses, freeing themselves from the original picture, e.g. the businessman had just got divorced because his wife was so obsessed with her appearance that she wore excessive face cream, causing her to skid across the pillow at night. The businessman was now contemplating producing a new skid-proof face cream!

It is interesting that, when interviewed, the teachers of these students said they preferred high achievers with high IQs, rather than high achievers who were highly creative. As a teacher of Sir Peter Ustinov once wrote: *He shows great originality, which must be curbed at all costs.* (Hurley, 2003)

Psychologist Liam Hudson (1966) used the work of Getzels and Jackson in his study of English schoolboys, published in a book entitled, *Contrary Imaginations.* With regard to the humour of the two types of thinker, Hudson found a distinct difference, *'...not so much in the quantity of their humour as in its quality.'* A divergent thinker is not content with finding a joke, he/she elaborates until he/she is confident that the effort is unique. However, although divergers are more likely to make jokes, some of the *'sharpest wit'* comes from convergers.

Edward de Bono, the man who invented the term *'lateral thinking'*, sees normal, convergent type thinking as a pattern which needs to be escaped from when new approaches are needed. We need to think laterally. As someone once said, *'Logic will get you from A to B. Imagination will take you everywhere.'*

De Bono argues that, *'Creativity and lateral thinking have exactly the same basis as humour.'* It is the movement across the main highway patterns that, *'is the essence of humour'*, and this movement is found with lateral thinking itself.

To illustrate his argument about pattern switching and humour de Bono cites this joke:

An eighty-five year old man dies and goes to hell. As he is wandering about he comes across a friend of a similar age who is sitting with a gorgeous young woman sitting on his knee. He greets his friend: 'Are you sure this is hell? You seem to be having a good time.' 'Oh, it's hell all right. You see I am her punishment.'

De Bono (2007) thinks that lateral thinking is both an attitude of mind and a number of defined methods. The attitude of mind is, *'...a willingness to try to look at things in different ways.'* The defined methods include provocation and random stimulation. With provocation, an idea is put forward in order to jolt existing thought patterns. De Bono uses the invented word *po* for this process, *po* being an abbreviation of *provocative operation*. A *po* can be absurd, an exaggeration, a distortion, wishful thinking or something outrageous.

An example of an absurd *po* is: *'Po cars would limit their own parking.'* That is, instead of the land owner imposing parking restrictions, it would be the car doing it. This absurd *po* led to the idea that cars could park for free so long as their headlights were left on, thereby enabling short term parking.

In the case of random stimulation, the mind is jolted off its existing pathway. A random stimulation can be a word, an object, a person, a magazine, etc. So, for example, a word found at random in a dictionary can spark off a new perspective.

These methods give you a way of starting, as de Bono (1990) puts it, *'If you give someone an open-ended creative problem there is great difficulty in getting started. There is difficulty in moving at all.'*

Brain storming, a form of random stimulation, was developed by Alex Osborn, an American advertising executive. It involves a group of people who throw out ideas about the topic under consideration. The hope is that some sort of synergy will occur and an idea from one person will stimulate the others to develop that idea into a great idea.

David Walliams describes comedic team working with Matt Lucas, and the creation of synergy as follows:

'...at our best as a writing team we made each other laugh. When one of us was laughing we knew we had something good. And most often we wrote something together that neither of us would have been able to come up with alone.' (Walliams, 2012)

Osborn had four basic rules for a brainstorming group. There should be no criticism. People should be encouraged to freewheel. A quantity of ideas is wanted. Combinations and improvements are desired.

Osborn was keen that ideas, however ridiculous, should not be censored or mocked. If they were, people would just stick to the conventional. Obviously, such a group needs a certain amount of trust as there is much potential for mickey taking and disapproval.

For Osborn, quantity of ideas led to quality ideas; the more ideas the better. Freewheeling off the subject should lead to a greater variety of ideas. In an actual brainstorming session there is a progression in the extent of the creativity. Initially, ideas reflect known solutions. Next, there are variations on existing ideas and some novelty. Finally, hopefully, high quality ideas may be generated (Thompson & Lordan, 1999).

One way to brainstorm on your own is to free associate by drawing a spider diagram. What you do is get a big piece of paper, and write the subject you are interested in, in the middle. You then link that to related sub-headings and keep going, writing down ideas, as single words, as they emerge. This is a very important technique, so I explain it further in the activities bit at the end of this section.

A very practical check list of questions to ask when brainstorming improvements to existing commercial products was also devised by Alex Osborn. Nowadays known as SCAMPER -*Substitute; Combine; Adapt; Magnify; Put to other uses; Eliminate,* and *Rearrange*, it can be used, in our case, for turning old jokes into new, which is what often happens in practice.

1) **Substitute? Who else? Other place? Other approach? Other tone of voice?**
With formulaic jokes there is often the possibility of thinking up a new person or place for the joke. Fresh takes on the light-bulb changer joke, for example, rely on this. Here's a couple I thought up, using football characters:

'How many football referees does it take to change a light bulb?' 'One, but he'll need his bloody glasses.'

'How many football subs does it take to change a light bulb? One, but he'll need to be on the bench.'

A man walks in a bar joke is usually located in an anonymous bar, but one I saw about a bar on the moon having no atmosphere, led me to consider other specified bars. A topless bar was a distinct possibility, which led to the surreal, *'A an walks into a topless bar.'*

2) **Combine? How about a blend?**
This happens with meta-jokes, jokes about a joke. For example:
An Englishman, an Irishman and a Scotsman walk into a bar. The barman says, 'What is this some kind of joke?'

3) **Adapt? What could I copy?**

Of course, from time immemorial, there has been a lot of copying of other people's jokes. For example, the legendary comedian, Tommy Cooper, bought hundreds of thousands of gags from American suppliers. To make the jokes work he had to modify them to a British audience.
So, this American joke:

'A Beatnik in Greenwich village rigged up a do-it-yourself charcoal grill on his fire escape and put a chicken on it to broil, when he heard one of his Beatnik pals yell up "Hey Dad, I don't wanna bug ya, but your music box has stopped and your monkey is on fire!" ', became:

'There's a guy having a barbeque in his front garden. He's turning the spit like this and the flames are getting higher and higher-higher and higher-and he's singing, 'O sole mio...O sole mio, farewell.' And the flames are getting higher and higher and this drunk walks by and says, 'Your singing's alright, but your monkey's on fire!' (Fisher, 2011)

There is quite an irony in this next Cooper gag: *'You know these jokes could be worse…they could be mine.'* They weren't…..This one was much closer to the truth, *'You know what you have to go through to be a comedian? A lot of old joke books!'*

4) Modify? New Twist?
Here some characteristic of the existing joke needs to be changed, for example by updating it, giving it a new setting, etc. For example, this Tommy Cooper joke, historically American, originally used Jewish names and accents:

'Two business men were having a drink. One said, 'I'm sorry to hear about the fire that burned down your factory.' He said, 'Hold your tongue! It's not until tomorrow!' (Fisher, 2011)

A new twist suggests taking an existing joke and changing the punch-line. Here are two Tommy Cooper jokes which have a similar set up but different punch-lines:

'Last week my grandfather celebrated his 103rd birthday. Unfortunately he couldn't be there…he died when he was thirty-nine!!'

'My grandfather passed away when he was 103. No one expected it. His father was broken up about it!'

The idea of adaptation also includes the Osborn idea of magnification, making it larger, exaggerating. Here, the idea is that big makes a joke more beautiful. The joke itself could be about bigness, or it could be made bigger, as for example, by lengthening a shaggy dog story, or by having a double punch line.
Let's take a joke, made in a Nigel Planer play on Radio 4, as an example:

A gynaecologist is examining a woman's vagina very closely. She hears him say, 'Gosh, that's big.' Then again, 'Gosh, that's big.'
The woman was exasperated by this and snapped, 'There's no need to say it twice.' The gynaecologist replied, 'I didn't.'

That's a rather good joke which requires some thought to work out. The listener is, in part, congratulating himself/herself on his own cleverness when he/she laughs at the joke. The joke is about bigness, the question is should the joke be made bigger, or is it best left alone? If a double punch is to be added, it is important that the first punch-line does not give any indication as to the nature of the second punch-line.

Here is my suggested double punch:
A male gynaecologist greets a female patient and to put her at her ease he asks what she does for a living. She says, 'Oh, I'm a psychologist, I specialise in asking people if they are happy in their jobs. Do you enjoy yours?' 'Well,' says the gynaecologist, 'I do'. 'Why's that?' asked the psychologist. The gynaecologist says, 'It's very hands on.'
The gynaecologist now starts examining the woman's vagina very closely. She hears him say, 'Gosh, that's big.' Then again, 'Gosh, that's big.'

The woman was exasperated by this and snapped, 'There's no need to say it twice.' The gynaecologist replied, 'I didn't.'

5) Put to other uses?

Jokes, especially formulaic ones, are very predictable. That predictability can be changed by playing around with the standard formula, and bringing another form of joke into play. For example, a man walks into a bar joke being put into limerick form.

Certain types of jokes are used in certain situations, but they can be put to other uses. For example, riddles and knock-knock jokes are typically found in the play-ground. But, it is possible to use riddles and knock-knock jokes in the adult playground as chat-up lines as we have seen.

6) Eliminate. Minify? Smaller, omit.

Comedians are always trying to make their jokes as economical as possible, seeing what they can leave out in order to reach the punch-line quicker. It's a sort of race to beat the audience to the joke. Comic Milton Jones made this observation about minification whilst touring:

'I even try out some new stuff about Kangaroos and pickpockets which works well enough, but I'll need to try it out a few more times to hone it down to a perfect economy of words.' (Jones, 2009)

A gag Tommy Cooper bought minified from:
'Boy, am I burned up. Last night I must have slept like a log. I woke up this morning in the fireplace!'
to:
'Last night I slept like a log. I woke up in the fireplace.' (Fisher, 2011)

7) Rearrange? Interchange components?

Groucho Marx came up with this rather neat rearrangement:

'Why don't we break away from all this and lodge with my fleas in the hills, I mean, flee to my lodge in the hills.' (Arnott & Haskins, 2004)

The idea of rearrangement also includes reversal. Turn it backwards? Reverse roles? Turn tables? It is very difficult to reverse a standard joke as the set-up always precedes the punch-line. You cannot have a joke where the punch-line comes first. Well, I don't think so. For example, this next one just wouldn't work the other way round:
'A comedian walked into a crowded wedding reception and laughed at the length of the punch line.'

You could possibly have it as a riddle the other way round, but it's not very funny:

'When did the comedian laugh at the length of the punch line?
'When he went to a crowded wedding reception.'
Reversals can be done on standard expressions, take this one:

A good man is hard to find, becomes A hard man is good to find.

I did manage an amusing reversal once when down the pub with a group of work colleagues, well friends really. We were speculating as to which one of us was likely to become Dean of the university school where we worked. I pointed out that to become Dean it helped to have a funny name. We had had two *Dean Martins* in the past. As none of us had a funny name none of us was a likely candidate.

I started playing with the name of the most likely future Dean, a Mr Forrester, and did a reversal. Hey presto, we had *Forrester Dean*. So funny, and yes, twenty years later he did become Dean.

It is possible to reverse roles and make the victims of standard jokes the victors. Take the case of the following Irish joke, classically, of course, the Irish are shown to be stupid in jokes:

An Irishman goes on to a building site and asks for a job. He is told by the foreman that he would have to undertake a brief test. 'Can you tell the difference between a joist and a girder?' 'Sure,' says the Irishman. 'Joyce wrote Ullyses, Goethe wrote Faust.' (Carson, 2009).

This reversal really adds to the joke as it is an additional surprise element which we didn't expect.

Finally, it's clear that humour itself enables creativity and, therefore, further humour production. It gets people in the right mood, and makes pattern switching easier. It also sparks off ideas in others. In particular, humour blocks negative emotions such as fear, which restrict creativity by steering thoughts into familiar channels (Morreal, 2009).

Kounious & Beeman (2009) confirm the importance of positive mood. They found that when people watch comedy videos they subsequently *'...solve more problems, and solve more of them with insight, than they do after they watch neutral and anxiety-inducing films.'*

Ziv (1976) found that after schoolchildren had listened to a humorous record, with a high laughter response, they went on, *'to perform significantly better on creativity tests than control groups.'* He didn't consider that the students had actually become more creative because of the record. It was simply that the humour enabled a mode of thinking, *'not bound to right and conventional answers.'* i.e. lateral thinking.

Similarly, Isen et al. (1987) found that subjects, who viewed a comedy film for five minutes, improved their performance on two tasks that required creative ingenuity. Kudrowitz (2010), in line with Isen et al., found that, after undergoing a comedy workshop, subjects who participated increased their idea output, on average by 37% in a subsequent brain storming session.

Reflection

It is clear that creativity has a close relationship with humour. People who generate their own humour are creative. Similarly, people can be more creative with the facilitation of humour.

Creativity is not an instant fix. It has to be worked at. Research has to be done, ideas explored, and most importantly, failure experienced, before that magical *aha* experience occurs. A practical tip for when this happens is to have paper and pen at the ready. It is far too easy to have a great idea then forget what it was.

Creativity techniques are important for those who want to be better at being funny. It is difficult to create really original jokes and humour, but there are ways, particularly using the SCAMPER checklist, to elaborate and be more creative. My own favourite from the checklist is reversal, as the surprise factor is magnified in this case.

The brainstorming technique may be the least useful approach because most of us work on our own at this sort of thing. However, you may be able to find a friend(s) to cooperate.

Activity

1)   What sort of creative mind do you have?

- Fluent?

If you were asked to think up uses for a house-brick, would you be stuck after two or three ideas, or would the ideas just keep on coming? More than 15 would be pretty fluent.

- Flexible?

Do you easily get stuck when thinking of new ways to do something, or can you spot different approaches. For example, the term *poka-yoke* is used by the Japanese to describe fool-proofing, such that it is impossible for something to go wrong. The overflow in a bathroom basin is a good example. Now, think of a practical problem in your life where something keeps going wrong, and work out a range of *poka-yokes* to solve that problem.

- Original?

Do you come up with ideas that are genuinely different, or are you rather conventional? For example, produce an idea for a television sit-com. To what extent is your answer really thinking outside the box?

- Elaboration?

Once you hear a joke or a story do you start thinking of ways to build on the original, or do you leave it at that?

2)   Do some incubation

Start a crossword puzzle and continue until you get stuck. Put the puzzle away and return to it a few hours later. Did you spot new answers more or less straight away?

3)   Are you a divergent thinker?

Can you join up the nine crosses using four straight lines?

X   X   X

X   X   X

X   X   X

If you managed to do it, you are likely to be a divergent thinker. (What you have to do is draw a line down the first column to an imaginary fourth cross. Then draw a diagonal line through two crosses and continue to an imaginary fourth cross along the top row. Finally, draw a diagonal from the top left to the bottom right).

Now, can you think of another way?

Yes, there is another way. You won't find it in any other book as it was devised by one of my students.

This student, by name Kapsalis, simply presented me with a completed rectangle composed of four lines going through the six top crosses. I pointed out that he had missed out three crosses. He retorted. 'Just stick a mirror on the rectangle.'

4)   How divergent is your problem solving?

Here is a short quiz concerning British towns and cities. You need to think out of the box to get to the solutions.

To help a bit, some science examples are: 007 007---Double Bonds; **CARBON**---Carbon Black; Conductor/2---Semi-Conductor.

1) **POOL**

2) LPYHFRDSIUNBVWALLS

3) £££££££££

4) ????

5) O NO

6) MHA (7 letters)

7) <u>TRO</u>

8) <u>O EAT</u>

9) N+O_2

10) /B

If you get between 7-10 correct, you've done pretty well, and you're likely to be quite divergent in your thinking.

The answers to the quiz are: 1) Blackpool 2) Wallsend 3) Stirling 4) Ware 5) Oban 6) Wrexham 7) Troon 8) Nuneaton 9) Ayr 10) Neath

5)   Produce an original joke using a spider diagram

A spider diagram is a way to free associate, such that ideas interact with other ideas so as to produce a new outcome, which can be made humorous. Sally Holloway, the comedian, explains this method very well in her book, *The Serious Guide to Joke Writing.*

What you do is write down the subject for a joke in the middle of a big piece of paper. You then think of words and ideas related to the subject. These can be big or small ideas, obvious or obscure. Lines are drawn on the paper, radiating out from the subject word/term.

So, the subject term could be *The World Cup*. The associations I came up with are: *Penalties; Alf Ramsay; Brazil; Hot; Bobby Moore; Goals; No Chance; Roy Hodgson; Qatar; Un-prepared;* and *Bribery.* You would, obviously, come up with different associations. Even so, you can see that a lot of humour lurks here, particularly with the negatives, like: *no chance, un-prepared and bribery.*

Next, you deliberately forget about the original subject word/term, and you repeat the exercise, using the associations made with the original subject. So, forget about *The World Cup* and use *no chance*. This gave me: bottom, also-rans, can't score, lower league, amateurs, losers, failure, sick as a parrot, back home, and long odds. You draw another diagram.

This time you think more funnily about the associations. You can use word play, opposites, clichés, etc. In fact, anything you want. Just forget the original subject---The World Cup. This forgetting is important. You can keep going on making more associations.

Next, we relate back to the original subject, The World Cup.

So, *'The World Cup, eh...disaster. The English team are like a load of virgins...none of them have scored yet.'*

'The World Cup, eh...disaster. The English team is rubbish. They're playing like a load of eunuchs... they'll never score.'

Clearly, this was playing around with who else *can't score*. They are not bad jokes, just a bit obvious. Actually, there could be a problem with the word *eunuch* as some people might not know what that means.

'I've got a new nickname for the England team....The Eunuchs.....That useless team have got no balls, and will never score.'

With these spider diagrams it's best to hone in on a specific aspect of the subject. Let's narrow it down to collecting *Panini* stickers, something many men did in their youth. *Panini* stickers gave me: *duplication, collecting, anorak, kids, rare,* and *addictive.* As addictive looked most promising I chose that, and got: *heroin, cold turkey, giving up,* and *narcotic.*

'I've got my World Cup Panini sticker book. You know, it gives you a chance to collect the very best footballers and managers in the world...The very best...The problem is that it's addictive and expensive. I'm going to have to give it up....but of course not until I've got Roy Hodgson.'

This is an important technique, so have a go at any subject that interests you. Remember to choose a specific aspect rather than something broad. It obviously works, but it doesn't work in all cases. Even if it does work, the joke may be fairly weak. No matter; in order to produce a good joke you will have to produce a lot of poor ones. It's all part of the process. The trick is to know which ones to discard.

The audience, creativity and chat-up lines

'Chat up lines with a high sexual content are more successful when used on men than women.' (Field et al, 2012)

What sort of chat-up lines do people want to hear? Do they really want crude ones? Or, do they want funny ones? Maybe they want funny, crude ones. Probably, different types of people want different types of approach. We must know what people want before we can go about devising effective chat-up lines, which is the objective of this section.

Academic research can help us here. There is general theory concerning factors that make for mating success. There is also laboratory based research where people are asked to rate chat-up lines, and there is actual field work, assessing chat-up lines in action.

Let's start with the more general theory. Theorists argue about why we developed a sense of humour in the first place. The argument is that, *'...the human sense of humor evolved at least partly through sexual selection as an intelligence indicator.'* (Greengross and Miller, 2011) That is, a person with an appropriate sense of humour is judged as intelligent and therefore has good genetic potential.

This theory has been tested by Greengross and Miller. They researched 400 university students and found that, *'...general and verbal intelligence both predict humor production ability, which in turn predicts mating success, such as lifetime number of sexual partners.'* This applied particularly to men.

It is not just intelligence that is being evaluated via someone's humour. It is also other underlying qualities, such as warmth. Not surprisingly, studies show that women report higher levels of humour evaluation than men, whilst men report higher levels of humour production (Wilbur & Campbell, 2011).

Provine (2000) studied 3,745 personal ads, seeking partners, in 8 U.S. newspapers. He found that, laughter or laughter related behaviour was mentioned in one eighth of the ads. Provine found that females were 62% more likely to mention laughter. He concluded that, *'Women seek men who make them laugh, and men are anxious to comply with this request.'* As Dawn French puts it, *'I love it when somebody makes me laugh—it's what attracts me to people.'*

So, it is obvious that humour display and evaluation is a key part of the romantic process, of course, it is not the only part. A man has to show he is funny, whilst a woman doesn't have to. Her job is to judge. This makes the production of quality humour an imperative for the male of the species.

Let's turn to the laboratory based research into the effectiveness of chat-up lines. Bale et al. (2006) gave students (N=205) relevant vignettes describing various amorous ploys. The students were asked to rank the ploys in terms of their likely dating success. The most highly rated 'introductions' were: 1) Character; 2) Culture, e.g. appreciation of art, and, 3) Wealth. The lowest rated were: Humour; Compliments, and Sex.

The researchers observed that, *'Openings involving sexually-based humor were rated as likely to be unsuccessful, as were 'chat-up lines' of the kind often found on web sites dealing with this topic.'* A direct request for sex was not the least effective gambit. Wit, i.e., spontaneous, appropriate humour, was valued, whilst pre-planned jokes, did not demonstrate intelligence.

This study was followed up by Cooper et al. (2007). A larger sample was used and this time non-students and students were included. The respondents had a much higher median age (38 vs 21). Even so, the findings of the first study were replicated.

Cooper et al. did have some pertinent findings and observations. They found that, *'...men over-estimated the effectiveness of sexually-loaded remarks and under-estimated the extent to which women valued humour.'*

Also, as in the first study, the standard chat-up lines were judged to be less effective than, *'...gambits which reflected the context of the encounter and revealed something about the man's character, personality, interests or wealth.'*

These researchers went on to classify the female respondents as being either extravert, neurotic or psychotic. They found that the different personality types favoured different types of man. The extraverts preferred leaders. The neurotics preferred *'nice'* guys, and the psychotics preferred *'bad mates'*—the conceited and fickle.

This finding led the researchers to conclude that by choosing to use compliments, or sex, men were seeking women who scored high on the *'bad mate'* factor. Also, by using humour they were able to eliminate introverts.

So, even though chat-up lines don't seem to score that well, they may be a rational strategy for men seeking to score with a particular type of woman.

Fortunately for chat-up line merchants, there is a flaw in this 'laboratory' research, and that is the absence of consideration of the real world, and the confusing influence of alcohol consumption-- the *'beer goggles'* effect. Lyvers et al (2009) investigated the effect of alcohol on attractiveness perceptions for intoxicated, and sober Australian students. They found that there was, *'A positive relationship between alcohol consumption and attractiveness ratings...'* There was no difference by gender.

Further, and most importantly, Weaver et al. (1985) found that as intoxication increased, the perceived funniness of *'blunt'* humour increased, whilst that for subtle humour decreased. The researchers considered that, on the one hand, alcohol frees individuals from inhibitions, and on the other, it impairs the cognitive skills to comprehend refined humour.

The implication of all this is clear. Wit is fine before nine. By ten thirty, move on to the flirty. After midnight, start talking shite.

Indeed, there is a time-based etiquette with *'chatting-up' humour.* Walle (1976) studied men's attempts to *'pick up'* waitresses when they came off a night shift, at an American all-night diner. The men would mask their intentions by employing three levels of humour: general humour; topical humour, and sexual humour. General humour might be a pun, or a one-liner, topical humour elicited beliefs, e.g. political persuasion, and sexual humour, indicated a degree of sexual knowledge in order for the listener to openly enjoy the joke.

These types of humour operated at increasing levels of intimacy, to which the waitress might or might not respond. Interest would be signalled by listening to and responding to each level of joke. Disinterest would be shown by ignoring the joke, or by displaying anger.

Perhaps the most important piece of academic research into real chatting-up is that reported by Field et al. (2012). The chat-up lines used by a very large sample of both men and women in a nightclub were recorded, and success rates noted.

The researchers found that:

1) *'You're more likely to get a phone number than not if you use a chat up line that demonstrates good moral fibre.'*
2) *'...as sexual content increases, women become less likely than men to hand out their phone number. Chat up lines with a high sexual content are more successful when used on men than women.'*
3) *'As sexual content increases women become less likely than men to go home with the person.'*
4) *'...as funniness increases, women are more likely to hand out their phone number than men.'*
5) *'As funniness increases, women become more likely to go home with the person than men.*
6) *'...the odds of a man giving out his phone number compared to not responding are 5.26 times the odds for a woman. Men are cheap.'*

So, if we try to make sense of all this research, we can see that quite clearly women favour humorous chat-up lines, and men prefer sexual chat-up lines.
Women are in a position to assess the quality of the male by his humour. That is why corny, dated lines are not that useful, and why spontaneous wit relating to the situation is preferable.
Humour is part of the mating ritual and it no doubt gives the male some confidence in approaching a woman if he has a decent, or indecent, chat-up line prepared. The woman may go beyond the chat-up line and rate the male for his confidence in delivering the line.
Males continue to use indecent chat-up lines as they hope they will enable them to locate a particular type of woman. Also, the males do not seem to understand that women are not smitten by smut. They are not smutterns.
Women, by and large, do not welcome the indecent lines. This seems to be particularly the case in normal, routine, settings, however, alcohol changes the rules, reduces inhibitions, and makes the blunt more acceptable.
To know where they stand, men can regard women's reactions like traffic lights. If the signal stays green they can progress up the scale. If the signal goes red, they should scale back the vulgar.

We are now in the position of being able to apply a number of standard creativity techniques to chat-up lines. The necessary preparation has been done and we know what is contained in many chat-up lines. We also know what people would like to see in a chat-up line. So, off we go, first by making use of Osborn's SCAMPER checklist.

1) Substitute? Who else? Other place? Other approach?

The word substitute rather suggests that you should send someone else on in your place to do the chat-up, like Steve Martin in the film *Roxanne*. Unfortunately, this is not how it works, although as a Wing-man you can benefit from a mate who is good at this sort of thing.

You could pretend to be someone else. If you are a good mimic you could ape a famous person trying out a pick-up line: *'Nice to see you, to see you nice.'*

Another approach, instead of using your 'best' chat-up line, would be to survey women and ask them to rate the worst chat-up line ever. Here are some suggestions:

1) *'Roses are red, dead weeds are sepia, I'm really quite odd, I couldn't be creepier.'*

2) *'Roses are red, ginger is ground, come to bed, and I'll give you a pound.'*

3) *'Five words….Two and a half inches.'* (a minification, or, just possibly, a maximisation)

4) *'I haven't got a chat-up line, because if I did impress you, I'd have to keep up that standard for the rest of your life, and I simply couldn't be arsed.'* (A modification of a W.C. Field quip)

5) And another one from W.C. Fields, *'My philosophy on life is that anyone who hates children and animals can't be all bad.'*

6) *'I hope you're better than your mother was.'*

7) *'Could you hold my drink for me, I need to go to the loo. I really need to shake a tit…'*

8) *'You know, Woody Allen once said that the last time he'd been inside a woman was when he visited the Statue of Liberty. You look easy, how about being my Statue of Liberty tonight?'*

Another completely different approach is to perform a simple conjuring trick. These normally get attention, and appreciation if performed effectively.

Try demonstrating your origami expertise. Gershon Legman, a famed dirty jokes man, was also an expert with origami:

'He used origami as an opening gambit when talking to strangers. In a train station or at a bus stop, he would sit down, pull a sheet of paper out of his pocket and begin a fold, and soon he and his new acquaintance were swapping jokes.' (Davis, 2008)

This approach is nice and quirky. Once you have completed your animal or design, give it to the woman who has been watching what you've been doing out of the corner of her eye.

2) Combine? How about a blend?

You could assemble a collection of chat-up lines and then ask the girl to choose which type she'd like to hear:

'Hi, some girls like funny chat-up lines, others like romantic ones, some like to be flattered, some even like dirty ones. Which do you prefer?'

Funny: *'Modesty is my best quality'* (A Jack Benny joke)

'I am not a vegetarian because I love animals. I am a vegetarian because I hate plants.' (A Whitney Brown joke)

Romantic: *'I could love thee to the depth and breadth and height my soul can reach.'* (Elizabeth Barrett Browning)
'You may fall from heaven. You may fall from a tree. But the best way to fall is in love with me.'

Flattering: *"Do you know John Cleese once said that, 'In Britain, girls seem to be either bright or attractive. In America, that's not the case. They're both.' Well, which American state are you from?"*

"Did you know that Joan Collins once said, 'The problem with beauty is that it's like being born rich and getting poorer.' Have you just left junior school?'

'Your smile is a curve that sets everything straight.' (Phyllis Diller)

Dirty: *'I'm taking Viagra and drinking prune juice—I don't know if I'm coming or going.'* (A Rodney Dangerfield joke)

'Do you like jewels' 'Yes' 'Suck mine, it's a gem.'

Hand the woman a card on which is printed, *'Smile if you want to sleep with me.'*

3) Adapt? What could I copy?

Direct quotes from films, particularly comedy films, have real potential. Richard Harris, an American psychology professor, has found that comedy film quotes are very often used in conversations as a way of building solidarity and getting a laugh (Pawlowski, 2009).

You could do these as a quiz, in which film…?

1) *'By the way is there anyone on board who knows how to fly a plane?'* (*Airplane2*)
2) *'Why so serious?'* (The Joker in *The Dark Knight*)
3) *'What's the difference between a wife and a job?' 'After ten years a job still sucks.'* (*What women want*)
4) *'Gentlemen, you can't fight in here. This is the war room.'* (*Dr Strangelove*)
5) *'We Romans are rich. We've got a lot of gods. We've got a god for everything. The only thing we don't have a god for is premature ejaculation, but I hear that he's coming quickly.'* (*History of the World Part 1*)

Similarly, a quiz on *The Simpsons* and who said the following lines could work:

1) *'Trust me Bart, it's better to walk in on both your parents than on just one of them.'* (Milhouse Van Houte)
2) *'Aren't we forgetting the true meaning of Christmas: the birth of Santa?'* (Bart)
3) *'Me fail English? That's unpossible.'* (Ralph Wiggum)
4) *'To alcohol! The cause of, and solution to, all of life's problems.'* (Homer)
5) *'When a woman says nothing's wrong, that means everything's wrong. And when a woman says everything's wrong, that means everything's wrong. And when a woman says something's not funny, you'd better not laugh your ass off.'* (Homer)

Catchphrases can be used as an introduction to the chat-up line. For example, *'And now for something completely different...Me'*, *'Are you sitting comfortably? Then, I'll begin...*Of these, the first has potential as it then allows for a discussion about favourite *Monty Python* sketches.

4) Modify? New twist?

All sorts of modifications are possible. One approach is to research quotations, and then modify them so that they suit a chat-up line. For example:

'Why are women like teabags'....'I don't know. Why are women like teabags?'... 'Only when they're in hot water do you realise how strong they are.'

This riddle is a modification of an observation by Nancy Reagan via Eleanor Roosevelt (See Oxford Dictionary of Modern Quotations). It is not particularly funny, but does have the merit that it praises, rather than denigrates, women. Hopefully, the woman should pick up on this positive character trait.

Here's another:

'Hi, I hope you agree that it's better to be looked over than to be overlooked. I particularly like looking at your....'

This is basically a quote from American film star, Mae West (Oxford Dictionary of Modern Quotations). It does enable a compliment about the woman's clothing/appearance, something which is pretty standard procedure when women are greeting each other.

Next we have a modification of a Rosamond Lehmann quote (Morgan, 1996):

'Do you know what they said about Ian Fleming, the guy who wrote the James Bond books? 'No' 'He got off with women because he couldn't get on with them. Me, I'm the other way round. Most of my friends are women. Would you like to join the circle?'

The roses are red ditty is very easy to modify as only two lines need to rhyme. I have a couple for nice guys to use:

'Roses are red, begonias are ruddy, I'd really like it, if you were my buddy.'

'Roses are red, sweet peas are grey, I'm really glad, I met you today.'

'Roses are red, hydrangeas are beige, I don't really care, that you're twice my age.' (Not too sure about that one! Never talk age to a woman.)

5) Put to other uses?

Here, we are looking for approaches that are not normally used in chat-ups, but could be used. For example, Knock-knock jokes are rarely used in a chat-up, however, they can be fun, they do require participation and they can be used in a sequence, reducing the problem of what to say next after using a chat-up line.

'Knock Knock' 'Who's there?' 'Ivor' 'Ivor who?' 'Either we have a drink or a dance. Which is it to be?'

(This structure is known in selling as the alternate close. It does not allow for a NO answer)

'Knock Knock' 'Who's there?' 'York' 'York who?' 'You're cute.' 'You're captivating' 'You're charismatic' 'You're coming home with me. Get your coat.'

'Knock Knock' 'Who's there?' 'Kanai' 'Kanai who?' 'Can I buy you a drink?'

'Knock Knock' 'Who's there?' 'Tat' 'Tat who?', 'Tattoo, if I show you mine, will you show me yours?'

Late night knock-knocks:

'Knock Knock' 'Who's there?''Can' 'Can who' 'Canoodling is allowed over there. Let's go'

'Knock Knock' 'Who's there?' 'Nicholas' 'Nicholas who?' 'Knickerless girls shouldn't climb trees' 'Fancy a root with my trunk?'

Limericks are not used as pick-up lines, but they could be very effective, particularly if they were relevant to the girl/guy being chatted up. If the other person's name is known then it could be slotted in to a standard limerick. For example:

Oh Cindy are you aware
of your lovely hair?
Don't tie it back
Or dye it black
For that wouldn't make it fair.

Although limericks look pretty easy to do, the devil is in the last line. This really has to have some sort of punch-line in it. Hopefully, you can start out with the punch-line, if not you have to make sure that there are a lot of potential rhymes, thereby allowing a greater number of punch-line possibilities. In this case I started with, 'I saw Cindy standing there' and played with that for a while as there are a lot of rhymes for 'there':

6) Eliminate. Minify? Smaller, omit.

The obvious minification is to get rid of the chat-up line completely:
'Hi, I hope you don't mind, but I didn't think you would be the type of girl who would be impressed by an insincere, corny chat-up line, so I won't insult you by using one. What I do have is some thoughts about the latest exhibition at the Tate. Have you been?'

That, of course, has everything, praise, but not that blatant, and an indication of your cultural interests; make no mistake, many girls are very interested in art.

7) Rearrange? Interchange components?

There are all sorts of possible rearrangements. Let's start with a play on the term, chat-up line:

'Hi, I haven't got a chat-up line. Why not you might ask, all the other guys have. Well, it's simple, just rearrange the letters in chat-up line and you get Chap, Nut, Lie, enough said' (point finger at head in a knowing way).

Existing jokes act as provocations for new ones. Take this interchange, based on dog breed names, and an original joke taken from the 1994 film, *Dumb and Dumber.*

Harry: 'One time, we successfully mated a bulldog with a Shih-Tzu'
Mary: 'Really? That's weird.'
Harry: 'Yeah, we called it a bullshit.'
A quick *Google* of the various names of dog breeds leads to these chat-up lines:

'Hi, I'm Joe and I'm a dog breeder'…'My favourite dogs are miniature poodles and Boxers. There's a bonus when you put them together. You get Boxer Shorts.' 'I have bred cocker spaniels and Bull terriers. You get a bullcock.' 'In my latest venture I crossed a cocker spaniel and a bull mastiff. I got a stiff cock.'

Obviously, you can now start a conversation about dogs, not boners, or maybe not. By the way, the last one can be toned down a bit: *'I have bred collies and whippets. You get willies.'*
A rearranged quote, which is just silly, rather suits a chat-up line in a pub, *'Hi, I'm not so think as you drunk I am'* (J.C. Squire, Oxford Dictionary of Modern Quotations). Also, you could say, sagely, *'Never let a fool kiss you or a kiss fool you.'*

Spoonerisms are an obvious rearrangement to use. Here are some adapted from the internet:

'Hi, I think the easiest way to get to know someone is to find out about their hobbies and their reading interests. My favourite book is written by Darles Chickens, A sale of two titties. Mind you, I also like, Pater Pen, The Bride of Miss Jean Prodie, Book lack in Ongar, Spaintrotting, and Bee men in a throat.'

'Would you like some cop porn? Oops sorry, pop corn.'

'It's roaring with pain. Oops sorry, pouring with rain.'

'Would you like a soul of ballad? Oops sorry, a bowl of salad.'

'He's a fart smeller. Oops sorry, a smart feller.'

'How did you get here? I rode my well-boiled icicle. Oops sorry, my well-oiled bicycle.'

'Would you like me to sew you to another sheet? Oops sorry, show you to another seat.'

'Would you like a nazal hut? Oops sorry a hazel nut.'

Moving on, I did try the random stimulation dictionary approach and found the following words: *guardian* and *tuft.* Well, *guardian* suggests the newspaper, which used to have a reputation for misprints. Now, these are funnier when read, but you can have funny spoken ones.

The funniest skit based on word ambiguity is probably the four candles skit by the *Two Ronnies*. Why not learn the key elements of the skit and try them out on a girl. Maybe, just maybe, she'll play along and feed you the responses.

Fork 'andles...No, fork 'andles. 'Andles for forks...Got any plugs? A rubber one, bathroom...Thirteen amp. Saw tips? Saw tips for covering saws...Got any O's....No O's. O's for the gate, Mon repos O's. Letter O's. Got any P's?...No, tins of peas...Got any pumps?...No, pumps for ya feet! Brown pumps, size nine...

To remember the order you could use a mnemonic, *FPSOPP*. This could be *Funny People Sing Opera Poorly.*

Tuft is not so easy. *Toughtitty* used to be a word we used when I was young. It means hard luck. This could be a punch-line in a limerick:

Her left breast was pretty
But so hard and gritty
She'd implanted her gland
With coarse builder's sand
And made it a really toughtitty

That's quite a respectable, saucy limerick, unfortunately not much use for pick-ups. Initially, I wasn't so keen on this sort of random stimulation, but if you keep the faith, stick at it, something pops up.

With the other pos, well they've rather been done. There are already so many pick-up lines which are: absurd, exaggerations, distortions, wishful thinking or outrageous, that there's not much point in inventing more of the same ilk.

Reflection

What we have been considering here is how to develop jokes using creative techniques. The chat-up lines are just a useful vehicle to consider this process. There is no doubt that work needs to be done before incubation produces a result. The subject matter must be understood, and it is vital to understand what the audience wants. It all takes time and this, no doubt, is why people tend to just copy other people's jokes.

The SCAMPER approach is very helpful as it allows you to consider, systematically, a range of scenarios for joke developments. What is really true is that it gets you started. Instead of just staring at a blank piece of paper, you have a line of attack.

Some elements of SCAMPER are more useful than others. 'Combine' and 'elimination' don't seem to be that good for new jokes, whilst 'modify' and 'rearrange' seem to be more effective.

It is very interesting that a random stimulation can be any joke. Any joke can trigger off a new line of thought, but there are some jokes which are especially good for this. I call these cue jokes. These jokes are those that give you a form which you had not previously considered. So, in this case, the first *roses are red...*ditty I read somewhere was all that was necessary to get me going, as was the first *dog breeds* joke.

Once this new form emerges it needs to be developed, in a problem solving way, in order to find new variations of the original joke. What is useful is a relevant list obtained via *Google*. Here, I used: lists of colours, dog breeds, catch phrases, and best-selling books. Each item on the list is considered to see if it works with the form under consideration. The new types of dog found this way were particularly pleasing. A stiff cock still makes me smile.

The random stimulation of selecting words from a dictionary works, but you have to persevere with this, and the results may not be suitable for the type of joke you are trying to develop at the time.

Activity

Invent some new chat-up lines. A skill is a practised ability, so practise as much as possible.

1) Complete the following ditties:

Roses are red, branches are tan...............?

Roses are red, violets are blue, orchids cost a bomb............?

2) Use random words

Select two words at random from a dictionary and see if you can use them to make up a chat-up line. Stick with it and don't just give up straight away. See where that word leads you.

3) Invent a new breed of bird.

For example, if you mate a blue tit and a skylark you obviously get a sky blue. Simply Google a list of bird names and see which ones go together. Don't get preoccupied with tits there are other types, like cockatoos, shags, and boobies. Try and go beyond the obvious and move to something like *'Boxer shorts'* where the word *'shorts'* alludes to a miniature poodle.

Gender humour

Comments made to a male *unicyclist* riding on the roads of Newcastle:

Around 95% of responses from women praised, encouraged, or showed concern, and women made few comic or snide remarks. In contrast, only 25% of the comments made by men indicated praise, appreciation, or neutrality, whereas 75% were attempts at comedy, often snide and proffered combatively as a put-down…'Wonderful'…'I am impressed'…'I wish I could do that' versus 'Hey do you know you've only got one wheel'…'Couldn't you afford the other wheel?' (Shuster, 2007)

Those comments more or less sum up the difference between typical female and male humour. For women, there is basically a respecting order, for men there is a pecking order. Women's humour is constructive, whilst men's is destructive.

We've already seen how male and female humour varies with respect to chat-up lines, now what I am interested in is examining, in some detail, the difference between female and male humour. This is because it is clear that your gender really influences the sort of humour you use and the sort you appreciate.

Historically, women were not assumed to be funny. It was not thought appropriate for women to, *'play the clown and fool around.'* They were supposed to be *'feminine'*, and *'caring'*. Aggression and aggressive humour were not expected. Women were simply the targets of male jokes (Kotthoff, 2006).

Nowadays, as Kotthoff points out, this, *'simplistic model of the actively jokey man and the receptively smiling woman has lost ground.'* Obviously, both sexes joke around, however, research shows a *'striking contrast'* between male and female humour. Men favour jokes with sexual and aggressive themes. In an early study, Brodzinsky et al. (1981) found that males preferred sexual humour, rather than absurd humour. The result was reversed in the female case.

Women, when they create humour, are thought to produce stories of, *'a personal, often self-effacing nature'*. They are more likely to laugh at non-sensical, non-aggressive humour (Lampert & Ervin-Tripp, 2006).

The self-deprecating joke is typically female. Richard Wiseman (2006) reports research that found that, whilst self-disparaging material made up just 12% of the scripts of male professional comedians, it made up 63% of their female counterparts' scripts.

The self-deprecating joke is seen as the most *'traditional'* form of women's humour. Regina Barecca (1991) argues that this sort of humour reflects power differences. When women joke about themselves as targets, such hostility is acceptable to the powerful. That is, the men.

Herzog et al. (2006) found that cruelty in humour matters more for females than it does for males. These researchers studied male and female appreciation of jokes about the disabled. They found that there was a negative relation for the females, and no such relation for the males.

Mitchell (1978) observes, however, that women do tell aggressive and/or hostile jokes, but these are likely to be saved for an all-female audience, and the jokes are less openly aggressive and hostile. Judge for yourself:

'Do you know how sex and a snowstorm are alike?'

'You never know how long it's going to last or how many inches you're going to get.'

The scholarly view is that *'respectable'* women, generally, do not tell dirty jokes. One factor here is that, as Bing (2007) points out, women are *'in a double bind.'* If they don't tell or laugh at sexual jokes they are accused of having no sense of humour, however, if they do, they are seen as being sexually available.

Most humour scholars are men, and, so, normally, do not have access to all-female groups. Bing, who is female, does have access to such groups, and reports that, *'many of the jokes I have collected (from a variety of women's groups) are about sex.'* She observes that women's sexual jokes tend to be a reversal of those of men. A man's joke starts clean and ends with a sexual punch-line, whereas a woman's joke starts suggestively, and ends clean. For example, a handsome man approaches a woman in a bar and, says, *'he will do anything for her, if she says three magic words.'* She says, *'Clean my house.'*

Interestingly, Mitchell (1978) considers that men will tell jokes that show the female body as *'disgusting and obscene'*, while women will rarely, if ever, make such reciprocal jokes about men.

Robinson & Smith-Lovin (2001) found that, *'men engage in humour at higher rates than women'*, however, that is not the whole story, as women only groups, compared to male groups, have, *'a significantly higher rate of humor.'*

These researchers found, similarly to Holmes (2006), that the female groups had a different type of humour from the males. In all-female groups they engaged in cohesive humour, *'merry and relaxed'*, whereas the men engaged in differentiating humour, that is, jokes either directed at self or others, which are more concerned with establishing relative status.

Hay (1995) found that in mixed gender groups speakers maintained boundaries by focussing their humour on the opposite sex. Men, in this situation, contributed more humour, with women being more reserved.

Barecca (1991) makes some interesting observations about mixed group humour. Firstly, the female reserve in this situation is not to do with power, but with men's vulnerability. Women do not want to embarrass the men by telling jokes that might undermine them. However, this logic does not seem to apply in the reverse situation.

Secondly, when a woman makes a joke in a mixed sex situation she is acting as a male. This could make others nervous as she is demonstrating that she is *'...unwilling to accept her role as passive onlooker.'*

Female humour can be concerned with status in a societal sense. According to Nancy Walker (1988):

'...a dominant theme in women's humor is how it feels to be a member of a subordinate group in a culture that prides itself on equality.' Such humour is linked to *'anguish and frustration.'*

Finney (1994) summarises the *'consensus of characteristics'* associated with women's humour:

...women tend to tell comic stories whereas men prefer telling jokes; that the primary aim of women's humor is communication and the sharing of experience in contrast to men's use of humor as self-presentation and the demonstration of cleverness; that comedy by women is less hostile than that by men: female comics are more prone to self-directed put-downs than to putting down others, the object of women's humor is the powerful rather than the pitiful, and women are less likely than men to laugh at those hurt or embarrassed; that women's stories are often non-linear...

When men joke with other men they banter. Men's banter can strengthen their sense of masculinity as it may well be about the superiority of *real* men and the inferiority of other groups. Gough & Edwards (1998) found that a group of working class young men used drinking sessions as an outlet for *'letting off steam'* against traditional male targets—women, gay men and men from different regions and origins. Such targets would be ridiculed as, *'weak and/or laughable.'*

Although women banter as well, male banter is so widespread and so typical, that Easthope (1992) claims that banter *'...must be considered an example of masculine style.'*

Easthope reckons that banter is how the male ego asserts itself, and what is really happening is an affirmation of, *'... the bond of love between men, while appearing to deny it.'* So, banter is both affiliative, and aggressive.

The female and the male brain process humour differently. Kohn et al., (2011), using neuroimaging, found that women's brains process humour by appraising, *'its emotional features'*, while men apply, *'more evaluative, executive resources'* to humour processing. Although both genders process the cognitive element of humour in the same brain area, there are differences in the affective processing. The female brain makes more use of the reward related centres. The male brain uses this area less, resulting in *'lower subjective ratings of funniness'*.

With regard to children, the differences between male and female humour shows up at a young age. Young (1988) studied 6-7 year-old humour in three religious schools in Texas (N=92). She found distinct differences between the humour and its relationship to the social competence of the boys and girls.

Girls, in contrast to the boys, who were rated by their peers as frequent humour initiators, *'were rated as likable by the children.'* Teachers rated these girls, and not the boys, as, *'high in perspective taking and social problem-solving ability.'* The boys were seen by the teachers as, *'high in need for approval'*, but not as being the most socially competent.

Young explained the differences as being due to sex stereotyped socialisation processes, with girls expected to be more passive and empathetic. Boys are expected to be more active and aggressive, using more unrefined humour in the process. Additionally, Young also mentions the differing developmental levels of the two genders at this age. Fuhr (2002) found that, when coping with problems Danish adolescent boys (10-16 years of age) used more aggressive and sexual humour strategies, whilst their female contemporaries, preferred, *'...to get cheered up by humor.'*

Foot & Chapman (1976) studied the laughter and smiling of Welsh schoolchildren, aged 7/8. They found that the presence of a companion enhanced laughter and smiling of either sex. Significantly, they also found that, *'girls laughed more in the presence of a boy than in the presence of a girl companion.'* Boy's laughter and smiling were, on the other hand, relatively unaffected by the sex of their companion.

Attention to others' laughter begins at an early age. Sherman (1975) observed 596 lessons for pre-school children, and found that group glee, which consisted of, *'...joyful laughter or screaming often accompanied by intense physical acts',* spread contagiously. This contagion was unlikely to be found in single sex groups. These were rarely gleeful. A gender mix seems to arouse *'excitement'*, even in preschool children.

Baxter (2002) found boys used humour in presentations to attract and sustain attention. It also helped them to assert their position by making *'cracks'* at other people's expense. Significantly, boys used humour to subvert other speeches, in order to *'stay in the limelight.'*

In contrast, Baxter found, *'very few examples in my study of girls using humour either to influence, ridicule or entertain other members of the class, or to aid the appeal and legitimacy of their spoken contributions.'* The girls weren't there for a laugh; they were there to make serious points in the discussion. Where girls did use humour was in semi-formal discussions.

Baxter notes that girls do not construct themselves, *'as witty speakers, entertainers or comics on the public stage as often as boys do...'* This all rather supports the classic stereotyped views regarding female and male humour.

Reflection

It is quite clear that male and female humour differ radically. Males have been socialised to be competitive and hierarchical, whilst, females have been socialised to be more solidaristic. In social situations men joke themselves up, whilst women joke themselves down. Women's humour is observational and about relationships, men's humour is about cleverness, superiority and things. It's all about *jestosterone*.

The stereotyped view of women's limited humour is changing, if indeed, it was ever true. It is interesting that the BBC has ended the practice of having an all-male cast on comedy panel shows, such as *Mock the Week*. This should make these shows less competitive and more cooperative, and help develop the ranks of female comedians.

Activity

Try out the following jokes on males and females, to see which they find funnier:

1) *What did God say after creating man?*

   'I must be able to do better than that.'

2) *Why do blokes like smart women?*

Opposites attract.

3) *What does a bloke have to do to keep you interested in his company?*

   Own it!

4) *Why are all dumb blonde jokes one-liners?*

   So blokes can remember them. (Johnson, 2002)

5) *'How do you make a blonde laugh on Monday morning?*

   Tell her a joke on Friday night.'

6) *Why did God create Adam first?*

   So he'd have a chance to talk before Eve came along

7) *Why do women live longer than men?*

   Because they don't have wives.

8) *Why do women have orgasms?*

   It gives them an extra reason to moan. (Arnott & Haskins, 2004)

I'm prepared to make a bet as to which of these jokes will be found the funnier. The women should prefer the first four and the men the second four. This, hopefully, is a demonstration of what is known as *'in-group bias'* . Abrams & Bippus (2011) found that both men and women rated jokes about the opposite gender, *'funnier and more typical than jokes about their own gender.'*

Of course, they may find neither joke funny as both are sexist, dealing in derogatory stereotypes which have no validity. We consider this ill humour later in the book.

Your sense of humour

'Humour is by far the most significant behaviour of the human mind.' (de Bono, 2001)

We have just seen that men's and women's humour differs quite a lot. Even so, it is not just our gender which determines our sense of humour. Our personality has a big part to play as well.

A key personality distinction is drawn between the introvert and the extrovert. Whilst the introvert is more inward looking, the extrovert is more outward going, more gregarious. Not surprisingly, the humour the two types appreciate, and produce, varies. The introvert appreciates humour that requires thought, but the extrovert likes the *'pure joy'* of laughter, and the satisfaction of the desire for superiority.

It's not surprising that Eysenck (1942) found that extroverts preferred *'sexual and simple'* jokes, whilst introverts preferred, *'complex and non-sexual jokes.'*

So, if you're introvert you should enjoy the parts of this book which deal with logic, such as word-play, and irony. If you're extrovert, you should enjoy the more social parts which deal with dirty jokes, banter, teasing and practical jokes.

Shy people are not able to relax enough in social situations and find it difficult to use friendly humour. Shy males are more likely to engage in aggressive humour, whilst shy females are not so inclined. They are much more likely to use self-defeating humour (Hampes, 2006).

Your humour preference, then, may be for either positive or negative humour, and that is the sort of humour in which you typically indulge and enjoy. There are, basically, two types of positive, and two types of negative humour. Positive humour may be either *affiliative* or *self-enhancing*. Negative humour is either *aggressive* or *self-defeating*. (Martin et al, 2003)

Affiliative humour is concerned with jokes and banter to amuse others. It can be self-deprecating, to put others at ease. If you prefer this sort of humour you probably like: Michael McIntyre, Sarah Millicam, Peter Kay, and Ken Dodd.

Ken Dodd, *'I feel people desperately want a laugh and what I offer them is optimistic comedy. Unlike some comics, I don't tell them what a rotten world it is. I say life is fabulous and wonderful and we should enjoy it while we can.'*   (Billington, 2005)

Self-enhancing humour is about maintaining a humorous perspective in the face of adversity. It can be the humour of the gallows and the trapped, where a brave face is put on in order to cope with their situation.

This is not standard comedy fare, but can obviously be found when people are sick or confined in some way. *Captain Blackadder*, in the first world- war trenches, spent his time mocking all around, particularly the generals:

'If you mean, "Are we all going to get killed?" Yes, clearly. Field Marshall Haig is about to make yet another gargantuan effort to move his drinks cabinet six inches closer to Berlin.'(www.imbd.com)

Jack Dee seems to be permanently oppressed by life, but tries to laugh at it, with himself as hero:

'The rainforest has Sting. Now Siberia has Jack Dee. Someone had to draw the short straw. In this case it was the rainforest.' (http://dave.uktv.co)

Aggressive humour relates to sarcasm, ridicule, and disparagement. It is likely to hurt or alienate others.

Well, we ought not to like this sort of superiority stuff, but *Fawlty Towers*, for example, was riddled with sarcasm and ridicule, and it was a very popular programme:

Basil in hospital, having suffered a concussion

Basil Fawlty (to nurse, a little groggily): *'My God, you're ugly aren't you.'*

Sybil Fawlty: *'Basil?'*

Sister: *'I'll...I'll get the doctor.'*

Basil Fawlty: *'You need a plastic surgeon, not a doctor.'* (www.imbd.com)

Frankie Boyle is even more hostile in his humour:

'Congratulations you're 18...On a list of 20 people I'd like to kill.'

'Congratulations on passing your test! You're HIV positive.'   (www.funnyordie.com)

Self-defeating humour concerns excessive self-disparagement and allowing oneself to be the butt of others' humour.

The blindingly obvious comedy candidate here is *Baldric*, the servant side-kick of *Blackadder,* but *Manuel* in *Fawlty Towers* is a pretty close second in the Butt stakes:

Captain Blackadder: *'I can't believe I've been so stupid.'*

Baldric: *'Yeah, that is strange cause normally, I'm the stupid one.'*

Blackadder: *'You really are as thick as clotted cream, that's been left out by some clot, and now the clots are so clotted, you couldn't unclot them with an electric de-clotter, aren't you Baldrick?'* (www.imbd.com)

To determine your sense of humour you can take Martin's test, which is accessible at: How do you use Humor? (www.psychology today. com/articles/200607/ how-do-you-use-humor.

Here are some of the test questions:

'I don't have to work very hard at making other people laugh—I seem to be a naturally humorous person. (Affiliative/smiling humour)

'If I'm by myself and I'm feeling unhappy, I think of something funny to cheer myself up. ' (Self-enhancing/laughing at life humour)

'If someone makes a mistake I will often tease them about it.' (Aggressive/Put down humour)

'I let people laugh at me and make fun at my expense more than I should.' (Self-defeating/Hate-me humour)

If you're male you probably scored fairly highly on all four scales (Martin et al., 2003). These researchers also found that males reported, *'a much greater tendency to engage in aggressive forms of humour ',* and a greater tendency to use self-defeating humour.

Your preferred humour style affects the way people perceive you and your satisfaction with life. Research, by Kuiper and Leite (2010), shows that the two positive senses of humour led to *'enhanced personality impressions'*, whilst the two negative styles led to *'strong detrimental effects.'* Affiliative humour led to a higher social desirability rating than self-enhancing humour. The aggressive style resulted in a more negative overall social desirability rating than the self-defeating style.

Yip & Martin (2006) suggest that use of affiliative, and self-enhancing humour, enables: the initiation of social interactions; provides emotional support, and helps manage conflict. These humour styles are also linked to personal disclosure, enabling the reciprocal process of disclosure and trust building.

Sense of humour is clearly related to social competence. Those who use aggressive and self-defeating humour are lacking in social competence. They have an inability to perceive emotions accurately (Yip & Martin, 2006). It may not surprise you to learn that married couples are less satisfied with their marriages when they, or their partner, use sarcastic humour. People are more satisfied when partners use more affiliative and less aggressive humour, in conflict discussions. (Winterheld et al., 2013)

People who use affiliative and self-enhancing humour *'experience greater life satisfaction and fewer depressive symptoms.'* Those who use more self-defeating humour, have *'lower life satisfaction and greater depressive symptoms.'* (Dyck & Holtzman, 2013) Further, self-defeating humour is related to *'...loneliness, shyness, depression.'* Those who prefer self-defeating humour are likely to have damaged self-esteem. (Stieger et al, 2011)

Some people, of course, don't have either a positive or negative sense of humour. They have a 0 sense of humour. Those with a 0 sense of humour don't even try.

One very famous zero-jeero was the renowned but grave scientist, Sir Isaac Newton. Newton was many things, but he certainly wasn't a joker. *'Isaac Newton was a humourless, solitary, anxious, insecure and private man with obsessional traits.'* Over a five year period he was heard to laugh just once. This was when he had loaned a copy of Euclid's *Elements* to an acquaintance, who had queried the benefit of studying Euclid, *'Upon which Sir Isaac was very merry.'* (Keynes, 1995)

People will probably deny being zero jeeros, for, as Lockyer & Pickering (2001) point out, to be so accused makes us vulnerable, *'as if there is something vital missing in our individual make-up.'* They add that it is thought that a sense of humour is, *'a required attribution in a mature and rounded personality. Having a sense of humour helps you identify yourself as someone worthy of being known.'*

Martin (2007) notes that, there is, *'considerable variability'*, in the extent to which, individuals possess a sense of humour. However, people think they are funnier than they actually are. Research by Levine & Rakusin (1959), found that people tend to rate themselves,'... *higher in their sense of humor, both in being humorous and in appreciating humor, than others rated them.'*

Reflection

There are four basic types of humour, two positive and two negative. They are: the affiliative—The Ken Dodd; the self-enhancing—The Jack Dee; the aggressive—The Frankie Boyle, and the self-defeating—The Baldrick.

Your personality rather predicts your humour style. The happy-go-lucky extrovert uses more affiliative and self-enhancing humour, whilst the shy, and more anxious neurotics, prefer mental gymnastics. They use more aggressive and self-disparaging humour. (Schermer et al., 2013)

It is clear that if you want people to like you, then you should develop a friendly, positive, affiliative sense of humour. You should get all of Michael McIntyre's dvds, work out what he does, and copy it. Conversely, you should destroy anything with Frankie Boyle in it!

People don't just stick to one style of humour. They can display both positive and negative humour, adjusting to the situation as appropriate. It is interesting that women are likely to laugh more at men who use affiliative humour, whilst men are more likely to laugh at women who use more self-defeating humour. (Winterheld et al., 2013)

Activity

1) Which of the following words best describe your sense of humour:

> *Slapstick; Juvenile; Tongue in cheek; Punny*
> *Sarcastic; Original; Deadpan; Clever; Sick;*
> *Dirty; Jovial; Warped; Teasing;*
> *Practical joker; Class clown; Biting; Witty;*
> *Old-fashioned; Dry; Clean; Non-existent;*
> *Satirical; Cynical; Ironic; Wind-up merchant.*

2) Building on your answer to question 1, how would you describe your persona when you are being funny?

> Persona means the *'public face you present to the world.'* (Murray, 2010)
> Are you: a *Comic Loser*--everything fails; a *Lovable Buffoon*—an idiot who gets everything wrong; a *Smart Arse*—a know all; a *Confrontationalist*—someone who takes on their audience; a *Genial*, all-round nice person—likeable and friendly; a *Deadpan*—never crack a smile; or, an *Outsider*—looks in from the outside? (Murray, 2010)
>
> Is your persona the same as your everyday self, or does it differ? Do you exaggerate and

become, for example, more biting or sillier?

Do you think you could develop more of a persona? If so, in which direction might you go? That is, on which section(s) of this book might you concentrate?

3) Write the following quote on the first page of your comedy notebook:

'The cardinal rule on humor is to make it natural to your style. There is nothing worse than trying to sound like someone else or use a form of humor that makes you look uncomfortable.'   (Mary Matalin)

4) Assess your sense of humour

Ask your nearest and dearest to assess your sense of humour:

Absolutely awful, Awful, Non-existent, Weak, Fair, Quite Good, Pretty Good, Great, Sensational

Compare and explain the difference between their estimation and yours.

5) Assess your positive and negative humour

Ask them again to assess you on the two positive, and two negative humour dimensions.

Again, compare and explain any difference.

6) Change

In the light of this section, consider whether you need to change and improve your sense of humour in any way. How might you do that?

Part 2: Jokes and their creation

This part of the book is about jokes and how you can create them.

A joke usually needs: a subject, a form, a technique and a theme.

It is up to you who you make the subjects of your jokes. The subject may be your friends, your parents, your boss, etc.

You have to decide which form you are going to use, that is are you going to use a riddle, a pun, a limerick or what? As you go through the book you will find out more about the various forms that are available. In this part I take a really close look at *A man walks into a bar jokes*. These formulaic jokes are nice and easy and are a user-friendly way into joke creation.

You have to think about which humour technique to use. How exactly are you going to make the joke funny? Will you use exaggeration, sarcasm, absurdity or what? A big chunk of this part is devoted to these techniques as they are so important.

Lastly, a joke needs a theme, what is the joke about? When it comes down to it, jokes are about our desires and our failings, particularly men's desires and failings. These are primarily sexual desires, or the desire to elevate ourselves, and relegate others. Of course, some jokes are just playful with no hidden message.

I look at joke themes early on in this part, but first I look at the joke. Jokes rely on an agreement between teller and listener that the normal rules of conversation don't apply. It's understood that the joke may not be true. It may be illogical or improbable. This doesn't matter. We have agreed to transport ourselves to a land of make-believe.

Normally, a joke has a set-up, which establishes the situation, and a punch-line that snaps the tension. To work, there has to be surprise. To get surprise you need incongruity, some deviation from the expected.

All sorts of things are incongruous. There is the abnormal, the immoral, the inappropriate, and so on. These incongruities all amount to some sort of deviation from the norm. They are unexpected. Unsurprisingly then, jokes usually have some sort of negativity at their core.

In jokes the incongruity may be in the set-up, and this incongruity is resolved in the punch-line. Or, it may be the other way round. In the first case we are led up the garden path, deceived in effect, and we discover the truth with the punch-line. In the second case, the set-up may be logical but it is destroyed by the punch-line, in what is known as a red-light joke. Some jokes, like riddles, even have incongruous set-ups and incongruous punch-lines.

So far I have rather indicated the theory of the joke; its practicalities, how it works. This is obviously useful. However, the problem comes when you sit down with a blank sheet of paper, and have to start producing your own jokes. Well, never fear, I have come up with a short cut, the cue joke. The cue joke amounts to intelligent cheating.

A cue joke is someone else's joke that stimulates you to make up further jokes. A cue joke is likely to be a good joke, but it doesn't have to be. It is a joke, good or bad, that lets you see a way forward.

Cue jokes are great for beginners. To start off you can just take someone else's joke and change it a bit. With experience you can change it a lot. Finally, you can change it so much that the original is unrecognisable. Copyability becomes Capability.

Jokes are all very well and important to know about, but, to some extent, they have had their day. The modern stand-up comedian relies less on jokes and more on stories and observational humour. So, I do look at anecdotal humour, particularly as I believe that beginners should concentrate more on story-telling as stories are less risky than jokes.

The modern comedian observes our society and comments about things we all experience. The comedian makes his or her point via an after-thought, a comment on the observation. The after-thought is the new punch-line. In all, the new comedy is a sharing.

It's very satisfying to invent jokes and stories, but a major problem comes when you start telling them and the joke cannot be remembered. So, I do have a section on how to recall jokes and stories.

I finish this part by looking at the audience. Anybody telling a joke or a story has to consider whether it is appropriate for that audience. Is it too difficult, too easy, too specialised, or too inappropriate? Not only do you have to consider these things before the presentation, you need to be monitoring audience reaction during the presentation. A skilled performer is able to adapt easily and move to plan B. An unskilled performer gets flustered, has no plan B, and so, is therefore more likely to fail.

Jokes

Two hunters are out in the woods when one of them collapses. He doesn't seem to be breathing and his eyes are glazed. The other guy whips out his phone and calls the emergency services, gasps, 'My friend is dead! What can I do?' The operator says 'Calm down. I can help. First, let's make sure he's dead.' There is a silence, then a shot is heard. Back on the phone, the guy says 'Ok, now what?'

In 2002, Professor Richard Wiseman asked people to submit their favourite jokes and requested ratings of the jokes. In all, 40,000 jokes were submitted, and 1.5 million ratings were received from a worldwide audience. The *Two hunters* joke had the most universal appeal. (richardwiseman.wordpress.com)

Well, I don't think that 'joke' is even slightly funny. It has a long build up. The punch-line is poor. It's about death, which is a bit morbid. There is not much wit. Really, it's just dumb, sardonic humour without the merit of laughability.

I should point out that rude jokes were not accepted by Professor Wiseman. The rudest submission that was rejected, involved *'two nuns, a large bunch of bananas, an elephant, and Yoko Ono.'*!! However, one rude joke did evade the censors and got a very high rating:

A guy goes to his priest and says, 'I feel terrible. I am a doctor and I have slept with some of my patients.' The priest looks concerned, and then tries to make the man feel better by saying, 'You aren't the first doctor to sleep with their patients and you won't be the last. Perhaps you shouldn't feel so guilty.' 'You don't understand,' says the man. 'I'm a vet.'

Men found that vet joke funnier than women did, and people from Denmark found it the funniest of all. The lessons to be learnt from all this is that people like jokes about sex, and people don't have identical senses of humour. The jokes that make others laugh, are not necessarily those which make you laugh. There can be a *'wit misfit.'*

It is so annoying when you make what you think is a good joke and the recipient doesn't understand it. To make matters worse they look at you as if you are stupid. For example, I remember being in a pub once and ordered some food. The system was that the person at the bar gave you a number and you displayed it on your table. Well, my number was 144. Straight away I exclaimed *'gross'*. Well, I thought it was funny. The barmaid didn't get it and gave me an odd look. I had to explain the joke and slink away.

That *gross* joke would be classified as a class 3 joke by Dewitte & Verguts (2001). A class 3 joke is one that misses its target because it is too unusual. The recipient of the joke does not have the presumed knowledge needed to understand the joke. The two other classes of jokes are: class 1, where a *'lame'* joke fails because it is too usual, and a class 2 joke which succeeds because it achieves a necessary *'delicate balance'*.

My favourite class 2 joke is this one from Bob Monkhouse:

'When I said I was going to be a comedian they all laughed. Well, they're not laughing now.'

I like it because it's sharp and witty. There is surprise and resolution, and there is and there isn't

superiority. On the one hand he is saying that he's not funny, on the other his wit tells us he is funny. Actually, I never thought that Bob Monkhouse was a great comedian. The quality of this joke was, in itself, an unexpected surprise. In all, it is a joke I wish I'd said--that criterion, for me, is the measure of a good joke.

Jimmy Carr, the comedian, explains that the best jokes:

'... use language with skill and economy to conjure up mental pictures which are hilarious by virtue of their incongruity, shock value or just sheer silliness.' (Carr & Greeves, 2007)

So, what is a joke? According to Berger (2010b) jokes are, 'short narratives, meant to amuse, that end with a punch line.'

Jokes may be spontaneous or ready-made--'learnt and repeated by a speaker to amuse an audience' (Coates, 2007). The ready-made joke is not necessarily about realistic characters, more about caricatures or types. There is usually a formula to the joke, starting with joke phrases like, 'A man walks into a bar'. This is followed by a predictable form in the body of the joke, which is skewed by the punch-line. (Norrick, 2003)

A joke often starts with a preface—'Have you heard the one about...?' accompanied by laughter. These prefaces are used to reduce the risk of the joke failing, and are a part of the whole joke performance. Bird (2008) studied these prefaces and concluded that they could be classified as either, interactional or evaluative.

An interactional preface enables a smooth transition into the joke. For example, there is a positive statement about the joke—'This is a really good one.'

An evaluative preface concerns the risk involved in telling a dud joke which the audience will reject. So, the teller might check if the audience has heard the joke before, or warn that the content is offensive. Bird observes that where prefaces warn that the joke may not be seen as funny, the end result is often, 'very successful jokes.'

Bird considers the preface to be part of a formulaic joke, for her it counts as the beginning of the joke. The preface assists the joke's effectiveness as the teller is judged on both the joke's content, and his/her performance.

Bird (2009) went on to consider the preface in relation to females telling jokes. She found prefaces which warn of possible poor telling, or forgetfulness, are used, '...almost exclusively by women.' Bird argues that this approach is, in fact, a clever exploitation of the female stereotype of woman being bad at jokes, in order to be funny.

The preface announces a conspiracy between joker and audience. In order to hear the joke, the listener implicitly agrees to suspend normal rules of conversation. It is understood that the joke need not necessarily be true, and that the listener will not evaluate it critically. Also, there is an understanding that illogical elements will be overlooked (Perlmutter, 2002).

The set-up is the premise of the joke. It provides necessary background. The usual recommendation is that it should be as tight as possible because what you really want is to get to the punch-line. A rambling set-up is confusing, so simplification is required. This stops distraction and the frittering away of tension (Koestler, 1976).

Jenny Roche (1999) suggests the following set-ups:

- A question—*"Did you know that...?"*
- A statement—*"Laughter can bring tears to the eyes..."*
- An observation—*"Ancient Egyptian pyramid builders used to drink beer morning, noon and night..."*
- A news item—*"Unemployment figures have fallen again this month..."*

The set-up doesn't necessarily have to be tight. The classic case where it rambles on is the shaggy dog story. Jokes with longer set-ups may contain *jab lines*, punch-lines that appear before the final punch-line. The *jab line* contributes to the build-up of humour in the total joke. It does not have the same form as the punch-line, that is, the punch-line cannot be anticipated via the *jab line* (Tsakona, 2003). In boxing parlance, the jab line is a light tap on the body, leading up to the punch-line, which is the knock-out blow.

A key element of the set-up, the *connector*, together with the *disjunctor* in the punch-line, completes the joke (Stark et al., 2005). So, if we take the following joke, *'I asked the bartender for something cold and filled with rum, so he recommended his wife.'* The *connector* is, *'something cold and filled with rum'*, and the *disjunctor* is, *'his wife.'* The connector is ambiguous.

The punch-line enables the release of built up tension. Critchley (2002) sees the joke as stretching time like an elastic band. We know the band will snap, but don't know when. It is the anticipation that is pleasurable.

{By the way the term 'punch-line' comes from *Punchinello*, a fat clown in the 16th century *commedia dell'arte*. Mr Punch, the puppet, evolved from Punchinello, Sanders (1995) }

Critchley (2002) emphasises the necessary *suddenness* of the mental shift occasioned by the punchline, *'both brevity and speed are the soul of wit.'* This suddenness is connected to surprise. For Koestler (1976), surprise depended on the originality of the joke in order that the necessary mental jolt is achieved.

Jokes are rated as funnier when hearers take a shorter time to appreciate them. There is a negative relationship between response time and funniness ratings (Kozbelt & Nishioka, 2010).

Legman (2006) points out that a joke may go beyond the punch-line to a further punch-line, what he calls the *clincher*, or harpoon-line. This extra punch-line, is supposed to turn a smile into a laugh.

A joke may have an unuttered punch-line, which, if uttered, would, in fact, ruin the joke. For example:

'What's the difference between roast beef and pea soup? Anyone can roast beef...'

The stated punch-line is a clue to the true punch-line, which we pride ourselves on detecting (Miller, 2009).

Legman (1974) gives us a clever limerick where the ending has to be devised by the listener:

There was a young maid of Boston, Mass.

Who stood in the water up to her knees.

(If it doesn't rhyme now,

It will when the tide comes in.)

Many jokes rely on ambiguity, and its resolution, but not all. The absurd and ridiculous are just that. For example:

'Why did Cleopatra bathe in milk?

Because she couldn't find a cow tall enough for a shower' (Bekinschtein et al., 2011)

Timing is vital for the joke teller. Mastery requires, *'a careful control of pauses, hesitations and silences, of knowing when to detonate the little dynamite of the joke.'*(Critchley, 2002)

The main timing is a pregnant pause, building up the suspense, before the punch-line is delivered. A pause can go on for 30 seconds. That's when professionals tell a joke. Amateurs, *'...tend to deliver the punch-line at a rate that is neither significantly slower nor faster than the setup.'* (Attardo & Pickering, 2011)

This timing business comes with experience. A beginner at public speaking is terrified of a situation where there is no noise happening, and so tries to speak all the time, often at quite a fast pace. The secret is to slow down, and, in the case of punch-lines, have the confidence to wait and say nothing for a moment or two. Such control of the proceedings gives the audience confidence that you know what you are doing.

Here's Steve Martin's take on timing:

'I'm not trying to brag. I'm not trying to be a big shot, but I have the gift that, uh, all the great comedians have, and I'm talking about this one element that is crucial to all delivery of comedy material. I'm talking about, of course, ti—ming, ti, timing, timing, timing.' (Wuster, 2006)

A successful joker has to reflect on feedback. Dewitte & Verguts (2001) argue that the development of humorous ability is a learning process. It has to be practised, and feedback has to be reflected on. Sensitivity to positive feedback, *'enhances joking frequency, whereas, sensitivity to negative feedback, enhances joking quality.'*

Those with the most experience of joking are stand-up comedians. Their performances were analysed by Rutter (1997). He found that their opening gambits are similarly organised, as are their closures. In the body of the performance, comedians draw on a small range of formats to signal a joke's ending. This reduces the audience's risk of laughing in the wrong place. Also, of course, these devices make a laugh more likely.

The initial part of the stand-up's opening is consistently non-humorous. The comedian rejects jokes at this stage in order to draw the audience into the performance. So, there are greetings, comments on the setting, and a request by the comedian for the audience to do something together as a group. The aim is to develop some commonality with the audience, and to unite them, so that they act as a whole. Double (2005) explains that dividing the audience up, and getting them to compete in some way, is a basic stand-up skill.

The comedian may develop a dialogue with an audience member, who is selected for his/her humour potential and appropriateness for what is to follow. The skill lies in taking the mundane, and converting it into the unusual, or comic.

Once the comedian has set up the audience, so to speak, and they have laughed together, he or she is now able to move into the body of the act, and begin with the first joke. Here, the comedian may use one or more of the following formats: contrast; list; puzzle-solution; headline-punch-line; position taking, and pursuit.

- With contrast, a state of affairs is presented, and then, an opposing viewpoint is given.
- A list usually comprises three items, and the audience is expected, and expects, to laugh after the third item. This is known as the rule of three, like, for example, *An Englishman, An Irishman and a Scotsman…*There is never a Welshman as well.

  The rule of three allows a basic pattern to be established in the first two parts, which is then destroyed in the final part. This is the most economical structure.
  In a study of 1157 jokes, researchers found that 72% followed the rule of 3. Jokes with a four part structure were quite rare, 7% (Rozin et al., 2006).
- The puzzle, essentially, follows a riddle format.
- The headline-punch-line is a more predictable type of puzzle, where a comedian answers his/her own question, maybe with a profanity.
  This is what Peter Kay says about swearing:

  'Listening back to a lot of my early performances again, I'm surprised at just how much I used to swear. A lot of the time swearing was a safe way of successfully punctuating a gag. You could tell a joke and get a laugh, but tell the same joke and stick a 'fuck' in the punch-line and it knocks it up a gear.' (Kay, 2009)
- Position taking is similar, in that the comedian states a position, and then evaluates it, probably with an expletive.
- Finally, pursuit is where a comedian passes a comment on a previous joke.

The comedian is most likely to make use of the first three formats: contrast, list and puzzle-solution. Rutter found that these were used 67% (151 of 226) of the time.

The comedian can make use of a number of specific stand-up techniques. Firstly, he/she can incorporate an earlier element into a later part of the performance. Then, there is the use of alliteration, assonance (similar sounds) and rhyme, particularly in the punch-line. Next, there is intonation. A comedian uses this for interest, and to signpost joke completion. Finally, the comedian can make use of different voices, throughout the performance, or occasionally.

The closing of the performance is signposted, and a final humour sequence follows. After which, there is a comment on the audience's quality. An assessment of the routine may be made. The audience is thanked, and the comedian states his or her name. There is an exclamatory finale, *'Goodnight', 'Bye, 'Cheers'*.

Reflection

By now you should know the recipe for successful jokes. A pinch of preface, a stem of set-up, and a twist of punch-line, should produce the necessary potion for the laughter emotion. The key thing is not to over-egg the pudding; economy is crucial.

There is quite a lot of advice for the trainee joke-teller in this section. It is useful to turn individuals into a group before telling them all a joke. A preface is the real introduction to the joke, and needs to be thought through. It is important that the audience is prepared for the joke.

The set-up should, normally, be economical, and the punch-line should be signalled by the use of rhetorical devices such as a list of three, or problem-solution. Think surprise. Think incongruity, shock, and/or silliness.

Feedback is vital. You must ask your listeners to tell you, honestly, what they think of your jokes/humour. Be encouraged if they enjoy it. Don't over-react when they are critical. Take heed and try to remedy your next attempts.

Activity

1) Look at the jokes submitted to Professor Wiseman

A thousand of these jokes can be found at, richardwiseman.files.wordprocess.com/2011/09. These are all clean jokes. They tell you something about what ordinary people, worldwide, find funny. However, there may be an over-representation of the young here.

2) Decide upon your favourite joke

Do this for the jokes in the Wiseman file. Try to analyse why that joke is the winner. Discuss favourite jokes with your friends.

3) Get feedback

Try out some jokes on someone and then ask them for their honest feedback, in particular, how they think you might improve your performance. Don't get upset if you hear things you'd rather not hear.

4) Produce a piece of graffiti

Economy is very important for the joke teller. There should be a minimum of word usage. In real life we find the most economical humour on toilet walls, graffiti.

Many years ago, I was sitting in a seminar room at a not very good teacher training college, waiting for the class to start, when a fellow student came in, grinning all over his face. He'd just been to the toilet and read a piece of graffiti. I grinned back, and revealed that I was the author:

Qu.: *'What is the difference between a cactus and this college?'*

Ans: *'A cactus has its pricks on the outside.'*

This must have been one of those rare instances where such humour got face-to-face feedback, although, funnily enough, there is research into graffiti which reveals that graffiti can become a dialogue (Green, 2003).

Green recorded graffiti from toilets and library study booths, at the *University of Otago*'s central library. He found that that there were strong gender differences:

'Graffiti from the female toilets tended to be more polite and interactive, whereas those from the male toilets were more argumentative and negative.'

There is a male bias in the writing of humorous graffiti. Bates & Martin (1980) conducted research at *Massachusetts University*, and found, *'Men also wrote much more humorous graffiti, across all categories, than did women.'* With regard to the sexual inscriptions, 40 of the 113 male offerings were humorous, whilst just 9 of the 163 female offerings were humorous.

Obviously, this one was found in a male toilet: *'If you can pee above this line, join the Rochester Fire Department.'* (Bartholome & Snyder, 2004)

Of course, much toilet graffiti is sexual in nature. A study of the graffiti in 4 Chicago schools, found there was a gender difference. For the boys, sexual activity was the emphasis, for the girls, the emphasis was sexual desire.

Normally, graffiti lacks the wit of *Banksy*, more the reverse.

Your task is to produce some economical graffiti for your workplace or educational institution. As few words as possible please.

For example, graffiti found in a school staff toilet after an Ofsted inspection, which rated the school as INADEQUATE:

Ofsted rules K.O'ed us

The Ofsted killjoy was here

I was busted by Ofsted

5) Work out a rule of three joke

'What kind of humour do you like?'

'Sight gags,' said the optometrist.

'Slapstick,' said the hockey player.

'Dry humour,' said the nappy maker.

'Corny jokes,' said the farmer.   (Kostick et al., 1998)

That joke is not that funny whatever you do with it, however, it is made worse by having four elements. An audience might start tittering after the third line, because this is where they expect to laugh. Meanwhile the teller has launched into the fourth part. So, one element should go, or it should be clearly signalled that there are four parts to the joke.

Here we have a three part Jo Brand joke: *'I read that book, Fat is a Feminist Issue. Got a bit depressed halfway through. And ate it.'* (Double, 2005)

Logan Murray (2010) explains what is going on in this sort of joke. First the subject is introduced. Then, it is reinforced. The logic is confirmed, not denied. That is, Jo Brand is a bit big, and people, women especially, are supposed to find that state depressing. Then, our expectations are subverted. Instead of going on a diet as the logic would suggest, Jo adds to her weight by eating the book.

So, it's: introduction---reinforcement---subversion.

Here's one of mine that a professor friend of mine reminded me about. I'd completely forgotten it, and was a bit surprised that I'd ever said it. Maybe it was someone else. He is losing his faculties:

'Well, it's five o'clock. I'm off to see my loved ones…. Then, I'll go home.'

6)   Produce a K or CK joke

Funny people say it is usually funnier to use words beginning with K, or that contain the CK sound. As Eric Morecambe once put it, *'Two words you can't go wrong with… kippers and Cockfosters.'* (Nordern, 2008) (So, even the name Eric was funny)

This is a bit weird this K business, but Professor Richard Wiseman (2006) confirmed it with an experiment he conducted. Wiseman took the following simple joke and substituted, in turn, tigers, dogs and ducks appropriately into the joke. Respondents found the duck joke the funniest. Wiseman suggests that this is because the K sound forces the face into a smile:

Two ducks were sitting in a pond. One of the ducks said: 'Quack'. The other duck said: 'I was going to say that.'

This CK business may partly explain why the following was amusing. One time I was working in Germany and I was showing off to some German colleagues. *'Britain,'* I said, *'has given the world many of its sports, for example: Football…Rugby… and… Cricket.'*

The Germans found the word *'Cricket'*, very, very amusing. Whoever said that they have no sense of humour?

Here's a list of K words that have humour potential:

Kagoul, Kaiser, Kama Sutra, Kangaroo, Karaoke, Karate, Karl Marx, Kazoo, Keg, Kent, Khyber Pass, Kick, Kilmarnock, Kilroy, Kinky, Klutz, Krakatoa.

'Read the Kama Sutra the other day

Changed my sex life completely

Now I do it by the book.'

Funnily enough, a few days after I'd made that joke up something similar was said by the then Education Minister, Michael Gove:

'[Tristram Hunt] has had more contorted positions on free schools than some Indian sex manuals.' (Anon., 2014)

That would have been a better joke if he'd used *Kama Sutra* instead of *Indian sex manuals*, because two words are better than three in jokes, particularly at the punch point. The listener needs less time and thought to get the joke, and a K word would have been used. And there I was thinking Gove was a real comedian!

Actually, CK words are better for punch-lines, as they have more sexual connotations.

Here's a list of CK words:

Bareback, Blowback, Brick, Bullock, Dick, Duck, Gamecock, Haddock, Joystick, Peacock, Poppycock, Prick, Nick, Suck, Wisecrack, Wristlock, and Yardstick. There are, when you think about it, quite a lot of swear words which contain CK or C, quite possibly there is a connection.

'Blowjobs suck.'

Joke Themes

Dad said, "Remember, son, those ethnic minorities—they're not like us!" I said, "I know Dad. Some of them have jobs." (Steve Hall)

What are jokes about? What are they telling us?

To find out, I have looked at the 640 jokes and anecdotes in Isaac Asimov's book, *Treasury of Humour*. Asimov's fundamental position is that, *'...in every successful joke is a sudden alteration in point of view.'*...A Surprise...

More specifically, jokes are about human nature, our desires and failings. As jokes are mostly constructed by men, they are about male desire. A key desire in jokes is the desire to be superior. There is a related desire to relegate others to the realm of the: stupid, inferior, or incompetent. Unsurprisingly, the first real theory of humour concerned superiority.

Another key human desire is sexual activity and fulfilment. There are many saucy jokes, indeed such jokes are the most popular, world-wide. Usually, in saucy jokes, the male dominates, and the female is the butt or victim. These jokes are often about sexual failure, reflecting basic male fears. They can be about the ridiculous, most notably with the fairly recent wave of *Viagra* jokes.

Marriage and its problems feature in many jokes. This is not surprising as the married state is still pretty normal. For many people it is their most important relationship, but it is not without its problems. As a result we get lots of jokes about sexual frustration and infidelity, as well as marital conflict.

A major human failing is our ability to put our own interests first, at the expense of others, even when their needs are much more important. Selfishness and meanness are key joke themes. When we put our own interests first, we may be forced to lie, or deceive ourselves, by holding contradictory views which suit our purposes. So, deceit and contradiction are commonly joked about.

Some jokes appear to be merely playful, dealing in the absurd, or simply playing with words, just for the fun of it. Although, of course, to display wit by skilful word play, does demonstrate mental superiority, and that may well be the point sometimes.

Specific joke themes found in Asimov's book:

1) The refined/superior becomes human/inferior

Asimov tells a joke about a sophisticated lady, who speaks and acts in divine ways, however at the punch-line she says, *'Brandy, on the other hand makes me burp.'* A completely unexpected statement, that makes us quickly reassess our opinion of the lady. The superior is debunked.

Asimov points out that the change in point of view, the surprise, should come with a minimum of warning, which is why the word *'burp'* is the very last to be uttered.

2) Delusions of grandeur

'It is reported that Madame de Gaulle, in bed one night, said, "My God it's cold." To which her husband, lying stiffly by her side, replied, "In bed, Madame, you may call me Charles."'

Those with delusions of grandeur will not admit to mistakes. For example, in another Asimov joke, a university boss was evaluating different departments, and he observed that the philosophers were the cheapest. Not only didn't they ask for paper and pencils, they didn't even ask for erasers.

These jokes are mocking the superior. Interestingly, the de Gaulle joke makes use of the idea of rigidity, a non-human form. The philosophy joke is really mocking the delusions of a group that appears to claim faultlessness.

3) Failure to meet expectations

In this Asimov joke, two psychiatrists are compared, one is exhausted and the other is relaxed. The first asks the second, *'doesn't it bother you when you listen to your patients?'* The response is, *'Who listens?'*

This is funny because we suspect it may well have a kernel of truth in it. Also, we may reflect that despite our more enthusiastic public statements about our own work, we may think very differently about it privately.

This humour is basically the humour of satire. We mock those in positions of power over us who fail to live up to expectations.

4) The put-down

Producing a witty retort to someone who has just insulted you is often associated with Winston Churchill. Here, Churchill is responding to Lady Astor, who says, *'Winston, if you were my husband, I would poison your coffee.'* Winston replied, *'If you were my wife Nancy, I would drink it.'* American wit, Dorothy Parker was good at the put down. Here, she uses a pun to squash a boring person, who says, *'What it amounts to is that I simply can't bear fools.'* Parker replied, *'Odd. Your mother apparently could.'*

A lawyer is giving a speech. He adopts an informal pose, with an open jacket and hands in his pockets. He notices a well-known speaker in the audience and greets him, mockingly. The well-known speaker responds, *'And how odd to see my good friend Henry on the podium, demonstrating that a lawyer can have his hands in his own pockets on occasion.'*

Lastly, we have the cleverest ever put down. It was made by philosopher, Sidney Morgenbesser, in response to a claim made, in a lecture in New York, by Oxford philosopher, J.L. Austin. The lecture concerned the significance of the double negative in languages:

'In some languages a double negative yields an affirmative. In other languages, a double negative yields a more emphatic negative. Yet, curiously enough, I know of no language, either national or artificial, in which a double affirmative yields a negative.'

Suddenly, from the back of the hall, in a round Brooklyn accent, came Morgenbesser's comment, 'Yeah, Yeah.' (Holt, 2008)

These put-downs are deflating those who have assumed the high ground of superiority. They are returned to the state of ordinary or inferior mortal.

5) Misunderstanding either deliberately or through ignorance/stupidity.

Asimov tells a story about Mrs Gladstone, the prime minister's wife, who misunderstands when someone says, *'Well, there is someone above who alone understands.'* Mrs Gladstone takes this person to be her husband.

Misunderstanding is a rich source of humour, perhaps the classic example is the *Two Ronnies* sketch *Four candles*, where the shopkeeper continually fails to understand the customer's words, and *four candles* becomes *fork handles.*

6) Stupidity, where the irrational is preferred to the rational

In this case, an adulterous woman tells her lover to leap from a 13th floor window in order to avoid detection. He refuses, and she says, *'...is this a time to be superstitious?'*

It is interesting that, in both this joke and the next, the female utters the ridiculous comment. This reflects the fact that jokes have been a man's world and, consequently, women become the butt. The male revels in feeling superior.

7) Stupidity, where someone appears to understand, but doesn't

'A sweet young lady'.....claims to understand the mathematics of astronomy, however, in the punch-line she admits she doesn't understand how astronomers find out the names of the stars.

Did you hear about the Israeli space mission to the sun? They intend to avoid the sun's heat by going at night.

At a nationalist level we seem to enjoy feeling superior to others; ours is the best gang. Each nation makes jokes about the inferiority of its neighbours. In the case of the English, we laugh at the supposed stupidity of the Irish, and the stereotypical meanness and drunkenness of the Scots.

8) The very serious accompanied by the mundane

Here, a man falls down stairs and dies. The punch-line is, *'Broke his glasses too.'*

We don't expect people to make such trivial comments in the face of something serious. We laugh at our surprise that someone would make such a silly comment. Again, this is the laugh of superiority. Sensible people know not to mix the sacred and the profane.

9) People put their own interests before those of others, which are, in fact, more important.

So, the Asimov joke is that, a very loyal, hard-working employee is, for the first time in 30 years, late for work. He's had a bad accident, but still turns up. In the punch-line the boss says, *'And to roll down two flights of stairs took you a whole hour?'*

Selfishness is a recurring theme in the jokes of Asimov. For example, he recounts a gallows humour joke, where a soldier is complaining to the prisoner that he has a long walk back after the execution.

The mathematician, Karl Gauss, is said to have told someone to tell his wife to delay her death as he was busy trying to solve a problem.

When we laugh at these jokes we are recognising that selfishness is a basic human fault, which, we recognise in others, but not, of course, in ourselves.

10) Coping successfully/unsuccessfully with a mistake

This joke is about a young army officer who complains about a general to a lady who turns out to be the general's wife. The young officer copes by asking the lady if she knows who he is. She doesn't, so the officer clears off.

Mistakes are a rich source of humour. Two classics can be found in *Only Fools and Horses*. Firstly, when *Delboy* goes to rest his arm on a bar, without looking, and falls down because the bar has been left open. Secondly, when a chandelier is removed from a ceiling with great care, only for us to discover, when it crashes to the floor, that the wrong chandelier has been removed.

Mistakes really are surprising. They shouldn't happen, but they do, suddenly and unexpectedly.

11) Sexual failure/inability

The joke is that a professor's wife defends her husband against taunts of possible infidelity with students. The punch-line is: *'He is too decent, too rational, too fine, too fastidious in his morality, and most of all, most of all, he is too old.'*

Interestingly, jokes about aged males and their sexual prowess, swing between the two extremes, either they are useless, or they are sexual champions.
Sexual failure is a male's greatest fear. Jokes about the failure of others, allow men to transfer that fear elsewhere. Have you ever noticed that a man will say something like, *'I've never had any complaints.'* I've never heard a man say, *'I was useless.'* Although I've heard women say it plenty of times!

12) Infidelity

In this joke, a man returns home, unexpectedly, and finds his wife in bed with his best friend. He staggers back and says, *'Max! I'm married to the lady, so I've got to. But you?'*

Similarly, a man returns home, unexpectedly, and finds his wife in bed with his best friend. His wife scowls, and says, *'Here comes Mr Big Mouth! Now the whole neighborhood will know.'*

Both husbands and wives fear that their partner will have an affair. The question is how will they deal with it if faced with the evidence? The surprise, in both these cases is that, firstly, the husband makes a rational rather than an irrational response, and secondly, the wife takes charge, when she should really be cowering.

13) Marital conflict/unhappiness

In this joke, a man at a party says to another man, *'Heavens, what an ugly woman that one is.'* *'That woman'* said the other, *'is my wife.'* The first man flushes painfully and stammers, *'I'm sorry.'* *'Not as sorry as I am,'* says the husband.

A husband says he makes the big decisions and his wife makes the small ones. He is asked what sort of big decisions he makes. He replies, *'I don't know. Big decisions haven't come up yet.'*

The institution of marriage is an endless source of humour, mainly because most adults are married, or in a partnership, and this is their most important, and probably, most complicated relationship. Marriage is something many people have in common. So, they can all share the joke.

Given the negative nature of the jokes, it is rather surprising that people remain married as long as they do!

14) Saucy

An old lady went to her psychiatrist and said she was worried about her husband's sexual potency. The psychiatrist asked for her and her husband's age, 80 and 83 was the answer. The psychiatrist asked when she first noticed this problem. She replies, *'Oh, I first noticed it last night, doctor; but what troubles me is that I noticed it again this morning.'*

A woman, at her psychiatrist's, wants to know what a phallus is. The psychiatrist unzips his trousers and shows her. *'Oh,'* says the woman, suddenly comprehending. *'I see. You mean it's like a prick, only smaller.'*

Sex is the classic material for jokes. It is just enduringly funny. If a comedian is stuck he just gets out his knob gags.

15) Reversal
In this neat reversal, two sardines were startled, in the depths of the ocean, when a submarine glided by:

Said one, 'Heavens, what's that?'
'Nothing' said the other. 'Just a can full of people.'

'Did you hear the one about the woman who grew so disturbed with everything she read about the connection between smoking and cancer that she finally simply forced herself to give up reading?'
In the first example we see the situation from an unexpected perspective, that of a sardine. In the second example, we expect the woman to take the rational course, and give up smoking. In fact, she takes what is rational course from her perspective, and gives up reading.

16) Contradiction

Here, a soldier complains about the food he is served. Not only is it slop, *'...they serve such small portions.'*

The ability to hold two contradictory opinions is a very human condition. We laugh at people's illogical attempts to have their cake and eat it.

A contradiction can come about as a result of a literal interpretation of an idiom. For example, a father criticises his son who is always eating apples, *'Listen, where do you think all those apples come from? You think they grow on trees?'*

17) Deceit

A Prussian king once visited a jail and found that nearly all of the prisoners protested their innocence. He only found one who admitted his guilt. The king released the guilty man as he didn't want him to corrupt the others!

A soldier about to go into battle gives a mate a letter for Mary. *'Tell her my last thought was of her and her name was the last word I spoke. And here's a letter for Helen. Tell her the same thing.'*

We know that people lie in all sorts of situations. They lie to save their skins and they lie in matters of the heart. We don't like it when liars get away with something, so there is joy when a liar is exposed.

There is more surprise in the prisoner joke as we are not too surprised to find a soldier two-timing.

18) Meanness

In this next joke, a rich man is criticised by a cabby for offering a small tip. The cabby points out that the man's daughter gives bigger tips. The man says, *'That's all right for her. She's got a rich father.'*

The man's response is a contradiction as he ignores the fact that he, himself, is rich. People who act in mean ways are not seen as fully human, and are generally ridiculed. Jokes about their meanness are basically attacks on their character, possibly in an attempt to get them to change their behaviour.

19) Word Play

A young woman was introduced to a naval surgeon. She says, *'Heavens, how medical men specialise.'*

Knock, knock! Who's there? Ammonia! Ammonia who? Ammonia bird in a gilded cage.
He: 'How do you like Kipling?'
She: 'I don't know, you naughty boy. I've never kippled.'

There is a joy in playing with words, particularly for young children, although adults are not immune. The pun is the king of word play, surrounded by a court of Spoonerisms, riddles, and knock-knocks.

20) Religious mockery

Joseph and Mary were on their way to Bethlehem when Joseph stumbled and hurt his ankle. He muttered, *'Jesus'*. Mary turned to him, eyes sparkling, and said, *'Just the name for the child.'*

Archangel Gabriel suggests to God that he might like a holiday on earth. *'God shuddered. "No no. It's a world of busybodies. I was there two thousand years ago and that's enough, thank you. I had an affair with a little Jewish girl and they're still talking about it down there.'*

The church is an institution that is easily mocked. One suspects that attacks by comedians, over the years, have added to the general decline in church attendance. It is not surprising then, that some religions forbid humour, in which case it is taboo. Humour is often a way we talk about taboo subjects.

Jokes about religion are on the decline. This reflects the increasing insignificance of religion for many people and the general decline of its power.

People make jokes about what is significant in their society and in their social life. So, for example, Americans make jokes about lawyers. America is a very contractual country, and very litigious; Britain less so, but maybe catching up a bit. It follows that Americans have a lot of lawyer jokes because lawyers are at the heart of American society, whereas Britain, doesn't really have lawyer jokes. (Davies, 2008)

According to Davies, meanness is the dominating theme of American lawyer jokes. Lawyers are, *'calculating, crafty and fond of money'*:

Santa Claus, the tooth fairy, an honest lawyer, and an old drunk are walking down the street together when they simultaneously spot a hundred dollar bill. Who gets it?

The old drunk of course, the other three are mythological creatures.

A key joke theme in British society is the mother-in-law joke, because this lady can have a powerful impact on a man's social and domestic life. She is an intruder, who can gang up with the wife to defeat the husband. There is a tension here, and jokes reflect tensions in life. Interestingly, there are very few jokes about: the wife's mother-in-law; fathers-in-law; sons-in-law, and men's mothers.

In mother-in-law jokes, the portrayal is that she is always, *'ugly, boring, interfering and generally unpleasant.'* (Christie, 2012):

A man went into a bar and ordered a mother-in-law. The barman brought him a stout and bitter.

In England they make fun of the mother-in-law but in Wales we've put her on our national flag.'

Reflection

Clearly, jokes cover a multitude of sins, particularly lust, pride, and avarice. Some are just ridiculous. Others are simply joyful playing with words. Relationships, sexuality and fears are commonly turned to comic effect.

Many jokes are made at the expense of others. We laugh at the failures of people to be human and humane, and we laugh at their mistakes, failures, and stupidity. We mock those who act in a superior fashion, and jokingly bring them down a peg or two.

Jokers, in effect, adopt a superior moral or intellectual stance, and use surprise to get to the laugh.

Surprise is an important element of all these themes. The greatest surprise comes when the most unexpected event takes place.

Activity

All of the activities that follow are about making up jokes based on personal experience. So, you have to rack your brains for funny things that have happened to you in the past. By the way, as you go through the book, you'll find plenty of suggestions as to how you might manufacture such jokes rather than just relying on experience.

If you find that you have not got enough experiences upon which to construct jokes, you should do something about that lack. Mix up with a wider range of people. Go travelling. Just do stuff.

1) Make up a surprise joke based on a mistake

Well, most jokes make use of surprise; the greater the surprise, the better the joke. Mistakes are a fertile source of surprises, for example, there are verbal blunders, mistaken identities, surgical mistakes, driving mistakes, etc.

Here is a totally true one, based on the personal statement of a sixth-former applying for university admission, which I had to assess:

'Please Sir', said this girl who had just finished a draft of her personal statement, 'could you check my draft please? The teacher picked up her work. 'Ah, I see you spend your holidays cycling around the peninsula of France. 'Just one thing,' 'Yes, Sir,' 'It's spelt peninsula, not penisula....

What a cock-up!'

Yes, the personal statement did have peninsula spelt as *penisula*.

So, have you ever misspelt words leading to unfortunate results? Have you ever mistakenly asked a large woman if she was pregnant? The most fertile mistakes for jokes are those that have caused someone much embarrassment.

Not all mistakes lead easily to jokes. For example, I was told the following story by a naval chaplain. I've found it difficult to turn it into a joke. Maybe you can do better than me?

The chaplain was officiating at a burial at sea. As the coffin was lowered into the water he gave the necessary blessing, and there was a fusillade of shots, into the air, from the dead man's comrades. However, the coffin wouldn't sink. It just floated aimlessly around. Someone had forgotten to drill holes into the bottom of the coffin. The ship's captain reluctantly ordered shots to be fired at the coffin, which eventually sank.

2) Make up a joke about lust

So, this guy goes to Ronnie Scotts to hear his favourite band. All of a sudden he sees this gorgeous woman, near the front, standing up, gyrating to the music. He's gob-smacked, she is so lovely. He can't take his eyes off her...transfixed. Then, a crowd of people come in and take a table near him, hiding his view. They just won't sit down, fluffing about. He's so angry. He stands up and yells, 'For God's sake, sit down....I can't see the music.'

This is based on a personal experience. I uttered the punch-line spontaneously in a jazz pub, when my view was similarly obscured. There was much laughter.

3) Make up a joke about deceit, based on personal experience.

Here, is a totally true story, from my time as an exam invigilator:

An exam invigilator is patrolling up and down, bored out of his skull. All of a sudden a girl sticks up her hand. He goes over to her, happy at the break from the boredom. 'Can I have more paper please?' she asks. As she lowers her hand, he sees there is writing on it. 'What's this?' he asks. 'Oh', she says, 'don't worry about that. It's for the next exam.'

That is so silly and so surprising. It is the sort of joke that is more or less impossible for a rational mind to invent from scratch. You couldn't make it up! A great virtue of jokes based on your own experience is that they are quite likely to be original and thus unique.

So, have you been deceived, or have you deceived others? The answer must be yes. Now, can you turn that deception into a joke?

4) Create a put-down that you could use in future

I was once at a bar in Chelsea talking about football with a mate. 'That ref. yesterday didn't need glasses, he was so far away from the ball he needed binoculars,' I said. 'Ah, sarcasm, the lowest form of wit...' said my mate. 'Dunno about that,' I said, 'I would have thought the lowest form of wit was using clichés.'

That put down actually happened with a student, who had butted into a conversation I was having with a colleague, in a college canteen. The student accused me of being sarky (not the first time this has happened!). I squashed him with the riposte.

I had previously worked out this response to the *'sarcasm, the lowest form of wit'* jibe. So, what appeared to be spontaneous was not. All too often we don't have a response to a joking attack. After the event we think of something we could have said, but by then, of course, it's too late. The solution is to have some ready-made ripostes.

5) Think of a time you successfully deflated someone and turn it into a joke.

This smart advertising executive was in a swanky bar trying to impress a glamorous woman he'd just met, but he was failing. 'Yes, I'm in advertising. I'm with a top agency with many blue chip companies as clients.' 'Oh, really,' she says, looking bored. 'I'm incredibly busy,' he says, 'I have to cope with so many calls that I have four telephones on my desk.' 'Oh really,' she says, 'So, how long have you been a telephonist?'

That one actually took place in a college staff room with a colleague who taught advertising and had worked in an advertising agency.

These deflations are best used with someone who is continually boasting about their prowess. The secret is to lower their status by comparing them to: the less prestigious/childish/amateur/animal.

6) Make up a joke based on your own selfishness

'These three brothers went to an uncle's funeral. They were all in their sixties, so they started talking about their own funerals. The oldest said, 'I want one of those funerals where horses pull the hearse, really classy.' The middle one said, 'I want one of those ecological funerals; lots of green and a cardboard coffin.' The youngest said, ' I was just wondering which one of you two would have the next funeral.'

Yes, I more or less said that to my two brothers at a funeral. They were not overjoyed, it has to be said. In fact, I was lucky to get out of that funeral alive.

7) Make up a joke based on a misunderstanding

'This husband and wife, Joe and Kate were out shopping in their local town, when Kate bumped into an old school friend, Judy. They started chatting and Judy complained that she never saw her husband as he was always working. Joe said he'd never actually seen her husband, what was he like? 'Oh, she said, 'He's tall, dark and quite handsome. His only problem is that he has a long neck.' Joe, jokingly said, 'Is he a giraffe?' Kate replied, 'No, he's human.'

That actually happened in Japan, when a Japanese friend of my wife, mistook the jokey giraffe reference, and interpreted it literally. This is quite likely to happen in cross cultural communication as listeners do tend to translate word for word.

I can't turn the following misunderstanding into a joke. Maybe you can. A Personnel Director, in the Potteries, told me about an odd incident that happened when he was recruiting a works manager. An interviewee was met at reception and escorted to the interview office. He was asked to *'sit over there.'* Over there was a table with a chair on it. Believe it or not, the interviewee clambered on to the table, and sat on the chair on the table! Something tells me he didn't get the job!

Incongruity

'How are Sri Lanka doing?

I have just got home after buying my morning newspaper at the local newsagent, which is run by a Sri Lankan couple. The man listens to cricket on the radio, whenever he can, however today he was listening to the reports from the Winter Olympics. *'How are Sri Lanka doing? I asked...*'He laughed, not a polite keep the customer happy sort of laugh, but a genuine laugh. Not hysterical laughter, just the sort of amused laugh that oils the wheels of our everyday short verbal encounters.

Now, why exactly is that observation about Sri Lanka and the Winter Olympics funny? Obviously, Sri Lanka never has any ice or snow, so what chance do people from Sri Lanka have to be competent at skiing or snow-boarding? They couldn't possibly have any chance of training or winning, so they don't have a Winter Olympics team.

The answer, then, is that the comment is absurdly incongruous. The two bits of the jigsaw, Sri Lanka and the Winter Olympics, simply don't fit. The two contrasting bits disturb our minds and what we expect as normal. We laugh at the confusion.

Incongruity is deviation. An incongruity is anything that is inconsistent, illogical, or inappropriate. When someone makes a joke they are often putting together things which are incongruous. In the punch-line they resolve the incongruity so everything makes sense.

Incongruity is associated with negativity. Research shows that jokes often include negative words like: *doesn't, isn't*, and *don't*, e.g. *'If at first you don't succeed, skydiving is not for you.'* Jokes also tend to contain negative type adjectives such as *bad, illegal* and *wrong*, or negative nouns like *error, mistake*, and *failure*. Indeed, negativity is pretty dominant in jokes. Nearly three quarters of a sample of 16,000 one-liner jokes were found to be negative in nature. (Mihalcea & Pulman, 2007)

Carroll (2005) gives us an extremely useful list of comic incongruities:

- The unexpected, The illogical, The improbable, The absurd
- The ambiguous, The abnormal, The immoral, The improper
- The ugly, The inappropriate, The impolite, The inapposite

This list of incongruities is what we mostly laugh about. It is so important that I've provided examples of each, below. This list is a great starting point for any humorist.

- The unexpected

Bonita: *'Somebody in DP (Data Processing) likes to play jokes on me in the computer room. They put a little rubber cockroach inside a cassette tape and when I opened it, it came out, and I started screaming. And they thought it was funny. I did too.'* (Gunning, 2001)

- The illogical

Stamp out quicksand.   (Rees, 1980)

- The improbable

A woman goes into a sex shop and asks the salesman where the vibrators are, and the salesman points to one of the walls, so she walks over to them and she sees a very nice big red one.

She asks the salesman, 'How much is this one?'

He replies, 'It's not for sale luv, it's a fire extinguisher.' (Jokes4us.com)

- The absurd

'Why do elephants paint their toenails green?'

'To hide in the grass.' (Brunvand, 1964)

- The ambiguous

Actor sent to jail for not finishing sentence.   (Bucaria, 2004)

- The abnormal

'A man and his dog are shipwrecked on a small desert island. After months of isolation, the man misses sex so much that he starts thinking about making love to the only other inhabitant, other than his dog, on the island, a wild pig.

One day, he gives in to his urges and walks over to where the pig is sleeping. Before the man can do anything, the dog goes nuts, barking at the man and biting at his legs. As soon as the man moves away from the pig, the dog quietens down.

This goes on for months. The man attempts to make love to the pig, and the dog goes nuts, not allowing the man near the pig. Finally, the man gives up.

Sometime later, another ship is wrecked on the reef, and the only survivor is a beautiful woman, who washes up on shore. The man thanks God for his generosity.

When she wakes up, the man says to her, "You are safe. I will make sure that you eat and that you are protected from the storms." Gratified, she says, "Is there anything I can do for you? Anything at all?"

"Yes," he says with an expectant smile. "Could you watch the dog for a while?" '

(van Munching, 1997)

- The immoral

A forward young fellow named Tarr

Had a habit of grooving his ma.

'Go pester your sister.'

She said when he kissed her,

'I've trouble enough with your pa.'

(Barrington-Gould, 1974)

- The improper

In 2003, Louisiana State District Judge Timothy Ellender arrived at a Halloween party costumed in black face make-up, afro wig, and prison jumpsuit, complete with wrist and ankle shackles.

When confronted with his actions, he noted wearing the costume was 'a harmless joke.'

(Mueller et al., 2007)

- The ugly

'...Just watched that Harry Potter film, but it's pretty unrealistic. I mean...a ginger kid with two friends.' (Manuel, 2006)

- The inappropriate

David Brent, *The Office*:

'Well, there's good news and bad news. The bad news is that Neil is taking over both branches, and some of you will lose your jobs. Those of you who are kept on will have to relocate to Swindon, if you wanna stay. I know, gutting. On a more positive note, the good news is, I've been promoted, so... every cloud. You're still thinking about the bad news aren't you?' (http://www.imdb.com)

- The impolite

A man walks into a lift, which already has a very attractive woman in it.

As the lift is going up he asks, 'Excuse me miss, can I smell your fanny?'

'Certainly not!' came her astonished reply.

'Ah! It must be your feet then.' (Manuel, 2006)

- The inapposite

'Never mind the Titanic—is there any news of the iceberg?' (Rees, 1980)

Carroll's list isolates the different types of incongruity. Clearly, what you can do when developing jokes, is take a cue joke and see if you can make it more absurd, immoral, impolite, etc, etc. the better and more surprising the incongruity, the funnier the joke. As Asimov (1972) noted:

'The sharper the incongruity and the more suddenly it can be introduced, the more certain the laugh and the louder and longer it will be.' (Asimov, 1972)

Asimov reckons that the incongruity should be introduced, *'...with as little warning as possible, in the last sentence.'* Surprise is clearly important, and theorists do see surprise as a necessary but not sufficient condition for humour (Keith-Spiegel, 1972). We can be surprised by many things which are incongruous, but some of them simply aren't funny, such as a young person dying suddenly, or a case of food poisoning in an expensive restaurant.

In a joke there can be three basic incongruous mechanisms: the garden-path, the red-light and the crossroads. (Dynel, 2012)

In the garden-path joke, the listener is deceived by the set-up into making an interpretation which is cancelled out by the punch-line. The listener ends up in a congruous situation only after realising that his/her faulty, but understandable reasoning, was incorrect. Dynel gives this example of a garden path joke:

The patient's family gathered to hear what the specialists had to say. 'Things don't look good. The only chance is a brain transplant. This is an experimental procedure. It might work, but the bad news is that brains are very expensive, and you will have to pay the costs yourselves.'

'Well, how much does a brain cost?' asked the relatives. 'For a male brain, $500,000. For a female brain, $200,000.' The patient's daughter was unsatisfied and asked, 'Why the difference in price between male brains and female brains?' 'A standard pricing practice,' said the head of the team. 'Women's brains have to be marked down, because they have actually been used.'

So, here we have been deceived by the set-up. We have probably assumed that this was a sexist joke, and that the female brain was worth less because it was inferior. The punch-line reveals that our assumption was wrong, and that far from denigrating women, it denigrates men; surprise, surprise.

In a red-light joke, the listener follows the logic of the joke until the surprising punch-line, which stops him/her in his tracks. A new route is then found via the punch-line, which could not have been predicted from the set-up. The punch-line, itself, in effect, is the incongruity. Dynel gives this example:

A naughty boy draws a penis on a blackboard. Lady teacher rubs it off. Next day he draws a bigger one and writes: 'REMEMBER THE MORE YOU RUB THE BIGGER IT GETS!'

Here, the punch-line is incongruous, and requires some thought to distinguish the two ambiguous meanings, which are resolved into the naughtier one. The humour resides in the double entendre. There has been no misdirection in the set-up.

Another example:

Winston Churchill to Bessie Braddock: *'Yes, I'm drunk and you're ugly, but tomorrow I'll be sober.'*

Here, there is no misdirection, no ambiguity. There is just a parallel to be drawn concerning the future state of both parties. The punch-line has stopped the listener in their tracks, and the only way to get going again is to make sense of the whole utterance.

In a crossroads joke there is an incongruity in the set-up. The listener cannot make sense of the joke, until the punch-line, which may also be incongruous, is heard. Dynel gives this example:

A tour bus driver is driving with a load of seniors down the highway when he is tapped on the shoulder by a little old lady. She offers him a handful of peanuts which he gratefully accepts and proceeds to eat. After a few minutes, she taps him on the shoulder again and she hands him another handful of peanuts. The little old lady repeats this gesture about three more times. When she is about to hand him another batch, he asks the little old lady, 'Why don't you eat the peanuts yourself?' 'We can't chew the peanuts because we've no teeth,' was her reply. The confused driver asks, 'Why do you buy them then? The little old lady replies, 'We just love the chocolate coating.'

Here, we have no idea where the joke is going, indeed, we are rather confused by the incongruity of someone buying something they can't use; maybe she's just generous. We can only make sense of this incongruity when we get to the punch-line. This enables us to cross the road to some sort of unsavoury sense.

So, jokes may have: deceptively ambiguous set-ups, logical set-ups or incongruous set-ups. Their punch-lines resolve the set-ups in either: fairly, very, or totally unpredictable ways. In the basic garden-path joke you may end up going one of two ways. In the red-light joke you end up going down an unexpected diversion. In the crossroads joke you might end up going anywhere, it's a mystery tour.

Although we know that incongruity is funny, we don't really know why it is funny. One approach to this issue is based on mistake. A joke gets us to commit to a belief. We then discover that the commitment was an error. The incongruity assists us in discovering the mistake, at which we laugh, maybe because we are admitting our own foolishness (Hurley et al., 2011). The problem with this approach is that it works well enough with garden-path jokes, where we do make a commitment to an assumption, but with a red-light joke there is no commitment, and so no mistake. In this case, it is the surprise that makes us laugh. The problem remains, why do we laugh at surprise, or mistakes, come to that?

Incongruity, to be funny, needs resolution, as with a punch-line. The mind, according to Leon Festinger (1957), is uncomfortable with dissonance (incongruity). It wants to reduce/eliminate any dissonance and achieve consonance, mental balance. Maybe we laugh at a joke because we are happy, relieved that we have been returned to consonance. In a joke telling session we revel in the constant adjustment of dissonance/consonance.

The *'mind reading'* hypothesis adds to incongruity theory in that the amusement, for the joke telling observer, lies in the *'resolution in the mind of the subject of the collision between old perception and new reality...the wheels turning inside the head...'* (Howe, 2002). The observed gains pleasure from mastering the joke, and the observer gains pleasure in observing the mental machinations involved, particularly if the joke is complicated, or, indeed, pathetic, as in, say, the shaggy dog story.

Finally, although incongruity, according to John Morreal (2009), 'is now the dominant theory of humor in philosophy and psychology', it doesn't explain all humorous events. For example, it cannot really explain why humour can be appreciated more than once. Of course, it is possible that a joke might have become forgotten, and a joke can be funny for more than one reason, so the extra dimensions might be seen second time round. It could be that the enjoyment of the first exposure is being recalled (Suls, 1972).

Reflection

Although this has been a short section, it is one of the most important in the book. Quite simply, incongruity is the backbone and the funny bone of humour. No incongruity, no humour. Congruity is no joke. Congruent triangles only have the same angles as each other.

There are various types of incongruity, and these types tend to be associated with different types of humour.

- The unexpected—Practical jokes/Observational humour
- The illogical—Word play/Irony
- The improbable—Dirty jokes/Sick jokes
- The absurd—Childish humour/Fantasy riddles
- The ambiguous—Word play/Puns
- The abnormal—Dirty jokes/Sick jokes
- The immoral—Dirty jokes/Sick jokes
- The improper—Satire/Sexist and racist humour
- The ugly--Sick jokes/Superiority humour
- The inappropriate—Sarcasm/Gallows humour
- The impolite—Sick jokes/Superiority humour/Teasing

- The inapposite--? Actually, this is the least useful of Carroll's categories. The word itself is not commonly used. It means, *'out of place, inappropriate.'* So, it covers all incongruous humour, and duplicates inappropriate humour. Therefore, inapposite is inapposite.

Of course, the different types of humour can go across the range of incongruity, perhaps the best example is limericks. These rhymes, which can be both clean and dirty, cover, and uncover the lot.

To be funny then, just take an ordinary situation and think of how it can be paired with something so that the two together are incongruous. In jokes, we put forward incongruities, negativities, and then resolve them in the punch-line, except in the case of absurd jokes. The punch-line is the prize and the surprise.

Activity

1) Study a newspaper for incongruities.

Whilst a lot of news is simply factual, much of it is about the incongruous, things which have happened that were not expected to happen. The unusual, the unexpected, the negative, these are the subjects that sell newspapers. People don't want to read that today, yet again, the rubbish bins have been collected. That's not news. It's *olds*. People want to read about the not normal—*'Freddie Starr ate my hamster!'*

The more an unusual item concerns an elite person/celebrity, the more likely it is to become news. However, ordinary people can make the news, for example when they get caught in unexpected situations, or when they achieve something remarkable.

At the time of writing this, the following events have made the news:

Judge sent to prison; Jeremy Clarkson caught up in a racism row via a nursery rhyme; UKIP leader gets an egg thrown at him; Max Clifford sent to jail for sexual offences; Dominique Strauss-Kahn sues a Belgian brothel for using the *'DSK'* name, and a school-teacher, Mrs Ann Maguire, is killed by one of her pupils.

Most of these events can quite easily be turned into a joke. However, a joke about a murdered school-teacher would be massively inappropriate; not all incongruity is funny.

2) Make up a joke based on an incongruity found in a newspaper

The great thing about making up jokes about the latest news is that they are fresh jokes, unlikely to have been heard before, however, whilst the character is new, the basic structure of the joke, and the punch-line may be old, or modified.

In the Max Clifford case, there was debate about his penis size, which gives us:

'Did you hear what Max Clifford's nick-name is in Wormwood Scrubs?'................*'Pin'*..........*'I don't get it.'*........*'Pin*........*short for pin-prick.'*

In the Chris Huhne case, we have:

'Did you hear what Chris Huhne's nick-name is in Wormwood Scrubbs?'.........'Rough'

I think the Max Clifford joke is much better. The hearer has been the stooge in the set-up, and the sexual element makes for humour. There is more surprise. The Chris Huhne joke is just word play, and more amusing than downright funny.

I explain where the pin-prick punch-line comes from in the *'A man walks into a bar'* section. I have actually stolen my own punch-line however I suspect that it is not original. It has probably been used many times by many others.

So, do what a lot of comedians do and scour the press for the incongruous, then make up jokes about what you have found.

3) Make up a red-light joke based on a cue joke

I looked at 580 dirty jokes on the internet, and 70% had a red light ending. Usually, a scene is set up which finishes with an unpredictable outcome. So, it's best to develop ability with red light jokes first:

A husband and wife were sitting watching a TV program about psychology explaining the phenomenon of mixed emotions. The husband turned to his wife and said, 'Honey that's a bunch of crap. I bet you can't tell me anything that will make me both happy and sad at the same time.' She replied, 'Out of all your friends, you have the biggest penis.' (Hurley, 2011)

Using Carroll's list of incongruities we can see that this joke is both unexpected and improbable. It is also immoral, impolite, improper, inappropriate and inapposite. Rolling all those incongruities into one makes it such a good joke.

Now, using the joke as a cue joke, can you make it either: illogical; absurd; ambiguous; abnormal; or ugly.

Illogical is not a good approach as the joke is a red light, which is logical in nature. Ambiguity is more appropriate for a garden path joke. So, we are left with absurd, abnormal and ugly. Absurd gives:

'....Out of all your friends you're the only one who can manage 10 times a night.'

You can see why a comedian would be tempted to use the F word instead of *times* in this joke as it has more impact and shock value, as well as having CK at the end.

Another approach is reversal, saying that the wife gives the best blow jobs out of all her friends, has the biggest breasts, etc. Remembering the K rule, *knockers* might be a better word to use than *breasts*. However, the K is silent in this case, so there is less impact.

4) Make up a garden-path joke, using a cue joke

Here, for a cue, I'm using a joke from the classic book on dirty jokes produced by Gershon Legman:

'Judge, he just reached over with the axe and hit him in the ass! 'You mean rectum?' 'Well, it didn't do him no real good.'

Here, we are directed, very firmly, down one path, only to be diverted elsewhere by wordplay. Legman actually considered that such use of Latin euphemisms for a tabooed organ in jokes was, the *'commonest trick.'*

Well, now, that cue joke is very rigid. It cannot be easily modified. More radical treatment is required, which means going down the road of Latin euphemisms for tabooed organs. The best Latin word for joke purposes is *coccyx*-the bone at the base of the spinal column. That word has everything. A C and a CK sound, an allusion to *cock*, and a reference to the backside, which is the funniest part of the body. Here, then, is another red-light joke:

'Sorry I'm late...bit hung-over...in fact last night I was so pissed I fell out of bed...ended up bashing my coccyx.'

I think that's still quite funny even though the punch-line had been given away beforehand.

And another:

'What's the surest way for a girl to lose her virginity?'

'Run into the Manchester United changing room, stark naked, shouting, hi men.'

Two Latin words which have potential are *testicle* and *vagina*. Here are two garden-path jokes, which are very reminiscent of Eric Morecambe.

'That octopus has nice tentacles'...'There's no answer to that.'

'Doctor, do I have something serious?' 'You have acute angina.' 'Oh doctor, lots of men say that.'

I know those two jokes are not very original. I suspect this particular territory has been thoroughly scoured by many before me. What is interesting is that the red-light jokes are technically better because the punch-line is at the very end of the joke, and cannot easily be guessed. So, there is more surprise. The ending of garden-path jokes can be more easily worked out.

Here are some Latin words you might like to play with: *clitoris, uterus, vulva, anus,* and *scrotum.*

'I see in the paper they are opening a new type of brothel in Soho. It's going to specialise in those sex toys...They're calling it UteRUS.'

That inapposite joke is an apposite red-light joke for a red-light area.

5)   Make up a crossroads joke based on a cue joke.

A Scotsman loans a friend a condom, and then asks for it back later. Embarrassed, the friend says, 'Why, Jock, I threw it away.' 'Where?' 'Do ye think we could find it again?' 'Well, hardly, I threw it out of the car window on the highway.' 'Eh mon, ye shouldn't ha' done it! That belonged to the club!' (Legman, 2006)

Hmmm. Well, that's pretty disgusting, albeit ecological in sentiment. The cue here is to concentrate on miserliness in order to invent a new crossroads joke, using the various types of incongruity.

I must admit I found this one quite difficult to do. One thought, which was very quickly discarded, was reusable tampons. (This topic did remind me of a very old joke. *The Sign outside The Tampax factory said—'Skilled fitters wanted.'*)

I went back to first principles, and used a spider-web. I started with MISER, and got associations like: *Scrooge, Spendthrift, Grasping, Tight*, and *Mean*. That didn't seem to be going anywhere. So, I concentrated on what misers don't like doing. That is, the opposite of their preferred behaviour. This led to GIFTS.

GIFTS led to: *Birthdays, Weddings, Charity, Gift Horse, BOGOF,* and *Reciprocation*. I then did the associations with *Charity* and didn't get anywhere much. I looked at *Reciprocation*, and didn't get much apart from *Back-scratching*. This seemed to me to have possibilities, like *baths* and *back-scratching:*

'My mate told me about a prostitute who ripped him off. She just gave him a shower—that's it, nothing else. She charged him a fortune for it as well, £80... I hate people who just sponge off others.'

I quite like that joke. What I particularly like is that it started out with a cue joke about miserliness, and that idea is the only vestige of the original joke.

Cue jokes

'What is the difference between a market gardener and a snooker player?
One minds his peas, the other minds his cues.'
'Doctor, Doctor, I think I am a snooker ball, what shall I do?'
Go to the end of the cue.'

Well, those are both jokes about cues, but they are not cue jokes. A cue joke is my term for any joke which stimulates you to make up further jokes. Those two jokes don't do that as they are too corny. A proper cue joke really takes your fancy. It makes you think can I expand on this? Where can I take this?

If you remember, I introduced this cue joke idea in: *The audience, creativity and chat-up line section.* One cue joke that got me going was what happens when you cross a *Bulldog* and a *Shih-Tzu?* You get: a *Bullshit.* I then went on to develop *Boxer shorts* from *Boxers* and *miniature poodles,* and *willies* from *collies* and *whippets.*

So, the cue joke provides the basic form and idea of the joke, but you change the details, making it your joke, sort of. In fact, as we have seen, you can move on so much that the original joke rather disappears.

Let's take a cue joke and see what we can do with it:

A visitor to a zoo, was being shown around by one of the officials. The pair came to a group of cages in which the products of hybridization experiments were kept.
The official said, 'Now this one's a cross between a tiger and a lion, and we call him a tiglon. And this one's a cross between a swan and a goose, and we call him a swoose. And this one's a cross between a pheasant and a duck.'
'What do you call him?'
'Charley.'   (Sackett, 1968)

Well, my first thought is that you could clean this up and turn it into a joke for all ages. You just have to go through relevant lists and see what works.

'...........................And this one's a cross between a meerkat and a kitten.'
'What do you call him?'
'A Kit-Kat.'

My second thought is that you can modify the cue joke so as to mock someone, preferably a boss, at your place of work, or school/college. You simply end the joke with the person's name. However, the ending isn't quite right for that, so the last two animals will have to change.

'...........................And this one's a cross between a prawn and a rat.'

'What do you call him?'

'Old Simpson.'

My third thought is that you could drop most of the joke, and just have a satirical attack on a boss:

'What do you call a cross between a clapped out beaver and a grouse?'

'Dunno.'

'Old Simpson'

'How come?'

'Obvious. A cross between a clapped out beaver and a grouse has to be a moaning old c—t.'

Next, we have a joke, which is an excellent joke, but has limited development possibilities. Really, a cue joke has to allow you the chance to add material in order to make it yours:

Dear Abby,
I've met this wonderful boy, and I'm terribly in love with him. We're engaged and plan to be married, but I have this terrible problem. He doesn't know about my family; my father's in jail, my mother's running a house of prostitution, my sister is a prostitute there, and my brother is a stockbroker. Dare I tell him about my brother?   (Joyce, 1982)

This joke only needs a change from *stockbroker* to the occupation you wish to mock. Obvious candidates are: investment banker; journalist, and politician. You could also use the name of a rival company or organisation. Depending on the audience, it may help to drop the prostitution references and add drug addict/long-term unemployed perhaps.

Some jokes, although they may be perfectly good jokes, are more miscues than cues as they have limited options for development. Let's look at this wordplay one-liner:

'Drama school needs acting principal'

Well, I think this is something of a miscue. It's a sound joke but it rather ends there as *acting* and *drama* have to go together. Film school is a possibility, but what's the point, and anyway the term drama school is more widely known. You could use the form of the joke as in *Brothel needs vice principal*, but that doesn't really work. Thinking more laterally, you could have *Football school needs substitute teacher*. Or, *Tourism school needs visiting lecturer*. These are OK, but nothing special.

You can find cue jokes that are rich in development opportunities, by searching through joke books, or, increasingly, nowadays, on the internet. Limor Shifman (2009) gives an interesting account of how an internet joke started, developed, changed and produced rivals, just like a cue joke.

Importantly, this joke can be fairly easily changed. It's a fluid, rather than a rigid joke.

Here is the basic cue joke, which started off on a long world-wide journey:

Dear Tech Support:
Last year I upgraded from Girlfriend 7.0 to Wife 1.0. I soon noticed that the new program began unexpected child processing that took up a lot of space and valuable resources. In addition, Wife 1.0 installed itself into all other programs and now monitors all other system activity. Applications such as PokerNight 10.3, Football 5.0, Hunting and Fishing 7.5, and Racing 3.6 no longer run, crashing the system whenever selected.

Reply

Dear Troubled User:
This is a very common problem about which men are complaining. Many people upgrade from Girlfriend 7.0 to Wife 1.0, thinking that it is just a Utilities and Entertainment program. Wife 1.0 is an OPERATING SYSTEM and is designed by its creator to run EVERYTHING!!! It is also impossible to uninstall or purge the program files from the system once installed.

A female response developed later, as a response to the cue joke. It was clearly closely based upon the original:

Entitled *"Upgrading from boyfriend 7.0 to husband 1.0"* The new wife in the latter version complains that *'husband 1.0'* severely limited *'access to wardrobe, flower and jewelry applications,'* which *'functioned flawlessly under boyfriend 7.0,'* and that it *'un-installed many other valuable programs'* such as *'Romance 9.5 and Personal Attention 6.5,'* replacing them with undesirable (sports) programmes such as NFL 7.4, NBA 3.2 and NHL 4.1"

The original joke obviously started in America, with male computer geeks being the likely originators. Once out there on the internet the jokes were widely circulated, and translated.

There were longer versions, shorter versions, and more sexist versions of the girlfriend/wife joke, whilst the boyfriend/husband joke was mostly unchanged.

Once the world at large got hold of the joke, there was a clear move away from *techie* content to terms that the general public could understand.

The jokes were translated into many languages, and whilst there was adaptation to suit local cultures, the basic ideas remained, indicating that, worldwide, *'...the detailed images and stereotypes of men and women seem the same...'*

In Germany the main changed elements were the sports references. NBA was replaced by *fussball.* Also, poker was turned into a German card game. The Indians introduced *saree* and *cricket.* The Portuguese added sexual connotations, for example, *lingerie 7.7* was changed in most texts to *lingerie 6.9.* The Chinese emphasised *gourmet food*, and either omitted *lingerie* or qualified it as *delicate and sexy lingerie.* The Chinese do focus on the importance of food, and they are rather reluctant to talk about sex openly.

The wife's mother appeared in versions of the girlfriend/wife joke. In China this was omitted as the key mother is the man's in China. Chinese wives traditionally lived with their mother-in-law, an arrangement which has not been without its difficulties. An understatement if ever there was one!

Arabia was the main area where the joke didn't catch on. The researcher suggests that this, '...may reflect opposition to some of the values encoded in it, such as pre-marital relationships.'

So, this *geekie* joke is a cue joke, which stayed fundamentally the same, but changed to adapt to different users and cultures. In particular, it enabled the production of a female version, based upon the original, but not sympathetic to it. Jokes begat jokes.

Cue jokes and their adaptation are how jokes evolve. If people like a joke they take it, repeat it, and maybe build on it. If they don't like it, they either ignore it, or develop a joke which opposes its basic values, paradoxically, in this last case, using the form of the original joke.

This takes us to where do jokes begin? Are there people out there whose hobby is to invent jokes? Some people say the joke-smiths are men with time on their hands, like prisoners, and even stockbrokers have been mentioned (Holt, 2008). However, the consensus seems to be that jokes evolve:

'Jokes are not made up but that they come into existence in the course of many interactions...the majority of jokes is not purposefully invented but grows slowly from a spontaneous remark into a real joke...the original anecdote or one-liner is embedded in the pattern a culture has for humorous narratives.' (Kuipers, 2006b)

Even so, Kuipers reckons that, *'There are few really new jokes. Most jokes that people tell have existed in one form or another for many years.'* She gives a Dutch example about a stupidity joke which had the same punch-line in the following cases: German immigrants, maids, farmers, Belgians, Surinamese immigrants, and, most recently, blondes.

This recycling happens with political jokes. You can get identical jokes across the centuries, amongst different peoples. For example:

The very amusing joke about the Jewish refugee from Nazi Germany who kept a portrait of Hitler on the wall of his one-room apartment in New York "to ward off homesickness," was also told about a man from East Germany escaping to the West with a portrait of Ulbricht, and about a Hungarian fleeing from the Kadar regime carrying, of course, the appropriate picture. (Speier, 1998)

This next one has been told about most dictators in the twentieth century: *'...the mighty man is saved from drowning by a brave fellow and, out of gratitude, extends him a wish. But the man, finding out whose life he has saved is shocked and cries out: "Please tell no one that I have saved you." '* (Speier, 1998)

Lastly, we have this one about Richard Nixon, which has also been told about the Clintons. It dates back at least to the 1890s, and continues because it is a very good joke:

So, Nixon's taking a walk around the White House grounds one winter day when he comes across the words 'I hate Tricky Dick' written in urine in the snow. He tells the secret service to investigate. A week later, they come back to him and say, 'Well, Mr President, we've analysed the urine, and it turns out to be Secretary Kissinger's. But we've also analysed the handwriting, and it's the First Lady's. (Holt, 2008)

We are still recycling jokes that the Ancient Greeks told more than a thousand years ago. The oldest joke book to survive is *The Philogelos* (laughter lover), produced around about the 4th Century A.D., and you can still find updated versions of some of the jokes in current joke books:

A dull witted man hears that ravens live more than 200 years. He decides to keep a raven in a cage to find out if he has been told the truth. (Speier, 1998)

'I had your wife for nothing,' someone sneered at a wag. 'More fool you. I'm her husband. I have to have the ugly bitch. You don't.' (Holt, 2008)

So, people tend to recycle old jokes when 'inventing' jokes. The old chestnuts are adjusted to the new situation, which may be one which is causing tensions in the society, or is significant for that society. For example, Kuipers does observe that the class obsessed British modify 'blonde' jokes into working class, Essex girl jokes.

So, who actually tells jokes? The simple answer is men. Kuipers surveyed Dutch people to find people who admitted to telling jokes:

'All the interviewed joke tellers, even the women, saw jokes really as something primarily done by men. Jokes, my respondents assured me again and again, are part of a 'man's world': the pub, the harbour, the soccer club, the billiard club and 'boys' nights out.' Joke tellers told their jokes mainly to other men.'

As *Harry*, the American owner of a small construction company puts it:
'Away from the office, yes on jobsites we tell dirty jokes. If we met away from the office it is okay. But not in the office.' (Ojha & Holmes, 2010)

So, manufactured jokes may be popular in particular work situations, involving working class men. Borman (1988) made an interesting observation in this respect, at American workplaces. Whilst she found practical jokes, and funny stories amongst groups who were working, she found 'memorized' jokes were only told during break times. Clearly, when having a break, people have time for sustained talking and may engage in joke swapping as part of that conversation. There may also be something of a ritual element to this in that this is the time people habitually tell jokes to each other. Also, if you run out of conversation, you have jokes to fall back on. On top of this, there is the relief and pleasure from not doing a repetitive task, so joking may be a natural thing to do.

Adolescents do engage in joke telling, but this seems to take place amongst large groups and less well-known friends. When Cameron et al. (2010) studied two youths, and their family and close friends, for a day, they found no evidence of memorised joke telling.

Kuipers found that her highly educated respondents rarely heard jokes. These people described jokes as:

'...crude, vulgar, simple, easy, predictable, and a forced way of getting a laugh.'

I must admit that in my career of 35 years of university lecturing I never once heard a fellow academic tell a pre-manufactured joke. Academics quite like displaying their mental superiority, so word play is rather favoured. I particularly remember one piece of word play I heard when returning from a training course at *Bournville,* which had been led by a Mr Tombs. *'Ah,'* said the psychology lecturer I was with, *'And what did you make of the sepulchral Mr Tombs?'*

So, the classic manufactured, non-spontaneous jokes are not associated with the educated classes. They are something for the *'lower classes.'* Kuipers takes this observation further and reveals an *'unexpected'* finding of her research, that jokes are particularly associated with those in trade, the *Del-Boys* of this world.

The relationship between trade and jokes is that jokes help break the ice and enable a relationship to be established quickly. I did once work with sales people in the commercial world, and indeed, there were many jokes. One I particularly remember was made by a Geordie at a sales meeting, *'Our family was so poor we used to sell pegs to the gypsies.'* Clearly, this was not original, but it got a big laugh. Maybe part of the laugh was a reward for increasing the stock of the other sales peoples' jokes. These jokes were often crude, for example confusing *Aer Lingus* and *Cunnilingus.*

So, outside of comedy clubs, the joke may be only found in certain parts of society, being shunned on taste grounds by many:

'...only about 10 to 15% of laughter in natural social contexts occurs in response to classically structured jokes that would seem funny when repeated out of context. Rather, most laughter occurs in response to short utterances or non-verbal micro-performances during informal conversation. These might seem funny in the immediate social context, but would often seem fairly mundane or stupid if repeated later.' (Greengross, 2008)

Reflection

It is very interesting that a joke can be, in creativity terminology, a random stimulation. Any joke can trigger off a new line of thought, but there are some jokes which are especially good for this--cue jokes.

Initially, when you are playing around with a cue joke you tend to produce jokes which are pretty similar to the original. Given a bit of time you get variations on the existing joke, and, finally, you can end up with a quality joke which bears little resemblance to the original.

Cue jokes are great for someone just dipping their toe into the murky waters of humour. What you have is a joke which you know is likely to work. If you just modify it a bit it is still likely to be successful. So, to develop your confidence this is where you should start, with the tried and tested. After a while you can become more ambitious and develop more radical versions of the original.

Most importantly, you end up telling your jokes, rather than someone else's. Here is Arthur Berger's (1998) take on this:

'But let me emphasise that I do NOT believe that telling jokes is a good way for the average person to be funny…When you tell a joke you are, in essence, generally performing someone else's material. Some people can do this very well, but many can't…why use other people's?

Finally, jokes snowball. Jokes develop by building on something someone said or wrote. They are a joint construction, much favoured by men, the working classes and those in trade. They are a way for men to relate to each other, without actually talking.

Activity

1)   Read a copy of *The Philogelos*, obtainable via Google.

Why? Well it's interesting to read about what the Ancient Greeks found funny. Also, if someone says your jokes are old, you have a response if you learn one or two of the oldest known jokes, e.g.:

'A miser writes his will and names himself as the heir.'

'A fool sits down next to a deaf guy and farts. The latter, noticing the smell, cries out in disgust. The fool remarks, 'Hey, you can hear all right! You're kidding me about being deaf' (Anon., 2008)

2)   See if you can modify this joke:

'What's the difference between Niagara and Viagra?'

'Niagara Falls.'   (Blake, 2007)

Have a serious go at this before reading my thoughts.

The best I could manage was:

'What's the difference between Victoria and Viagra?'

'Victoria Falls.'

Now, is that a better joke? The *Niagara* one has the benefit of rhyme, whilst the *Victoria* one has the benefit of alliteration, which is not quite as good as rhyme for impact and memorability. However, the *Victoria* joke gives much less of a clue as to the punch-line, so should be more surprising, and therefore funnier. But, Victoria is also the name of a female, so the joke doesn't make complete sense. Of course, you can only be sure about which is the funnier by testing both jokes out on audiences.

If you cannot modify that joke it isn't a problem. It is a rigid joke which doesn't allow that many options, although, hopefully, you have considered flags, droops and wilts.

'What's the difference between Salisbury and Viagra?'

'Salisbury, Wilts.'

3) Improve a random joke

Go to a joke web site, select 5 jokes at random, and see if you can improve some of them. Don't give up straight away. Use SCAMPER.

Gap analysis and A man walks into a bar…

Knock, knock, 'Who's there?' 'The Chicken' 'The Chicken who?' 'The Chicken who crossed the road.' 'Why did the Chicken cross the road?' 'To get to the other side' 'What did it do on the other side?' 'It walked into a bar, and the bartender said, 'Get out we don't serve your type' 'So, what did the chicken do?' 'It Eggs-itted.'

We've all heard plenty of knock-knock jokes, and *'man walks into a bar'* jokes, not to mention *'How many----does it take to change a light bulb?'* jokes. These formulaic jokes have a standard set up which alerts us to the fact that a joke is about to be told. We can predict the basic structure of the joke and that there will be a final punch-line that changes the pattern of the joke abruptly.

Here, I am going to concentrate on *'A man walks into a bar jokes'*, and consider what they are and how they work. To do this, I have taken 207 of these jokes from the internet and books, and have then analysed them looking out for characteristic patterns. The overall aim is to try to generate completely new jokes of this type by detecting what they do not cover, the gaps. In fact, there are 18 original jokes in this section, or, at least, I think they are original.

The gap searching technique is known as *Gap Analysis*. Here, you look for gaps in the existing coverage and work out feasible ways to plug those gaps. These gaps are either specific to the joke or more general about the sort of humour being used/not used. So, specific gaps might be a lack of women walking in, the absence of a specified bar, or whether the barman is the butt or not. General gaps might be whether double punch lines are used, satire is used or topicality indicated. The actual analytical framework you use depends on your frame of reference, what you are particularly looking for in the joke.

The actual framework emerges after reading a sample of the jokes. Indeed, you can find that you missed something and so you have to go back over the jokes looking for some category you hadn't initially considered.

This approach is very rational and logical in nature. What emerges at the end is a list of areas not covered by the existing jokes that can then be explored creatively. As a result I have produced jokes: where a woman is the victor; that have double punches, and a limerick, etc.

This is one of my favourite man walks in..:

A man walks into a bar and points at a beer tap. 'Do you want a pint?' asks the bartender. The man nods, and the bartender notices that the man has a huge scar across his throat. 'Where did you get that?' he asks. The man manages to croak, 'Falklands.' 'Blimey', says the bartender. 'Well, have this one on the house, mate. You boys did a great job over there.' The man says, 'Muchos gracias.'

Well, be honest, you didn't really expect that ending did you? This joke is pretty typical however it does have two unusual elements. Firstly, the bartender is rarely the butt/victim of the joke. He/she (the gender is not usually specified), is more likely to have the role of questioner or punch-line imparter. Secondly, these jokes are most unlikely to be topical. They are timeless and so can be handed down through the generations.

A MAN walks into a bar, on his own, in about half the jokes. Otherwise he is with an animal or an object. A woman doesn't walk into a bar very often. Animals can go into bars and talk, as can inanimate objects, and abstract concepts.

A Bear walks into a bar and says to the bartender, 'I'd like a beer………………………………………………… and a bag of crisps, please.' The bartender replies, 'Sure, but why the large pause?'
The Bear says, 'I've always had them.'

A giraffe walks into a bar, orders a drink and leaves.

A monocle walks into a bar. The bartender says, 'That's amazing. A monocle just like you came in half an hour ago. We've never had a monocle in here before, and now we have two. Why don't you go and talk to him? He's over there drinking a Guinness.'
The monocle says, 'Don't you know, monocles never mix up together.'
The bartender says, 'Why ever not?'
The monocle replies, 'We don't like to make spectacles of ourselves.'

I thought that one up after considering the various occupations, sited in the local high street, which could feature in these jokes. I eventually got to the opticians and the fairly obvious punch-line. The joke was constructed on the punch-line.

Here is one derived from consideration of the local restaurants:

A spoon walks into a bar. The bartender says, 'We don't want your sort in here.' The spoon replies, 'Why not?'
The bartender says, 'You're always stirring things up.'

Actually, the bartender does sometimes refuse service in these jokes. Usually the customer is inanimate.

A nose walks into a bar and asks, 'Can I have a pint of lager please?'
The bartender replies, 'Sorry, I can't serve you. You're already off your face.'

William Shakespeare walks into a bar. The bartender says, 'Get out, your Bard.'

Celebrities/The famed do not usually feature in these jokes, however, they can be found in about 6% of them:

Jesus walks into a bar. The bartender says coldly, 'Shut the blooming door, what's the matter with you? Were you born in a barn?'
So this relative absence of celebrities presents an opportunity for original jokes:

Tracey Emin walks into a bar and orders a bottle of whiskey, a bottle of brandy, a bottle of gin, and a

bottle of cocktail cherries.
She then gets completely undressed and pours the whiskey, brandy and gin over herself, and then sticks the cherries all over her body.
The bartender asks, 'Tracey have you moved on to performance art?'
Tracey replies, 'No, I just can't stop making an exhibition of myself.'
The bartender says, 'We all know that. It's just that I thought you might have started a new art movement.' 'What might that be?' says Tracey.
'The Pubists.'

Well, that one came about because I decided to consider famous artists as possible candidates for inclusion, and Tracey was the first to come to mind. What is unusual about this joke, apart from the use of a celebrity, is the use of a double punch-line. These jokes normally end in a single punch-line.

Here's another double punch, based on an existing joke:

A dyslexic walks into a bra, has six pints, stumbles out and goes arse over itt.

(Actually you could use tit in this case) (This does lead to: A breast and a buttock walk into a bar, fall over, and go arse over tit)

There are, of course, a great variety of punch-lines. What is interesting is that a quarter of the punch- lines are puns: a fairly simple ending for a fairly simple joke. It is as if the format was devised to enable pun usage.

The past, present and future walk into a bar. It was tense.

Although, puns are very common, idioms are pretty rare as punch-lines. So, opportunity for new jokes exists here as we shall see in the activities section at the end.

Sex, surprisingly, doesn't feature that much. It appears in about 11% of the jokes:

A rather confident young man walks into a bar and takes a seat next to a very attractive young woman. He gives her a quick glance, then, casually looks at his watch for a moment. The woman notices this and asks, 'Is your date running late?'

'No', he says, 'I just bought this state-of-the-art watch and I was testing it.' Intrigued, the young woman says, 'A state-of-the-art watch? What's so special about it?' 'It uses alpha waves to telepathically talk to me', he explains.

'What's it telling you now?' 'Well, it says that you're not wearing any panties....' The woman giggles and replies, 'Well it must be broken then, because I am wearing panties!'

The man exclaims, 'Damn—this thing must be an hour fast!'

I've seen that fairly long joke compressed as a chat-up line. Maybe that chat-up line formed the basis of the above joke.

Where a female does appear in these jokes she is more likely to be a victim/degraded than be a victor:

A woman and a duck walk into a bar. The bartender says, 'Where did you get the pig?' The woman says, 'That's not a pig, that's a duck.' The bartender says, 'I was talking to the duck.'

Here, then, is an opportunity for new jokes based on female victory:

A man and wife walk into a bar. The wife orders the drinks and tells her husband, 'Sit down Newt.' A woman sitting near-by hears this and asks, 'That's an unusual name, 'I've only ever heard of one other Newt, Newt Gingrich. His real name is Newton. How did your man get that name? Is it short for anything?' 'Oh yes,' the wife says, it's real short for something. I call him that because he's my newt.'

The standard way for women to win is to disparage the male apparatus. I lifted the punch-line in this case from a joke about a man taking a newt called *Tiny* into a bar.

3 months after writing that joke I was reading the newspaper and came across the word *pinprick*. Straight away the connection to the *My Newt* joke was made. So, ...'*Sit down Pin*'......'*I call him that because he's got a pinprick.*'

Once you really get into this joking lark it's as if you develop a joke-radar. There is a chunk of your mind constantly scanning the world round about you, and every so often something pings, giving you a new joke.

A few of these jokes focus on the bar itself:

A woodworm with no teeth walks into a bar and says, 'Is the bar tender here?'

A ballerina walks into a barre.

That one is unusual in that it works when read rather than when spoken. The classic BAR joke is:

A man walks into a bar, Ouch!

This has been developed:

A horde of lemmings walk into a bar, 'Ouch', 'Ouch', 'Ouch', 'Ouch', 'Ouch', 'Ouch', 'Ouch'...

It would be very difficult to come up with a new joke using the bar itself, although nothing is impossible as the limbo dancer said when he walked into the bar, and was disqualified.

It is very unusual for the bar to be located anywhere in particular. Normally it is just an anonymous, placeless bar. Sometimes a location is given as the place of action is required for the joke to work:

A guy walks out of a bar on the moon, complaining, 'The drinks were OK, but there was no atmosphere.'

This does mean that new jokes are possible using a located or specified bar:

A an walks into a topless bar.

All manner of weird things happen in the bar. Maybe it's the alcoholic arena that facilitates the surreal. Here, we have a classic example:

A man walks into a bar with a slab of asphalt under his arm and says, 'A beer please, and one for the road.'

Alcohol itself is integral to about 13% of these jokes:

A screwdriver walks into a bar and the bartender says, 'Hey, we have a drink named after you!' The screwdriver responds, 'You have a drink called Brian?'

Brand names are rarely used. When they are they usually have the same punch-line as the screwdriver one.

It is very unusual to find a satirical element in these jokes. Here is a rare example:

A man, using Apple Maps, walks into a bar, or maybe a hospital, or possibly a church.

That joke then, offers real potential for the creation of original satirical jokes, as rivals do not exist:

A clown, an adulterer, a toff, and a blonde walk into a bar. The bartender asks, 'What will it be Mr Mayor?'

To create this joke I made use of someone else's clever device of pretending that four different people were involved, when in fact there is only one person. The original cue joke was a rather poor affair about Barack Obama being an illegal immigrant, a lawyer, a pathological liar, and a communist.

The Mayor joke will become out-dated, but no doubt can be updated...Prime Minister?

Here's another in the same vein:

A toff, an eccentric, an adulterer, and a long suffering waiter walk into a bar. The bartender says, 'We don't see you in here much, Prince Charles.'

Three items is the expectation in a joke, so 4 elements can be reduced to 3:

A priest, a paedophile, and a rapist walk into a bar, and he has a drink.

I only came across one example of a limerick and a bar, and, oddly enough, not one bar was located in *Limerick*. The one example was very poor, maybe because there is not much that rhymes with bar. Here is my effort:

Alan Partridge walked into a bar
And ranted loudly, over a jar,
'God made Adam and Eve,
Not Adam and Steve.'
Alan's funny peculiar, not funny ha ha.'

This limerick started with thought as to what rhymes with bar. *Ha* soon emerged, and led to Alan's standard catchphrase. A bit of *Googling* led to the third and fourth lines. This left the second line which is fairly weak because of the lack of rhymes.

You can find jokes of this type aimed at a particular type of audience, and not the world at large. Here, the listener requires specialist knowledge to decipher the joke. Clearly, the joke teller must be pretty sure that the audience will get the joke, otherwise the joke will fail:

Two chemists walk into a bar. The first one says to the bartender, 'I'd like some H_20. The second chemist says, 'Oh that sounds good. I'll have some H_2O, too. The second chemist died.

A teacher walks into a bar. He says to the barman, 'Two half pints of lager in pint glasses, to go please.' The bartender says, 'Are you having a laugh?'
The teacher says, 'No, I'm just taking the Piaget.

This one I devised for the benefit of educational psychologists. It refers to Jean Piaget, a Swiss researcher, who found that children experience stages of mental development. At around the age of 7 they recognise that volume is conserved when liquids are transferred from vessel to vessel, before that they think there is more in a taller vessel, irrespective of the vessel's diameter. Jokes just don't work when you have to explain them.

Reflection

It is obviously very useful to absorb yourself into different types of jokes. You see how they work, what they concentrate on, and what they ignore. What are the gaps? As a result you can more easily create new jokes or develop new ones based on the existing jokes.

Gap analysis reveals that *'The man walks into a bar'* joke uses a lot of puns in the punch-line but few idioms. It never uses a double punch-line. It is rarely satirical and mentions few celebrities. It downgrades women. It is not, typically, a sexual joke. It is rather surreal in nature. So, new joke potential lies in these gaps: idioms, satire, celebrities, double punch-lines, female victory, and sex.

Activity

1) Work out set-ups for the following punch-lines. (Suggested answers are at the bottom of the next page.)

a) *So, the bartender showed him a picture of his naked wife*

b) *'I can't serve you, what are you, nuts?'*

c) *'I hope you're not going to start anything with that.'*

d) *'I'm just a little hoarse.'*

e) *'I'll have anything as long as it's not a Canadian Club.'*

2) Work out a likely punch-line for the following jokes. In each case the bartender has refused to serve the customer. Why? A pun or idiom is integral to the punch-line:

a) *A pork chop walks into a bar.....*

b) *A golf club walks into a bar......*

c) *A brain walks into a bar (idiom)......*

d) *A ghost walks into a bar and orders a whiskey.....*

e) *A group of fonts walk into a bar......*

3) Work out a joke on a man going into a bar near Buckingham Palace

4) Work out a joke which has the following idioms in the punch-line. It might be best to consider refusal to provide service for b, c, d and e:

a) *Barrel of laughs*

b) *One over the eight*

c) *Off the wall*

d) *Elephant in the room*

e) *Too close to the knuckle*

Possible answers:
1)
a) A man walked into a bar to have a few drinks. The bartender says, 'What'll you have? The man said, 'Surprise me.....
b) Two almonds walk into a bar and order drinks. The bartender looks at them incredulously and exclaims....
c) A man walks into a bar with a chequered flag. The bartender looks at him warily and says....

d) A pony walks into a bar and coughs, 'hey gimme a beer (coughs). The bartender serves him and says, 'What's with your voice?' The pony says….

e) A baby seal walks into a bar and the bartender says, 'what will it be stranger?' The baby seal replied……

2)

a) 'Get out we don't serve food in here.'

b) 'I'm not serving you because you'll be driving later.'

c) 'I'm not serving you as you're out of your skull.'

d) 'We don't serve spirits here.'

e) 'We don't serve your type in here.'

3) A man walks into a bar near Buckingham Palace, sits down, and says, 'Give me a beer. I've had a rough day at work.' And the bartender says, 'Oh, What do you do?' The man says, 'I take care of the corgis--you know the dogs the royal family owns. The bartender asks, 'Tough job, huh?' The man says, 'Yeah. All that inbreeding has led to low intelligence and bad temperaments. And the dogs aren't too smart, either.'

4)

a) A man walks into an empty bar and orders a pint. As he starts drinking he hears a chuckle, then a giggle, next a chortle, and finally a guffaw. He asks the barman, 'Are you a ventriloquist?' 'What?', says the barman. The man says, 'Where's that noise coming from?' The barman points to the beer keg, 'From that, it's a right barrel of laughs.'

b) The number 9 walks into a bar. The barman says, 'I'm not serving you.' 'Why not?' replies the 9, 'You're already one over the eight.'

c) Two bits of graffiti walk into a bar. The barman says, 'I'm not serving you. You're totally off the wall.'

d) A mammoth walks into a bar. The barman says, 'This is a happy bar, I'm not serving you.' 'Why ever not? I'm quite amusing', says the mammoth. The barman says, 'The last thing we need is an elephant in the room.'

f) A finger nail walks into a bar. The barman says, 'This is a respectable establishment, I'm not serving you.' 'Why not?' replies the fingernail. The barman says, 'You're too close to the knuckle.'

Berger's techniques

Humour is like a frog; if you dissect it, it dies. (Mark Twain)

Arthur Berger, an American professor, decided to make a detailed study of those things that make people laugh. He carried out an analysis of a wide variety of humorous materials and found that there were precisely 45 techniques of humour, which he categorised under four headings: Language, Logic, Identity, and Action. (Berger, 2010)

It is these techniques that all humorists make use of in order to be funny. From: Shakespeare to Shaw; Woody Allen to Woody Woodpecker, and Spike Milligan to Sarah Millican. All of them only have only 45 techniques to play with.

This list of techniques can be used to analyse humour and, by acting as a catalyst, a provocation, create it. Usually, more than one technique is in operation when we see or hear something funny, so when we come to creating humour with this approach we have to decide which techniques to combine.

Berger explains that many of these techniques can be reversed. So, if we take *'exaggeration'*, its opposite, *'understatement',* can also be understood to be part of the list.

In this section I will explain the list and in the next section I will look at how to use the list in order to be funny.

<u>Language</u>

Allusion; Bombast; Definition; Exaggeration; Facetiousness; Insults; Infantilism; Irony; Misunderstanding; Literalness; Puns/Wordplay; Repartee; Ridicule; Sarcasm; Satire

<u>Logic</u>

Absurdity; Accident; Analogy; Catalogue; Coincidence; Comparison; Disappointment; Ignorance; Mistakes; Repetition and Pattern; Reversal; Rigidity; Theme and Variation

<u>Identity</u>

Before/After; Burlesque; Caricature; Eccentricity; Embarrassment; Exposure; Grotesque; Imitation/Pretence; Impersonation; Mimicry; Parody; Scale; Stereotypes; Unmasking

<u>Action</u>

Chase; Slapstick; Speed

(Source: Berger, 2011)

Language Humour

Looking at the language part of the list first, it seems that verbal humour is rather geared up to making fun of someone else, attacking them, and/or being, or attempting to be, superior to them. Still, not everything on the language list is an attack or about superiority. Puns and wordplay are usually just silly, whilst irony and definitions are more sophisticated forms of wordplay. Exaggeration is a fundamental humour technique which is not necessarily antagonistic.

So, when we *'Ridicule'* someone, we adopt a superior position, and mock, deride and humiliate them. Cartoonists do this when they show politicians falling, failing or farting. They are usually making a satirical comment as well.

Satire is a general technique that uses the humour of: irony, exaggeration, insult, invidious comparison, or ridicule to expose the stupidity or vices of others. The satirical magazine *Private Eye* is famed for its attacks on the powerful, particularly via its front cover, which usually has a photograph, a caption, and a speech bubble.

A particularly good one had a photograph of George W. Bush, with the caption—'Bush: Countdown to war.' The following speech bubble came out of his mouth---*'10, 9, 8, 7, 6, 5, 4, 3, 2, er....'*

Sarcasm is another superiority mockery, this time an exaggerated contemptuous verbal attack on another. It is clearly related to the insults category such that the dividing line may not be clear...*'He has no enemies but is intensely disliked by his friends.'* There is no masking of the aggression.

Insult humour can be quite nasty:

A woman gets on a bus with her baby. As she pays for her ticket, the bus driver says. 'That's the ugliest baby I've ever seen. Eeuuugh!'

The woman sits down fuming. She says to a man next to her: 'The driver just insulted me.' The man says, 'You shouldn't take that. You tell him off—go ahead. I'll hold your monkey.'
(www.smileofthedecade.co.uk)

That poor woman was left speechless, without any comeback, any repartee. Berger sees *Repartee* as *'a technique which counters aggression with aggression.'* Repartee must be made immediately following an attack. Because of this it is seen as clever and witty. Comedians, to cope with attacks have a ready supply of put-downs for hecklers. Really, if you are not sharp witted enough to answer an attack immediately, it is best to have your own supply of prepared answers.

Here's one developed from a put-down by George Bush Sr. ....*'That answer was about as clear as Boston Harbour.'* Using that as a cue we get, *'That answer was about as clear as the Manchester Ship Canal.'*

The name of your local polluted river can be substituted, but canal is better as we have the magic C sound and canals are often murky. In this case we also have assonance based on the sound of the word *ship (shit)*. So, a nice generic come-back for virtually anything someone else says attacking you.

Bombast is an attempt at superiority, using exaggerated high sounding language with little meaning in order to impress others, just like *Del Boy* in *Only Fools and Horses....'Si danke schon, bonjour.'* We laugh at his pretentiousness.

Jokes based on *Literalness,* often involve mockery of the less able. The victim is not able to comprehend the meaning of language, and takes it at its face value. Berger (1998) gives the following example:

'Why did the moron bring a ladder to the party? He heard the drinks were on the house'.

We mock those adults whose humour is childish and *'Infantile'.* They seem to have arrested mental development so act like children. The jokes they produce are not appropriate. We laugh at, rather than with them. Infantile jokes often have weak word play and a toilet reference:

'Why did the sand blush?'

Because it saw the sea weed.'

That 'joke' relies on the ambiguity of language. It is this ambiguity that works in *Puns/Wordplay.* Although the pun isn't usually used to deride others, it is rather derided. However, it can work when it is surprising, and relies on a double meaning, rather than a double sound. Also, it is often a key part of a longer joke. The pun is the basis of much childish humour, notably in riddles and knock-knock jokes. Here's quite a nice pun joke:

'I did a theatrical performance about puns. Really it was just a play on words.' (punoftheday.com)

Definitions are what you find in a dictionary, but a humorous definition is a defining technique that contains an element of trickery, wordplay. A nice example is, *Pundit* –Milton Jones. Definitions do allow for insult. Berger gives an example from Ambrose Bierce:

'A bore: someone who talks when you want him to listen.'

Misunderstanding is concerned with people not communicating effectively with each other. It is about the language we use and its ambiguities:

A man walks into a book shop and says, 'Can I have a book by Shakespeare?' 'Of course, sir,' says the salesman. 'Which one?' The man replies, 'William.' (Arnott & Haskins, 2004)

When we are being *Facetious* we treat serious issues with deliberately inappropriate humour...*'If the unemployed got jobs they wouldn't be so poor.'* The facetious person probably doesn't mean what he or she says. So, the technique of *Irony* is not a million miles from the facetious. Here, we reverse the rules of language by saying the opposite of what we really mean. We might say *'Nice day today'*, when there's a blizzard. Irony is a dangerous humour as others may take what we say ironically at face value, and consequently regard us as odd or lying.

That just leaves *Allusion, and Exaggeration* in the language humour category. These don't seem to have much to do with superiority, however, Berger points out that, allusions *'are tied to mistakes, errors, gaffes, stupid things people say.'* An allusion enables us to recall something that is embarrassing for someone. Frequently, this is about something sexual—*'on the job training'*, *'at it all night'*, etc., etc.

It is funny when someone doesn't get the allusion. Margaret Thatcher was famed for this, for example, she once claimed that, *'Jim Callaghan couldn't organise pussy!'* (Cameron, 2013)

Finally, *Exaggeration* is one of the basic techniques of humour. Exaggeration distorts and makes something more ridiculous. It is not necessarily an attack, but may be used as part of one. The classic case of exaggeration is the tall story, which is typically American:

The mosquitos of Alaska are world famous for their size and ferocity. During the mosquito season no Alaskans go out at night, except in cars. One night, an unsuspecting visitor was seized by two gigantic mosquitos. 'Shall we eat him here or take him to the swamp?' one of the mosquitos asked the other. 'Here,' said the other. 'If we take him to the swamp, the big mosquitos will take him away from us.' (Berger, 1998)

Logic Humour

Logic humour is essentially about things not being right. It is incongruity humour where an orderly world becomes disorderly, and that is often, but not always, funny.

Logic humour covers: the totally illogical, things going wrong, comparisons and contrasts.

The most illogical humour is the *Absurd* as it totally ignores the laws of logic. It is about nonsense and confusion, with no resolution. The absurd is puzzling. It is appealing to children, and to the child in adults:

Q. *'How do you hide an elephant?'*

A. *'Paint its toenails red and stick it in a cherry tree.'*

Spike Milligan is perhaps the best absurdist of recent times. The *Goon Shows* were simply ridiculous, but funny. Spike also appealed to children with his fantastical verse:

'Mountains should have holes in

To see the other side.

By observing the view thru this aperture

Would save a considerable ride.'

Absurdity is out on its own, however quite a lot of techniques relate to things going wrong.

Accidents and *mistakes* make the world disorderly. A logic accident is not a mistake as such. It is a failure to say something properly, when the correct pronunciation is known. Such slips of the tongue are due to stress, intoxication, etc. So, *'...my awful wedded wife.'*

Typos obviously qualify here as well. Also, there are grammar failures where a sentence is, inadvertently, poorly constructed: Butcher's sign. *'Try our sausages. None like them.'* (www.guy-sports.com)

A mistake stems from inattention, ignorance or foolhardiness. We laugh in a superior way at those who make mistakes, particularly where slapstick and embarrassment are involved:

During the service, the pastor asked if anyone in the congregation would like to express praise for prayers which had been answered.

A lady stood up and came forward. She said, 'I have a reason to thank the Lord. Two months ago, my husband Jim had a terrible bicycle wreck and his scrotum was completely crushed. The pain was excruciating, and the doctors didn't know if they could help him.'

You could hear an audible gasp from the men in the congregation as they imagined the pain that poor Jim experienced. She continued, 'Jim was unable to hold me or the children and every move caused him terrible pain. We prayed as the doctors performed a delicate operation. They were able to piece together the crushed remnants of Jim's scrotum and wrap wire around it to hold it in place.'

Again, the men in the congregation squirmed uncomfortably as they imagined the horrible surgery performed on Jim. She continued, 'Now, Jim is out of the hospital and the doctors say, with time, his scrotum should recover completely.'

All the men sighed with relief. The pastor rose and tentatively asked if anyone else had anything to say.

A man rose and walked to the podium. He said, 'I'm Jim and I would like to tell my wife the word is sternum.'   (http://poddys.squidoo.com)

A pretty good joke, made better by the tension it causes, particularly amongst men. Laughter may come about as relief of that tension.

Berger classifies *Coincidence* alongside accidents and mistakes. A coincidence is sort of accidental as it wasn't planned, but it just happens because of the randomness of life. A coincidence may be funny because someone ends up in an awkward situation and so becomes embarrassed:

A man walks into a bar, sits down and orders a triple martini. The bartender says 'What a coincidence, the only other person at the bar is that beautiful woman at the other end. She is also drinking triple martinis.'

After a few sips of his drink, the man walks up to the woman and says, 'Isn't it a coincidence that we are both having the same drink.' She replies 'Yes!' I am here because I am celebrating. After 20 years of trying I am finally pregnant!' 'What a coincidence' the man replied. 'I am also celebrating. After years of experimenting, I have invented a multi-coloured chicken.' At this the woman asked 'How did you ever accomplish that!?'

'I had to try a lot of different cocks' he said.

The woman replied 'What a coincidence!!' (www.jokebuddha.com)

Well, that's a joke about coincidences, but it's not much of a joke. This is because the punch-line has been revealed before the end of the joke. As a result there is no surprise, so no merriment.

Jokes about *Ignorance* as such, deal with fools, or normal people who have been made to appear foolish through the trickery of others. So, this is very much superiority humour where people end up doing something stupid.

I shall avoid Irish jokes. Here is one about the old, who appear to be fair game still;

'A guy walking down the street one afternoon passes an old man sitting on the side of the road with a large sack. The younger guy says to the old man, 'Watcha got in the sack?' The old man responds, 'I got some monkeys in that there sack.' The younger man asks, 'If I guess how many monkeys you got in the sack, can I keep one?' The old man replies, 'Son, if you guess how many monkeys I got in this sack, I'll give you both of 'em.' (http://www.arwscripts.com)

That joke is not a million miles from an all-time classic, Dad's Army joke. The one where Captain Mainwaring says, *'Don't tell him Pike.'*

The ignorance of normal people is often revealed by what the Americans call a snipe hunt. Here, a young newcomer to an organisation is given an impossible or imaginary task. One such task is to obtain an ID 10T form to be filled out for the government. The gullible person will go off and ask someone for such a form.

Other tasks, of which there are many, include obtaining a: bacon stretcher; soufflé pump; glass hammer; brass magnet, and a left-handed screwdriver. (http://en.wikipedia.org)

Jokes about *Disappointment* are often sexual in nature. They involve leading people up the garden path, and then denying them their logical expectation. Berger considers that disappointment humour is similar to teasing. It is fooling people:

A little sexy housewife was built so well the TV repairman couldn't keep his eyes off her. Every time she came in the room, he'd near about jerk his neck right out of its joint looking at her.

When he'd finished she paid him and said, 'I'm going to make a...well...unusual request. But you have to first promise me you'll keep it a secret...'

The repairman quickly agreed and she went on. 'Well, its kind of embarrassing to talk about, but while my husband is a kind, decent man—sigh—he has a certain physical weakness. A certain disability. Now, I'm a woman and you're a man...' The repairman could hardly speak, 'Yes. Yes!'

'And since I've been wanting to ever since you came in the door...'

'Yes, yes!'

'Would you help me move the refrigerator?' (http://www.nairaland.com)

That joke's quite a tease, and not funny for the listener. It collapses like a lead balloon. These disappointment jokes are best avoided.

One type of disappointment is sexual failure, which is directly countered by Viagra jokes about *Rigidity*. These jokes are funny because of the incongruity of old men with long-standing erections. The old men become machine-like, non-human, and it this which is at the base of rigidity humour.

Rigidity is about a lack of human feeling, when acting in an automatic, absent-minded or obsessive way, and so things go wrong:

A man is walking along the street when he is brutally beaten and robbed. He lies unconscious, bleeding.

While he is lying there, a police officer passes by, but crosses to the other side of the road, without trying to help. A boy scout does the same. As do a number of pedestrians.

Finally, a psychologist walks by, and runs up to the man. He bends down and says, 'My God! Whoever did this needs help.' (http://home.spynet.com)

Turning to the logic jokes that deal with comparison, we have:

Analogy and *Comparison*, which are much the same as each other for an analogy is a type of comparison eg., *The heart is like a pump.* An analogy shows how one thing is similar to another. On its own an analogy isn't funny, to be funny the analogy has to be *'invidious,'* most likely insulting or ridiculous:

The doctor was caught in bed with the farmer's wife and explained to the shocked husband that he was only taking her temperature.

The farmer took his shotgun off the wall, primed it and said grimly, 'I guess you know what you're doing, but that thing had better have numbers on it when you take it out.' (Pease, 2005)

A *Comparison* is more direct than an analogy, and more critical:

Q. *'What's the difference between a shopping trolley and a university vice chancellor?'*

A. *'You fill them both up with as much food and alcohol you can but it's only the shopping trolley that has a mind of its own.'* (http://richardwiseman.files.wordpress.com)

Theme and variation humour compares the ways in which different types of people vary with respect to a belief, behaviour or activity. The people may differ by nationality, social class, religion, age, etc. Berger points out that this technique is best combined with other techniques like stereotyping, insult, and exaggeration:

An Englishman, a Frenchman and a South Korean are viewing a painting of Adam and Eve frolicking in the Garden of Eden.

'Look at their reserve, their calm,' muses the Englishman. 'They must be English.'

'Nonsense,' the Frenchman disagrees. 'They're naked, and so beautiful. Clearly, they are French.'

'No clothes, no shelter,' the South Korean points out, 'they have only an apple to eat, and they're being told this is paradise. Clearly, they are North Korean.' (http://poddys.squidoo.com)

Next, we have language jokes that contrast.

Repetition creates a tension as a series, a pattern, is established. We wonder if the series is going to be maintained or destroyed. In jokes, a humorist often spins out a logical development, involving a pattern, which is then destroyed by a contrasting punch-line:

'There are lies, damned lies, and statistics.'

That famous quote from Mark Twain has been around for more than 100 years. It has survived the test of time, and must, therefore, be very good. It is amusing. We suspect there is truth in it, particularly when we find a statistic inconvenient. It is memorable because of the brevity and the pattern. The pattern leads us to expect the word *'lies'* in the third instance and an even worse word than *'damned'*, but our expectations are shattered by destruction of the pattern.

To just say *'statistics are a load of lies'* would not be anywhere as near as good. Of course, the trouble with using the Twain quote is that it is now a cliché. We need a new cliché:

'There are liars, damned liars and Richard Nixon.'

You can substitute any name you fancy here, although you have to be careful. You cannot libel the dead, only the living.

Reversal is about events turning out in unexpected, contrasting ways:

A woman goes to a lawyer and says she wants to divorce her husband. 'Do you have grounds?' asks the lawyer. 'Yes,' says the woman, 'six acres.' 'Do you have a grudge?' asks the lawyer. 'No,' says the woman. 'We have a carport.' I'd better get more specific thinks the lawyer. 'Does he beat you?' asks the lawyer. 'No,' says the woman. 'I get up before he does.' 'Well, why do you want to get divorced?' asks the lawyer. 'Because my husband doesn't understand me,' replies the woman. (Berger, 2010)

That joke centres on misunderstanding, but relies on the final reversal to work. Many punch-lines are reversals.

Finally, a *Catalogue* is a rather specialist technique where a comic plays with the items in a list. The use of a sequence of funny names is one example of this approach. I guess the best case of this in recent times is the *Schoolmaster* sketch performed by Rowan Atkinson (available on *YouTube*). Here, Atkinson reads out a list of incongruous names when taking a school register: *'Buttock…Haemoglobin…Loud Hailer…Orifice…Sediment.'* The humour lies partly in the silly names and partly in the way Atkinson uses his face to show contempt and disgust.

This does remind me of the time I used to take registers in classes for students studying printing. One student said his name was *'Honeymonster.'* Each week I announced his name, and he would reply *'present.'* It was only at the end of the course that I discovered that the *Honey Monster* was a comic character used to promote *Sugar Puffs*. Hmmmmmmmmm.

Identity humour

Humour in this category involves: 'unusual' identities; copying of identity; changes of identity; mockery of identity; revelations about identity and the consequences of such revelation.

The *Eccentric* is a commonly used 'unusual' character in comedy situations. The normal sort of image of an eccentric is someone who is not concerned with what others think, and acts in strange ways. However, Berger has a much broader range of people who qualify as eccentrics: *'misers, misanthropes (people who dislike others), drunkards, liars, braggarts, poseurs.'* Victor Meldrew is quite a good example of this more general type.

These eccentrics usually end up being outsmarted and having to learn some sort of lesson:

A man goes into a shop to get his wife a present. He points out a bottle of perfume and asks how much. 'That's £50, sir,' says the assistant. 'Oh no. That's too much,' says the man. 'What about that smaller bottle?' 'That's £30, sir,' says the assistant. 'No,' says the man, 'That's still too much. What about that really tiny bottle?' 'That's £15,' says the assistant. 'No,' says the man. 'Still too much. I'd like to see something cheap.' So the assistant hands him a mirror. (Arnott & Haskins, 2004)

A *Grotesque* person is at the outer edges of eccentricity. He/she is absurd and single-minded. A grotesque may be physically deformed or terribly ugly.

The cartoonist often makes someone grotesque by using exaggeration and invidious comparison in *Caricatures*. A politician, for example, ends up with a really big nose or extended teeth, etc., looking like the village idiot, or whatever. Here's the great cartoonist, Gerald Scarfe, explaining his scarface approach:

'When I start to caricature someone, I exaggerate their features or I may imagine them as something else entirely, a wombat or a vacuum cleaner. What I'm trying to do is simply to bring out their essential characteristics. I find a particular delight in taking the caricature as far as I can.' (Scarfe, 2005)

A caricature doesn't have to be an image. We can exaggerate some aspect of someone's behaviour and act it out. This is part of the copying of identity which involves: mimicry, imitation, parody and impersonation.

Mimicry is where someone takes on the identity of another, but at the same time maintains his or her own identity. The entertainers we call impersonators are really mimics. They rely on famous personalities who have distinctive voices, mannerisms and personality. The bland are no use to them. Of course, the mimic needs jokes as well, so really we're getting double value from these guys.

Rory Bremner is the best political impersonator in Britain of the present era. His take on George Bush was particularly good:

George Bush: *'What time's my 11 o'clock?'*

George Bush: *'I'm proud to be a merkin.'*

(A merkin is a pubic wig, and sounds like *American* the way George Bush pronounced it. It may interest you to learn that when I was at college I had a Mr Merkin as an economics tutor. His first name gave him a double whammy as it was Jerry!)

A *Parody* is an imitation of the characteristic style of an author or a work for comic effect or ridicule. So, you can parody an author like Enid Blyton, a genre like *EastEnders*, or a particular text like *James and the Giant Peach.* Parodies can be funny in themselves, which is fortunate if the audience doesn't know the original which is being parodied.

Recently, some Chinese wits have taken delight in making fun of British cuisine. To do this they have used the style of a successful cooking programme, called: *A Bite of Chinese.*

The parody focuses on our obsession with potatoes. The parody explains:

There is one secret known throughout all kitchens in Great Britain...From an early age the British are taught that small potatoes cook faster than big ones.'

The host of the programme, when sprinkling salt on a potato, explains that, '...a tasty snack like this can keep British people going 'literally all day long.'   (www.bbc.co.uk)

The parody went viral. It does seem that we appear potato dependent to the Chinese, and let's be honest, there's a lot of truth in it. However, it's a bit rich coming from a country that insists on eating rice with every meal, and has a joke, *'The only four-legged thing a Chinese won't eat is a table.'*

Imitation involves a person pretending to be someone or something else, or in a different state, such as sleeping. The key thing is that the person keeps his or her own identity.

The best example I can think of here was when ex-M.P. George Galloway was a contestant on *Celebrity Big Brother* and his task was to pretend to be a cat. This involved him licking milk out of actress Rula Lenska's cupped hands. She proceeded to stroke his ears and moustache as you would with a pet cat. Galloway was branded a 'laughing stock' for his feline failings. There is a clip on *Youtube*. Watch this if you are at all tempted to vote for Galloway's party, *Respect.*

Impersonation involves a character pretending to be someone else—taking on their identity or profession. In the process the impersonator is likely to reduce the person he/she is impersonating in some way.

One of the best at impersonation is Barry Humphries, who diminished the status of Australian diplomats with his take on the uncouth cultural attaché, Sir Les Patterson. However, when he became Dame Edna Everage, there was a personality magnification, to housewife-Superstar.

Dame Edna was something else. The impersonation of an Australian suburban housewife went to the extreme. 'She' wore: acres of make-up, spectacular spectacles and garish gowns. Dame Edna revelled in mocking 'her' guests. For example, Joan Rivers got this one:

'Tell me the secret of your successful marriages.'   (http://news.bbc.co.uk)

In *Before and After* humour there is a transformation in the identity of the person, for example from loser to winner, or vice versa.

After three years of marriage, Kim was still questioning her husband about his lurid past.

'C'mon, tell me, she asked for the thousandth time, 'how many women have you slept with?'

'Baby,' he protested, 'if I told you, you'd throw a fit.' Kim promised she wouldn't get angry, and convinced her hubby to tell her.

'Okay,' he said, 'One, two, three, four, five, six, seven—then there's you—nine, ten, 11, 12, 13......'
(www.Bigfunnysite.com)

Of course, the joke in this case is that there has been no transformation in the character of the husband after his marriage.

Mockery of identity takes place when that identity is seen as deficient or incongruous in some way. One way this is done is by stereotyping and tarring everyone, negatively, with the same brush. Another way to mock identity is to compare, ludicrously, that identity with something which is much bigger, or much smaller.

Stereotyping is a type of rigidity, forcing people into boxes which don't necessarily fit them. Comics make much use of the stereotype as it is a convenient way to humanise a joke they have invented. The stereotypical identity of someone will, inevitably, be mocked.

Heaven is where the police are English, the cooks are French, the mechanics are German, the lovers are Italian and everything is organized by the Swiss

Hell is where the police are German, the cooks are English, the mechanics are French, the lovers are Swiss, and everything is organized by the Italians. (www.nbc.news.com)

Scale involves using large or small objects or people to create humour through incongruity. A good example of this can be found in the film *Twins*. Here, a genetic experiment goes wrong and the small, tubby Danny DeVito turns out to be the twin of the very large Arnold Schwarzenegger. The humour further develops through the contrast between DeVito being streetwise and Schwarzenegger being intellectual.

Scale often crops up in sexual humour:

A man and a woman are lying in bed after a disappointing bout of sex. 'You've got a very small organ,' says the woman. The man replies, 'Well I didn't know I'd be playing in the Albert Hall.' (Arnott & Haskins, 2004)

In *Exposure* humour, something about the person's identity is revealed, often as a mistake. Revelations about someone's sexual life are common, but you can also find revelations about liars, cowards, frauds, etc. Bodily exposure is included in this category:

A blonde is walking down the street with her blouse open, exposing one of her breasts.

A nearby policeman approaches her and remarks, 'Ma'am, are you aware that I could cite you for indecent exposure?'

'Why, officer?' asks the blonde.' 'Because your blouse is open and your breast is exposed.'

'Oh my goodness,' exclaims the blonde, 'I left my baby on the bus.' (jokes.cc.com)

So, that joke has two lots of exposure, a bodily one, and one revealing the woman to be a bad mother. We laugh at her failings.

Unmasking is very close to exposure and could really be the same category. With unmasking, something which someone is trying to conceal is brought out into the open. It may be that someone is pretending to be someone else, in order to fool them. Usually the person is revealed for what they are:

A college student picks up his date at her parents' home. He's scraped together every penny he has to take her to a fancy restaurant but, to his dismay, she orders everything expensive on the menu. Appetisers, lobster, champagne—everything. Finally he says, 'Does your mother feed you like this at home?' 'No,' replies his date, 'but then Mother's not looking to get laid.' (Arnott & Haskings, 2004)

Embarrassment humour follows from exposure and unmasking. It concerns situations where people are *'...uncomfortable, shamed, self-conscious or ridiculous.'* Naturally enough they seek to escape, which can be a messy business:

Mrs Jones lived on the second floor of an apartment building in Chicago. One morning she woke with a start when she heard the downstairs door open. She remembered she had forgotten to put out a milk bottle so she rushed to the kitchen, just as she was--al fresco-- and stepped out across the hall. Suddenly she realized that it was too late to get back into the apartment so she slipped behind a door which closed on the water meters and waited for the milkman to depart. But it wasn't the milkman. It was the water inspector, who opened the door and found, to his surprise, Mrs Jones standing naked. 'Oh, I'm sorry,' she said, 'I was expecting the milkman.' (Berger, 1998)

Here we have an exposure joke leading to embarrassment, ending with a coincidence. It is a moderate joke because the references are unfamiliar to an English audience. Milk bottles and milkmen have disappeared. There needs to be a reason why a woman should be outside and naked.

Finally, we come to *Burlesque*, which, according to Berger, is a catch-all category. It is more of a description than a technique. Berger included it to show how techniques relate to each other. These techniques make literary works incongruous by satirising and lampooning them.

However, he then changes tack completely and writes, *'For our purposes, it is best to reserve the term burlesque for a kind of theatrical production featuring sexually provocative skits, slapstick humour and nude or seminude dancers and chorus lines. This is the way it has been traditionally understood.'*

So, this is just a tad confusing. Berger himself admits that the burlesque category is problematic. So, I shall ignore this category, as satire is covered elsewhere, and burlesque Windmill Theatre humour is very dated, and not politically correct. Also, we have no humour technique associated with burlesque as such.

Action humour

Berger lists three types of action humour: chase, slapstick, and speed. Obviously, the first thing you think about when these words are mentioned together is the slapstick comedy of the silent movie era, starring The Keystone Cops, Buster Keaton and Charlie Chaplin, amongst many others.

Chase, well, involves chase. The character being chased finds ingenuous ways to avoid capture. There is plenty of opportunity for confusion and accidents.

Slapstick is about pies being thrown, banana skins being fallen on, collisions, and things being destroyed. It is a crude but commonly used comedy. There is a very good take about such action on YouTube: *Monty Python's, History of the Jape.*

Speed is really about changing speed from the normal, an exaggeration. So things either go too fast or too slow.

All this is rather basic humour, but still funny for all that. I won't bother with it any further as it is rather outside my remit, but we do touch on it again in the Bergson and the practical jokes sections.

Reflection

Arthur Berger has shown us that humour techniques are concerned with the manipulation of: language; logic; identity, and action. That is, who we are, how we think, what we say and how we act.

Berger has done us a great service in working out the list of humour techniques. The list is available for us to use in two main ways. First, we can analyse any piece of humour we encounter and work out how it is constructed. This may be a bit academic, but you can use the list to analyse your own humour, and thereby confirm your style, and how you might improve it. So, which of the techniques do you mainly use, and which have you never tried, which you might now try?

Second, we can use the list to construct humour. As an aide memoire the list enables us to consider approaches we would not, normally, have considered. Also, it allows us, systematically, to think about a variety of technique combinations that could be funny. We do this in the next section.

Berger points out that the list isn't perfect. He admits he might have missed something. For instance, I think rhyme has a place, notably in the case of limericks. Berger also thinks that some categories are very broad, such as satire, and some are very narrow, like catalogue. On top of that I have no idea why burlesque is included as it does not seem to be a technique. Also, if satire gets a place, why doesn't cynicism?

A list is just a list. It doesn't tell us which items are more important than others. Which items do you really need to master in order to be humorous, and which can you safely ignore? Still, at least, you now know what is out there to master.

Activity

1) Which techniques are in these jokes?

Look at the following jokes and decide which of Berger's techniques are mainly being used. My suggested answers are at the bottom of the page.

a) 'Scientists have discovered a certain food that diminishes a woman's sex drive by 90%

....Wedding cake.' (This uses: Exaggeration, Before/after, Stereotype)

b) 'What does a 75 year old woman have between her breasts? That a 25 year old doesn't?' 'Her navel.'

c) 'Why does your boyfriend have a hole in his penis?'
'So his brains can get some oxygen now and then.'

d) A man comes home with a bouquet of flowers for his girlfriend and she says 'I guess I'll have to spread my legs now. And her boyfriend asks 'Why, don't you have a vase?'

e) 'What's the difference between getting a divorce and getting circumcised?'
When you get a divorce, you get rid of the whole prick.'   (www.Jokes4us.com)

f) The latest statistical survey of golfer's height, conducted on behalf of a major sportswear company, reveals that the average player is seldom as tall as his stories.

g) 'Why the long face?' 'My husband says I must choose between him and golf.' 'Sorry to hear it.' 'Me too—I'm really going to miss him.' (Exley, 1992)

h) Actress: 'I fell in love with my husband at second sight.' Gossip columnist; 'Don't you mean first sight?' Actress: 'No, when I first saw him I didn't know he was a billionaire movie producer.'

i) 'Why am I so lucky at cards and so unlucky at the race track?' 'Probably because they won't let you shuffle the horses.' (Kostick et al., 1998)

j) 'Work is the curse of the drinking classes.'

k) 'When God was creating the world. He realised that France had turned out perfect, which was not his plan. So, he made Frenchmen.'

l) A man calls home from his office one day, and his phone is answered by the maid, Maria. 'Maria,' says the man, 'I'd like to speak to my wife.' 'I'm sorry senor, but she cannot come to the phone. She is making love to a man in the master bedroom.' 'My God, Maria. Can that be true?' 'Yes, senor. I am sorry.' 'Maria, I must ask a favour. You have been with me many years, and now I need something from you.' 'Yes, senor what is it?' 'Maria, are you in my study?' 'Si, senor.' 'In the upper right drawer of the desk you will find a loaded revolver. Take it to the bedroom and shoot them both.' 'The phone goes dead for a few minutes, and then Maria's voice comes through. 'It is done senor.' 'Good, Maria. I am in your debt. Now take the revolver, wipe off the handle, and throw it into the swimming pool.' 'Senor? We have no swimming pool.' 'Is this 555-4694?' (Cohen, 2001)

Answers: b) Stereotype, exaggeration, before/after, ridicule c) Stereotype, insult d) Misunderstanding e) Pun, insult f) Wordplay, unmasking g) Reversal h) Unmasking i) Exposure j) Reversal k) Stereotype, insult l) Mistake, coincidence, ignorance.

This is not a perfect science and you may well find some of your answers are different and correct.

2) Determine your humour techniques

Go through Berger's list and work out which of his techniques you tend to use, and which you don't. Decide if you're happy with the result and work out at least three humour techniques you will now try to use more often.

3) Analyse the techniques used by successful comedians

Here, you should record your favourite comedians and then analyse their performance using Berger's list. Work out the techniques they favour and which they ignore.

Humour creation using Berger's techniques

Prince Charles: *'Marriages are like Shakespeare's plays. Some are romances, some are tragedies, and some are comedies….. Mine was a farce.'*

In this section I will look at how to use Berger's list to create jokes. Essentially, the list gives you a starting point, a point of departure, which is just what Edward de Bono recommends for lateral thinking.

A few years ago I decided to try out this approach, using the idea of the *'Grotesque'*, just to see if it worked. Well, the human body is always good for a laugh, so I decided to use a grotesque body with three heads as a joke subject. Two heads would have suggested conjoined twins which is/are not funny. Four heads would have been plain silly. Three heads, I thought was just right, particularly as jokes often make use of the rule of three.

So, now I tried to fit a three-headed man into a standard joke format. A three-headed man walks into a bar, didn't go anywhere. I tried him going to other places. The barber's didn't work, best I could manage was *'short, back and sides'*. Then, I had him going to the police station, "ello", "ello", "ello", not too awful that one.

Then I got distracted by sex. Berger doesn't actually have a 'sex' category as such, as his categories are about technique, so, obviously, there is little or no overlap. I guess 'disappointment', 'exaggeration' and 'chase', cover most of the 'sex' genre, oh, and there is 'slapstick'. Anyway, my guy could obviously have a threesome on his own, and, in dating ads, he could write he had a good sense of humours.

Moving on, the three-headed man would be popular with school governors as they would be able to appoint three heads for the price of one.

Turning to riddles:

'What is the difference between a lady's handbag and a man with three heads?'

'One has six lips and the other has lip-sticks.'

Clearly, the process of joke creation using this approach can be a bit chaotic. There is also a lot of failure.

When you get stuck and nothing is working you can use Berger's list to initiate a new line of thought. In this case, I looked at satire in relation to the three-headed man, and that's how I got to this MP joke: Did you hear the one about the man with three heads?

He was elected to parliament. Of course, he was much cleverer than the other MPs as he had an IQ of 3.

As far as three headed man jokes go, I don't think you can cap that. Well, actually, I thought it was ok, and tried it out on some friends, more 'so so', than 'ho ho', they said. Clearly it is too contrived and non-sensical. Maybe the grotesque is rather linked to the infantile; back to the drawing board.

At least I had a punch-line of sorts. I decided to stick with that and satire. Prince Charles soon emerged as a distinct possibility. You have to feel a bit sorry for him as he is often mocked. A key reason for this is that everyone knows him, and his past. So, a comedian knows that listeners are likely to understand any allusions.

I soon got to this superiority joke about Charles:

'Did you see that Prince Charles isn't as clever as you and me? They measured his intelligence and found he's just got an IQ of one'.

OK, but still not good enough. I then went for elaboration using Berger's scheme. I picked on the conversations Prince Charles might have had with Prince William just prior to his wedding. Remember, it's always best to be specific with jokes. The Shakespeare witticism (at the start, above) came about by concentrating on analogy. Then, absurdity:

'William, that Pippa is a bit of hot stuff. Have you, umm, got her telephone number?'

Prince Charles: *'Congratulations, William my boy, you're marrying a woman who is both clever and beautiful...Snap!'*

Clearly, it is possible to use Berger's categories as a provocation to create new jokes. However, so far it has been a bit of a random process; a ramble rather than a guided tour. Very often we need more focus with humour generation. We want jokes about particular subjects. Let's do one about the English football team.

The first thing that comes to mind is *Disappointment* jokes, but these are an anti-climax, and not funny. Let's do *Catalogue* and play with the players' names:

'The English football team to play against Germany in the World Cup final has been announced by the manager, Walter Winterbottom. As expected, Mr Winterbottom is backing a 4-2-4 formation.

Starting with the defence, there is Mocking, the goalkeeper. The back 4 will be Hulk, Skull-crusher, Animal and Pansy. The mid-field pairing are Cow and Gate. Finally, the 4 attackers are, Rob Lunt, Ron Punt, Richie Hunt and Aright.'

As you can see this catalogue contains, ridicule, comparison, word-play, repetition and variation.

Another way of using the list of techniques is by taking a cue joke, and changing it by applying different techniques. Here is a useful cue joke because we have all been in this basic situation:

A professor gave his class an assignment for over the weekend, and said the only acceptable excuses for not handing it in on Monday would be if you were sick or a close relative died.

One student raised a hand and asked 'What about sexual exhaustion?'

The professor patiently waited for the other students' supportive laughter to subside and then replied, 'Maybe you should consider using the other hand!' (Hurley et al., 2011)

So, that cue joke uses repartee, facetiousness, exaggeration, unmasking, stereotype, ridicule, and embarrassment. It's a good joke, and difficult to improve, but it is fluid and can be easily changed.

What could we do? Well, looking at Berger's list we could use *definition*, for the academic relies on defining terms.

This professor walks into a seminar room, holding a newspaper. He says, 'I like to start my seminars with a consideration of today's news. Today, the paper tells me that there has been a decline in the popularity of belly dancing in the Middle East. That's interesting. First, how would you define a belly-dancer?

A student shouts from the back of the room, 'A flop stopper.'

Not bad. Discards here included: A gutsy performer, and a mid-riff performer. The idea for belly-dancing came from the day's newspaper.

A cue joke can contain a technique which you are interested in using, like insult for example. So, just find an appropriate insult cue joke and adapt it. Recently, there was a television advert with the punch line:

'You're so stupid you studied for your blood test.'

Obviously, this covers insult, ignorance and literalness. So, building on the test theme we get several jokes:

'He's so thick he thinks he has to take an I.Q. test at a bus stop.'

'He's so thick he thinks the River Test is an exam for canooists.'

'He's so thick he thinks a test tube is a new type of underground train.'

'He's so thick he thinks any man who dies intestate must be American.'

'He's so thick he thinks he has to take the bar exam in a pub.'

Exaggeration is a basic humour technique. Here is a nice cue joke which is not about exaggeration, but easily could be:

'My penis was in the Guinness Book of Records...until the librarian kicked me out.'
(http://unijokes.com)

So, we get, by first leafing through the *Guinness Book of Records*:

'My penis is in the Guinness Book of Records...It's the most juggled.'

'My penis is in the Guinness Book of Records...It's the longest dormant.'

'My penis is in the Guinness Book of Records...Longest tattoo ...Llanfairpwllgwyngyllgogerychwyrndrobwyllllantysiliogogogoch...Goes round nicely.'

'My wife said my penis should be in the Guinness Book of Records, in the financial section...biggest write off ever.'

'My underpants are in the Guinness Book of Records....longest skid marks ever.'

Cue jokes do make life easy. They cut out half the work. Still, we should try and be original if possible. I do like lists as a way of generating humour. You just go down a list and see what happens. Of course, in this case it helps to have a relevant technique in mind. The pun is a basic technique, so let's go down a list of idioms, something I found useful with *A man walks into a bar joke*. In each case here, the idiom forms the punch-line:

Jim Davidson's jokes; no laughing matter.

'I met that Mary Portas. She said, 'let's talk shop.'

'My brother cries a lot at night. He's a real wet blanket.'

Reflection

Berger's categories can be used to generate humour, as he suggested, but didn't actually do. Using his list you can start with any of the words, and see where that takes you. Or, you can be more focussed.

I think the focus provided by a cue joke is most useful however you are rather dependent on what the cue joke is about for your subject matter. So, you may have to spend some time finding a relevant cue joke.

You can, of course, avoid the cue joke entirely and just select the subject you are interested in and apply Berger's categories to that.

Activity

1) Create a *Catalogue* joke

These are fairly easy to do, maybe because English names are so rich and varied.

You could try naming a cricket team, and develop the classic line, *'The batsman's Holding, the bowler's Willy.'*

A rugby team would be better as there are more names needed, and hence more potential jokes. You could go further and name the opposition as well. Such a joke would be great for any speaker at a sport's club function. The inclusion of some current players' nicknames would be a bonus.

2) Create an *Exaggeration* joke and a put-down (*Repartee*)

Exaggeration is a basic humour technique. It has to be considered for inclusion in all jokes. Here is an exaggerated cue joke you can modify, possibly in relation to where you live:

A Texan is bragging as usual. 'You know,' he says, 'I can get in my Cadillac at 7 a.m., drive all day

long and still be on my property.' 'Yes,' replies his listener, 'I had a car like that once.'

(http://richardwiseman.files.wordpress.com)

3) Create a *Mistake* joke

I have seen several jokes that use, as their basis, this cue joke:

A business owner has just moved places and was reopening soon. A friend of his wanted to congratulate him so he went to the local florist and asked if he could have some flowers delivered to the man. He then asked the florist worker to write something clever to go with the flowers.

A few days later the florist receives a phone call. It was the business owner. 'I am sure there was a muck up in your delivery service, my flowers came but the message said: 'Rest in Peace.' 'Well I'm sorry' was the reply, 'But what about the mourners at a funeral at the moment with flowers with a card saying; 'Congratulations on your new place.' (http://richardwiseman.files.wordpress.com)

4) Create a *Reversal* joke

In this case, we have a political joke, where a liability becomes an asset. Try and do this for any established politician:

In 1984, Ronald Reagan at the age of 73, and already the oldest American President of all-time, ran for re-election against Walter Mondale, who was 56:

'…I will not make age an issue in the campaign. I am not going to exploit, for political purposes, my opponent's youth and inexperience.' (The auditorium filled with laughter.)   (Rhea, 2007)

So, is it possible to turn an Eton education into an electoral asset? Can the name *Balls* be turned into an advantage? Can being a nerd in any way be made to be a good thing?

5) Create a *Comparison/Analogy* joke

I have a cue joke which I'm afraid I'll have to explain. The joke concerns the structure of the South Korean economy. This economy is severely unbalanced. There are a few very large conglomerate firms like Hyundai and LG, which totally dominate. Their tentacles are everywhere. As a result, smaller firms find it difficult to compete, and don't do that well.

So, the joke is, *'The South Korean economy has the body of Arnold Schwarzenegger but the legs of Woody Allen.'*

A bizarre image is created, which is accurate. By combining two film stars to describe something else we end up in the land of the Beauty and the Beast.

To do one of these you need to think of something which has good and bad characteristics at the same time, and then work on the relevant film star combinations.

It may be a very small technical point, but originally with that South Korean joke I had written, *'…and the legs of Woody Allen.'* The word *but* is an improvement as it indicates contrast, a negative.

6) Create a *Theme/Variation* joke

Berger (1998) gives us a nice example:

An Irishman was digging a ditch in a notorious red light district when he noticed a Protestant minister entering one of the houses of ill-repute. 'So what I've heard is true,' he thought. Then he notices a rabbi entering the house. 'Six of one, half a dozen of another,' he thought. Then he saw a priest enter the house. 'Must be someone sick in there,' he thought.

This is an Irish joke, but it doesn't portray the Irishman as stupid, rather he is shown to favour his own group. This is a very human failing, and as such is so open to ridicule.

Football managers are the most obvious example of bias, so they could be your characters. Obviously, you will make a rival team's manager your victim. So, that's the ever objective Arsene Wenger then.

Anecdotal and Observational Humour

'Telling a story is always better than telling jokes.'   (Jay Leno)

'Oh you're one of those new comedians like Ben Elton, are you? All those stories instead of proper jokes.' (Manford, 2011)

Anecdotal and observational humour has rather taken over as far as stand-up comedians are concerned. The stand-up has become a sort of anthropologist, telling people tales about their society and how it operates— *observerstories.* Unlike the anthropologist, the comic is an *insider* looking at what people do and say in an insightful way:

'Why do mums buy crap pop?' he said, as the room heaved. I caught myself smiling. Oh my God, I thought, that's what my mum does – that Rola Cola stuff from Netto. 'That Rola Cola stuff from Netto!' he boomed. The audience lapped up every word of his slick Bolton brogue...

He told stories from his life and told us about his family, building up all the characters and colouring the parts with lush northern language...

I watched the audience. Not only were they laughing and clapping but they were nodding 'yes'. They were thinking, this guy is one of us, he's lived our life. But what was unbelievable was that they were all doing it, from the single geography teacher to the married Asian sign-writer, from doctors to kies to bankers.'   {Jason Manford (2011) describing Peter Kay}

Clearly, the audience identifies with Peter Kay. He reveals information about himself and his life, which relates to the lives of others. His humour does not appear to be invented. It appears authentic.

In the *observerstory*, the comedian,

'...talks about everyday phenomena that are rarely noticed or discussed. To work properly, the routine must be based on shared experiences...Sharing is built into the very language of observational comedy. 'Have you ever noticed...?' has become a comedy cliché.'   (Double, 2005)

It helps to have an *attitude* when telling *observerstories*. Logan Murray (2010) notes:

'What the professional comic tends to do is to talk about how they see things and what their attitude to it all is. It is personal to them.'

Attitude derives from persona. So, if we take Jack Dee as a cynic, we get a variety of attitudes, such as: disappointed, world-weary, and self-serving. These attitudes shine through in the stories he tells.

Logan Murray gives us some examples of attitude comedy and a comic's love life:

Disappointment: *'I've just fallen in love again...She's not my first choice, but beggars can't be choosers.'*

World-weariness: *'I've just fallen in love again...I suppose it'll keep me occupied for a brief while between the cradle and grave.'*

Devious: *'I've just fallen in love again...although to tell you the truth, I'm only going out with her so I can sleep with her best friend.'*

The punch-line in these observations are not really punch-lines, they are afterthoughts. Afterthoughts are continuations of previous thoughts, moving the initial comment in a different direction. Take this one by Jo Brand:

'My husband never learned to drive...in my opinion.'   (Brand, 2010)

A variation on observational comedy is comedy based on a *'found'* object. This involves the use of a prop which is brought on to stage and discussed:

'I'd bring onstage with me to get laughs: an English-French phone book, a misleading headline from the front page of The Guardian, the Highway Code booklet, a set of inflatable Spice Girl dolls...' (Double, 2005)

This use of props is very helpful for someone who is not used to performing in front of an audience. You can use the prop to take the pressure of yourself and divert attention to the prop. I recommend it highly.

Anecdotes, in real life, are on a continuum with regard to their effect on listeners. They can be more or less funny, or they may not be funny at all, but still be more or less interesting. Jokes, on the other hand, are either funny or not funny. The audience laughs or it doesn't. So, anecdotes are less risky to tell than jokes.

An anecdote is far less likely to obviously fail because, even if the audience doesn't find it funny, they may find it interesting. Importantly, an anecdote isn't necessarily signalled as funny in the way that a joke is. A failed joke can be quite difficult to overcome, particularly if is made at the start of a presentation. The joke teller has said this is what I find funny, and the audience has disagreed. The two have become distanced, their difference tellingly revealed.

So, you should think anecdote first if you are going to do any sort of public presentation. It is far less risky, and it is more human and authentic.

Norrick (2003) points out that a personal anecdote may contain more than one element of humour, which helps differentiate the anecdote from the joke. Such anecdotes generally give some new information about the teller. They humanise the teller. They demonstrate he or she has a sense of humour, and, depending on the anecdote, *'present a self with an ability to laugh at problems and overcome them.'*

Interestingly, the type of stories that Peter Kay tells present a self which is more typically female than male. Men's stories focus on action, whilst women's focus on people and relationships. Coates (2003) analysed the narratives of both male and female conversations. Women's stories tend to be about mundane, everyday experiences, such as *'comfortable shoes'*, however male stories tend to be about, *'heroism, conflict, achievement'*, anything but the mundane. Whilst women, in their stories, disclose personal information, with an emotional impact, men's talk avoids the personal.

Men tend to *'top'* the story of another male, *'...tell you what, I'll beat all of that'*; women build on the story of another female.

Sir Clement Freud was one male presenter who told plenty of quality anecdotes. Here is one of his, which is difficult to top, that appears in a collection of his writings, *'A feast of Freud'*. As rector of *Dundee University*, Sir Clement had to deal with a complaint by a final year physics student, about his exam marks. The complaint revolved around the following question, *'How would you gauge the height of a skyscraper, using a barometer?'* The student's answer was failed.

The student had written that he would lower the barometer from the top of the skyscraper to the ground, and then measure the length of string involved, adding the length of the barometer.

The court of the university, of which, Sir Clement was chair, accepted that there were grounds for appeal, and called in an external examiner.

The examiner, in a viva, asked the student the original question. The student replied that he could measure the time it took for the barometer to fall from the top to the bottom, and hence estimate the height of the skyscraper. Or, he could measure the barometric pressure at the top and at the bottom, and calculate the height.

But, the student said, he would actually go to the caretaker, and, say to him, *'If you tell me the height of this skyscraper, I will give you a barometer.'* (Freud, C., 2009)

A nice story to tell, particularly to a scientific audience, however, I should point out that that barometer story is, well, a tall story, in that, it actually happened around 1905, in a physics exam at the *University of Copenhagen*. The candidate was *Niels Bohr*, a man who went on to win a Nobel Prize in Physics in 1922.

The details in Bohr's case are exactly the same as in the Dundee case, as described by Cropley (2001). Indeed, additional scientific methods of measurement are said to have been given by Bohr. One was to calculate the ratio between the length of the barometer and its shadow, then measure the length of the shadow of the building and multiply that by the same ratio. Another method was to use the barometer as a pendulum at ground level and at the top of the building, then calculate the difference in gravity and thus calculate the height. The final, simple, method was to use the barometer as a ruler against the side of the building.

This *'tall-story'*, reveals something about the nature of story-telling. People appropriate the stories of others and pretend they have actually happened to them. In the process they may well exaggerate and embellish the story, to make it more impressive or funnier. This makes the individual more interesting and amusing to others.

There are all sorts of stories you can tell, perhaps the most appreciated are those that involve a mistake:

In September 1985, the Post Office launched a quiz designed to familiarise the public with their post codes. There was only one question and prizes were awarded simply for getting one's post code right. Sadly, few of the replies got through. Ironically, when giving the return address the Post Office got its post code wrong. The Post Office explained: 'It was a printing error.' (www.anecdotage.com)

At the time, cock-ups such as this one, are disastrous for those involved, however, over time, cock-ups take on a humorous dimension, and become anecdotes; as Jimmy Carr puts it: *'comedy is tragedy plus time'* (Carr & Greeves, 2007).

For example, a focus group member, interviewed by Wilkinson et al. (2007), recounted a mistake he had made in a presentation he had given to a group of *Women's Institute* ladies. He managed to thank them from the *'heart of my bottom.'* He observed, that, in later presentations, *'it's something I can illustrate and they remember it.'*

Such self-deprecating humour allows the speaker to cope with his/her own errors, which, itself, is likely to have favourable consequences. Self-deprecating humour makes the speaker appear more human by lowering his/her status.

Goodson & Walker (1991) give a pertinent example of a young science teacher who was trying to gain order by banging a bottle, which contained red lead, on a table. The bottom of the bottle fell out and she ended up covered in bright orange powder. First, there was absolute silence, then howls of laughter. The teacher fell off the rostrum because she was laughing so much. She commented, *'...after that I have no problems with the kids at all because they were impressed that I could laugh at myself.'*

There can be a reciprocal effect with self-deprecating humour, for example, Gordon (2010) cites a professor of poetry who observed that laughing at his own efforts, enabled students to open up to constructive criticism.

Zajdman (1995) elaborates on self-deprecating humour. He explains that a person who engages in this potentially face threatening act is usually seen as courageous, unafraid to uncover weaknesses. Paradoxically, by revealing a weakness, the self-deprecator may give the impression that this is his/her only weakness, and thereby, demonstrate superiority. Zajdman reckons that the person who laughs at him/herself is in control of the situation.

Self-deprecation is, however, risky. For example, in matters of the heart, self-deprecation works for high status people, but not for those with low status. Those with high-status can more easily afford to bring themselves down a notch or two. For low status people, a self-deprecating joke may simply confirm their: low intelligence, physical defects or lack of moral fibre.

Interestingly, men find high status women especially attractive, *'...when they use self-deprecating humor'*. Conversely, men find high status women, *'... especially unattractive when they use other-deprecating humor.'* (Greengross, 2008)

You do have to be careful to avoid self-denigration humour as people will mock or avoid you. Take this odd comment by Woody Allen:

'My one regret in life is that I am not someone else.'

Or this one: *'If my films make one more person miserable, I'll feel I have done my job.'*

Woody is better at self-deprecation: *'I'm such a good lover because I practise a lot on my own.'* (http://listverse.com)

Reflection

In the world of comedy, the anecdote and the observation have taken over from the joke. When comedians tell stories they relate more to the audience and reveal their human side. There is a connection.

The anecdotes comedians use may be borrowed or authentic. Obviously, technically, the authentic anecdotes are better because they are easily remembered and can be told with real feeling.

Anecdotes are a vital part of any presenter's armoury. As big guns they can be used to signal the start and end of an encounter. As grenades they can be lobbed at suitable intervals to wake and enliven the listeners. As sniper bullets they can focus on individuals and be used for explanation and encouragement. Tales of flash-in-the pan mistakes, and guns going off half-cock, can be used to entertain and enlighten. In all, anecdotes help presentations go with a bang.

For novice presenters the anecdote is the best bet by far. Although they can go wrong, they are less likely to fail than jokes. Jokes are either/or; anecdotes are on a continuum. So, always go for the anecdote.

Perhaps the best anecdotes to tell are those that involve a personal mistake or failure. When you become the butt of your own story you can gain respect because of your bravery. Still, it is best to explain how you overcame any problem as you don't want people thinking you're a complete loser.

Activity

1) Watch a professional comedian and work out what % of his/her time is devoted to anecdotes/observational humour/jokes. Compare that result with a calculation for yourself.

2) Work out an attitude joke about your love life.

Take a positive attitude statement and add a negative ending. For example, a self-serving attitude gives:

'I've just fallen in love with a rich widow, least that's what I tell her.'

Positive attitudes to work with: Caring; Enthusiasm; Generosity; Sensitivity, and Trust.

3) Work out some afterthoughts

Logan Murray observes that definitive statements are quite good for generating afterthoughts. Some examples he gives are:

'I've been married five times'......Every one a success! (Ronnie Rigsby)
You could have, 'I've been married five times'.....I keep a photo of all five on my desk, to remind me of who each one was.'
'I think you should get to know someone properly when you start dating them......before you use them and degrade them.' (Steve Martin)

You could have, *'I think you should get to know someone properly when you start dating them…….That's the surest way to avoid ever getting married.'*

Some definitive statements to play with:

'I don't believe in the life hereafter…'

'I like drinking a lot….'

'You can't beat a good sex life…..'

'The secret of success in relationships is listening…'

4) Construct a joke based on observation.

5) Go in your local corner shop and observe what people say to the owner. Work out a short comedy routine based on your observations. Comments on the weather are the most obvious way to go. Here, in particular, watch out for the phrase, *'wrong sort of weather/snow/rain/sun,'* etc. This is a very popular joke for the British.

6) Select likely props for a presentation

Look around your house and list 5 objects you could use as effective props in a presentation. The best laughs I ever got were when I used books from the *Munch Bunch* series – *Wally Walnut/Professor Peabody/Lucy Lemon,* etc. I guess it was the incongruity that made this approach work.

6) Read a comedian's biography and work out 3 anecdotes you could use in a presentation. Start a library of anecdotes.

7) Compare male and female anecdotes

Watch the T.V. programme *Loose Women* and see if female anecdotes are geared to the more mundane and personal. Compare your findings with those for any football programme presented by males.

8) Work out a self-deprecating joke

The diminutive Warwick Davis says: *'I do a lot of public speaking and I'll always start with a self-deprecating joke to make everybody feel more comfortable with my size because there can be hang-ups and anxieties.'* (www.Brainyquotes.com)

How would you start a talk in his situation?

Here is a cue joke that might help: *'In today's performance, the role of the idiot will be played by myself.'* (Dynel, 2009)

Recalling jokes and stories

An elderly man was talking with a friend: 'My wife and I tried a new Chinese restaurant the other night. It was really good. I think you and your wife would enjoy it.'

Friend: 'Really. We'll have to try it. What was the name of the restaurant?'

Elderly man: 'Oh, let's see...what was the name...I just can't quite think of it...hmmm...uhhh, what's the name of a flower...real popular...long-stemmed...thorns...flowers...?'

Friend: 'Rose?'

Elderly man: 'Yes! That's it!...Rose, hey Rose, what was the name of that new restaurant we went to the other night?' (http://margiesmessages.com)

A nicely surprising joke that one, much better than the usual, rather predictable jokes about old people and memory:

'There are 3 things that indicate you are getting older, first there is loss of memory................ (www.agelessfx.com)

The thing is, which one of those two memory jokes are you more likely to remember? Probably, you'd remember the second joke because it is shorter and less complicated. Maybe, even more likely, you'd forget both. How often do you hear people say, *'Oh, I can never remember jokes?'*

Indeed, Tony Buzan notes that, in studies of business people and students, *'...nearly 80% thought they were not particularly good joke tellers.'* He adds that all wanted to be good joke tellers, and, *'...all listed memory as their major obstacle.'* (Buzan, 2006)

In this section then, we look at how to go about remembering jokes/humour, obviously a crucial skill if you want to become more humorous.

Probably the most important thing for memorisation is motivation. If we couldn't care less about a joke, then we will not be bothered to remember it. Barecca (1991) argues that this is why women are poor at remembering jokes. Jokes are male things which simply don't appeal to women, *'...most of the jokes women have been told haven't been worth remembering.'*

Normally, we don't watch comedy in order to remember it. We watch comedy to be entertained. Joke follows joke and we cannot keep all the information in our short term memory, even if we wanted to. The jokes rather disappear.

More exactly, a clever punch-line seems to confuse our brains. Ricky Gervaise observes that:

'Jokes work like a magician's tricks. When the punch-line comes, you just gasp at that and you forget where the magician put his hand before or what he did before.'

Research confirms that the, *'...final twist and surprise in the joke makes us remember the punch-line, but forget the run-up to the gag.'* This doesn't apply to all jokes though, *'...the structure and punch-lines of clichéd gags are so predictable it makes them easy to recall.'* (Cockcroft, 2009)

It seems that we are more likely to remember punch-lines with the rest of the joke being something of a haze. Harvard psychology professor, Daniel Schacter, considers that we tend to remember:

'... the general meaning or gist of things; this is why we can remember anecdotes. With jokes, we have to remember details like nuance and timing.' (Cockcroft, 2009)

The fact is, as Liberman et al. (1972) observe, *'...recall is always a paraphrase.'* When people recall spoken information their words will differ from the original, except in special cases, for example, where they use rote memory.

Joke tellers don't learn jokes and anecdotes by heart. When recalling jokes in actual joke telling, tellers repeat themselves, correct themselves, hesitate, backtrack, re-start, but, *'...the punch-lines themselves typically come off without a hitch.'* Joke-tellers rely on a *'skeletal joke structure'*, using a few phrases from memory in order to present a joke. (Norrick, 2001)

It is not a good idea to learn a joke word for word. The audience can detect the robotic delivery and lack of spontaneity. Sometimes, you can spot the rote learners' eyeballs reading the joke in their head.

With formulaic jokes you don't have to learn every word anyway. The set-up words like, *'A man walks into a bar'*, or, *'How many? do you need to change a lightbulb?'* are known. Technically, these routine words are said to be constrained.

Constraint means that there is little alternative to a particular word, given the other words. So, for example, in a limerick, the very last word must rhyme with the last words of the first two lines, so, normally, not many alternatives are possible.

Constraint also operates in the case of verse, and humorous verse. Alternative words and meanings are limited. The memory load is thereby reduced. A pattern is learnt and recalled. This is why rhyme is one of the most used mnemonics. (Rubin & Wallace, 1989)

How then can you go about remembering jokes/anecdotes that are not constrained? Well, in the first place, you must pay attention to the humour. The ignored cannot be remembered. Van Munching (1997) recommends that you should repeat a joke as soon as possible after you have heard it. Rehearsal is so important for memory.

Secondly, you have to encode the joke/anecdote. Encoding means that you work out a way of storing the information in your brain. Effective encoding should provide cues; hooks, that enable recall of the information.

Various encodings can be used. A visual picture can be created, and/or, the new material can be related to material that already exists in the brain. Mnemonics, word devices that aid recall, can be deployed. For example, the following acronym gives the exact order for the spelling of mnemonic – Memory Needs Every Method Of Nurturing Its Capacity.

Tony Buzan explains that when you associate – link -- something with some known idea:

'The more funny, ridiculous, absurd and surreal you make your images, the more outstandingly memorable they will be' (Buzan, 2006).

So, for example, to remember a shopping list of: bananas, eggs, and soap, the shopper could build a visual transformation of themselves slipping on the banana skins and the soap, and breaking the eggs messily, producing a bubbly, banana omelette.

Or, maybe, an image of *Guy,* a gorilla, washing himself with scented soap, in the shape of a banana, whilst using stolen birds' eggs to shampoo his head. This more extreme version meets Buzan's requirement of the ridiculous, absurd, and surreal; what psychologists call the *bizarre.*

Worthen & Deschamps (2008) researched the effect of the bizarre on long-term memory with relation to humour. They found that, *'...the facilitative effect of bizarreness on free recall is dependent on the level of humorousness of the bizarre elaboration.'* Simply put, the bizarre is more likely to be remembered if it is funny, and, as Worthen & Deschamps point out, the great thing about the highly bizarre is that it is likely to be funny.

Distinctiveness then, is important for memorisation. Eysenck (1988) notes that:

 '...encodings that are distinctive or unique in some way are more likely to be remembered than encodings that are not distinctive.'

Distinctive mnemonic techniques mostly use imagery, just as with Tony Buzan's link approach. Roediger (1980) tested such techniques, and found that they all showed a recall advantage, particularly where order of items in a list was important.

The *loci* and the *peg* methods scored best where order was important. The *loci* method is basically the link method, but in addition the memoriser has to take a well-worn personal path, where he/she links particular locations in order with the material to be remembered. So, as you walk around your house/flat, you enter through the door go down a hallway, then, up the stairs, turn left for the bathroom, and so on. At each notable point on this journey, there is something to be remembered. The whole is turned into a story.

The *peg* method associates the material to be remembered with a list of known items. For example, one *peg* approach requires the initial learning of a rhyme, to which items are subsequently linked. The rhyming pegs are: 'one' -- *gun*, 'two' -- *shoe*, 'three' -- *tree*, 'four' – *door*, 'five' – hive, 'six' – Sticks, 'seven' – heaven, 'eight' – gate, 'nine' – vine, 'ten' – hen. The first item to be learnt is associated with a gun, then, subsequent items are linked to *shoe* and *tree*, etc., and a story is developed. What is happening is that a narrative is being created, an episodic memory, which may be recalled as an ordered sequence.

Recall is problematic. It may be impossible, difficult, patchy, or spot-on. It does depend on retrieval cues, which relate to how the initial encoding took place. Lockhart et al (1976) note that , *'...a failure to recall might just as well be viewed as a consequence of inappropriate initial coding as due to an inadequate retrieval use.'* A rich initial encoding is obviously important.

Even so, with time, we do tend to forget. This is either because the memory trace simply fades, and decays, or, because subsequent learning interferes with what was previously learnt (Baddeley, 1994)

To stop the fading away, it is important to practice. Psychologists call this practising, *rehearsal*. There is little disagreement that elaborate rehearsal improves long-term memory (Eysenck, 1988). That's why wives shouldn't stop husbands telling anecdotes that they've heard a hundred times. The anecdote is getting rehearsal time, or maybe they should!

And, finally,

Whatever memory technique you use, make sure that it works, so rehearse it before the event. Don't make the sort of mistake that Peter Kay once made:

'One night I devised a clever method of colour-coding my material. I wrote down my set list as usual but then circled the different topics in a variety of colours. For example, holidays would be coloured in yellow felt tip, working in a video shop in red, my mum and the video recorder green, and so on in a variety of colours. Then, and here's the clever bit, I colour-coded them in the same order on the back of my hand, so now I had six coloured stripes that corresponded with my set list. I thought this was revolutionary and nobody would even suspect that the small rainbow on the back of my hand was my encoded crib sheet. That night I confidently bounded on stage, stared down at my hand and thought what the hell does red stand for? I couldn't remember what any of the colours meant. Suffice to say I never used that method again.' (Kay, 2009)

Reflection

The recall of a joke/story is helped by a rich encoding and subsequent rehearsal. Cues used in the encoding help with the retrieval, as does constraint, which limits the possibilities for punch-lines and endings generally.

The quality of the encoding is vital. Essentially, it is important to create stories that are personally meaningful and progress in some logical order. This may be best for joke content. An acronym may be better for remembering a list of jokes to be told in order. Actually, professional comedians are quite likely to use a set list, which is a list of the topics to be covered, that is kept on a stool or at some other convenient place. So, they don't have to bother about order, although they still have to memorise content.

There is one thing that doesn't need much encoding and that is funny things that have actually happened in your life. This explains one reason why anecdotes are so popular with comedians.

Activity:

1) Work out an encoding

Now, can you recall the joke we started this memory section with? Your task is to work out an encoding that improves its recall. For example, we could have a linked story:

'Methusulah went into our new local caff which is still nameless, so he called it Rosebud after his wife.'

Or, a ridiculous rhyme:

Two old Joes,
Memory froze,
Wife knows,
She's called Rose.

Van Munching (1997) recommends that a memorable title be developed for each joke to be remembered. This should be a distillation of the important elements of the joke, into something short and snappy. *Blank-spot Rose* would be OK. (Black spot is a rose disease)

2)   Here we have a memory test:

a) How do you spell Tony Buzan's name?

b) What is on the tip of your tongue?

c) (Not for women as it's pointless asking.) Do you usually remember punch-lines of jokes? Yes—No—N/A

d) (For married women only) Can you remember all of your husband's indiscretions during the past year? Answer Yes or Yes.

e) (For men only) How many birthdays/anniversaries have you forgotten in the past 5 years? All/Most

f) (For men only) Do you remember that bit in *Carry On Camping* when Barbara Windsor lost her bra? Yes/I'm too young, but my dad told me about it.

g) Name the 39 steps (in order please)

h) Why does the term *memory stick* stick in our memory?

i) Is EU a nonsense syllable?

j) My bank identification number is: 10661588181519141939. How on earth can I remember that? I'm having a real battle with my wits on that one.

3)   Work out a reliable way of remembering your various computer based passwords, using rhyme

For example, take the following rhyme about the kings of England. Once it is learnt it is very difficult to forget. Now, select a name that is significant to you. For men, this is obviously *Willy*. Use this as the basis of the password, e.g., *Willy1Willy2,* or *Willy1rex*. When you come to change passwords just move along the list.

Willy, Willy, Harry, Ste

Harry, Dick, John, Henry 3

1, 2, 3 Neds, Richard 2

Henry 4, 5, 6, then who?

Edwards 4, 5, Dick the Bad,

Harrys twain and Ned the Lad.

4) Create an acronym mnemonic

Say you were going to tell the following types of jokes in this exact order, create an acronym mnemonic: Riddle, pun, knock-knock, dirty joke, limerick, satire, anecdote, joke, Spoonerism. Example: *Really Pretty Kate Does Love Some Amusing Jokes and Spoonerisms.*

5) Use the peg method on the same list. Example:

The sphinx had a gun and shot it so it punctured my shoe. In agony I knocked the gun out of her hand with a small tree and she played dirty and hit me with a door. Then some Irish bees stung me. I mocked the sphinx, mud sticks. I told the story about heaven and joked with St Peter at the gate. He was boiling his icicle

6) Work out a standard response for when you've forgotten someone's name

This problem will begin to afflict you after about the age of 30. It is bound to happen sometime. It can be really, really embarrassing when it happens, so a face-saving escape route is useful.

Jon Macks (2005) recommends the following:

- *'Look forgetting your name is bad enough. I forgot the pill three times and we ended up with Frank Jr., Cindy, and Brittany.'*
- *'This is the second most embarrassing time I blanked on someone's name. But, if the Pope can forgive me, so can you.'*

How about making sure you place yourself in an inferior position:

- *'I'm so sorry, please give me a clue. Does it rhyme with I've got a sieve like a memory?'*

Or, how about playing with words and terms connected with memory, such as: elephant, tip of my tongue, etc.

- *'I'm so sorry, please give me a clue. Does it rhyme with Alzheimers?*

The comedy audience

'A jest's prosperity lies in the ear of him that hears it, never in the tongue of him that makes it'
(Love's Labour's Lost)

'I had a gig in Aldershot on Saturday night and they were a slightly older audience and a slightly smaller audience and...maybe less comedy savy, you can just tell. And so I wasn't quite as grumpy about it...was slightly more upbeat...They needed to know I was enjoying it rather than hating it.

...So you have a persona but you have to, sort of, scale it up or down depending on where you are or what the situation is.' (Joe Wilkinson quoted in Quirk, 2011)

A skilled humourist is someone who studies and understands their audience, producing appropriate jokes/stories that work with that audience. The audience is crucial. All the humour skills in the world are useless unless the joke is appreciated by the audience.

Something is only funny if other people laugh or smile at it. Of course, you may find something funny, but if others don't, you are in a minority of one, and your humour will be rejected.

There isn't a massive amount written about audiences and humour, particularly stand-up humour, but there is some research that is relevant. What I've mainly done here is take comedians' thoughts about the audience, from www.brainyquote.com, and used them as the basis of this section.

There is some useful research about why people go to comic performances, carried out by Lockyer & Myers (2011). These researchers found five factors were important: respect; the unexpected; intimacy; interaction, and sharing the experience.

Apart from respect for the comic skill of the comedian, there is respect for someone who is prepared to stand up on their own and attempt to entertain an audience:

'I like a really good laugh & I like to see somebody brave it, as it were, in front of an audience...I think it's the bravery of the stand-up comedian because he or she is all on their own and they're braving the whole storm.' (50 year old female)

Stand-up comedy also appeals because of *'...its unexpected and unpredictable potential'*:

'It's the unexpected that I enjoy with stand-up, not knowing what's coming, what the material is.' (Male, 32)

Indeed, some people deliberately go out of their way to avoid seeing the performer on TV or DVD in order that their material is unexpected. Of course, this idea of the unexpected isn't always true. *Monty Python* sold out the *O2*, promising to use updated versions of old material. John Cleese observed, *'...they're actually disappointed if you do new material.'* (Anon., 2013)

In fact, the *O2* fails on grounds of intimacy:

'Everyone that I've gone along with have all said the same thing, '...fantastic venue the O2 but not for stand-up comedy.' (Male, 32)

The closeness and intimacy of the stand-up performance is important for the audience:

'It's the spatial closeness that I find rewarding because it makes me feel more part of what's going on.' (Male, 32)

The spatial closeness allows for participation and interaction:

'...you've around the table, you've got a few drinks, you've had a good chat with your friends, and then a comedian comes on and they interact with the audience...' (Male, 43)

However, there is a danger of being too close, as the individual might be picked on by the comic, something some people wish to avoid because of shyness and potential embarrassment:

'I don't want to be picked on, who does? They can be cutting can't they?' (Female, 50)

So far, so general, we now know why the audience goes to stand-up, but we don't know much about what sort of humour they like, and their importance in the process, shaping, as they do, the comedian's performance. Let's look at comedians' observations about their audiences:

'You perform for a different audience each night. People who don't understand just think that you go out there every night and do the same thing, but you don't—you have to find out who they are and give it to them.' (Rik Mayall)

'You do something you're really quite proud of, and the public doesn't like it. Then you do something that perhaps you're not at all happy with and the public loves it. And that's the moment of truth, because it's the audience that's the final judge.' (Les Dawson)

These observations sum it all up really. Essentially, comedians are market researchers: 'Does this joke work?' 'What about this one?' 'Oh, you like that, really?' The feedback is instantaneous and obvious, ha ha or ah.

Some very elementary research would have saved a comedian observed by Andrea Henry:

'...the comic before me did a bit about how he hated and plotted against his girlfriend's cat...The show was a fund-raiser for an animal shelter.' (Briedbart, 2011)

The audience, particularly in a smaller setting, has a big influence on what jokes are included in the set:

'...I basically let people dictate what jokes I'm going to do.' (Gabriel Iglesias)

If something isn't working, a skilled performer can, swiftly, bring in material that is more likely to work. An unskilled performer is quite likely to be stuck with the routine that was planned at the outset. He/she cannot adapt so easily and is more likely to fail. The implication is clear, a rookie performer, if they are going to use humour, should have a plan B.

The unskilled performer is at another disadvantage, and that is the expectancy effect:

"...new comics need to 'win over the audience' whereas established comedians can rely upon the expectation of humor derived from past experiences." (Johnson & Mistry, 2013)

There is another disadvantage for the newcomer and that is lack of confidence. If you demonstrate that you are confident, then audiences will pick that up, and be confident that you know what you are doing, and will make them laugh. As soon as they spot hesitation and confusion they lose that confidence. As Billy Crystal once said:

'...if you lack confidence in a joke, the audience will know it right away. I think Henry Kissinger said that.'

The newcomer may well blame the audience for not understanding the humour, however:

'In comedy it's the audience that rules. You can never blame them for being wrong.' (Walliams, 2012)

None of us like to attribute blame to ourselves, so the audience is the obvious candidate. Even so, it is the comic who has failed to deliver material suitable for the audience. The very worst thing a stand-up can do is abuse the audience, calling them *'stupid'* or whatever. There is no way back after that.

After you do a joke a few times, you have material that you know works. Although sometimes I have a joke that has worked a bunch of times, and then one night it'll flop.' (Aziz Ansari)

This is simply a consequence of the fact that audiences vary, but it is very perplexing when the audience doesn't laugh when it should. Comics will often gloss over a failed joke and move quickly on to the next, without looking embarrassed. For a beginner, there may well be a feeling of panic, a loss of confidence and a deteriorating subsequent performance. Comic Simon Dunn advises not to say something like, *'Not doing that one again'*, rather, just shrug, which *'...can get a laugh.'* (Dunn, S.)

Perhaps the best audience reaction ever to a failed performance happened in the case of Kirk Douglas' son, Eric, who had *'...an ill-fated stand-up career.'* Eric is said to have once lost it on stage, and took to shouting at the audience, *'I'm Kirk Douglas' son.'* In response, *'One audience member stood up and said, 'No, I'm Kirk Douglas' son, followed by another and another...'* (Daniels, P.)

The advice for the beginner is to start with some of their best material. It builds up confidence and wins over the audience such that they will give the benefit of the doubt when a subsequent joke bombs. Of course, if the best jokes fail there is a real problem, and a major rethink is required.

'After a while, a joke, if you say it too much, just becomes contrived, or fake-sounding.' (Dave Chappelle)

'There are lines that I know are going to get a belly laugh, but after a few shows I get sick of hearing myself say them so I drop them.' (Sammy Davis Jr.)

These two quotes indicate why a favourite joke may fail and why it is important to keep discarding jokes and stories and develop new ones. The teller gets bored with the joke, tells it mechanically, and the boredom transmits itself to the audience.

'You have to learn the crowd. I just pay attention to them so I can make sure I can make them laugh.' (Dave Cook)

That's a nice phrase, *'learn the crowd.'* For a skilled presenter it is second nature:

'Are they listening? Is something else distracting them? How is their body language? Are they alert or slumped? Are they getting bored? Should I change my approach? Are there particular people in the audience who need to be tamed? Do they need the eyes, or a put down?'

Victoria Wood explains:

"While one side of your head is performing, the other half is thinking, 'Oh, that didn't go so well, 'I'm going to miss out the next bit,' or, 'I'd better speed up, some quick laughs are needed." (Double, 2005)

Talkers in the audience can be a problem. American comedian Eddie Brill deals with them by going to the talker's side and then talking more slowly. If the talkers shut up he moves on, if not he says:

'It stinks when you come out for a chat, and they build a comedy club around you.' (Breidbart, 2011)

American comedian Fred Stoller got into real trouble with talkers once, in a club in San Antonio. Two women at the front wouldn't stop talking, so he got the bouncers to throw them out. The problem was that one of the women used crutches... *'The crowd booed me off stage.'* (Gladstone)

The implication for the beginner is that they must focus on the audience. This is a real problem because beginners tend to focus on themselves: their nerves, their next utterance, how they are doing. It is only by practice that this problem can be overcome.

The brain of the stand-up is in overdrive, although it may not look that way:

'When I'm on stage, it's really intense. My mind is going a million miles an hour, trying to remember my act, trying to say it all the right way. It's funny how different it looks and how it's happening...outwardly it looks like I'm going to get a bagel.' (Steven Wright)

Next, we look more at how audiences differ.

'If you want to make an audience laugh, you dress a man up like an old lady and push her down the stairs. If you want to make comedy writers laugh, you push an actual old lady down the stairs.' (Tina Fey)

You cannot expect different audiences to laugh at the same things. Each audience will laugh at things they have in common, which includes themselves in, and excludes others out. This makes it easier to present to a homogeneous audience like, for example, company salespeople or architects. The comedian finds out what they have in common and focuses on that.

Specialist jokes are ok for a group of specialists. However, jokes about subjects the audience are not likely to know much about are to be avoided. The problem comes when the comic knows a load of specialist stuff which the audience doesn't. There is the possibility of going off on one, leaving the audience floundering. A random audience is much more difficult, for the comedian doesn't know so well that which they have in common. This is why a stand-up comic may not start with a joke but instead says something which creates some sort of group identity… *'Manchester/Liverpool/Swindon is my favourite town'*

The actual physical shape and size of the space is important for group development. People laugh in crowds so it is best if the audience is in a compact space rather than spread around. This helps with the intimacy experience and is a very important practical consideration.

Groups, once they've formed, have continuing jokes, in-jokes. Simon Dunn reckons that these are the best jokes, known in the comedian's trade as *call-backs.* Dunn's advice is to develop an in-joke early on and then refer back to it later, *'you generally get a second wave of laughter.'* (Dunn, S.)

'London audiences are tricky, too. They don't laugh as much as the Northern audiences because, and I hate to say this, they are a bit cleverer normally, and they are picking up on all the little details and listening more carefully.' (Steve Coogan)

This Steve Coogan quote indicates three important ways in which an audience can differ. Firstly, there can be regional, and indeed, national differences in the type of humour an audience enjoys. Secondly, a more educated audience will have different expectations and standards with regard to humour. Personally, I don't tend to laugh at jokes very much, because I am more engaged in judging the standard of the humour, and that may be what is going on with an educated audience. Also, there could be more assessing of whether the material is politically acceptable. Maybe, it's just that educated people don't find it so acceptable to engage in belly laughs at the slightest opportunity.

Friedman (2011) questioned educated people about their non-laughing. Most people said you needed some laughter, but that it wasn't necessarily essential. Something could be funny, but you didn't always need to laugh in order to appreciate it. Indeed, laughter could get in the way of artistic appreciation of some comedy.

Finally, different social classes are amused by different kinds of humour. Class is a fundamental reality of British society, it therefore permeates our comedy. We laugh at what our class laughs at. We laugh at the other classes because of what they laugh at.

This class thing is very important for anyone attempting to amuse an audience. Fundamentally different rules apply to the various groupings. Take the way the middle and working classes perceived the *Carry-On* films. These bawdy films were anti-bourgeois. Working class characters dominated. They were jovial, dirty and sexy.

The films were aimed at a working-class audience. They celebrated *'the (low) body rather than the (high) mind as a source of humour (smut, not wit.)'*

Consequently, according to (Healy, 1995) they were, *'…reviled by the middle-class establishment on grounds of prudish, political and intellectual snobbery as trash for the masses.'*

Researchers have found, in the case of both Holland and Britain that *'…comedy taste is strongly class-specific.'* To understand more sophisticated humour people need the necessary knowledge to decode what is being said. Without this knowledge the less educated and knowledgeable are excluded. (Friedman & Kuipers, 2013)

The well-educated may well regard sophisticated humour as a status marker that distinguishes them from less educated groups. For them, humour has to be *'intelligent'*, *'complex'*, *'intellectual'* and most of all, *'clever.'* That is, it has to be *'difficult.'*

This all shows up in a quote from *Dale*, a journalist, explaining why he likes Stewart Lee:

'To be perfectly honest he makes me feel like I'm in an in-crowd of comedy nerds. It is almost like sitting an exam. You go in and you know you're going to be challenged, you know a few people in the audience won't get him. Overall, it makes you feel a bit smug, and it's an awful thing to say, but you look down on the people who don't get him.' (Friedman, 2011)

For less educated people, laughter is a key part of comedy, *'You've got to laugh.'* Laughter and comedy is more of an escape, a way of *'relaxing after a stressful day at work.'* Consequently, positive comedy is valued as a counterbalance to the negative things in life:

'To be honest with you I see enough shit in the newspaper and the news every day, I'd rather see things that make me laugh, that I get enjoyment out of. I don't want to see anything too highbrow or too morose. I just want to be entertained in a light-hearted way.' (Duncan, electrician) (Friedman, 2011)

Different social classes frequent different venues, so the comedian can predict the nature of the audience accordingly. Arts Centres, for example, attract, *'A civilised and politically aware audience, albeit prone to over-intellectualising and showing off…'* (Quirk, 2011)

People go to see comedians that they like, probably because they have seen them on television. So, established comedians can assume that much of the audience enjoys their humour. Those that don't like their humour will not turn up. I rather fancy comedian Arthur Smith doesn't go to many of Jimmy Carr's gigs:

'He makes jokes like little clocks. He has no interest in their context or meaning, only that they cause an explosion of laughter. I want a comedian to have a hinterland. The best comedians are interested in jazz, poetry and the world.' (Arthur Smith in Powell, 2010)

There can be then, a desire for the comic to move out of role and the planned routine, and reveal something personal:

'I like seeing what the comedian thinks is funny, not just what they think I'll think is funny.' (Anthony Jeselnik)

Appreciation of sexual humour is a universal constant, but the exact form that is appreciated will vary by age group. 'It's the teenage and university crowd, so we give them lots of sex jokes and gross humour.' (Keenan Ivory Wayans)

Obviously, this age group is very interested in sex, and by extension, sexual jokes. Gross humour, sick humour, is very much the humour of the young.

"I've definitely become smuttier. When I first started out, I had these aspirations: 'I'm not going to do jokes about anything crude because I'm bigger and better than that.' But then, I don't know—It makes me laugh, so I started doing it.' " (Jack Whitehall) As Mae West once put it: 'I used to be Snow White, but I drifted.' Clearly, it's best that a comic jokes about things which he/she finds funny. The interest and the amusement shows. Whitehall's downwards slippage couldn't have been maintained unless audiences enjoyed the smuttier material.

'I've always been fascinated by the difference between the jokes you can tell your friends but you can't tell to an audience. There's a fine line you have to tread because you don't know who is out

here in the audience. A lot of people are too easily offended.' (Billy Connolly)

Billy Connolly is pointing to another difference in the treatment of audiences, essentially the greater sensitivity you need to display in the public than in the private arena. On the one hand the comic doesn't really know the public audience and what will upset them, on the other hand, he/she knows the private audience very well, and so knows their limits.

'I do try to have my own standards: I don't do everything the audience wants, and I do try to surprise them.' (Gallagher)

Gallagher is indicating that some audiences want the comedian to go deeper into the mire of mirth- the Roy "Chubby" Brown swampland, something which Gallagher is not prepared to do. So, the audience is not always completely right if the comic wishes to maintain a sense of personal integrity.

(Referring to Morecambe & Wise) *'...they'd calculated that the worst nights tended to fall on a Monday when the house was full of people who had a week of work ahead of them and so weren't much in the mood for laughing. This bizarre logic actually made some kind of sense since on Friday nights, the beginning of the weekend, laughs were much easier to come by.'* (Sellers & Hogg, 2011)

This quote indicates that the psychological state of the audience can vary, in this case according to the day of the week. Jo Brand has a different take on Fridays, with a more sociological explanation:

'Comedy nights held on a Friday are always dodgy; you often have groups of people who know each other, so the pack mentality is heightened. (Brand, J. 2009)

There is also the inebriation state to consider. The later the session the more likely there is to be intoxication and audience aggression. As Mark Thomas explains, The Comedy Store attracts:

'...wall-to-wall pissed accountants', 'who demand a crude and uninspiring type of comedy—by two o'clock in the morning, he's just shovelling off knob gags to stay afloat.' (Quirk, 2011)

The audience can be aggressive, although Quirk (2011) considers that this is not typically the case as there is a vested interest in a successful performance. Where there is aggression, it can be displayed as passivity, humiliating heckles, or abuse.

The Glasgow Empire was famous for being a grave yard for English comedians. Des O'Connor is said to have '...fainted on stage under the withering glare of its audience.' The brothers, Mike and Bernie Winters, were once humiliated by silence, followed by a heckle. In their act, Mike went on first, did some patter, and played his clarinet. He was met by, 'a total and not exactly respectful silence.' Bernie then came on stage, and commenced with his trademark 'eeeeh'. The heckle came, 'Christ! There's two o' them.' (Goldie, 2003)

Skill at handling a heckler is vital as Jo Brand explains:

'Once a heckler has spoken, something clicks in the audience's brains. They collectively hold their breath to see how you deal with it. If you struggle, they turn against you, because they lose confidence in your ability.' (Brand, 2009)

Clearly, the comedian needs a range of comebacks in reserve to deal with the various likely heckles. For example, when Jo Brand, got the rather predictable, *'You fat cow'*, she replied, *'I deliberately keep my weight up so that a tosser like you won't fancy me.'* (Parry, 2011)

Jo lost out in this interaction:

Punter: *'You're shit!'* Jo Brand: *'Oh we have a comedian in the house.'* Punter: *'We fucking wish.'* (www.b3ta.com)

It is not recorded what Jo said after this heckle: *'Don't get your tits out.'* (www.qi.com)

Lee Mack once produced this ingenious comeback. He started by asking the crowd what they thought his career had been before he went into stand-up. A voice is heard, *'Comedian.'* Lee, stops, looks stunned, and praises the heckler, all the time taking off his shirt. He reveals a T shirt, upon which is written: *'One wanker always says comedian.'* (www.b3ta.com)

Male comedians have an easier time than their female counterparts. Female comedians are routinely subject to sexual comments and comments that assume women are not funny.

Welsh stand-up Sian Bevan observes:

'...as a broad generalisation I think men get banter-y heckles and the ones for women tend to seem more aggressive. There's nothing you can do with them. It's very much like a gang of little boys in a playground. It feels like there are some gigs when the woman couldn't have done anything. She was up against a brick wall the minute she walked, with her tits on to stage.' (Lavery, J.)

Not surprisingly, there are far fewer female stand-ups than males. Chortle, the stand-up industry's web site, reports that just 20% of entrants for its student comedy award are female (Benedictus, 2012).

Catherine Tate has addressed this issue. She considers that there are:

'...lots of funny, brilliant women out there...but I do think, perhaps, the ones that have pushed through have had to do it with quite a male attitude.'

Tate explains: *"...I do think, socially, people are conditioned to think that it's actually not a woman's place to stand up...to demand the stage, to say 'what I'm going to tell you is funny and it's OK to laugh at it.'"* (jarrahodge.tumblr.com)

I'll end this section with an ironic quote from Ricky Gervais, or is it?

'Anyone who thinks women aren't funny is an idiot: two of my favourite comedians of the last twenty-five years are Lily Savage and Dame Edna Everage.' (Powell, 2012)

Reflection

Quite obviously, it's not an easy job being a stand-up comedian. Audience understanding has to be acquired, good material has to be developed all the time, and unruly audiences have to be dealt with. No wonder Jerry Seinfeld says, *'Being a good husband is like being a good stand-up comic—you need ten years before you can call yourself a beginner.'*

Eventually, after much practice, the comedian becomes a skilled performer, where his/her act appears effortless, as Milton Jones puts it:

'...I don't rehearse what I'm going to say anymore, I just get up and do it...A lot of gigs in a short time have made me sharp, like an athlete who knows what he's good at; confident, or perhaps just tired of being nervous.' (Jones, 2009)

Clearly, a successful comedian monitors audience feedback in order to judge his/her effectiveness. When the audience is laughing there is no need to change gear, when there is silence, a different gear needs to be engaged. The skilled comic does this effortlessly, the newcomer crashes.

The problem for the newcomer is that, just like Henry Ford, he/she is probably saying, *'You can have any colour so long as it's black.'* – There is no alternative. As a result the audience loses confidence and starts heckling. If there is no effective response then the performance fails.

Now, what can normal people, with no aspiration to become stand-ups, learn from this section? Apart from attempting to understand the audience, and monitoring, and responding to their feedback, I guess the most important thing is to create a group out of the audience; groups laugh, individuals just smile. So, people should be seated close together, comments should be made about what the audience has in common, in-jokes should be developed.

Activity

1) Devise jokes for a particular audience

Select an audience, preferably one you know something about, and make up jokes that they might appreciate. If you're stuck, hospital workers have a lot of potential; much dark humour lurks there.

Here's a cue joke to get you started:

'Who are the most decent people at the hospital? ....The ultrasound people' (David O'Docherty in Powell, M., 2010)

Here, I will have a go at the police force as an audience, not I hasten to add because I've had anything much to do with the law, although I have taught police officers from time to time.

Now, I happen to live close to a major London police station. This station doesn't seem to have a canteen on site and consequently police officers are always in the local cafes. Today I saw a big police paddy wagon parked outside their favoured caff, although, usually there are three or four police cars outside, sometimes with their engines left running.

This then would seem to provide a way in to an amusing talk involving those local police officers:

'Evening all, I'd like to start by thanking you all for keeping the local area safe and sound. We rarely have burglaries or muggings. I must say I feel really safe walking the streets around here and that must be due to your efforts. Thanks very much.

One place I used to be really scared of was Dave's Caff. You know the one at the end of Belmont

Parade. It used to be full of all sorts of riff-raff. Well, it's not scary now, thanks to you. It was a masterstroke to always place at least 4 police officers in there. That's scared the villains away.'

(Not wildly funny, but a start with a mild bit of teasing.)

'Not so long ago I was in Dave's Caff and watched what the police officers were eating. Predictably enough, the men all went for fry ups and the women went for salads. They all had a pudding, except for one guy. I wondered why? So, I asked Dave. "Dave, why did one of those PCs miss out on a sweet, is he on a diet? Has he got a GENTOC coming up?" "Oh, that's John Kay, he sticks to the letter of the law." "How do you mean?" "De minimus non curat lex." "You what?" "The law doesn't bother with trifles." '

Not bad. It would have been a lost opportunity not to make some comment about food once the café had been introduced. GENTOC, by the way, is an assault course that has to be completed by some police officers in order to demonstrate their fitness.

This anecdote does show the benefit of immersing oneself in humour. The punch-line is lifted from the following limerick:

There was a young lawyer named Rex

Who was sadly deficient in sex.

Arraigned for exposure

He said with composure

'De minimus non curat lex'

(Baring-Gould, 1974)

2) Make up a joke attacking middle class pretentiousness

Here is a cue joke from Basil Fawlty:

I can certainly see that you know your wine. Most of the guests who stay here wouldn't know the difference between Bordeaux and Claret. (Powell, 2010)

Wine is a goldmine for pretentiousness. Go through a glossary of wine terms, and see what emerges:

'He told me that a master sommelier had recommended buying a case of Silverado Merlot, 1995. Unfortunately, he pronounced Merlot as in harlot, not as in Harlow.'

(The punch-line is a bit of a cheat as it is basically a famous riposte supposedly made by Margot Asquith to film star, Jean Harlow. Harlow had called Margot, Margott, stressing the final 't.'

Offended, Margot replied, *'The final 't' in my Christian name is silent, unlike your family name.'*)
(http://quote investigator). To get round accusations of plagiarism, *'shallot'* and *'shallow'* could be used instead.

3) Make up a joke mocking the ill-read

How about using book titles as a source for these?

To do these, just go to a list of famous books and see what happens:

He thinks *Don Quixote* is a breakfast cereal for horses.

She thinks Evelyn Waugh's novel *Scoop* is about life in an ice-cream parlour.

She thinks *Mill on the Floss* was written by a dentist.

He thinks Nabokov's *Lolita* is some sort of text message.

Part 3: Word-play and humour

In this part I look at the wonderfully rich English language and see how its multiple ambiguities can be used to generate laughs.

The first section is about words, spelling, and grammar. The pun is the big boy in this playground, but there is also fun in Spoonerisms, grammar failures, and ignorant responses.

Then, linguistic blunders, accidental, or deliberate, are examined. These can be hilarious, for example when a news-reader is telling us about a serious subject, gets a word mixed up, and ends up saying something rude. The giggling fits, or attempts to control the giggles, are particularly infectious.

Spoken or written blunders occur either when sounds or letters are added, deleted, or transposed, or when a different word is used instead of the correct one. So, we are in the weird world of George W. Bush, Freudian slips, and Malapropisms.

Next follows a section on the pun. Here, we are in the land of the good, the bad, and the ugly. The really awful pun just plays with sound. For a pun to be any use at all there must be a play with meaning.

I then take the liberty of going off on one, and play around with collective nouns, as puns. This is good punning practice, and demonstrates the superior quality of puns based on ambiguous meanings, rather than sound.

The next section is also a bit of a punning lark, as it is about *Daffynitions*, which are alternative definitions for standard words. A genre much loved by devotees of Radio 4's comedy programme, *I'm Sorry I Haven't a Clue*. For example, *Imitate*—Fake art gallery.

We finish with knock-knock jokes and riddles. You may well want to skip this section, but an understanding of this humour is useful for any parents and teachers out there. It is interesting that complicated jokes may well start out as simple riddles. Over time they get elaborated such that their humble origins are hidden away.

Language Jokes

Man eating chicken   (Restaurant sign)

Language jokes play with words, spelling or grammar. The pun is the main variety, but there are several other types, such as spelling jokes and Spoonerisms. These sorts of jokes are the staple material for children's humour such as knock-knock jokes and riddles, however, more sophisticated adult versions are not uncommon. The pun itself is often the staple part of a one-line joke.

Lew (1997) worked out a way of classifying language jokes:

1) Word-play jokes

A word-play joke relies on the language providing a word with two differing, and hence, ambiguous, meanings, that is, the pun. Lew considers that these jokes are the most frequent.

Did you hear the one about the butcher who backed into the bacon slicer and got a little behind with his orders? (Metcalf, 2009)

How do you make an elephant stew?
Keep it waiting for two hours.   (Lederer, 1991)

Church wants men to help lay women.

Nurses needed to help stroke victims. (Blake, 2007)

In the above cases, a noun and a verb get confused. Lew also points out that ambiguity can extend to a string of words, notably an idiom. In the following case the idiom is interpreted literally.

Recruit, after physical: 'Well, Doc, how do I stand?'

Doc.: I don't know. It's a mystery to me.'

'Anger. It's all the rage.' (Vine, 2010)

2) Grammar jokes

A grammar joke makes use of the ambiguity arising from a word meaning different things according to differing grammatical usage. Lew gives the following example:

Miss Wornout wrote on Bobby's report-

'Bobby's trying-very'

In this joke the ambiguous word is *trying*. It functions, initially as a verb, but the addition of *very* turns it, in effect, into an adjective. That joke appears to be an afterthought, and therefore spontaneous. So, for maximum effect, it does need a pause after the word *trying* in order to make it appear some reflection has taken place. To make it even better the end should be *very trying.*

A couple more in the same vein:

'Look! That policewoman is arresting'…'highly'

'The lawyer said she is appealing'…'clearly.'

There can be ambiguity as to which word is acting as the subject or object of the sentence:

If the baby doesn't like cold milk, boil it. (Roche, 1999)

Jokes based on grammar failure, deliberate or not, should be included in this category. For example, here we have: a hyphen failure, verb agreement failure, an incorrect placement of a clause containing a preposition (with), and two conjunction failures:

Dicks in tray

(Dick's in-tray) (Truss, 2003)

George W. Bush –*'Rarely is the question asked: Is our children learning?'* (Weisberg, 2001)

'I saw a man digging a well with a Roman nose.'

In the far West a man advertises for a woman, "to wash, iron and milk one or two cows."
(Anon,1883)

Errol has, of late, shown an interest in girls, in particular, he hangs around their toilets and dribbles.

That little word *and* can cause all sorts of problems if it is associated with a failure to put a comma in the right place. Take the book title, *'Eats, shoots and leaves'*. If we write *'Eats, shoots and leaves'*, we mean someone had something to eat, then shot a weapon, then goes. If we write, *'Eats shoots and leaves'*, we mean someone ate two things.

My local school, which is supposed to be *outstanding*, had this on its website:

'The school has a well-stocked library and librarian.'

I e-mailed the school and asked if I could reference her section. There was no reply, but there was a rapid change to the website.

3) Longer grammar jokes

Here, much the same thing is happening as with grammar jokes, it's just that longer grammatical units are involved. Lew gives this example:

A charitable woman gave a down-and-out a dollar, and whispered, 'Never Despair. 'The next time she saw him he stopped her and handed her nine dollars. 'What does this mean?' she asked. 'It means ma'am,' said the man, 'that Never Despair won at 8 to 1.'

Here, the clause *'Never Despair'*, has acquired a new meaning as a noun, the name of a racehorse.

A ditto joke: *Local police were indebted today when they acted on information received—and it fell at the first fence.* (Roche, 1999)

4) Sound-play jokes

The ambiguity in this case stems from two words having the same or similar sound. The sound pun is a very elementary joke type, enjoyed by younger children, but rather scorned by adults.

Why did the house go to the doctor?

Because it had window pane.

In what direction does a sneeze travel?

Achoo! (Lederer, 1991)

5) Spelling jokes

Here, spelling, or, more likely, misspelling is the essence of the ambiguity. Such a joke is best read, as telling it, as in the joke below, ruins the joke. Odd, when you think about it in that, in effect, the recipient tells the joke.

Yy u r yy u b I c u r yy 4 me.

'F U NE X?' ('Have you any eggs?')

'S, V F X.'

'F U NE M?'

'S, V F M.'

'OK, L F M N X.' (Lederer, 1991)

Translation:

'Have you any eggs?' 'Yes, we have eggs.' 'Have you any ham?' 'Yes, we have ham.' 'OK, I'll have ham and eggs.'

How can you tell the difference between a chemist and a plumber?

Ask them to pronounce unionised.'

'There are only 10 kinds of people in the world—those who read binary and those who don't.'(Hurley et al., 2011)

6) Context jokes

In this type of joke the meaning of a word or expression depends on the context in which it is used. The context is ambiguous. For example:

She: ' Would you like to see where I was vaccinated?'

He: 'You bet!'

She: 'OK, we'll drive past it in a minute.'

Teacher: 'Susie, where is the ocean deepest?'

Susie: 'At the bottom!'   (Kostick et al, 1998)

The key ambiguous word in these jokes is *where*. Its function is to divert the location of the action, to change the context. In the next joke the key word is *in*.

'Were you hurt in the melee?'

'No, in the stomach.' (Blake, 2007)

7) Do you mean me? Jokes

In this case, two interpretations of a class of things/people are possible. The first interpretation implies a general class is meant, whilst the second interpretation is more specifically about an individual. For example, Lew gives this joke:

'In Los Angeles a man is hit by a car every five minutes.'

'Boy, I'll bet he's pretty beat up.'

A: 'There's a report in the paper here that in New York a man is mugged every three hours.

B: 'But after the first mugging he would have nothing left.' (Blake, 2007)

'A Newfie friend of mine heard that every minute a woman gives birth to a baby. He thinks she should be stopped.' (Wiseman, 2008)

8) Literal/ignorant response

Here, a statement is derailed by an inappropriate literal or ignorant response. For example: *Plumber: 'Where's the drip?'*

Housewife: 'He's in the bathroom trying to fix a leak.' (Metcalf, 2009)

Producer: 'I'm not sure about the script of his comedy. It's too caustic.'

Sam Goldwyn: 'The hell with the cost. If it's good, we'll go ahead.' (Blake, 2007)

The real purpose of the communication is ignored, either through ignorance or malice, or, to make a joke.

9) Manner of speech jokes

In this case a statement, in the form of a directive, is made whose intention is ignored, and an unexpected response, which challenges the original, is substituted.

Teacher: 'Consider this sentence: I don't have no fun at the weekend. How should I correct this?'

Pupil: 'Try and find a boyfriend.' (Metcalf, 2009)

Teacher: 'Jeremy, please use "I" in a sentence.'

Jeremy: 'I is---

Teacher: 'Don't say "I is." Say "I am."

Jeremy: 'Okay. I am the ninth letter of the alphabet.' (Kostick et al., 1998)

10) Elaboration jokes

Many jokes contain more than one ambiguity. Here is a series of puns from *Richard Whately* (1787-1863), one time Archbishop of Dublin:

'Why can a man never starve in the Great Desert? Because he can eat the sand which is there. But what brought the sandwiches there? Why, Noah sent them, and his descendants mustered and bred.' (Tartakovsky, 2009)

Dr. William Spooner is said to have said the following:

'Mardon me padam, you are occupewing my pie, may I sew you to another sheet?' (Lederer, 1991)

N.B. Lew actually used rather academic terminology for the various types of language/linguistic humour. Word play = Lexical; Grammar = Syntactic; Longer grammar = Lexico-syntactic; Sound-play = Phonological; Spelling = Orthographic; Context = Deictic; Do you mean me? = Specific or non-specific; Literal/ignorant response = Pragmatic ambiguity; Manner of speech = Type of modality expressed; Elaboration = Multiple ambiguity.

Reflection

Lew's classification is useful for understanding which language jokes are possible. If you needed to construct a range of language jokes you could simply use the list to provide you with appropriate cue jokes.

Clearly, language is inherently ambiguous. This ambiguity can be easily exploited by anyone in order to generate humorous impact. For example, in teaching:

'I decided to watch 'Match of the Day' with my boy and the commentator began to use some very funny language—'a square ball', 'the referee blew up', 'he left his foot behind' (laughter). Well, we have some special language that we use in science that you will need to learn.' (Wragg & Wood, 1984)

Activity

1) Invent a funny or rude car registration plate number

You can use any of the numbering systems which have been used since 1903. For example: T34 BAG; PEN 15; PA55GAS; P155OFF. Remember 3=E, 4=A, 5=S; 6=G; 7=T; 8=B.

Actually, to do this easily it would be a great help to have a list of the registrations that the DVLA disallows because of their offensive nature. For example, in 2007 TN07 was issued instead of SN07 (snot). VA61ANA and BL03 JOB are not allowed, although BO11 LUX has been allowed

2) Make up some punny adverts

Adverts make much use of the pun. A short, eye catching, humorous message gets viewer attention and aids memorability. For example, *You can't keep quiet about a Wispa*; *You shop. We drop* (Tesco home delivery); *Taste not waist* (Weight watchers frozen meals), *It 'asda be Asda* (www.adslogans.co.uk)

Your task is to watch/listen to some TV or radio ads and spot the puns. Once you've worked out which advertisers like to use puns, devise some for their use in ads. Send them to the companies concerned.

3) Make up a joke using the punch-line, *eats, shoots & leaves*.

This is the answer: *A panda walks into a café. He orders a sandwich, eats it, then draws a gun and fires two shots in the air.*

'Why?' asks the confused waiter, as the panda makes towards the exit. The panda produces a badly punctuated wildlife manual and tosses it over his shoulder.

'I'm a panda,' he says, at the door. 'Look it up.'

The waiter turns to the relevant entry and, sure enough, finds an explanation.

'Panda. *Large black-and-white bear-like mammal, native to China. Eats, shoots and leaves.'* (Truss, 2003)

4) Make up some ambiguous newspaper headlines

Often this is because a noun gets confused with a verb e.g.: *Squad helps dog bite victim* (Lederer, 1996)

One way to do this is to use the *Squad helps* line as a cue. The key part is *dog bite*. All you have to do now is to consider other words ending in bite…frostbite…love bite…snakebite.

So, a very simple change would be *Doctor helps snake bite victim.*

Now, you can be more ambitious and think of two words, one of which is a verb, which together constitute a noun. How about *ring-fence*, to protect cash?

Careful crooks ring fence

Actually, these are not that easy to generate. Starting is easy, but finishing is difficult. You just have to allow some incubation time:

Lame playboy bed hops

Snooker club black balls potter

If that is too difficult sound puns are an alternative. Just find a word, or words, with the same spelling, that have alternate meanings: *'Sappers blow up doll'* *'Stable boy commits suicide.'* On a lighter note how about using *jock-strap*, a piece of safety clothing which has humorous potential? At the moment Scottish independence and the financial implications are in the news, so:

Jocks strapped for cash

Puns using people's names can be used in headlines:

Peter Brook babbles in interview

Alex Salmond leaps for joy

Try: Doris Day; Hugh Grant; Jodie Foster and Brad Pitt

You can have ambiguous proper nouns, *Queen Mary having bottom scraped; Queen in affray at Palace* (This was a *Guardian* headline concerning a footballer at *Crystal Palace*)

Ordinary nouns can be ambiguous: *Men recommend more clubs for wives*.

Linguistic blunders

1) *Missippi's literacy program shows improvement*   (www.viralread.com)

2) George W. Bush -- *'They misunderestimated the compassion of our country.'*

3) Qu.: *'What's the difference between an OFSTED inspector and a plastic surgeon?'*

Ans.: *'Well, the plastic surgeon tucks features....'* (www.est1892.co.uk)

4) Alimony: *Bounty from the mutiny*

   Carp-to-carp walleting   (Redfern, 2000)

5) *'Illiterate him quite from your memory.'* (Mrs Malaprop)
6) Al. Gore – *'We all know that a leopard cannot change his stripes.'*   (http://freedomkeys.com)

7) *A Freudian slip is, 'when you say one thing and mean your mother.'* http://tvtropes.org)

8) Rodney: 'Why do you call me Dave, 'Trig'? My name's not Dave, It's Rodney.' (Harey, 2014)

9) '...and I've had a rimful of the Catholic Church.' (brimful)   (http://eggcorns.lascribe.net)

These examples illustrate the main sorts of spoken and written blunder. Such errors are of two main types. Firstly, there are errors where sounds or letters are added, deleted or transposed, e.g. *Spoonerisms.* Secondly, there are errors where a different word is used instead of the correct word, e.g. *Malapropisms.* (Vitevitch, 1997)

A slip of one small letter can make a big difference to something which is written and spoken. Take this quote from Labour politician, *John Prescott,* a man who finds the English language something of a challenge:

'My roots, my background and way I act is working class, but it would be hypsocritical to say I'm anything else than middle class now.'   (www.totalpolitics.com)

That slip was a mistake, but additions/deletions can be deliberately constructed, maybe for satirical effect, eg. *Both Boris Johnson and David Cameron went to Eliton.*

I live near Potters Bar, just north of London, and I was taken in once by the writing on a tradesman's van, as, initially, I thought it was a terrible spelling mistake:

Potters Barthrooms

Unintentional printing errors, which change just one or two letters, are quite common: *A story that appeared in Sunday's Argus Observer contained an incorrect spelling of a name. Pastor Dick Bigelow was incorrectly identified as Dick Bigblow. The Argus Observer regrets the error.* (www.oddee.com)

Misprints can be constructed deliberately in the pursuit of humour. For example, during the war, Norwegians used humour as a way of resisting Nazi power and propaganda. The collaborator puppet leader, *Vidkun Quisling* was a particular butt of jokes. There were many puns on his name, using *'usling/uisling'*, Norwegian for scoundrel. A newspaper editor managed, deliberately, to print a headline: *Vidkun 3/4uisling*. He persuaded the Nazis that rarely used typefaces, like Q & Z, were kept next to the fractions, and that was how the *'mistake'* occurred (Stokker, 2001).

Blends are another simple form of sound blunder. Blends are words formed from two other words e.g., *'frowl'*—frown and scowl, and *'refudiating'*—refuting and repudiating. Blends can be an anticipation of the next word to be said, such that a transposition occurs, e.g. *'slagged slightly'*. (Wells, 1973)

American president George W. Bush was famed for his problems with language, indeed they came to be called *Bushisms.* Not only would he produce blends like *misunderestimate* , he would also blend phrases. For example, *'I know how hard it is for you to put food on your family.'* (Cloud, 2003)

Politicians are often under great pressure and come in for close scrutiny. So, it's not surprising that they make gaffes, and that these gaffes are widely reported. For example, Mrs Thatcher was not immune to this problem. She once used the dialect word *'frit'* in Parliament, instead of frightened, and commented on the birth of her first grandchild, *'We are now a grandmother.'* Such mistakes are picked on with great glee by opponents and satirists, in this case Sir Clement Freud named a racehorse, *'We are a grandmother.'*

Sarah Palin, the American politician, and author of the word *'refudiate'*, is much mocked. One commentator predicted of a Palin presidency:

Her first act will be to cancel the agreement between nouns and verbs. Next, she'll replace the English language with Palinese: a language known only to her.' (Zimmer, 2010)

The classic transpositions are those associated with Dr Spooner:

'You have tasted your worm, you have hissed my mystery lectures, and you must leave by the first town drain.' (Knowles, 2004)

'I'll damn you for sewages.' (Nash, 1985)

'He's out at the back---boiling his icicle.'   (Watkins, 2002)

'When I see before me these rows and rows of beery wenches' (supposedly said by Spooner at a temperance meeting).

Spoonerisms are named after The Reverend William Archibald Spooner (1844-1930), an Oxford University academic, who is supposed to have made many of these transpositions. A man who set out to be a bird watcher, but ended up a word botcher! Spooner's biographer, Sir William Hayter, records that the term *Spoonerism* was in colloquial use in Oxford from about 1885. Hayter considers that many Spoonerisms are apocryphal, but does provide a telling quote from Spooner, made at the end of a speech, *'And now I suppose you will expect me to say one of those things.'* This does rather suggest that Spooner did make slips, and that they were not planned.

In fact, the only Spoonerism that can be tracked directly back to Spooner, is, *'weight of rages'* (Bockenhauer et al., 2007), although the New College, Oxford oral tradition is that Spooner admitted to *'Kinquering Kongs'* but denied the rest. It seems that many of his supposed Spoonerisms were invented by students-the *Shining Wits*.

I wonder which clever student invented this variety?:

As wine drinkers everywhere know, sprinkling salt over spilled wine is said to prevent a stain.

During dinner one evening the famously absent-minded William Spooner accidentally upset the salt-shaker on an immaculate white linen tablecloth. Without a moment's pause, he took up his wine glass and dribbled its contents over the spill. (www.anecdotage.com)

My favourite deliberate Spoonerism was made by *The Right Honourable Lord Justice Ward*, a judge in the Court of Appeal. He began his judgement as follows; *'This case involves a number of—and here I must not fall into Dr Spooner's error-warring bankers...'* (www.inform.wordpress.com)

It is the sheer surprise that makes for additional humour. Judges, particularly the most senior ones, are not supposed to joke about and, in particular, are not expected to be crude.

A word exchange error is similar to some *Spoonerisms* in that two words are switched. For example:

I let the cat out of the bag.

I let the bag out of the cat.

The shit hit the fan

The fan hit the shit

Exchanges are double shifts, and so can involve the shift of parts of words:

'...getting your nose remodelled.'

'...getting your model renosed.' (en.wikipedia.org)

The real humour with these shifts is when you hear them at the time they were made. Blake (2007) reports a TV news announcer saying: *'British police are refusing to confirm media reports that a man was killed in last night's bum boss--bus bomb--in London.'*

My favourite news-reader blooper, was one made by both James Naughtie and Andrew Marr. This concerned a Spoonerism over the pronunciation of *'Jeremy Hunt, the Culture Secretary.'* The not very cultured result was first said by Naughtie, who giggled about it through the news. The mistake was further compounded by Andrew Marr, who, soon after, when talking about Freudian slips, made the same transposition. Both made profuse apologies. Marr said, *'...it's just very hard to talk about it without saying it.'* (Hough, 2010)

Humorists can make good use of word exchange. For example:

'Work is the curse of the drinking classes.' (Oscar Wilde)

'A critic said that he never panned the opening show of a new theatre season because he didn't want to stone the first cast.' (Lederer, 1996)

Mae West, the witty American actress, was particularly good at word exchanges:

A hard man is good to find.'

It's not the men in my life that count, it's the life in my men.'   (www.brainyquote.com)

The other main type of linguistic blunder is word substitution, where an incorrect word is used as a substitute for a correct word, either by ignorance or by mistake.

A lady who more than slightly exceeded her linguistic grasp was, *Mrs Malaprop*, a Richard Brinsley Sheridan (1751-1816) invented character, who invariably managed to use a similar, but wrong word, with comic effect-*'Sure, if I reprehend anything in this world it is the use of my oracular tongue, and a nice derangement of epitaphs!'*

Sheridan wasn't the first to use the *Malapropism* form. There are several examples in Shakespeare's work-*'Comparisons are odorous.'*

The *Malapropism* has been much used by comic writers up to the present day as it an easy device to spell out pretentiousness and intellectual/educational inferiority. For example, Del-Boy the market trader-*'Good to be back on the old terracotta'*, and Adrian Mole- *'My schoolwork is plummeting down to new depths. I only got five out of twenty for spelling. I think I might be anorexic.'* (Townsend, 1992)

The *Malapropism* is found in everyday life as people quite often make such mistakes, giving mirth to observers who feel superior. For example, a head teacher friend of mine was once asked by a parent if, *'the school had any acoustic students.'* (The parent meant autistic)

The *New Scientist* reported a rather special one, where an office worker described a colleague as *'a vast suppository of information'*. The worker then apologised for his *'Miss-Marple-ism'*. This was possibly the first time anyone had uttered a *Malapropism* for the word *Malapropism*. (http://en.wikipedia.org)

Children are especially prone to the *Malapropism*. As their mastery of vocabulary is limited, they can easily substitute a known word for a more rarefied term. Here are some taken from student work:

'Socrates died from an overdose of wedlock'
'Ancient Egypt was inhabited by mummies and they all wrote in hydraulics'
Solomom had three hundred wives and seven hundred porcupines'   (www.mb21.co.uk)

A selection error is similar to a *Malapropism*, in that an incorrect word is selected. This is not due to ignorance, but memory lapse, pressure, etc. Al Gore, for example, managed to say a leopard couldn't lose its stripes in 1995, despite, in 1992, saying: *'A zebra does not change its spots.'* (http://freedomkeys.com/gore)

There is a word for when someone continues to use a *Malapropism* or other blunder, even though they have been told they are wrong, and that's a *Mumpsimus*. This occurs when someone sticks to an action or language that is incorrect. The classic case is *Trigger* in *Only Fools and Horses*, who persisted in calling *Rodney, Dave*:

Trigger: *'If it's a girl they're gonna name it Sigourney, after the actress. And if it's a boy they're gonna name him Rodney, after Dave.'* (Hodgson, 2014)

There is much humour in the *Mumpsimus*. We laugh at the rigidity of the fool, or old person who is unable to change, characters like: *Old man Steptoe, Alf Garnett,* and *Victor Meldrew.*

The term *Mumpsimus* itself is said to derive from an old monk in ancient times, who insisted on saying *Mumpsimus* instead of *Sumpsimus,* when reciting the *Eucharist.* (http://en.wiktionary.org)

The cause of the linguistic blunder may be simple error, stupidity, bloody-mindedness, or it could be more complex. For example, Yang (2002) reports a university professor who *'stunned'* a graduation audience of students and parents, by congratulating the students on the achievement of their, *'tremendous amount of scholarly and tremendous amount of sex—success.'* Now, was this a simple slip of the tongue? Or, was it an envious admission of the truth? Or, was it about some deeper, personal issues of the professor? A Freudian slip?

Freud (1973) found, when psychoanalysing patients, that they might make a slip of the tongue, which revealed underlying, repressed thoughts, *'a mode of self-betrayal'*. For example, a patient was talking about her family, saying they were unusual in that they all possessed *Geiz* ('greed'), when she meant to say *Geist* ('cleverness'). Freud observed, *'this (greed) was in fact the reproach which she had repressed from her memory.'*

The Freudian slip is a source of jokes:

'One of my patients had a rather amusing Freudian slip: he was having dinner with his wife, and he meant to say 'pass the salt', but instead he said 'You've ruined my life, you blood-sucking shrew' – Niles Crane, Frasier   (http://tvtropes.org)

Having one wife is called monotony (monogamy)   (examples.yourdictionary.com)

Mishearings

Sometimes there is humour in deliberately mishearing what someone has said. Comedians can take knowing advantage of this process. They deliberately say words like *mastication* or *castigation* and know they will get a laugh as the audience makes a *masturbation* or *castration* interpretation.

Where a word or phrase is innocently misheard, or not understood, and another word is substituted, we have what is known as a mondegreen. For example, *'Jeff's nuts roasting on an open fire,'* (Chestnuts roasting on an open fire), or *'Six geezers laying,'* (Six geese a-laying).

Usually, mondegreens are mishearing of song lyrics: 'Excuse me while I kiss this guy', should be *'Excuse me while I kiss the sky.'* (Jimi Hendrix, Purple Haze)   (www.snopes.com)

The term *mondegreen* was invented by a writer called Sylvia Wright, who misheard a line from a 17th century Scottish ballad:

Ye Highlands and ye Lowlands

Oh, where hae ye been?

They hae slain the Earl of Murray.

And laid him on the green.

Wright thought the last line was: *And Lady Mondegreen* (http://www.quickand dirtytips.com)

The *eggcorn* is similar to a *mondegreen*. In this case, a meaningful word or term is substituted for the original, and whilst the *mondegreen* is restricted to songs or poems, the *eggcorn* has no such restriction. For example:

Old timer's disease = Alzheimer's disease; *Rest-bite* = Respite; *Lame man's terms* = Layman's terms (uwelingo.wordpess.com)

Erard (2007) reports the following: '...from the beginning Camilla approved of Charles marrying Diana while she remained his power mower.'

An important factor in mishearing is the denseness of a word's neighbourhood. The more words that resemble a particular word, the denser its neighbourhood is said to be. Words with dense neighbourhoods need more time to be recognised, whilst words with sparse neighbourhoods are more accurately recognised (Vitevitch, 1997). Just compare *Zimbabwe* with *write/right/rite/riot*.

Some words are particularly problematic. Adrian Room calls these confusibles, such as: their, they're and there. Not only do confusibles have similar spelling and pronunciation, they have similar meaning, eg, fraction and faction; effect and affect. (Redfern, 2000)

Finally, we have simple failure to construct a sentence that is sensible. Although each word may be correct, the whole is incorrect, or not worth saying as it is a statement of the obvious:

George W. Bush: *'The problem with the French is that they don't have a word for entrepreneur.'*

George W. Bush: *'I think we agree, the past is over.'*   (Rudd, 2009)

Reflection

Once we start talking we are on a precarious trek through a jungle of words. Usually, our brains are clever enough to cope with the complexities of language but, there are so many words to cope with that it's no surprise we get them confused now and again, often with humorous effect.

Our deficient performance reveals educational, memory and hearing failure. Slips reveal our efforts to conceal that we are under stress. Indeed, if Freud is right, they reveal our inner secrets.

Although there seem to be loads of linguistic errors, and we are all guilty of them from time to time, it is reassuring to know, in fact, that *'...speech errors in normal subjects (are) rare.'* The average person makes a slip of the tongue only about twice in every 1,000 words spoken. (Erard, 2007)

The brain's mechanisms enable self-monitoring of one's own speech production. When we hesitate, *'covert repairs'* may be being carried out-*'the error has been detected even before articulation.'* (Moller et al. 2007)

Even so, for the novice presenter, the fear of making a fool of him or herself, partly through speech errors, might in fact lead to those very errors. I was conscious of this once when I was interviewed by *Angela Rippon* for a radio programme. So, I made absolutely sure I had relevant written material to hand to ensure that things went as smoothly as possible. Still, I was surprised by the number of *ums* and *ers* I managed to produce. {Actually between 5-8% of what we say each day involves an *'uh'*, *'um'*, or some other pause filler, or a repair to what we have said. (Erard, 2007)}

There is a lot of fun in linguistic blunders. We can deliberately use the ambiguities of language to amuse others. We can point to the mistakes of comic characters like *Del-Boy* to illustrate the correct usage of words-*a faint accompli*. We can use Spoonerisms to fight a liar. We can literally use printing errors to make a pint. They are a powerful weapon in the humourist's charmoury.

Activity, this is the pun fart:

1) Create new funny words

The Washington Post newspaper invites readers to submit new words which are alterations in existing words. Only one letter can change. For example:

Joke Biden—Vice President

Foreploy—Any misrepresentation about yourself for the purpose of getting laid.

Kinsane—What your spouse's family is.

Giraffiti—Vandalism spray-painted very, very high.   (www.washingtonpost.com)

Your task is to create such new words. To do this, open the dictionary at a random point and start searching for suitable words. One syllable words are not much use as any slight change distorts the word and makes it unrecognisable. Also, the 'new' word may well not be new, eg. Sex, six, sax, sox.

You do need to invent an amusing word so, for example, *coinflab* isn't much use—*a chat about money*. I came up with: *nul de sac—turning infertile*; *fuckold—husband of an ageing adultress*, and *sex gratia—prostitute's tip.*

You can then go on and use your new word in a witticism:

I reward my mistress sex gratia

Shotgun wedding: a case of wife or death

When you dream in colour, it's a pigment of the imagination. (Blake, 2007)

2) Create a *'What's the difference'* Spoonerism

Actually, it is quite hard to do a decent one of these. Take this one:

'What's the difference between a book worm and someone whose rabbit follows him around?'

Ans.: 'One has a reading habit, the other has a heeding rabbit.'

The reading habit is fine, but the heeding rabbit is a bit strained. It possibly doesn't matter so much if you are aiming at a young audience, as they are not as discriminating as adults, and they may well enjoy the silliness and incongruity.

Richard Lederer (1996) gives us some useful Spoonerisms which could be used for these jokes:

Baits his hook/hates his book; dangling monkey/mangling donkey; bad salad/sad ballad; speeding rider/reading spider; money bags/bunny mags.; curried horse/hurried course; nooks and crannies/crooks and nannies; bunny hair/honey bear; cute mitten/mute kitten; big pin/pig bin; leaping wizard/weeping lizard; brown cattle/crown battle; stuck door/duck store; gate crasher/crate gasher; four socks/sore fox.

If you want to create your own Spoonerisms, this is what you have to do:

Step 1 – Select a word which has plenty of rhymes, which does not begin with a vowel, is 'interesting', and has joke potential. (Word A, e.g. *'choose'*)

Step 2 – Select a new word that makes sense when combined with word A. Again, this must not begin with a vowel, and it must have lots of rhymes. (Word B, e.g. *'beer'*)

Step 3 – Select a word that rhymes with the first word, and starts with the same consonant as the second word, B (e.g. *'booze'*).

Step 4 – Write out the final word, by combining the first consonants of the first word (A) and the letters that follow the first consonants of the second word (B). There is no choice as this is determined by what you have already done (e.g., *cheer*).

So, you end up with: *choose beer.........booze cheer* -- an acceptable Spoonerism that can be turned into a riddle.

'What is the difference between a brewer and his customers?

'A brewer is always choosing beers, his customers are always boozing, cheers.'

It is so important to pick words with a lot of potential rhymes, as Spoonerisms rely on rhyme.

Here's another, using the same method, and the same type of rhyme:

'What is the difference between the Daily Mirror and a smart dresser?'

'The Daily Mirror is a news sheet, a smart dresser likes his shoes neat.'

If you have a word in the punch-line in mind, you simply reverse the above process, e.g. 'Why do they call *'pay loos'*, *'pay loos?'* 'I don't know, why do they call *'pay loos'* *'pay loos?'* 'Simple, in *'pay loos'* you *'lay poos!'*

3) Create your own modern day malapropisms

Here are a couple of the winners of the *New York* magazine's competition 348 for modern day malapropisms:

Absinthe makes the heart grow fonder

Sitting and trading antidotes   (Zwicky, 1980)

This is a relatively easy task. Just take a list of proverbs, select the key noun in the proverb and modify one or two letters to create, hopefully, an amusing variation. You do have to have a fairly unusual word to modify, *'A safe pair of hands'*, for example, gives you nothing to work with:

A plaque on both your houses (plague); *A riddle wrapped in an enema* (enigma); *Anus horribilis* (annus).

4) Invent a Mondegreen

Go through some music lyrics and try and invent a *Mondegreen*. I should warn you that this is very difficult to do, because popular music uses very short words which are easy to understand. For the most part, the words that are sung seem to be some sort of combination of the following: *I want you baby, La La, La, Can't live without you. You turn me on, Yeah*

I did have some moderate success:

One Thing by *One Direction*: *'Shot me out of the sky, You're my kryptonite'* can be heard as: *'You're my crib tonight.'*

Hand on heart by *Olly Murs*: *'We mend, we break, And so the cycle goes'* can be heard as *'And so the sigh call goes.'*

5) Watch an edition of *Only Fools and Horses* and work out how much of the humour derives from linguistic blunders.

6) For those new to public speaking, it is very reassuring to have a prop. In the case of linguistic blunders, amusing newspaper headlines and misprints can be used as part or all of a presentation. Start a collection of headlines and misprints for future use.

Puns

Harry sent ten different puns to a friend in the hope that at least one of the puns would make him laugh. Unfortunately, no pun in ten did. (Arnott & Haskins, 2004)

Puns are strange things. They can be both funny, and not funny, and still be funny. In the first case the wit is appreciated, in the second, the awfulness is recognised, and groans erupt. There is a laughing *at*, but even the laughing *at* can be a laughing *with* as well.

To explain, if we take a teacher's pun from a *Jennings* book, we can see a laboured development and a fairly obvious, scripted pun-chline, which is not spontaneous, and doesn't quite work:

'Allow me to explain, Bromwich, in words so simple that even you can understand.' He pointed to his handiwork. 'These creatures are both weevils--grain eating insects which do great damage to crops. As you can see, one is larger than the other. Therefore, the smaller one is the lesser of two weevils.'

'The pun was greeted with the usual derision. All round the room boys groaned, sighed, winced, held their heads in their hands or collapsed in mock fashion.' (Buckeridge, 1990)

If the boys had considered that the teacher knew the pun was awful, and that is, in fact, the joke, they would have laughed with him.

How about this shocker told by Richard Whiteley of *Countdown* fame:

'Two eskimos were on a wooden boat and it was so cold that one of them lit a fire. Unfortunately the boat caught fire and sunk which just goes to show that you can't have your kayak and eat it.' (Apanowicz, 2006)

It is the faulty sound play that really causes the problem. Hempelmann (2004) considers that puns that rely just on playing with sound have a pariah status. To be effective, he argues that the sound play must be accompanied by a play with meaning.

A play on meaning isn't found in the *'shaggy dog story'*, a long, somewhat rambling story, which ends in a distorted version of some proverb or saying. *'Usually this final line purports to summarize or draw a moral from the preceding story.'* (Binsted & Ritchie, 2001).

Partridge (1954) reckons the shaggy dog story was invented in the 1930s. He relates a story, about a shaggy dog, which is thought to have given its name to the genre. To cut a very long story short, a rich man in London lost his valuable dog, which was *'rather shaggy'*. He advertised for its return, with little luck. However, a man in New York read the ad., and decided to give the Englishman a replacement for the lost dog. After encountering many difficulties, the American finally delivered the replacement dog. The butler glanced at the dog, and in horror exclaimed that the lost dog, *'...was not so shaggy as that, sir!'*

Binsted & Ritchie give a shorter example of a shaggy dog story, what they refer to as a *'strong pun'*:

'Once upon a time, many years ago, there was a chieftain in a remote tropical village who owned an old battered throne of which he was very fond. One day, a visiting dignitary gave him a brand new and ornate throne, which the chieftain had to adopt immediately out of politeness. However, he could not bear to part with the old throne which had served him so well, so he stored it away in the roof area of his grass hut, in case it should be useful in the future.

Unfortunately, the interior structure of the hut was too flimsy to support the weight of the large object, and it crashed through the grass ceiling, falling on to the chieftain and killing him.'

The moral of the story is: *'...people who live in grass houses shouldn't store thrones.'*

Not surprisingly, Binsted & Ritchie note that the listener's reaction is *'often to groan rather than to laugh.'* Actually, the listener may look forward to the groaning, and that is the point of the shaggy dog story. Everyone involved knows the rules. That is what is funny. Clearly, shaggy dog stories are jokes, but not as we know them!

Brunvand (1963) argued that the shaggy dog story is, in essence, a trick played on the listener after enduring the pointless narrative. The trick lies in the verbal double cross of the punch-line.

Given the awfulness of the shaggy dog story, it is not surprising that the humour experts don't have much time for the pun. Sigmund Freud (1991) considered that puns were regarded with contempt, as the lowest form of verbal joke, *'... because they are the 'cheapest'—can be made with the least trouble.'*

Norrick's (2003) damning assessment is:

Punning in particular enjoys a rather poor reputation traditionally. Puns count as frivolous and superficial even among the various types of humor, and they rank quite high in the scale of aggression, because they disrupt topical talk by misconstruing and redirecting it. Moreover, puns often revolve around rather managed, less salient senses of a word, those related to arcane or abstract areas of knowledge.

Not all the experts are so withering, Arthur Berger (2010) claims:

'Puns are often attacked as being "the lowest form of wit." This is not true; good puns are excellent examples of wit. It is only when the pun stretches too far or is too far off base that puns elicit the customary groan from people...'

Perhaps the cleverest pun of all time is that said to be have been produced by Sir Charles Napier (1782-1853), when, in 1843, he took armed control of the province of *Sindh* in India, which is now Pakistan. In a telegram to the British government he is supposed to have sent one word, *Peccavi*, Latin for *'I have sinned.'* Actually, the pun was published in the humorous magazine *Punch* in 1844, a witticism created by teenager, Catherine Winkworth (Byrne, 2012).

Dorothy Parker, the renowned American wit, was a noted punster. She was once asked to use the word *'horticulture'* in a sentence and promptly said, *'You can lead a horticulture but you can't make her think.'* (Asimov, 1972). If it is indeed true that that quip was instantaneous, the audience would have laughed, not just at the pun, but at the quick-wittedness of the response.

So, what is a pun? According to Lederer (1981) a pun occurs when, *'...two or more meanings are packed into a verbal space which they do not ordinarily occupy.'* He considers there are six methods of pun making: the single-sound pun, the double-sound pun, the Spoonerism, the meld pun, the palindrome, and the acronym.

The single-sound pun is the simplest. If the same spelling is used, the pun is a homograph (same writing), e.g., *'A butcher backed into a meat grinder and got a little behind.'* Where the spelling differs, the pun is a homophone (same sound), e.g., *'I'm on a seafood diet. Every time I see food, I eat it.'* (Lederer, 1981)

In the case of a double sound pun a sound generates two meanings, but the second meaning only has a link to the first. Here is rather a good example, *'The Bronte sisters engaged in a scribbling rivalry'* (Lederer, 1981). Simply, *'scribbling'* and *'sibling'* sound much the same.

It is these double sound puns (also known as near puns) which give the pun such a bad name. They are, of course, the staple of children's knock-knock jokes, e.g.:

Knock-knock: 'Who's there?' 'Quacker' 'Quacker who?' 'Quack another bad knock knock joke and I'm leaving!'

Spoonerisms *'... compress two or more meanings into a relatively small verbal space.'* Lederer gives a nice example, *'It is kistomary to cuss the bride.'*

A meld pun is where two words are compressed so that the meaning is preserved e.g. *chortle* derives from chuckle and snort. Withington (1939) provides us with some clever examples, taken from the *Reader's Digest*:

She slipped away to her clandestination
She's so tomboystrous
He majored in alibiology
She glamoured for attention

Palindromes and acronyms are not usually humorous, but they do meet Lederer's definition of a pun, e.g., Madam, I'm Adam; and S.A.N.E.—Students Against Nuclear Energy.
Dynel (2009) gives us some funnier ones: SINK SCUM = Single Independent, No Kids...the Self-Centred Urban Male; SINBAD = Single Income, No Boyfriend, Absolutely Desperate; DNA = National Association of Dyslexics.

Maybe puns aren't so much for the adult, but children love them, and that's one good reason why adults should be able to pun—to amuse children. Opie & Opie (1973) have a nice turn of phrase when considering the commonplace use of puns by schoolchildren amongst themselves. They observe that the, *'... pick-pocket of wit the pun is a common ingredient of juvenile jokelore.'*

An example the Opies give is: *'My ice-cream is dripping'*—*'Oh that's funny. I thought it was ice-cream.'*

As puns appeal so much to children, they are an effective way for a teacher to hook pupil attention. Tatum (1999) explains how he uses puns in an English class. Firstly, he asks for the correct usage of a word, then a punning usage. The best example he gives is the use of the word *'refractory'*. A student replied, *'a place where they manufacture prisms.'* Tatum argues that this approach gets pupil attention, develops creative thinking skills, and improves pupils' vocabulary.

Of course, the British vocabulary is very rich, and so lends itself readily to the pun. According to Lederer (2013) there are 616,500 words in the *Oxford English Dictionary*. This far exceeds any other nation's word stock. Actually, the Germans are next with 185,000, followed by the Russians, weighing in with 130,000.

We shouldn't get too carried away with our bragging rights. The average Brit. only recognises between 10,000 and 20,000 words. The average British conversation is made up of the most frequently used words, which number just 737. (Lederer, 2013)

Of course, if you are teaching or learning Shakespeare you cannot avoid the pun. Punning, or quibbling, as it was known, was a *'universal habit'* in Elizabethan times, and this is reflected in many of Shakespeare's works. (Rot, 1983) For example, *Pistol* in *Henry V,* says, *'To England will I steal, and there I'll steal.'*; *Falstaff* in *Henry IV Part 2* says to *Prince Henry, 'Were it not here apparent that thou art heir apparent.'*

Finally, we mustn't forget that puns are a staple part of jokes, so, to become a jokester, you do need a facility with puns:

'Conjunctivitis.com – that's a site for sore eyes.' (Vine, 2010)
'I just got a text from Heaven. That was a Godsend.'

Perhaps the funniest puns are those that are unintended. Their sheer surprise, especially if there is a sexual implication, can cause hysterics:

Harry Carpenter at the Oxford-Cambridge boat race, 1977, 'Ah, isn't that nice. The wife of the Cambridge President is kissing the cox of the Oxford crew.' (forums.digitalspy.co.uk)

Reflection

Puns can be funny, but they are often the rather obvious joke, so are not seen as the wittiest, indeed, Freud reckoned they were inferiority humour. The worst puns are based on the faulty use of sound, where no double meaning is involved. Such puns then, may be better never, than late (Withington, 1939).
Puns are at the basic end of the spectrum, and this simplicity makes them particularly appealing to children. Not surprisingly, they are a crucial element of many knock-knock jokes, and riddles.

Teachers, and parents come to that, can make use of puns as a teaching tool. Puns illustrate double meanings and so can be used to develop vocabulary in an amusing way. Even so, they should be careful not to use them too often; no one likes a tired wit.

Activity

1) Construct some *Tom Swifties*.

Tom Swift was the lead character in some children's adventure stories, published before the second world-war. The stories made use of a sentence structure, where the adverb finishes the sentence in a punning way. For example:

'This might be a good place to camp', said Tom tentatively.

'I suppose I like modern painting', said Tom abstractly. (Lippman & Dunn, 2000).

These are standard *Tom Swifties*, where there is only one pun, however, a double pun can be used and, for more surprise, witty sound puns can be deployed, as well as reversals:

'I'd like to help you have a good time,' she said, solicitously.

'This is a draft shopping list,' he said, provisionally.

'This bouquet doesn't have many flowers,' she said, lackadaisically.

'There is no more coal in there,' the geologist said, mindfully.

'They are completely wrong,' she said, positively.

Complete the following (The answers are lower down the page):

   a) *'This beer is too expensive,'* said Tom, ...
   b) *'I'll have an ice-cream,'* said Tom, ...
   c) *'Mine is eight inches,'* said Tom, ...
   d) *'I want to kiss you a thousand times,'* said Tom, ...
   e) *'I really love jelly,'* she said, ...

Work out appropriate set-ups:

   f) ....he said, *reflectively*.
   g) ....he said, *lamely*.
   h) .... he said, *grouchily*.
   i) ....he said, *overemotionally*.
   j) ....said, Captain Hook, *offhandedly*.

Answers: 1) Bitterly, 2) Sweetly, 3) Cockily, 4) Grandly, 5) Firmly, 6) 'I wonder if I should look in the mirror,' 7) 'I deliberately fell over because I thought it would be a laugh, 8) 'Marx is my least favourite writer,' 9) 'We won the match with the last ball,' 10) 'I wonder where Peter Pan is,'

2) Pair up the following meld puns:

Anagrambo – Endless piss-take
Cannabistro – Gravitas
Bintercourse – Drug baron
Madolescence –Oxymoron
Dildoting – No class, no money
Affixture – Drunken behaviour
Computerine – Study of Chinese gambling
Tabooze – Rigged football match
Ridicule de sac –Tough crossword clue
Estrangel – Blow job
Cracketeer – Very keen on manual stimulation
Titilatex – Drug café
Bistoic –Satan
Limpotent – Teenage
Casinology – Sex with an Arab woman
Chiantics – Internet porn
Chavenots – Boob job
Oxygenital – Alcoholics Anonymous slogan

These meld puns are quite tedious to do, but satisfying when an apt one emerges. To construct them you have to plough your way steadily through a dictionary. It is easier to add elements at the end of a word as you can easily check in the dictionary, or you can just spot an appropriate ending, e.g. *titilatex*.
Use the internet for additions at the front of the word, e.g., *anagrambo*, was constructed on *Rambo*, and used Scrabble word finder at www.scrabblefinder.com

3) Invent a Naming pun

Naming puns are puns which consumers invent in order to mock a company because they are dissatisfied or frustrated by its product or service. For example:

Aer Lingus—Air Fungus; *Delta Airlines*—Don't Even Leave The Airport; *FIAT*—Fix It Again Tony (Nilsen & Nilsen, 1991).

Devise naming puns for companies and organisations that annoy you. See how amused they are when you send them your efforts in letters of complaint.

How about:

TESCO—Takes Every Site; Closes Opposition;

WONGA—Worships Obsessive Naked Greedy Avarice.

Collective Nouns

Qu.: *'What do you call an underground train full of professors?'*
Ans.: *'A tube of smarties.'*
That is a fairly respectable use of two puns, tube and smarties, in order to liken a group of academics on a train to a well-known brand of confectionery. A tube of *Smarties* becomes a new collective noun for academics travelling on the underground.

This section is about inventing amusing collective nouns, using puns. The aim is to turn you into punning stars via stunning parse.

We begin by looking at puns that I have devised in order to describe groups in schools and colleges. To qualify as a collective noun pun, the pun must relate to the person(s) specified and must also refer to some sort of collection. Only some of the puns here meet that test. You might like to have a go using the job titles at your work place.

The punning starts:

There is a term for teachers:

(*'Term'* is a word with two meanings, but there is no collectivity. The whole sentence is not funny as, without priming the audience that there is a joke coming, this same writing pun could easily be missed. It is just moderately clever.)

A muse of funny teachers

(This pun is a bit better, making use, as it does, of the indefinite article *A*. It is quite clever, using the word *'muse'*-- a source of inspiration. The listener has to work out what is going on, and that is part of the fun of it. There is no collectivity involved)

A void of boring teachers

(This pun is similar to the previous one, but it is better as we have all been there, and there is a distinct ring of truth about the whole sentence. With luck there might be a smile of recognition and nostalgia. There is no collectivity involved.)

A shower of P.E. teachers

(This pun is acceptable, as a shower is slang for a nondescript group.)

A repast of history teachers

(This one is more dubious. It is clever in the sense of referring to the past, but it fails in the other sense of a meal, as this doesn't relate to history teachers. There is no collectivity involved; so, too clever by half.)

An OMG of R.E. teachers

(Well, this is up to date. It is an acronym, which qualifies as a pun, but there is only one meaning; so, so-so.)

A division of maths teachers

(This is acceptable, but not particularly funny as it is too obvious; a same writing pun.)

A tense of English teachers

(This is not that good as there is no reason why English teachers should be particularly tense. You could have, *A pretense of unqualified English teachers*, but this is a rather unrealistic set-up.)

A babel of language teachers

(Not really a pun, just a reference to multiple tongues. It might be a good term to describe a group of language teachers, but it is not that witty.)

An in-continents of geography teachers

(Well, I think this is funny, but it is a strain. The term *'in-continents'* doesn't really exist, so this is not a naturally flowing joke.)

A charge of physics teachers

(This is ok, nothing special; a same writing pun.)

A cell of biology teachers

(Ditto)

An exodus of Newly Qualified Teachers

(Not a pun, just a comment on teacher retention.)

A pallet of art teachers

(This is quite good. It is a same sound pun, which requires a little effort to work out.)

A Liszt of music teachers

(This is the best one so far. It is a same sound pun which also makes use of the indefinite article.)

A queue of drama teachers
(Again, quite good; it's a same sound pun)

A cache of economics teachers

(Ditto)

A crew of accountancy teachers
A cruel of accountancy teachers

(The first one of these meets our requirements; however, whilst the second one doesn't, it does have more bite.)

A diet of domestic science teachers

(This meets requirements, but is not that funny; a same writing pun.)

An interlude of staff room banter

(I like this one. There is a pun on lewd, but interlude is only a collectivity of time, not people, however, staff room banter does take place at interludes when groups are present.)

A diatribe of lecturers
(Quite a good sound pun, although something of a slur on lecturers.)

An absence of professors

(Not a pun. I heard this one from an external examiner. It is a comment on the difficulty of finding a professor as they tend to be absorbed in their research, or they are off at conferences.)

A meddle of v.c.'s

(This is my favourite, but it is an insider's joke. A v.c. is a vice chancellor, the person who has executive responsibility for a university, however meddle is not a collective word.)

An eyeful of pupils
 (This is clever but fails the collectivity test.)

A mind field of students

(Here we have a mine field and a filled mind. This is pretty good and would make lecturers laugh as students don't usually have filled minds and they can be something of a mine field. You do have to step carefully. Even so, we have no real collectivity.)

A William Hill's of librarians

(This is a little complicated and presents a challenge to a listener. If they ask you what it means, you may well get a laugh when you say *'bookies'*. This one fails the collectivity test.)

A score of examiners

(Technically, there is a lot going on here. A score means 20, and therefore the pun passes the collectivity test. Score also means how many marks you get. It also means to strike out, to mark wrong. Unfortunately, they are just same writing puns.)

An ice-cream of burnt-out teachers
A scream of class clowns
A scram of truants
A cram of examinees
A ram of male computer teachers
An am of philosophy teachers
An a of star pupils
An   of Zen Buddhism teachers

(This collection is a consequence of pushing the envelope to see how far a joke could go. Only one actually meets our collectivity requirement, a cram.)

Reflection
 It is absolutely clear that same sound puns are far better than same writing puns. The same sound puns require some thought to decipher. Conversely, the same writing puns are just not very clever. They are too easy to construct and they may not even be noticed by the hearer.

Derivative puns are interesting. We have seen the *Bookies* one in relation to librarians. They can be used to involve the audience and they do easily become riddles. So, *'Why are librarians like William Hills, the betting shop? They're both bookies.'*

To construct one of these, you simply think of an occupation or type of person, consider their key characteristic, which has a pun possibility, and then play with that word and see what other occupation or person relates to that word. So...actors...roles...rolls...baker...knead...need. *'Why is an actor like a baker? They both need rolls.'*

Activity

1) Produce a collective noun

Here is an anecdote reported by Isaac Asimov (1972):

'Four scholars, on a walk off campus, encountered a group of ladies clearly of that class described as being of easy virtue.

'Ah,' said one of the scholars, 'a jam of tarts.' 'Not at all,' said the second, 'say, rather a flourish of strumpets.'

'Or,' said the third, 'an essay of Trollope's.'

And the fourth said, 'Rather, I think, an anthology of pro's.'

Asimov added his own idea, 'How about a frost of hoars?'

Your task is to devise a new collective noun for prostitutes. Words you could consider are: *harlot, hooker, bawd, floozie, call girl, and tom* {*Tom Tart* is Australian rhyming slang for sweetheart, and *Tommy Tucker* is cockney rhyming slang for a loose woman (Jack, 2011)}.

2) Construct a collective noun pun

Select three occupations and three animals and devise a collective noun pun for each. Submit your efforts to www.ojohaven.com. This is a website that collects collective nouns, *'The goal is not (yet) to be comprehensive—merely entertaining.'*

There are some good ones in this collection: *a band of gorillas; a body of pathologists; a brace of orthodontists,* and *a clutch of kleptomaniacs*

You could also try submitting descriptive common nouns for animals, birds and insects. The English language is rich with these: *a gleam of herrings; an ostentation of peacocks; a quiver of cobras; a murmuration of starlings* and *a cornucopia of slugs,* etc.

Daffynitions

Daffynitions, are word-plays, often involving puns, which are alternative meanings for standard words.

My all-time favourite is *willy-nilly* – impotent; but *impotence* – no hard feelings, comes close, too close for comfort. *Aperitif* – French dentures, is good, as is *adenoid* – irritated by TV commercials. (Blake, 2007)

Such *daffynitions* are a staple part of the *Radio 4* comedy programme, *I'm Sorry I Haven't a Clue* – the antidote to panel games. Here, four comedians suggest *daffynitions* for the *Uxbridge English Dictionary*. Some examples:

Edelweiss – An unused bench clamp

Matrix – Practical jokes executed by your best friend

Paperback – What a masseuse earns

Triangle – Have a go at fishing

Romantic – An Italian flea   (www.alspcs.com)

Producing these *daffynitions* develops punning skills. Also, a new definition can be used as the basis of a longer joke. Sally Holloway (2010) gives us examples:

'I really love language. I used to think bumbling was jewellery for your arse.' (Tiernan Dooyab)

'When I was a kid I thought 'racist' meant someone who was good at running. I'd go up to black kids and say, "You're good at running. I bet when you grow up you are going to be a great racist." ' (Jason John Whitehead)

To produce *daffynitions* just go to a dictionary and run your eye down the words. Avoid long words as they are too difficult to use. Break up each word into its component parts and see if there is a pun lurking there somewhere. Here are some very simple ones, where no great thought is involved. There is no change in the sound:

Horseback – A bet

Pungent – Milton Jones

Changing the stress of the syllables in the word is a good approach. For example:

Finicky — A sick fish

Normally, when we say finicky, we stress the first syllable and the rest of the word is not stressed. With the new definition the rest of the word is stressed and the first syllable is pretty quiet.

Exactly the same process is going on in this case: *Icy* – Understanding

You can be more ambitious and go for the double pun, for example:

Hypnotise – Fashionably open necked.

This is a bit more sophisticated, a bit more surprising, so, a better gag.

It is not necessary for a pun to be involved. You can have a literal description, for example:

Gasworks – Intestines

Golfer – Balls hitter

This golf one can easily be turned into a joke, trouble is you already know the punch-line.

'A golfer I once knew, Tom Barker, was pretty good. He could drive a ball for miles. He really did have a great drive, not such a good putter, though. The trouble was he often fiddled his score, saying he went round below par, when he was usually about 5 over. People got really fed up with him, but I shut him up one day. I told him his nickname, "Balls hitter!" '

This next one is very similar. The end or start of a word is transferred to the other word:

Full stop – A dunce's cap

Reflection

These *daffynitions* are fun. They are fairly easy, and can turn into the building blocks for jokes. What you really need to do them is a change of perspective, so as to look at a word differently. The trouble is we are so used to seeing words in certain conventional ways that a perspective change is quite difficult.

Activity

1) Suggest *daffynitions* for the following words (Answers over the page):

   a) Macabre
   b) Madame
   c) Maidenhead
   d) Mailbag
   e) Meander

2) Which words do these *daffynitions* define? They all begin MA…..(Answers below):

   a) Male Dyson

b) Mother's Ruin
c) Clans
d) Second helpings of flan
e) Gay assignation

3) Produce your own *daffynitions*

Submit them for inclusion in the *Uxbridge English Dictionary* at www.alspcs.com

4) Make at least one joke out of a *daffynition*.

Answers: 1) a) Scots Pine, b) Self-confessed lunatic, c) Idea, d) Scrotum, e) Couple

2) a) Manoeuvre, b) Margin, c) Mascots, d) Mawkish, e) Mandate

Knock-knock jokes

In September, 2013 someone with the nickname, *ChipsattACK* wrote to *AskReddit.com* with this request:

'I have never heard a knock-knock joke that was actually funny. Reddit please prove me wrong.'

A response was submitted by *UndeadGilroy*:

'When going to a production of Hamlet, just before the show starts lean to the person next to you and say "Knock Knock." The first line of the show is "Who's there." '

It's true. In Act 1, Scene 1 of *Hamlet*, in front of the castle at Elsinor, *Bernardo*, on guard, shouts out *'Who's there?'* and is answered by *Francisco*.

Well, *ChipsattACK* got his answer, but maybe, he's also got a faulty memory. As an adult, he sees through a glass darkly, and cannot remember being six or seven years old, at which age knock-knocks are hilarious.

'Knock knock''Who's there?''Cargo''Cargo who?''Cargo BEEP BEEP!'   (Zipke, 2008)

A grown-up Marcy Zipke is here reflecting on her obsession with knock-knock jokes when she was 6 years of age. She says she would, *'laugh uproariously'* whenever she heard one, no matter how inane. In particular, she remembers a Eureka moment when she realised it was funny that language was there to be manipulated, as one word could have two meanings. She recalls seeing the word *'tennis'* on the side of a building, and then developed her own joke:

'Knock knock' 'Who's there?'Tennis''Tennis who?''Ten is my favourite number'

Knock-knock jokes are some of the first jokes that children tell. They are their entry point into the world of humour. Through knock-knocks they can revel in word play, engage in social joking, and be superior to another by treating them as the butt of the joke.

Knock-knocks are relatively easy to remember as they are formulaic. They don't have to be that funny, so they can be easily invented by the child. They are more than adult word play. They are play at words, where children realise that language can be considered as a *'thing-in-itself.'* (Fowles & Glanz, 1977)

Technically, knock-knock jokes are usually puns based on word sound alone. They are also close to being riddles, albeit rather unsolvable ones.

Typically, a person's name is the source of the sound pun:

'Knock knock' 'Who's there?' 'Arthur' 'Arthur who?' 'Arfur got!'

'Knock knock' 'Who's there?' 'Henrietta' 'Henrieta who?' 'Henry eat a worm that was in his apple!'

'Knock knock' 'Who's there?' 'Mikey' 'Mikey who?' 'My key doesn't fit the keyhole, let me in!'

The pun doesn't necessarily have to revolve around a name. Any object/person/idea is fair game:

Knock knock' 'Who's there?' 'Waiter' 'Waiter who?' 'Waiter minute while I tie my shoelaces!'

'Knock knock' 'Who's there?' 'Police' 'Police who?' 'Police stop telling knock-knock jokes!'

'Knock knock' 'Who's there?' 'Goat' 'Goat to the door and find out!'

The knock-knock can focus on the door/knocker/bell:

'Knock knock' 'Who's there?' 'Nobel' 'Nobel who?' 'No bell so I knocked!'

'Knock knock' 'Who's there?' 'Theodore' 'Theodore who?' 'Theodore is stuck and it won't open.'

One type of knock-knock specialises in punning on the 'who' sound, with the obvious ones being *Doctor Who* and *The Who*:

'Knock knock' 'Who's there?' 'Lass' 'Lass who?' 'That's what cowboys use!'

'Knock knock' 'Who's there?' 'Cash' 'Cash who?' 'No thanks, but I would like a peanut instead!'

'Knock knock' 'Who's there?' 'Boo' 'Boo who?' 'Gosh don't cry, it's only a knock knock joke.'

This last joke rather makes fun of the stooge, and indeed, knock-knocks can be used to attack/mock others:

'Knock knock' 'Who's there?' 'I am' 'I am who?' 'You mean you don't know who you are?'

'Knock knock' 'Who's there?' 'Cows go' 'Cows go who?' 'No, cows go moo!'

Young children have an abiding interest and delight in jokes defecatory. Here, this interest is combined with knock-knocks:

'Knock knock''Who's there?''Centipede''Centipede who?''Centipede on the Christmas tree'

'Knock knock' 'Who's there?' 'Europe' 'Europe who?' 'No, you're a poo!'

'Knock knock' 'Who's there?' 'A pile up' 'A pile up who?' 'You said it!'

Enough already! Let's face it, for adults, knock-knock jokes are not that funny, as they are rather predictable and lack sophisticated wit. There can be ironic amusement at the joke's awfulness. For grown-ups they are groan-ups. In their way they are a juvenile *Shaggy Dog* story.

Knock-knock jokes are clearly the preserve of the child, however, originally, they seem to have been designed for adults. Here is rather a good, early one, from 1936:

Knock knock. 'Who's there?' 'Edward Rex.' Edward Rex who?' 'Edward wrecks the coronation.' (Wikipedia. org)

Nowadays, you can still find adult varieties of knock-knocks. Some are whimsical, others are vulgar:

'Knock knock''Who's there?''Sam and Janet''Sam and Janet who?''Sam and Janet evening'

(Sung to the tune of *Some Enchanted Evening*)   (Norrick, 2004)

'Knock knock' 'Who's there?' 'Yah' 'Yah who?' 'Nah, I prefer Google!'

'Knock knock' 'Who's there?' 'To' 'To who' 'To whom!'

'What school do comedians go to?'

'The school of hard knock-knock jokes'

'Knock knock' 'Who's there?' 'Little boy blue' 'Little boy blue who?' 'Michael Jackson!'

(Girl) 'Knock knock'   (Boy) 'Who's there?'   (Girl) 'Pussy'   (Boy) 'I don't get it'   (Girl) 'No, and you never will!'

And, finally:

'Knock knock' 'Who's there?' 'Amsterdam' 'Amsterdam who?' 'Amsterdam tired of these knock-knock jokes I could scream.'   (Dirks, 1963)

Reflection

Knock-knock jokes are a child's passport into the realm of humour; the rite of passage away from slapstick into the world of word play. Children should be encouraged to tell knock-knocks as they help with their sociability as well as developing their sense of humour and word proficiency.

For adults, knock-knocks are a cross to bear, still there is a joy in seeing kids get a joke and telling one competently. Don't knock-knock it.

Activity

1) Construct a knock-knock joke for a family member.

2) Construct knock-knock jokes using the following words:

a) Iva; b) Aida; c) Iona; d) Needle; e) Canoe; f) Tara; g) Cuckoo Catch; h) Armageddon; i) Tennis; j) Ears.

Possible answers are below.

3) Construct a Christmas knock-knock, e.g.:

'Knock knock' 'Who's there?' 'Carol singers' 'Carol singers! Don't you know what flaming time of night it is? 'No, but if you hum it we'll sing it.'

(Anon, 2013b)

Answers:

a) 'Knock knock' 'Who's there?' 'Iva' 'Iva who?' 'Iva a sore hand from knocking.'

b) 'Knock knock' 'Who's there?' 'Aida' 'Aida who?' 'Aida a sandwich for lunch today.'

c) 'Knock knock' 'Who's there?' Iona 'Iona who?' 'Iona a new car.'

d) 'Knock knock' 'Who's there?' Needle 'Needle who?' 'Needle a little money for the cinema.'

e) 'Knock knock' 'Who's there?' Canoe 'Canoe who?' 'Canoe help me with my homework?'

f) 'Knock knock' 'Who's there?' Tara 'Tara who?' 'Tara-ra boom-de-day'

g) 'Knock knock' 'Who's there?' 'Cuckoo catch who?' 'Cuckoo catch who...Mrs Robinson, Jesus loves you more than you will know...wo wo wo.'

h) 'Knock knock' 'Who's there?' 'Armageddon' 'Armageddon who?' 'Armageddon out of here.'

i) 'Knock knock' 'Who's there?' 'Tennis' 'Tennis who?' 'Ten is five plus five.'

j) 'Knock knock' 'Who's there?' 'Ears' 'Ears who?' 'Ears some more knock knock jokes for you.'

Riddles

Adrian Mole: *There is a new joke craze sweeping the school. In my opinion these so-called jokes are puerile. I watch in amazement as my fellow pupils roll helplessly in the corridors with tears of laughter coursing down their cheeks after relating them to each other.*

Q. What do you call a man with a seagull on his head?

A. Cliff

Q. What do you call a man with a shovel on his head?

A. Doug

Q. What do you call a man without a shovel in his head?

A. Douglas

Q. What do you call an Irishman, who's been buried for fifty years?

A. Pete

Q. What do you call a man with fifty rabbits up his bum?

A. Warren

Come back Oscar Wilde. Your country needs you. (Townsend, 1992)

Sue Townsend could have added, *'What do you call a spy who goes underground?' 'A Mole.'* That one probably won't become part of our cultural riddle stock, relayed by successive generations of school-children, as it isn't very funny. Also, it is too easy to solve, and will become dated.

Riddles, according to Dienhart (1999) are, *'...part of human culture in all areas and all ages.'* Probably the best known riddle, historically, is the riddle of the *Sphinx of Thebes*. The *Sphinx*, a Greek mythological creature, with the face of a woman, the body of a lion and the wings of a bird, would ask travellers the following riddle: *'What has one voice, and is four-footed, two-footed and three-footed?'* Failure to answer correctly would lead to the *Sphinx* devouring the traveller. The complex riddle was solved by *Oedipus*, who said, *'Man'*. This caused the *Sphinx* to commit suicide. (www.users.globalnet.co)

In the British case, we can trace riddles as far back as the Anglo Saxons. One of the few surviving literary texts from the tenth century, the *Exeter Book*, contains some 90 riddles, as well as many poems. See if you can solve this riddle, number 25, and no, it's not what you think:

'I am a wondrous creature: to women a thing of joyful expectation, to close-lying companions serviceable. I harm no city dweller except my slayer alone. My stem is erect and tall—I stand up in bed, and whiskery down below. Sometimes a countryman's comely daughter will venture bumptious sir, to get a grip on me. She assaults my red self and seizes my head and clenches me in a cramped place. She will soon feel the effect of her encounter with me, this curl-locked woman who squeezes

me. Her eye will be wet.'...Say what I am called. (http:// Penelope.uchicago.edu)

The answer is at the end of this Riddles section.

These Exeter riddles were probably intended for an educated audience, such as monks. Maybe they were the dirty jokes of the day. Possibly, they were educational, explaining sexual matters to an ignorant audience. Maybe they were only cracked at Christmas. Actually, most of the riddles were concerned with the more mundane, and were more likely to have been part of an intellectual game to test the wits of others.

The Exeter riddles are, nowadays, sometimes bewildering. Experts mull over them and try and come up with solutions that work. It is of course extremely difficult to adopt a tenth century mind set, so therein we have a problem.

Here is one interpretation of riddle number 74:

I was once a young woman,

A glorious warrior,

A grey-haired queen

I soared with birds

Stepped on the earth,

Swam in the sea

Dived under waves,

Dead amongst fishes,

I had a living spirit.

Well, what do you make of that? We have a fighting queen that could fly, walk and swim; maybe some sort of powerful aquatic bird? The various solutions that have been put forward include: water; cuttle-fish; sun; siren; barnacle goose; swan; oak-boat; a ship's figurehead, and soul.

Bolding (1985) suggests the moon as the answer. In Germanic myth, the moon had a female spirit. The British saw the moon as a warrior. The moon changes shape and colour. It 'dies' at dawn.

I guess we will never know the definitive answer. The listener is left baffled as is the case with many modern riddles. They are too ambiguous, lacking vital information. We simply have to wait to be told the answer in most cases.

The modern riddle usually has a question form, beginning with Why, When, Where, What or How. It has a two part structure with a misleading element, which makes the answer difficult to guess, and a resolution that makes sense of the answer. (Green & Pepicello, 1979)

Another W is important for the riddle and that is Wit. There should be, *'...an artful device for the creation of confusion.'* (Green & Pepicello, 1979). This device is referred to as *the block*, the misleading element. It is ambiguity that confuses the riddlee (Pepicello, 1980).

There are various levels of ambiguity in riddles: sound, word and sentence. A sound level ambiguity is found in:

What turns but never moves? Ans. *Milk.*

A word ambiguity, a pun, is found in:

When is coffee like the soil? Ans. *When it is ground.*

A sentence-level ambiguity is found in:

What do you call a man who marries a man?' Ans. *A minister.* (Pepicello, 1980).

One of the key things about the riddle is that it is so constructed that, usually, the riddlee, the hearer, finds it difficult to solve. This gives the riddler superiority. Also, the riddler may well have the joy of explaining the joke to the riddlee, who then has to work out how the riddle really does make sense (Shultz, 1976).

The automatic *I don't know* response to the formulaic riddle opening such as, *'What do you call…',* or *'Why did the…'* can sometimes be exploited to make the riddlee look ridiculous.

'What's the difference between an elephant and a watermelon?'

'I don't know.'

'You'd be a fine one to send to the store for a watermelon.' (Dienhart, 1999)

The riddler has other tricks up his/her sleeve in order to manipulate language. He/she can place a juncture in the answer. For example:

'Why is a man clearing a hedge in a single leap like a man snoring?' Ans. *'He does it in his sleep' (his leap).*

The riddler can make use of minimal pairs which differ only marginally, so are not quite puns. For example:

'What is the difference between a baby and a coat?' Ans. *'One you were. The other you wear.'*

Another trick is to just use an element of a word as the answer. For example:

'What kind of bow can you never tie?' Ans.: *'A rainbow.'* (Pepicello, 1980)

Riddles can be divided into three main types: conceptual tricks, language ambiguity, and absurdity riddles. (Dienhart, 1999; Yalisove, 1978)

Conceptual trick riddles reside in reality, and do not involve word play. For example:

'How many balls of string would it take to the reach the moon?' Ans. *'One, but it would have to be a big one'.*

By the way, that moon riddle dates back to 1511 at least, when it appeared in *Demaundes Joyous*, printed in *Fletestrete* by *Wynkyn de Worde* (Opie & Opie, 1973). The Opies call such riddles, catch riddles, tricks without word play. They give an example: *'What water never freezes?' 'Hot water.'*

Language ambiguity riddles, as we have seen, include puns, and, also, riddles like:

'Where do you always find money?' Ans. *'In the dictionary'*; and, *'Why do birds fly south?'* Ans. *'It's too far to walk.'*

I quite like this pun one:

'Why did the football manager give his team a lighter?'

'Because they kept losing their matches.' (Dienhart, 1999)

In absurdity riddles there is something ridiculous, either in the question, or in the answer. For example:

'How do you fit six elephants in a car?' Ans.: *'Three in the front, and three in the back.'*

The authorities on the riddle, Green & Pepicello (1979) do not consider these absurdity riddles, *'Joking questions'*, to be true riddles. For them, a riddle has to be *'potentially solvable'*. An elephant joke is simply a device that allows the teller to deliver a punch-line.

Opie & Opie (1973) are in agreement with Green & Pepicello (1979). They refer to *true riddles*, where some creature or object is described obscurely, and the solution fits all the characteristics of the description. An example the Opies give is:

'What goes up when the rain comes down?' 'An umbrella.'

Children's understanding of riddles develops gradually. At the age of 4-5 there is a pre-riddle stage, where children tell 'riddles', that seem to be riddles but, crucially, lack the incongruous element (Bergen, 2009). For example:

'How come the straw talked to the box?' 'Cause it wanted to say goodbye.' (Park, 1977)

Yalisove (1978) studied 208 American children, from first grade to college age. He found that conceptual trick riddles were comprehended first, language ambiguity at an intermediate age, and absurdity riddles were comprehended only by the oldest children.

Yalisove suggests that different levels of sophistication are required for comprehension of the riddles. The youngest children focus on the silly. As the child develops he/she learns that language does not have to refer to reality, and can refer to the hypothetical, which can be logical. Absurdity riddles, according to Yalisove, are understood on this basis.

Shultz (1974) found that 6 year olds couldn't detect the hidden meanings and just enjoyed the incongruity of a riddle. Eight year olds appreciated the resolvable nature of the riddles' incongruities.

As children age they have increased comprehension of riddles, but there is decreased enjoyment.

Older children (aged 10-11) have more complex cognitive structures, so find riddles less interesting (Prentice & Fathman, 1975).

Park (1977), who studied children of various ages, in four schools for three years, argued that, children at different ages, use riddles for different purposes. These purposes are: to exchange information; to entertain, and to compete. For children, at the age of 7, riddles were playful, but not very funny. However, they did allow the exchange of facts. The children at this age were particularly concerned with the rules surrounding the competitive interaction of riddling.

Children at around the age of 9-10, were less interested in rules, and were more playful with riddles, which could be quite complicated. For example:

'Why did the chicken cross the road?' 'To get the Daily News' 'I don't get it.' 'Neither do I. I get the New York Times.'

At around the age of 12, riddles of psychological relations predominated. In particular, riddles about sex and aggression are popular. One girl's riddle was: *'Why did the boy bubble chase the girl bubble?' 'Because he wanted to see her bust.'* The girls' riddles enabled the exchange of information and allowed the girls to have fun.

The boys riddles at this age were mainly aggressive, and concerned *'...sex, excretion, and some violence.'* Superiority humour predominated, with disparagement of friends and others.

Children are not particularly competent at creating their own riddles. McGhee (1974) tested children between the ages of 6 and 11 and found:

'...neither boys nor girls appear to have gained much insight into the nature of the joking relationship in wordplay riddles as late as the sixth grade (11-12).'

It follows that most, if not all, playground riddles are cultural transmissions rather than original creations.

Finally, it is worth acknowledging that the riddle form can be used in adult humour as well. For example:

'What's grey and smells of curry?'

'John Major's dick.'

'What do you call a man with half a brain?'

'Gifted.'

'Why do elephants have big ears?'

'Because Noddy wouldn't pay the ransom.'

'What's a shitzu?'

'A zoo with no animals.' (Manuel, 2006)

What is the subject of the following statements?

George Bush has a short one.
Arnold Schwarzenegger has a big one.
The Pope has one, but doesn't use it.
Cher doesn't have one at all.
What is it?

Ans: A second name   (Blake, 2007)

Reflection

Riddles are an introduction to joking for children. They are a half-way house between problem solving and joke appreciation.

As children age their mental equipment changes quite dramatically; whilst youngsters prefer the silly, older children prefer more complexity, and enjoy understanding resolutions. Eventually, a clear distinction between male and female humour emerges, as boys use riddles, and humour generally, in a more aggressive way.

It is interesting that superiority is woven into the riddle process. Riddles allow the verbally competent to dominate others through jokes. Anderson (2008) does point out that it is enjoyable for any young child to have all the answers. This is a change from their usual subordinate position.

The riddle is clearly ideal for teaching literacy in an interesting and amusing way. Through word play the children actively discover more about language. They learn, via the riddles, how to manipulate language and understand the multiple meanings of words.

Activity

1) Use the cue joke approach to create new riddles.

For example: *'What did the teacher say when the student wrote WETHR?'*

Ans.: *'That's a terrible spell of weather.'*

That good joke gives us a riddle with a different set up but same punch line:

What did the nice witch say when the bad wizard wrote, UZE POIZON.

Ans.: *'That's a terrible spell.'*

Here are some cue jokes for you to use:

'What happens when a ghost is set on fire? Ans.: 'You get roast ghost.'

'What birds are always unhappy?' Ans.: 'Bluebirds.'

'What do you get if you cross an insect with a rabbit?' Ans.: 'Bugs Bunny.'

2) Use the dictionary to create a joke using a juncture:

When is it difficult to get your watch off your wrist?

Ans: *When it's ticking there (sticking)*

So, for example:

By going through the verbs beginning with S, we get:

When is an owl dangerous?

Ans: *When it's hooting.*

You don't have to stick to S:

'When can you hear me and I'm not there?'

'When I'm 'issing.'

3) Create idiom riddles

Terban (1992) gives a way of using idioms as the punch-line for riddle type jokes. First an idiom is selected, e.g., *'She swept him off his feet.'* Then the set-up is worked out. In this case, *'Why did the millionaire marry the cleaning lady?'*

The basic format to create an idiom riddle is:

(Why did/Why didn't) _____(A relevant person/character) _____(Do something)

The idiom punch-line is: *He got cold feet*

The set up then could be: *Why didn't   the abominable snowman   ask the girl for a date?*

Terban suggests working out jokes based on the following three idioms: *Giving someone a piece of your mind; giving someone the cold shoulder; throwing one's weight around.*

Using his approach I came up with:

Why did the psychiatrist cry?

He'd given a patient a piece of his mind

Why did the snowman know the snow-woman didn't like him?

She'd given him the cold shoulder

Why was the sumo wrestler unpopular?

He kept throwing his weight around.

It seems to me that it is quite easy to make fairly good jokes using this system. Have a go with some idioms obtained via an internet search.

(The answer to the Exeter Book riddle No.25 is Onion.)

Part 4: Sexual Humour

Let's face it, people like the rude and crude; some more than others, which is code for men more than women. So, hands up if you turned to this section first!

I start by looking at why the world's favourite humour is the dirty joke. The man who dug deepest and came up dirtiest in this area is, believe it or not, *Sigmund Freud*. He wrote a classic book on jokes and why we tell them.

For *Freud*, the dirty joke emerged from the subconscious. Such jokes trick the censors of the conscious mind, and allow built-up tension to be released.

In his book, *Jokes and their Relation to the Unconscious, Freud* considers joke technique and stresses the importance of brevity. He distinguishes between innocent and non-innocent jokes—these latter jokes are basically hostile or obscene, and are the ones we laugh at more. Freud considered that we tell these jokes for the pleasure they give us in satisfying our sexual and hostile instincts.

I then change tack and move on to look at double entendre and dirty jokes. The British have loved the double entendre since time immemorial. Great writers like *Chaucer* and *Shakespeare* had their way with it. In more recent times the *Carry On* films, seaside postcards and *Julian Clary* have relied on saying one thing and meaning another.

As society has become more liberal, the double entendre has been rather pushed out by the more blatant dirty joke. Men are usually sexual supermen in dirty jokes, whilst women are their victims. Men are insatiable, whilst their wives are passive. The consequence is that men dream of nymphomaniacs in their fantasy jokes, which they tell each other as part of male bonding.

Many dirty jokes are about superiority. The wise, experienced joke-teller displays his competence by mocking the beginner or the virgin. Hence, the popularity of honeymoon jokes and jokes about fools and love-making.

Women, basically, have two superiority jokes in their armoury. The absolute classic is the small penis joke, closely followed by jokes which show that a man's brain resides just beneath his navel.

The old do badly in this joking world. Sex for O.A.P.'s is seen as ludicrous; something which is performed by the incapable and the ugly. The advent of *Viagra* has added to the ridiculousness of over-age sex.

This small part ends with a section on Limericks. Really, these should be dirty to get a good laugh, but clean ones can be witty and are good fun to compose. There is plenty of advice as to how to go about producing your own Limericks.

Freud and jokes

Ken Dodd—'Freud's theory was that when a joke opens a window and all those bats and bogeymen fly out, you get a marvellous feeling of relief and elation. The trouble with Freud is that he never had to play the old Glasgow Empire on a Saturday night after Rangers and Celtic had both lost.' (Knowles, 2004)

It may come as something of a surprise to find that the great psychoanalytical theorist, *Sigmund Freud*, devoted an entire book, *Jokes and their Relation to the Unconscious*, to jokes and humour. Surely, he had better things to do? Obviously, he must have seen jokes as a significant element of the conscious and subconscious mind. A realisation he may well have developed whilst working on his classic book, *The Interpretation of Dreams*. *Freud* considered that dreams and jokes had distinct similarities. He argued that the same *'psychical process'* is at work in both.

Freud's big idea is that jokes make possible the pleasurable satisfaction of an instinct, be it sexual or hostile, *'in the face of an obstacle that stands in its way.'* Normally, forbidden sexual and aggressive ideas and feelings are locked away in the subconscious. The brain, according to *Freud,* uses psychic energy to repress these feelings. However, both the joke and the dream allow the trapped feelings to escape, and built up tension is released. (Lynch, 2006)

Freud's work has given us insight into why people engage in jokes. His book, which contains plenty of jokes, and is a fascinating read, is divided into 6 main sections. The first section, *'The Technique of Jokes'* is concerned with how a thought is transformed into a joke, causing laughter. *Freud* refers to a process of *'condensation'*, (a blend) using the following joke as an illustration:

A poor lottery agent, *Hirsch-Hyacinth* boasts of his relationship with the wealthy *Baron Rothschild*, saying: *'...I sat beside Salomon Rothschild and he treated me quite his equal-quite famillionairely.'*

Freud gives other examples of condensation: *'anecdotage'*, and *'alcoholidays'*. He notes a rather good insult witticism. A man is commenting on the weaknesses of another: *'Yes, vanity is one of his four Achilles heels'*. This is a compression of the fact that the speaker thinks the vain man is something of an ass, together with a belief in his vanity.

Freud goes on to consider various joke techniques. In addition to *'Condensation'*, he lists, *'Multiple use of the same material'* (reversal), and *'Double meaning'* (pun). An example of *'Multiple use'*, which *Freud* describes as *'diabolically ingenious'*, is:

'Mr and Mrs X live in fairly grand style. Some people think that the husband has earned a lot and so has been able to lay by a bit; others again think that the wife has lain back a bit and so has been able to earn a lot.'

An example of double meaning is taken from *Shakespeare*: *'Discharge thyself of our company, Pistol!'*

Freud concludes that all the techniques are *'dominated by a tendency to compression, or rather to saving. It all seems to be a question of economy'*.

Indeed, brevity is the soul of wit, however, something more than just brevity is needed for funniness.

In the next section of the book, *'The purposes of jokes'*, *Freud* draws a distinction between *'innocent'*, non-tendentious jokes, and tendentious jokes. In the former case, the joke has no particular purpose. It is an end in itself. It is just fun. In the latter case, there is a purpose, which may be resented by others.

Innocent joking, for *Freud*, was an activity aimed at, *'deriving pleasure from mental processes, whether intellectual or otherwise.'* Even so, he observed that such jokes do not cause the sort of humorous outbursts occasioned by tendentious jokes.

Tendentious jokes are either: hostile, obscene, cynical (critical, blasphemous), or sceptical. In the case of hostility, *'By making our enemy small, inferior, despicable, or comic, we achieve in a roundabout way the enjoyment of overcoming him...'*

In the case of obscenity, educated people turn smut into a joke, so that it may be tolerated. For *Freud*, cynical jokes attack moral regulations, in particular, the institution of marriage.

'The Mechanism of Pleasure and the Psychogenesis of Jokes' section, gets rather technical. One comment made by *Freud* though, shines through, *'man is a tireless pleasure seeker'*. He/she wants to access sources of pleasure which are suppressed. For example, under the influence of alcohol, *'the grown man once more becomes a child, who finds pleasure in having the course of his thoughts freely at his disposal without paying attention to the compulsion of logic.'*

In the case of tendentious jokes, pleasure is liberated by getting rid of inhibitions. Repression is slain. Jokes, as such, *'produce new pleasure by lifting suppressions and inhibitions.'* *Freud* does go on to argue that all jokes, not just the tendentious, are related to the *'unconscious.'*

In *'The Motives of Jokes-Jokes as a Social Process'* section, *Freud* argues that pleasure is the main reason for jokes, but admits that other motives are possible.

One additional motive for joking, is, *'an ambitious urge to show one's cleverness.'* *Freud* suggests that this equates with exhibitionism in the sexual field. Another powerful motive lies in the social realm, *'A joke...must be told to someone else.'* In the case of innocent jokes, this is to test the quality of the joke. There is a compulsion to tell someone else a joke because *'we are unable to laugh at it ourselves.'* The laughter of the other arouses our own laughter.

The penultimate section of *Freud's* book is, *'The relation of jokes to dreams and to the unconscious.'* *Freud* observes that jokes, like dreams, can be involuntary, they just appear, thus, indicating their origin in the *'unconscious.'* However, a joke, unlike a dream, is social and has to be intelligible.

The final section of *Freud's* book is, *'Jokes and the species of the comic.'* Here, firstly, *Freud* considers the naïve comic, which is most likely to be found with children, and then, with uneducated adults. The child may have said something that the adult finds funny, but did not intend that result. The child lacks inhibitions, whilst the adult does not.

Freud goes on to consider the *'comic'* in more depth. The individual can make himself comic, as well as other people. To make others comic we use mimicry, caricature, parody, etc. *Freud* points out that these techniques give pleasure, and may serve, *'hostile and aggressive purposes.'*

When we laugh at others as comical we feel pleasure at our superiority. Where we find others are superior to us, we admire.

Freud ends his book poignantly, stressing that we engage in a quest for the euphoric mood of our childhood, *'when we were ignorant of the comic, when we were incapable of jokes and when we had no need of humour to make us feel happy in our life.'*

Freud's book was quite a breakthrough in terms of scope, analysis and theory-making. It was rather as if, previously, only amateurs had been playing the humour game. A hundred years have passed since the publication of *Freud's* joke book. This has given plenty of time to test his assertions, particularly with regard to the key point repression, but, generally, the research findings are not always on his side:

...limited support has been found for some Freudian hypotheses, there is little evidence that the level of enjoyment of jokes and cartoons is directly related to the degree to which the impulses they convey are repressed. Instead, the bulk of the evidence suggests that people laugh most at humor relating to impulses that they themselves express *overtly in their behaviour and attitudes, rather than repress* (Martin, 2007).

Cross cultural studies of humour have found that the more sexually repressive a society is, the less likely it is to use sexual humour. This is the direct opposite of what a Freudian would predict. Incidentally, of the 186 societies studied, sex was, *'the most often mentioned subject of humor.'* (Finnegan & Alford, 1981)

Eysenck (1985) observes that, the research evidence, generally, is *'highly critical'* of *Freud's* subjective work. Experiments and observations do not support his claims. The *'unconscious'* is a *'highly speculative construct'*. Research has conspicuously failed to detect the supposed *'powers and tendencies'* of the subconscious.

Reflection

Freud is probably the most important theorist to have considered humour. Indeed, McGhee (1971) noted that, *'The most influential theory of humor to date continues to be that advanced by Freud...'* Freud recognised the importance of humour as a result of his quest to discover how the sub-conscious mind functions, and as a consequence of his analysis of dreams.

For Freud, jokes are either innocent or not. He, of course, was mainly interested in the non-innocent. He wanted to know what these *'tendentious'* jokes really meant. He decided that, deep down, people repress violent and sexual urges. One way the libido surfaces, is, under the disguise of jokes. In so doing, the conscious mind loses the battle for control to the subconscious. The joke unyokes.

However tempting it is to agree with *Freud's* analysis, we do have to recognise that not everyone is convinced by his approach as it is too speculative, and not necessarily based on experimental support.

Another humour theory that deals with what goes on in the deeper brain is known as tension relief theory, which developed particularly with Herbert Spencer in 1860. Drawing on Darwin, Spencer saw laughter as, *'the discharge of excess nervous energy stemming from a disappointed expectation'* (Hill, 1993).

There certainly can be relief connected to laughter. In particular where, initially, there is arousal because of distress and fear. If, subsequently, the person realises that there is no danger, then laughter relief can occur (Rothbart, 1973).

Shurcliff (1968) found that, the greater the anxiety, prior to relief, the greater was the judged humour. This researcher placed 36 students in three differing anxiety groups. The task was either to pick up a rat, take blood samples from a rat, or, take blood samples and face the risk of the rat escaping, and being bitten. The punch-line was that, although the subject could see real Norwegian rats, the actual 'rat' that was picked up was a toy.

And, finally:

An erotic neurotic named Syd

Got his Ego confused with his Id

His errant libido

Was like a torpedo

And that's why he done what he did.

(Legman, 1974)

You'd never have guessed

Freud failed the test.

Laughter surges

Aren't real purges

Of filth that's deeply repressed.

Double entendre and dirty jokes

A woman goes into a bar and asks for a double entendre, so the bartender gives her one.

Well, blow me, this is the hard part. Hopefully, if I keep banging away at this section, I'll get a result. Know what I mean, nudge, nudge…..

A double entendre is a phrase that can be understood in two ways, one of them being sexually suggestive. As *Ronnie Barker* commented, *'The marvellous thing about a joke with a double meaning is that it can only mean one thing.'* (Knowles, 2004)

The British love the double entendre. It has a long past in these isles. In literature, we can trace it as far back as *Geoffrey Chaucer* and *William Shakespeare.*

For example, *Chaucer* uses the word *'queynte'* in the *Canterbury Tales*. This had two meanings, a woman's domestic duties and the female genitalia. Indeed, *queynte* is the ancestor of the modern day C word. (www.urbandictionary.com)

The Bard used many a bawdy joke in his works. For example, *Malvolio* in *Twelfth Night* says, when picking up a hand written letter:

'By my life, this is my lady's hand there be her very C's, her U's and her T's and thus makes she her great P's' (the *and* was pronounced 'n').

In *Much Ado About Nothing*, Benedick says, *'I will live in thy heart, die in thy lap, and be buried in thy eyes.'*

Where's the joke you might well ask. Actually, there are two. In Elizabethan slang *'to die'* was a term for sexual climax. *'Nothing'* was a euphemism for a woman's private parts. (Damschen, 2014)

Much more recently, but continuing the tradition, the double entendre was the staple of the seaside postcard:

Female artist to naked male model -- *'You're getting a bit stiff, Mr O'Toole. Would you like to stop for a bit?'*

It's amazing that some of these postcards were banned by local censorship committees. The artist, Donald McGill, actually pleaded guilty to publishing obscene images in 1954. For example:

A man is selling newspapers in front of a sign which says, *'Big Strike, 10,000 men down tools.'* A woman remarks to another woman, *'You know dear, it's the wives of those strikers that I feel sorry for!'* (Kelly, 2010)

The *Carry On* films of the '50's and 60's relied on the double entendre. So, in *Carry on Camping* we have:

'No Barbara dear…tent up first, bunk up later.'

In *Carry on Doctor* we have:

Kenneth Williams (Doctor) *'You may not realise it, but I was once a weak man.'*

Hattie Jacques (Matron) *'Oh don't worry, once a week's enough for any man.'*

The comedian who stands out, to my mind, as the leading double entendre merchant of the present day, is *Julian Clary*—*'I like a nice warm hand upon my entrance.'*, *'I went to the kind of school, where, when they called out "Head Boy", half the school knelt.'* (Ash, 2010)

Double entendre may be intentional or unintentional. One place they are intentional is in pantomime, where children get one meaning, and their parents get the joke, or that's the theory! Television sit coms can also go down this route.

Where the double entendre is unintentional, the surprise, embarrassment, and sheer inappropriateness, can cause giggling fits:

A female news anchor who, the day after it was supposed to have snowed and didn't, turned to the weatherman and asked, 'So Bob, where's that eight inches you promised me last night?' Not only did he have to leave the set, but half the crew did too, because they were laughing so hard!'
      (http://forums.digitalspy.co.uk)

Sometimes people produce unintentional double entendre because they simply do not know the alternative sexual meaning. Mrs Thatcher was famous for this:

'I don't know what I would do without Whitelaw. Everyone should have a Willie.'

(Inspecting a field gun in the Falklands) *'Will it jerk me off?'* (Ash, 2010)

(On a factory visit, remarking to a group of young lads) *'That's an enormous tool you've got.'* (Brand, 2010)

Such innocence, displayed by the more powerful, undermines notions of their street-wiseness, and allows subordinates moments of superior glory. This is particularly true of adolescent school children. For example, Woods (1990) found a class at *Old Town* comprehensive, reduced to laughter when a young, female teacher referred to, *'Vikings stop-motion screw'* in a sewing machine, and when she advised students to, *'Touch-up your stencil points.'*

School-kids of a certain age love this sort of stuff. Willis (1984) observed a class where:

'At the vaguest sexual double meaning giggles and 'whoas' come from the back accompanied perhaps by someone masturbating a gigantic penis with rounded hands above his head in compressed lipped lechery.'

Experienced teachers learn to monitor their intended speech and delete possible double entendre. New comers soon learn not to call themselves that (titters). Even so, school-kids can make a double entendre out of almost anything, a single entendre. Take this instance, noted by Dubberley (1993):

...then Mrs Galton mentions the need for agitation to achieve political change. 'What's flagelation? asks the slim girl. 'Agitation', corrects Mrs Galton. 'Oh', says the slim girl, grinning wickedly.

School-children also use risqué humour to taunt and embarrass teachers, particularly the females. In this next example, students are *'sussing out'* a teacher at the start of a year:

'...They laugh at O'Malley and King bellows out: 'Miss, Miss, he's called O'Tool, Miss.' (Beynon, 1984)

Actually, Woods (1990a) notes that it is at the stage before puberty onset that, *'deviance and naughtiness become popular topics of humour.'* At this age there is a keen interest in sexual activity and bodily functions.

Research by Fuhr (2001) indicates that *'sex'* jokes reach a peak of importance for 12 year olds. Fuhr also found, in his study of Copenhagen adolescents, 12-16 years of age, that, *'Both genders obviously like sex related jokes, but boys prefer them more than girls.'*

Sanford & Eder (1984) studied the humour of American adolescent school-girls, aged 11-14. They found that the ambiguous nature of humour allowed the girls to explore a sensitive area like sexuality, *'...without having to reveal explicitly the extent of their actual knowledge in this area.'* Sexual jokes enabled information exchange about topics that were not clearly understood. The telling of risqué jokes, enabled the teller to be treated as mature, as the assumption was that the teller understood the behaviour described in the joke.

The girls told dirty jokes when they wanted to *'make conversation'* and it was unclear what else to talk about. Significantly, Sanford & Eder found that swearing and sexual joke telling was frequent, and those who engaged in such behaviour, were, *'admired in many groups.'*

Young men seem to find a particular fascination with big breasts, so they joke about them a lot, as they reduce women to just the physical. Indeed, women may just get referred to as a series of body parts, *'seemingly designed for the purpose of male surveillance and titillation.'* (Gough & Edwards, 1998)

The fact is that it is not just adolescents and young men who like sexual humour, most of us do. We have seen *Freud's* explanation for this, sex jokes are release valves for psychic energy, that otherwise would have been repressed. However, this is not the only explanation. For example, Kuhlman (1985) found that people enjoyed jokes about taboo subjects, such as sex, profanity, and violence, more than other types. He concluded that taboo violation is funnier because it is concerned with the surprising violation of rules of *behaviour*, rather than the violation of the rules of *logic*, which is found in standard word play.

Asimov (1971) observes, *'...it is so easy in the dirty joke to confuse the merely shocking with the funny. There is undoubted pleasure in defying convention, a certain thrill in using forbidden words, detailing forbidden acts...The pleasure of all this may induce laughter.'*

Easthope (1992) agrees that there is a pleasure in talking about sex, and dirty jokes allow that pleasure to happen. He sees the dirty joke as a part of *'masculine style.'* Told among men, the joke teller enjoys the fantasy of seducing a woman, egged on by his audience. In men's dirty jokes, told to men, women are mastered, and a male bond is confirmed.

As men are normally the heroes of dirty jokes, they *'...are assumed to be permanently lecherous...Women, on the other hand, are assigned to two quite different categories. Married* women are generally represented as being insufficiently interested in sex to satisfy their husbands' libido, whereas unmarried females are either virgins or nymphomaniacs.' (Blake 2007)

Here we have a joke about insatiable males:

There is an Italian, a Frenchman, and an American sitting in a bar talking and the Italian is bragging that last night he made love to his wife 3 times and this morning his wife made him breakfast in bed and told him how amazing he was the night before.

The Frenchman said 'That's nothing. I made love to my wife 5 times last night and then this morning to show her appreciation she made me breakfast in bed and told me how much she loved me and gave me head while I ate my breakfast.'

Then the men turned to the American and asked him how many times he made love to his wife the night before and he said 'Only Once.' The two men started laughing and the Frenchman asked him what his wife said to him this morning and the American smoothly replied 'Don't Stop.' (www.jokes4us.com)

Married women's disinterest is summed up neatly in the following joke:

'How do you cure a Jewish nymphomaniac?'

'Marry her.'   (Dundes & Hauschild, 1983)

Another lifeless wife joke:

'You'll have to take it easy, if you want to live,' says the doctor.

'What about smoking? Asks the man.

'No smoking,' says the doctor

'What about drinking?'

'No drinking,' says the doctor.

'What about...?'

'Only once a fortnight,' says the doctor. 'and with your wife. You mustn't risk any excitement.'

(Blake, 2007)

Talking about leg-overs, let me tell you about *Gershon Legman* (1917-99). Are you sitting erotically? Then, I shall begin. According to Davis (2008) *Legman* was, *'the greatest scholar of the forbidden, historian of erotica, cult icon of the beat generation and world expert on dirty jokes and bawdy songs.'*

Legman, wrote *Rationale of the Dirty Joke: An Analysis of Sexual Humor*. He produced a second edition, purchased by subscription only, which contained the *'dirty'*, dirty jokes. The first edition contained about 2,000 *'clean'* dirty jokes.

In addition to that, *Legman* was an expert on origami and wrote several other works, including a book of bawdy limericks. He is supposed to have devised the slogan, *'Make Love, Not War'* (Anon, 2011a)—Some legmancy. According to *Wikipedia*, *Legman* died in appropriate fashion, suffering a heart attack after *'excessive sexual effort.'*

Legman reckoned that:

'Erotic humour is far and away the most popular of all types, and an extremely large percentage of the jokes authentically in oral circulation, in this, and apparently all centuries and cultures, is concerned with the humor-often unwilling, unpleasant, and even purposively macabre-of the sexual impulse.' (Legman, 2006).

Legman took a very Freudian approach to why people told dirty jokes, agreeing that they were an *'outlet for hostility and anxiety.'* He considered that, *'The teller is often forcing his joke on his audience and passing his fears on to them. When you laugh, he's reassured.'*   (Vinocur, 1973)

Interestingly, he reckoned that, American dirty stories tended to have *'racial or homosexual themes,'* whilst the German and Dutch are *scatological*, and the French are preoccupied with *'adultery and impotence.'* Whatever the subject matter, British jokes are, *'essentially aggressive and full of one-upmanship.'* So, it looks like we worry about class even when we're on the job.

Although he tried to make the various chapters of his book much the same length, *Legman* found that the chapter on *'Marriage'* turned out to be twice as long as any other. He reckoned that this emphasis reflected the fact that marriage was, *'...the principal focus of male sexual anxiety.'*

Legman recognised that jokes were created by men and that women were only treated as the butt of the joke. He uses the term *grossly anti-women* to describe the sense of dirty jokes.

In dirty jokes, all women are assumed to be available to men. This is for the purpose of coitus which is taken to be, *'more important than anything else in the world.'*

The penis is seen as weapon, not as a device for pleasure. It is taken for granted that the man is able to satisfy the woman with his weapon. The man always brings the woman to orgasm, except in the case where the failure is her fault. The man is assumed never to be sexually satisfied:

A man feeling run down describes himself to the doctor as having sexual relations with five or more women three times every day. The doctor tells him this is the cause of his trouble. 'I'm glad to hear it, Doc. I was afraid it might be the masturbation.' (Legman, 2006)

Legman found that foolishness connected to sex was the subject of many of his collected jokes. That is, the teller is adopting a superior position. The superiority theory of humour holds that we laugh at the behaviour of someone whom we consider inferior. They are the ignorant and foolish. We are the experienced and wise. This theory obviously applies to the dirty joke, as much fun is made of those who do not understand sex, or are unable to perform sexual acts competently.

Two Italian virgins marry and go on their honeymoon. Unfortunately, neither knows what to do when they get there. The newlyweds call the groom's mother for advice. The mother says that they should sit on the bed together, snuggle, and things should happen from there. The newlyweds do this, but nothing happens. The groom calls his mother back. She says they should take their clothes off, get under the covers, and nature should take its course. The bride and groom take his mother's advice, but still nothing comes to mind.

He calls his mother a third time. Getting frustrated with the situation, she says, 'Listen, just take the biggest thing you have and stick it in the hairiest spot!'

The groom is quiet for a moment and then asks his mother, 'I've got my nose in her armpit—now what?' (www.nairaland.com)

The virgin is mocked for his/her lack of competence, and lack of a vital experience which signifies adulthood. The nun, but not the priest, is often taken as the archetype virgin, so appears in many jokes where a virgin is needed for the joke to work. This next joke, told on a factory floor in Sweden, concerns the local ice-hockey team:

'...they've signed a 65-year-old nun...if she hasn't let in anything for that long, she won't do it now.'

(The response, at the factory, was, 'The group of women burst into laughter, on-going for several minutes. They are crying and falling over with laughter.') (Stromberg & Karlsson, 2009)

Clearly, young children have no real understanding of sex. However, their ignorance is used in jokes to reveal something about others:

One night a little girl walks in on her parents having sex. The mother is going up and down on the father and when she sees her daughter looking at them she immediately stops.

'What are you doing, Mommy?' the mother is too embarrassed to tell her little girl about sex so she makes up an answer.

'Well, sweetie, sometimes daddy's tummy gets too big so I have to jump up and down on it to flatten it out.'

The little girl replies, 'Well, mommy you really shouldn't bother with that.'

The mother has a confused look on her face, 'Why do you say that sweetheart?'

The little girl replies, 'Because mommy, every time you leave in the morning, the lady next door comes over and blows it back up.' (http://academictips.org)

The child is not always so innocent:

During recess Willie Jones, the bad boy, has chalked on the board, 'Willie Jones has the biggest prick in school.' The teacher indignantly orders him to stay after school. The gang wait an hour for him to appear, and anxiously ask him what had happened. He merely winks and says, 'It pays to advertise.

Misunderstandings feature in dirty jokes. For Legman, they took place in shops or with certain jobs, like plumbing. Here's one in a hotel:

Being a very religious kind of person, when I checked into my hotel, I said to the woman at the desk; 'I hope the porn channel in my room is disabled.'

'No.' she said, 'It's regular porn, you sick bastard!' www.unijokes.com

Legman devotes a chapter to sex with animals. In such jokes, the bull is often the dominant animal, and the sheep is often the submissive one. Women are seen as being more interested in donkeys because of penis size. When men have sex with animals there are various excuses, including laziness and the lack of females. Here's one animal sex joke based on misunderstanding:

Two old ladies were outside this nursing home, having a smoke when it started to rain. One of the ladies pulled out a condom, cut off the end, put it over a cigarette and continued smoking. The other lady said 'What's that?' The lady smoker said, 'A condom. This way my cigarette doesn't get wet.' The first lady said, 'Where did you get it?' The second lady said, 'You can get them at any drugstore.'

The next day the first lady hobbles to the local drug store and announces to the pharmacist that she wants a box of condoms. The guy looks at her kind of strangely (she is, after all, over 80 years of age), but politely asks what brand she prefers. She replies, 'It doesn't matter as long as it fits a Camel.' (www.jokes4us.com)

There is much bragging about penis size in dirty jokes. For Legman this exaggeration provided reassurance that the penis was not as small as feared.

In line with superiority theory, however, there are many, many jokes about the small penis. This type of joke is the fundamental way a woman can mock a man:

I've smoked fatter joints than that.'….'Ahhhh, it's cute.'….'Wow and your feet are so big.'….' Can I be honest with you?'…. 'How sweet, you brought incense.'….Maybe if we water it.' …. 'This explains the car.' ….'I guess this makes me the early bird.' (www.funnymail.com)

The earliest example I have found is from the eighteenth century:

Calmly urinating against a horse, a gentleman looked up to find two young ladies laughing at the window. 'What was so funny?' 'O Sir, said one of them, a very little thing will make us laugh.' (Dickie, 2011)

Here is a more modern one that makes use of a psychiatrist. This is a nod to Freud and the allowed discussion of sexual matters in psychiatry:

The young lady nodded her head at what the psychiatrist was telling her, and said, 'Yes, I see, Dr Schmidt. At least, I see everything but one point. The one thing I'm hazy about is this phallic symbol you mentioned. What's a phallic symbol?'

'A phallic symbol,' said the psychiatrist, 'is anything that can be used to represent or symbolize a phallus.' 'But what is a phallus, doctor?'

The psychiatrist said, 'I think I can explain that most clearly by a demonstration.' He stood up, unzipped, and said. 'This, my dear young lady, is a phallus.'

'Oh,' said the girl, suddenly comprehending. 'I see. You mean it's like a prick, only smaller.' (Asimov, 1971)

Mitchell (1977) got men and women to rate the following small penis joke, and reached some interesting conclusions:

There was this man who was an exhibitionist. And he was going to take a trip on this airplane. And

there was this stewardess who was waiting at the top of the stairs that go onto the plane, and she was collecting tickets. So when this man got to the top of the stairs, he opened his coat and exposed himself. And the stewardess said, 'I'm sorry sir. You have to show your ticket here, not your stub.'

Of the 150 male and female respondents, all the women enjoyed that joke, with 80% giving it a high rating. No woman gave the joke the lowest rating. The males were generally positive, but did not consider the joke as funny as the women did. Some men gave the lowest rating.

The interesting thing is that the men and women liked the joke for different reasons. The women identified with the stewardess and admired her calmness and quick wit. They thought the man, *'got what he deserved.'*

The men enjoyed the *'witty put-down'*, but none of them mentioned that he *'got what he deserved.'* Men also focused on the small penis insult, something which was mentioned by very few women.

Women don't just ridicule the small penis, they mock men, and, in particular, the way their brain seems to be located in the scrotal area.

'The useless piece of flesh at the end of a penis is called a man.' (Jo Brand)

In retaliation for the small penis jibe, men respond with attacks on the giant vagina:

A farmer and his daughter are driving along the road in a waggon when they are held up by robbers, and everything is taken from them but some jewels that the daughter manages to hide in her vagina. Afterwards she gives them to her father, and tries to console him for his loss. 'Oh' he says, 'if only your mother was here, we could have saved the horse and wagon too.'   (Legman, 2006)

Both superiority and incongruity theory relate to the old and their sexual performance. Old men are treated in one of two ways in sex jokes. They are either seen as clapped out, or as still rampant. Of course, the advent of Viagra has assisted here. The rampant old man is an absurd, incongruous idea, particularly when he turns into a machine powered by a blue pill.

'...the sexual life cycle of man: Tri-weekly, Try weekly, Try weakly.'   (Palmore, 1971)

'I used to ask women to come upstairs and have sex, but now it has to be one or the other.' (Clement Freud)

'Now that I'm seventy-eight I do tantric sex because it's very slow. My favourite position is called the plumber. You stay in all day but nobody comes.' (John Mortimore)

'Did you hear the one about the 85-year-old man in hospital who was given Viagra with his hot chocolate at night? The chocolate made him sleep and the Viagra stopped him rolling out of bed.' (Vares and Braun, 2006)

The most popular stereotype of the old man is that he is impotent. Bowd (2003) argues that jokes displaying the old man as virile are in fact a consequence of this, and such jokes are just paradoxical, and not credible. The absurdity adds to the funniness:

A priest in the confessional hears an old man's voice on the other side of the screen. 'I'm 79 years old, married to the same woman for 50 years, and always faithful-never looked at another woman. Yesterday, I made passionate love to a pair of 18 year-old twins.'

Priest: 'And when was the last time you went to confession?'

Old man: 'What confession? I'm Jewish!'

Priest: 'So why are you telling me?'

Old man: 'I'm telling everybody.'

According to Richman (1977) jokes about coupling between an old man and a younger woman are quite common. He gives this one, which I've heard *Joan Collins* use:

A man goes to his doctor and tells him that he is going to marry a much younger woman. His doctor warned that too much sex could be fatal. The old man shrugged and responded, 'If she dies, she dies.'

Jokes about the aged are generally negative, particularly in the case of women. However, there is some positivity. Palmore (1971) considers that:

'This may indicate that many people both fear declining sexual abilities in old age and cherish the hope that their abilities will not disappear.'

Palmore analysed 264 jokes about the aged and found that many more jokes were positive with regard to men than to women. More than 75% of jokes about women were negative. In particular, old maids were usually seen as *'lonely, frustrated, shrivelled'*, which suggests that, *'...society views ageing among women more negatively than ageing among men.'*

A couple of old ladies were sitting on the patio in their twilight home. Both were very bored. One turned to the other and said, 'Nothing ever happens here. All the men are half dead. There's no fun. The other nodded. 'Very well, let's do something to liven the place up.'

So they agreed to streak across the lawn to attract the attention of the old fellows sitting around sunning themselves.

One old guy looked up and said to his neighbour, 'Did you see that?' The other replied, 'I think so. Couldn't say for certain. My eyes aren't too good these days. What were they wearing?'

'Can't say for sure. But whatever it was, they needed ironing.'   (Bowd, 2003)

Of course, you can still find jokes that indicate that old women are still sexually active:

An 80-year-old lady was complaining to a friend that she had a lot of trouble during the night because a man kept banging on her door. When her friend asked, 'Why didn't you open the door?' the lady replied, 'What and let him out?'   (Palmore, 1971)

That sort of joke about the old woman being randy, may just be paradoxical, an illogicality. Let's face it, sex and the aged is quite an incongruous notion. Thinking about your grandparents banging away is rather absurd, inappropriate and pretty ugly. That is, jokes about the old and sex are full of comic incongruities.

Let's return to the list of incongruities suggested by Carroll (2005) to analyse dirty jokes generally:

- The unexpected

A girl asks her boyfriend to come over Friday night and have dinner with her parents. Since this is such a big event, the girl announces to her boyfriend that after dinner, she would like to go out and make love for the first time. Well, the boy is ecstatic, but he has never had sex before, so he takes a trip to the pharmacist to get some condoms. The pharmacist helps the boy for about an hour. He tells the boy everything there is to know about condoms and sex.

At the register, the pharmacist asks the boy how many condoms he'd like to buy, a 3-pack, 10-pack, or family pack. The boy insists on the family pack because he thinks he will be rather busy, it being his first time and all.

That night, the boy shows up at the girl's parent's house and meets his girlfriend at the door. 'Oh, I'm so excited for you to meet my parents, come on in!'

The boy goes inside and is taken to the dinner table where the girl's parents are seated. The boy quickly offers to say grace and bows his head. A minute passes, and the boy is still deep in prayer, with his head down.

10 minutes pass, and still no movement from the boy. Finally, after 20 minutes with his head down, the girlfriend leans over and whispers to the boyfriend, 'I had no idea you were this religious.'

The boy turns, and whispers back, 'I had no idea your father was a pharmacist.'
(www.activejokes.com)

- The illogical

'My sister was with two men in one night. She could hardly walk after that. Can you imagine? Two dinners!'   (Sarah Silverman)

- The improbable

'What do you call a man with a twelve-inch tongue who can hold his breath for ten minutes?'
'Nothing, just keep hold of his ears.'   (Smith, 2004)

- The absurd

(This joke is from the *Lucky Pierre* joke cycle that flourished in America in the 1920s, a consequence of American soldiers' experiences in war-time France.)

'And now, Madam,' Lucky Pierre says, 'I am going to kiss you on ze breasts.'

The American woman giggles as Pierre does so.

'And now, Madam, I am going to kiss you where you have never been kissed before.'

'Where's that?' she asks..

'On ze navel,' he answered with a leer.

'Oh,' she answers, dismissing the thought, 'I've been kissed on the navel before...'

'From ze inside?'   (Carnes, 1986)

- The ambiguous

The bowler's Holding, the batsman's Willey (Brian Johnson)

- The abnormal

Hymie, the mortician, is preparing a body with the biggest penis he's ever seen. 'I have to show this to my wife,' he says. So he cuts it off and takes it home in a box. He gives it to Becky. 'Take a look at that' he says. Becky opens the box. 'Oh my God!' she screams,

'Schwartz is dead!' (Winner, 2012)

- The immoral

I told a joke about incest to my wife. She didn't get it...but my daughter did. (www.sickipedia.org)

- The improper

The Rodeo sexual position

As you're doing the girl doggy style, reach forward and gently cup her breasts in both of your hands. Because you've been extremely suave this far, she'll mistakenly think you're about to say something erotic. Instead, you lead her on with a sultry voice and say, 'these are not as big as your sister's.'

Try to hold on for eight seconds. (www.reddit.com)

- The ugly

'What sex position makes an ugly baby?'

'Go ask your mum.' (www.reddit.com)

- The inappropriate

How can you make your wife scream for hours after sex?

Wipe your dick on the curtains.

(Arnott & Haskins, 2004)

- The impolite

A man was travelling in a crowded bus. A young lady was standing in front of him. After a while the man said, 'Wow, what a big arse!'

Then the girl turned back and slapped him in the face. While she was turned back however, the man said again, 'Wow, what small boobs!'

The girl turned back again and slapped him one more time.

After a while the man said,

'Excuse me for what I said a moment ago, but if you want I can give you advice on how to make your boobs bigger.'

The girl thought it over and said, 'Okay, tell me how.'

'Every morning when you get up, take a piece of toilet paper and start rubbing it on your boobs.'

Does it work?'

'I don't know, but I see it worked on your arse.' (www.bonusjokes.com)

- The inapposite

This beautiful woman one day walks into a doctor's office and the doctor is bowled over by how stunningly awesome she is. All his professionalism goes right out the window…

He tells her to take off her pants, she does, and he starts rubbing her thighs.

'Do you know what I am doing?' asks the doctor?

'Yes, checking for abnormalities,' she replies.

He tells her to take off her shirt and bra, she takes them off. The doctor begins rubbing her breasts and asks, 'Do you know what I am doing now?' She replies. 'Yes, checking for cancer.'

Finally, he tells her to take off her panties, lays on the table, gets on top of her and starts having sex with her. He says to her, 'Do you know what I am doing now?'

She replies, 'Yes, getting herpies—that's why I am here!' (www.lotsofjokes.com)

I rated 580 dirty jokes on the internet and found that most jokes fell into the unexpected category (45%), reflecting the common use of the red light formula. Second place went to the ambiguous (24%), indicating the popularity of word play. The absurd (9%) and the improbable (8%) were some way behind. All the other categories featured, but not very highly, with the illogical and the ugly hardly registering.

And finally, the British seem to have a basic awkwardness when discussing sexuality. We get embarrassed and end up using allusion and euphemism. The consequence is that our language is littered with words that can mean genitalia or sexual behaviour. Lloyd (2007) observes that there are over 1,000 synonyms for male and female genitalia. Erection is the most obvious behavioural word, and it is interesting that that word is rarely heard in its more formal, construction sense, except when someone wants to make a double entendre.

So, the result is that, *'...our language is overbuilt for punning that is sexually allusive.'* (Lloyd, 2007) This is great for jokers as they have a rich resource to draw on. Here is a list of the many ways we have to describe intercourse and the sexual organs, which you may find useful. It comes from a book about double entendre written by *Russell Ash*, entitled *It Just Slipped Out*. The list is not comprehensive but it is pretty extensive, if you know what I mean.

Sexual acts:

a bit; all the way; at it; banging; be in; beating the meat; bedridden; blow; blow job; both ways; bunk up; check-up; come/coming/comes/come up; current affairs; discharge; do it; down; drill; each way; ejaculate; enter/entry; feel/felt; fiddle; filling; finger; get it in; get off; give you a hand; go down; go higher; a good seeing to; grind; happy ending; hard up; having it; having relations; how's your father; in action; in frequently/infrequently; it's in; jack off; jerk; kneel; knocked off; leg over; liquor; make advances; mass debating; master bates; mount; on the job; poke; positions; pull it off; pull out; ram; relief; ride; roger; score; screw; shag; sixty nine; slip in/slip out; seeing to; stuck into; stuff/stuffing; suck it and see; sunk in; take advantage; toss; touch up; tug; up/up your alley/ups and downs; whip it out; whole board; wild oats; withdrawal; yank

Backside

aris/Aristotle; asphalt; ass; bum; Khyber; rear; ring; Uranus

Female Organs

acute angina; baps; bargain basement; bazookas; beaver; boobs; bouncers; box; bush; bust; crack/crack of dawn; down under; dumplings; fan/fancy/fanny; handful; hole; in between; in the pink; knockers; muff; opening; pair; pussy; snatch; tight; tit-bit; verge. (Blake {2007} adds *jugs, doughnut, slit, slot and tits*)

You might like to know, that around about 1730, *'...the word joke was a bawdy name for the female genitalia.'* (Roberts, 1962) Just remember that when a dirty joke is on the tip of your tongue.

The term *'coal black joke'* referred to pubic hair and the genitalia. It could also refer to a prostitute. There was a tune, *The Black Joke*, c.1755, which had the following lyrics:

We are got in a joke, in a joke we are born.

From a joke we proceed, to a joke we return. (Dennant, 2013)

Male Genitalia:

appliance; banana; bullocks; chopper; cobblers; cock/cocky/cox; cockatoo; dick; ding-dong; donkey; endowment; equipment; extension; hampton; hung; instrument; joystick; knob; large; a large one; length; limp; long sausage; member; nuts; old fellow/old man; package/package holiday; pecker; plums; pole; prick; regalia; shortcomings; tool; weapon; willy. (Blake {2007} adds *roger, dong, lance, rod, poker, shaft, stick, sword, dagger, sausage)*

Erect penis:

boner; early riser; erection; grand prix; hard; horn; inflation; rigid; rise; semi; stand/stand out/stand to attention; stiff; upright organ; upright/uprising

The other:

Bit of fluff; broke it off; camp; cherry; clap; coccyx; crumpet; drawers; dripping; ho(e); hormone; hot; in the altogether; maiden over; out/get it out; privates; scouting for boys; scrubber; seamen; tart.

You can use this list when inventing sexual jokes. You might like to bear in mind that the backside is probably the funniest part of our anatomy, as it has the ability to both arouse us and turn us off. Moore (2004) comments:

'The penis and vagina come closest to the ass in this respect...but neither has the power to make us laugh as hard as the butt.' So, if you're engaged in slapstick in any way, it is the arse that should be kicked, and it is the arse that should be fallen on.

If you are in the business of inventing satirical names for a boss, etc., you can't go far wrong with *Winterbottom*. Jimmy Edwards, an English comedian of the 1950s and 60s, maintained that the following joke could be used in all sorts of contexts, because it appealed to everything in the English sense of humour: dignity deflation; the pun; the backside, and the weather:

'*His name was Winterbottom. A cold, stern man.*' (Nordern, 2008)

Reflection

The double entendre is a dirty pun. A play on the myriad of words we have in English to describe sex, and the sexual organs. The double entendre is as English as roast beef and Yorkshire pudding, and it has gone down well throughout the ages.

The double entendre has allowed comedians to get away with dirty talk, but in these more liberal times, there is less need to rely on such verbal deceptions. Comedians can be more blatant in their approach.

Jokes about sex start to become important as we enter our teenage years. Dirty jokes, are, in their way, educational tools, explaining who does what with whom, in graphic ways.

There is no doubt that many adults, worldwide, find dirty jokes very appealing. This is nothing new, Cicero (106BC-43BC) noted, *'An indecency decently put is the thing we laugh at hardest.'*

There is the thrill of breaking taboos and talking about pleasurable subjects. Dirty jokes are very much part of the relationship that exists between males. When telling such jokes, men are often careful to restrict the audience to other like-minded males. This is no doubt a recognition that it is very important not to tell dirty jokes to an audience that does not want to hear them, or should not be exposed to them.

Men are usually the heroes in dirty jokes, and women the objects to be conquered. Wives are written off. Other women are seen as either virgins or nymphomaniacs.

Jokes can reflect our anxieties. A major anxiety is decline in sexual potency as we age. We tell jokes about the old and randiness in order to express these fears, and maybe dispel them. Fortunately, the magic pill *Viagra,* has come to the rescue of this sadness. It's no wonder that quite a joke cycle developed as a result.

Dirty jokes are a stamping ground for those who wish to demonstrate their superiority—their competence versus the incompetence of the mocked. For women, a small penis joke is the gag (but not a gag), to use to humiliate a man.

Activity

1) *It* is such a simple little word, but it can be a very ambiguous and so allows for many jokes:

A woman walked into a pharmacy and spoke to the pharmacist.

She asked, 'Do you have Viagra?'

'Yes,' he replied

She asked, 'Does it work?'

'Yes,' he answered.

'Can you get it over the counter?' she asked.

'I can if I take two,' he answered.   (Blake, 2007)

Invent a *Do It* joke...*Teachers do it with class*

Usually, these jokes relate to an occupation, but they can refer to a religion, sport or hobby, etc. Hence, *Catholics do it on their knees, kayackers do it, roll over, and do it again,* and *naturists barely do it.*

To construct one of these you have to focus on a sexual activity/desire/ability, and then relate that back to an appropriate group, or vice versa.

So, *solicitors do it willingly, drunks do it incapably, Bach did it with a passion, Arsenal fans do it in the way their name suggests,* and *magistrates do it in sessions.*

2) Play a game of *Innuendo Bingo*. Get your friends to fill their mouths with water, and then tell them dirty jokes and stories. The winner is the one who still has water left in their mouth.

3) Invent a *'She was only a...'* joke.

She was only a tobacconist's daughter, but she was the best shag in the shop.

She was only a statistician's daughter, but she knew all the standard deviations.

Obviously, what you have to do with these jokes is to work out a double entendre based on a particular trade, occupation, etc. To do this you can go to the list of words for sexual acts, in this section, and work out an appropriate occupation, etc., e.g.:

She was only a Good Samaritan's daughter, but she would always give you a hand.

She was only a miner's daughter, but she loved going down.

Or, you can go to a list of occupations and see what comes up:

She was only a dentist's daughter, but she loved getting drilled.

She was only a training manager's daughter, but she loved learning on the job.

4) Prepare a caption for a *'Dick Joke'* competition. At the turn of the century, *The Wellington Evening Post*, New Zealand, ran a competition where a naked man, with his penis, suitably hidden by some object, was engaged in some activity. Readers had to supply an appropriate caption, which turned out usually to be a double entendre concerning the penis.

So, *Naked Man* conducting an all-female orchestra:

'Once again the ensemble did not need a metronome.'

'There was a stunned silence as he raised his baton.'

Naked Man meets the vicar:

'J. Thomas withered under ecclesiastical scrutiny.'

Other *Naked Man* situations included: Walking up the steps at a girls' school, with three girls also on the step; *Naked Man* at a jumble sale, and *Naked Man* playing rugby. (Lloyd, 2007 & 2011)

Limericks

The limerick's birth is unclear
Its genesis owed much to Lear
It started as clean
But soon went obscene
And this split haunts its later career

(O.E. Parrott, cited by Vallely, 2007).

That limerick gives a nice overview of the career of the limerick. No-one really knows where and when limericks began. They had definitely been around for a long time before they were popularised in the nineteenth century by the humourist Edward Lear, however, he didn't really write limericks as we know them today. Lear's nonsense rhymes were squeaky clean, but they were adapted and a rash of vulgar limericks erupted. The sleazy ones are seen as the best by some observers:

The limerick parks laughter anatomical
Into space that is quite economical
But the good one's we've seen
So seldom are clean
And the clean ones so seldom are comical   (Metcalf, 2009)

With regard to the history of the limerick, there is a suggestion that the limerick form can be found in *The Wasps*, a work by the Greek comic Aristophanes (448?-?380 B.C.) (Baring-Gould, 1974). A very early record of the limerick form is from an Irish source, *The Song of the Sea*, by Rumann MacColmain, published in the 8th Century:

When the wind comes from the south,
Over the shield-bearing Saxon stout
It drives waves up Skiddy
Makes high calad Nit giddy,
Pounding the grey-green of Shannon's mouth   (Anon, 1968)

Bawdy limericks were common entertainment in English taverns, as early as the 15th and 16th centuries (Vallely, 2007). Indeed, a drinking song is said to be the earliest limerick to be printed in English, in 1622 (Herben, 1963). This is from Othello, Act 2, Scene 3, when Iago declaims:

And let me the canakin clink, clink;

And let me the canakin clink.

A soldier's a man;

A life's but a span;

Why, then, let a soldier drink.   (A canakin is a small can or cup)

Legman (1974) pinpoints the first limerick, in modern form, as appearing by 1640 as a broadside ballad, *Mondayes Work* from the *Roxburghe Ballads*:

Good morrow, neighbour Gamble,

Come let you and I goe ramble:
Last night I was shot
Through the braines with a pot
And now my stomacke doth wamble   (Wamble means to be nauseous)

In 1822 a book entitled, *Anecdotes and adventures of fifteen gentlemen* was published. It contained a limerick which was to prove important:

There was a sick man of Tobago,
Who liv'd long on rice gruel and sago;
But at last, to his bliss,
The physician said this—
To a roast leg of mutton you may go.

(Baring-Gould, 1974)

Not a very inspiring limerick you might think, but it inspired humourist Edward Lear (1812-1888), who became known as *The Poet Laureate of the Limerick*. Although he never used the term limerick, he published 212 in various nonsense books, which proved very popular.

Typically, Lear repeated a first line rhyme in the fifth line, making the verse rather fizzle out:

There was an old man with a beard,
Who said, 'It is just as I feared—
Two owls and a hen,
Four larks and a wren,
Have all built their nests in my beard!

(Baring-Gould, 1974)

To be honest, by today's standards Lear's nonsense rhymes are not that good because of the last line fizzle:

With respect to the great Mr Lear,
Inventor of rhymes without peer.
His limericks are fine
Until the last line,
When the muse seems to leave him, I fear. (Rees, 2008)

Edward Lear's nonsense rhymes were soon parodied, notably by Algernon Charles Swinburne (1837-1909). So this following sweet nothing was radically transformed:

There was a young lady of Norway
Who casually sat in a doorway;
When the door squeezed her flat,
She exclaimed: 'What of that?'
This courageous young lady of Norway

There was a young lady from Norway
Who hung by her toes in a doorway,
She said to her beau:
'Just look at me, Joe,
I think I've discovered one more way!' (Rees, 2008)

The limerick's connection with the town of Limerick seems to have come about via an early 19th century singing game, popular in Ireland. In this game, each singer contributed a different line about the exploits of imaginary people, from different towns in Ireland. The chorus, sung by everyone, began with the line, *'Will you come up to Limerick'* (Vallely, 2007). This singing game is said to have been popularised by members of the Irish brigade who had returned from France where they had been attached to the French army for a period of nearly 100 years from 1691.' (Baring-Gould, 1974)

Legman (1974) suggests that the limerick name was accepted, at some time between 1882 and 1898, possibly in the columns of a sporting newspaper, *The Pink 'Un*. The word first entered the *Oxford English Dictionary* in 1898. (Baring-Gould, 1974)

The limerick had become established and all sorts of people, including notable authors produced their versions, e.g., Lewis Carroll, Mark Twain, and William Gilbert (Gilbert & Sullivan). George Bernard Shaw complained that so many of his favourite limericks were *'unfit for publication.'* (Baring-Gould, 1974). Indeed, limericks are frequently rude, often involving young women from *Bude*, *Venus*, or wherever.

Legman (1974) considers that the real limericks are the vulgar. This is how they started, and clean versions are just, *'insipid'*, of no *'real interest to anyone.'* He reports Don Marquis, who said limericks are of three kinds:

'Limericks to be told when ladies are present; limericks to be told when ladies are absent but clergymen are present-and LIMERICKS' (Legman, 1974).

Gershon Legman's classic book, *The Limerick,* contained 1700 vulgar limerick verses. The contents list included: abuses of the clergy; zoophily; organs, and assorted eccentricities. Legman does point out that the limerick was the preserve of the educated class. Here are some examples from the 1700:

Said a lecherous fellow named Shea
When his prick wouldn't rise for a day
'You must seize it and squeeze it,
And tease it and please it,
For Rome wasn't built in a day.'

A pansy who lived in Khartoum
Took a lesbian up to his room
And they argued all night
Over who had the right
To do what, and with what, and to whom.

The nipples of Sarah Sarong,
When excited, are twelve inches long
This embarrassed her lover
Who was pained to discover
She expected no less of his dong.

We now move on from the past to the present, and advice on how to construct your own limericks. So, firstly, what exactly is a limerick? Normally, limericks amount to a memorable anecdote, with a set-up that establishes: the Who, the Where, and the What. The final punch-line, the Why, resolves the set-up.

According to Baring-Gould (1974), the: *'...first line sets the scene and introduces the main character; ideally, the rhyme word at its end is an unusual one...The second line rhymes with the first, making a couplet (a a). It may introduce a second character and it should open the action which is to precipitate the crisis...The third and fourth lines are shortened to intensify the suspense, and they introduce a new rhyme, hopefully startling, which again make a couplet (b b)...The fifth line, enhanced by the end rhyme (a again) brings the climax and denouement of the plot.'*

A teacher called Hughes has begun
To make her lessons more fun.
As she reckons that jokes
Are best left to blokes
She sticks to misusing the pun.
I devised this limerick for a colleague whose teaching I had observed as part of her assessment. I suggested using more humour as a way of maintaining interest.

To start with I didn't have a punch-line, just her name. Hughes is a good name for limericks as it has a lot of rhymes, but I couldn't get anywhere with *'A teacher called Hughes'*. So, I changed the rhyme and immediately pun came into the picture for the punch-line. It was only walking through woodland a few days later that the whole punch line suddenly emerged. The third and fourth lines were quickly rattled off.

So, to construct a limerick it is best to have a punch-line, starting bottom up, failing that you need end words which have a lot of potential rhymes, and just hope that a punch-line emerges.

Clearly, the following limerick started with the punch-line. There is the additional benefit that *'tat'* has a lot of potential rhymes:

On a maiden a man once begat
Bouncy triplets named Nat, Tat, and Pat;
'Twas fun in the breeding
But hell in the feeding:
She hadn't a spare tit for Tat.

(Baring-Gould, 1974)
Technically, the pattern of the limerick is three anapestic trimeter lines, and two dimeter anapests. A trimeter is a line with three stresses, with greater stress on the final syllable, and, a dimeter has two stresses. (Loomis, 1963).

There <u>was</u> / a young <u>la</u> / -dy from <u>York</u>
Who <u>had</u> / a great <u>fond</u> / -ness for <u>pork</u>
She <u>ate</u> / it all day
And <u>ne</u> / -ver could <u>play</u>
Cause her <u>hand</u> / would not <u>put</u> / down her <u>fork</u>   (www.cnr.edu/home/bmcmanus/meter.html)

This knowledge should help with understanding the following limerick:

Ann bragged that her limericks were best-
A-a-b-b-a with a jest-
Whatever she'd hum
Would come out dee-dee-dum
And that, of course, made An (n)-a-pest!   (Miller, 1979)

It is important that a limerick moves to a climax and doesn't just fizzle out, for example:

There was an old girl of Kilkenny
Whose usual charge was a penny.
For half of that sum,
You might fondle her bum.
A source of amusement to many.

(Baring-Gould, 1974)

You can use a pun as the punch-line, although this is not typical:

There was an old man of Kilbride,
Who slipped in a sewer and died,
His stupid young brother,
Went into another,
And the verdict on both was 'sewercide'

(Anon, 1968)

An idiom works quite well:

A fellow who lived on the Tyne
Saw some fish on which he wished to dine;
But how to invite them?
He thought: 'I shall write them!'
And sat down and dropped them a line.

(Rees, 2008)

A multiple use of rhyme in the fifth line adds to the effect:

A happy young colleen from Derry,
On ale was loving and merry,
She dallied with sin,
On vodka and gin,
But was rigid and frigid on sherry

(Anon, 1968)

You may want to write an obscene limerick. Research by Virdis (2010) helps us understand what is involved in such rhymes. She analysed the limericks which appeared in the first issue of a gentleman's erotic magazine, *The Pearl*, 1879-1881. This publication was, in fact, shut down by the authorities, because of its rude and obscene nature. Virdis found that the limericks demonstrated male power, and control of women and animals. Normally, the limerick contained some comic setback for the main character. Any manner of sexual or obscene activity might be involved.

The place where the action took place was usually foreign, in line with the orientalist consideration of the time, that, the foreign is more erotic. So, the following places featured: *Bombay; Peru; Calcutta; Santander; Ostend,* and *Sark*. Somehow or other though, *Wood Green, Dundee* and *Hitchin* managed to be included.

Here are some examples:

There was a young man from Peru
Who had nothing whatever to do;
So he took out his carrot
And he buggered his parrot
And sent the result to the zoo.

There was a young lady of Troy,
Who invented a new kind of joy:
She sugared her thing
Both outside and in
And then had it sucked by a boy.

There was a young man of Dundee
Who one night went out on the spree
He wound up his clock
With the tip of his cock
And buggered himself with the key.

Here are some rhymes used in naughty limericks, taken from Rees (2008), which you could consider copying or adapting:

Adam, madam, had 'em; Aird, bared, Be prepared; Wheeling, feeling, ceiling; Hall, ball, call; Jones, moans, zones; Divine, fine, mine; Kent, bent, went; Strewed, rude, nude; Humble, tumble, fumble; Czechs, sex, wrecks; Belgrade, maid, laid; Herts, tarts, parts; Rhyl, fill, pill;

Hunts, punts, grunts; Bits, tits, fits; Claire, dare, pair; Bude, rude, protrude; Duff, muff, rough; Bermuda, shrewder, screwed'er; Cock, clock, frock; Ewing, screwing, doing; Venus, seen us, penis; St Just, lust, bust; Ealing, kneeling, feeling; Goring, whoring, boring; Stoke, joke, stroke.

The internet is very useful for finding lists of rhymes. Two useful sites are: www.rhymezone.com and www.rhymer.com

Reflection

Good limericks need to build to a crescendo. The first two lines are routine, as they simply set the scene. The third and fourth, very quickly morph, into the last, which is often obscene.

Although the limerick is perhaps a little quaint, it still has a place in the humour pantheon. The limerick allows you to be acceptably crude by converting the smutty into witty. Indeed, it gives you a chance to display your humour craft, to be admired by others. Why don't you try and do one for someone's leaving card? *'Best wishes'* is so pathetic.

Limericks are fun to do. They are particularly good for making fun of a friend or colleague, that is, if you can find a useful rhyme based on their name, job, or location, etc.

Activities

The limerick is fun, and quite easily done. Now spend your time, constructing a rhyme. You'll find it's second to none.

1) Select a word starting with A/B/C/D/E and construct a limerick around it. Then, submit your work to www.oedilf.com. This is the site of the *Omnificent English Dictionary In Limerick Form*. The aim here is to have one limerick for every word in the English dictionary. The estimated date for completion of this project is 12th December, 2043. Here is one of the entries for aardvark:

When longing for treats hot and steamy
A Wild Westerner's thoughts could turn seamy
'Is that Davy Crockett,
An aardvark in your pocket,
Or are you just happy to see me?'
2) Complete the following, from a competition run by the *West Cumberland Times,* in 1907:

A man in the island of Skye/Had a notion he knew how to fly/Some wings he contrived/from a steeple he dived/........

The winner and runner up lines were: *'Tempus fugit' (Time flies), said he, 'Why not I?'* 2) *And his wife added 'P' to RI.*

3) Here is another competition to complete:

There was a young lady of Ryde/Whose locks were consid'rably dyed./The hue of her hair/Made everyone stare/...

One winner wrote: *'She's piebald, she'll die bald! They cried.* (Baring-Gould, 1974)

4) Here are the first 4 lines of a limerick submitted to a *Sunday Mirror* limerick competition. Provide the 5th:

There was a young lady from Cheam/Who tried out a breast-growing cream/She woke in the night/With a terrible fright....

Answer: Another had grown in between

(Rees, 2008)

5) Have a go at writing a limerick in text speak:

Thr wnce ws a grl frm SX
Who cdnt stp usin hr txt;
She ws gtin a bor,
I cud nt take no mor,
So I fd hr phn 2 my dg Rx   (Violet Macdonald, 13, in: Rees, 2008)

Part 5: Group humour

If you tell a joke in a forest and there is no-one there, is it funny? Well, it may be to you, but trees don't laugh, unless they are really barking mad. No, a joke needs an audience, and that is what this part is about, the audience. For most of us, our audience is the groups to which we belong, primarily our families, and then our friends, and then the people at work. After that, it is any group of which we are a member, like a football team or book club.

I begin by looking at a bit of relevant theory contributed by a French philosopher, Henri Bergson. His big idea was that our laughter is a social corrective. We mock and ridicule others until they learn to live properly in our groups.

It is therefore the potential of mockery that forces us to conform. On top of that we have blushing and embarrassment, which is the way our bodies and minds have to tell us that we have stepped out of line in some way.

Whilst the young are easily embarrassed, older people try to appear unembarrassed after they have made a mistake, or been deliberately provoked. This is usually done by laughing off the situation, and showing that they are good sports.

After looking at embarrassment we turn to an examination of groups and their humour. Here, there is a distinct difference between newly-formed groups and groups which have been long established. The new group flails around with its humour attempts, whilst the long-running group has a joking history, with everyone knowing their place.

Usually, the boss of the group sets the humour tone and the others respond, often building on what the boss has said, in rather a deferential way. Others, less politically astute, can use veiled humour to criticise the boss.

People in groups often tease each other. Although teasing looks like fun, there is sometimes a nip or a bite in the tail, making the tease more of an attack. I take a good look at teasing, particularly that carried out by the young.

The thing about teasing is that you have to judge the intent of the teaser. Is it a fun tease, having a laugh, or is it malicious? Is it your mates mucking about, or is it a bully come to rough you up?

Next, we have a bit of fun with nicknames, which can, of course, be teases in themselves. The nickname given by a group, establishes the fact that one is a member. The nickname indicates the relative status of a person in a group.

Those who are mocked by a group get derogatory nicknames. Very often, in organisations, insulting nicknames are bestowed on managers, with the nickname indicating a lack of competence, etc.

Understanding of teasing and nicknames helps with the next subject, which is workplace banter. This, very often for workers, is their main humour outlet. It dispels boredom, builds relationships, relieves tension and generally helps make work worth doing.

The closer you get to the shop-floor, the more likely it is that the banter is raunchy in nature. This is especially the case with a male workforce. The banter of a female workforce is likely to be much more friendly and cooperative in nature.

Banter is invariably subversive. Workers unite against the common enemy, management. They laugh at their mistakes, mock their behaviour, and mimic their accents, etc.

Banter relies on what I call *duptrix*. This term covers all the sorts of tricks people play on each other- hoaxes; practical jokes, leg-pulls, wind-ups and tall stories. New recruits get told to go and get a bucket of sky-hooks. The gullible get their legs pulled. The wind-up merchant goes around annoying people. April 1st, and many other days come to that, sees a multitude of pranks being played on the unsuspecting.

In all, the group is the arena for your humour. As a new recruit your attempts are more likely to fail or be ignored, indeed, you may be the butt of other people's humour at this stage. With time, you work out what works and what doesn't, and you establish your role in the joking hierarchy. You begin to tease and join in the banter and the pranks. Finally, if you end up as boss, you have the pleasure of everyone laughing at your jokes, but watch your back. They will be laughing behind that as well.

Bergson and laughter

'A man dressed in a suit complete with bowler hat comes into a shop. He has a silly walk and keeps doing little jumps and then three long paces without moving the top of his body. He buys a paper, then we follow him as he leaves the shop.' (www.orangecow.org/pythonet)

The Ministry of Funny Walks sketch is a classic comic piece from the *Monty Python* shows. In 2005 It was rated in the top 50 of Britain's greatest comedy sketches (www.aberdeen-music.com). Essentially ridiculous slapstick, it was later adapted by John Cleese as a goose-stepping routine, meant to amuse some German guests at *Fawlty Towers*. Funnily enough, they didn't find it so funny.

Silly walks aren't always funny, although perhaps the most famous funny walk was that of Charlie Chaplin's tramp. Here, Chaplin, bowler-hatted like Cleese, walked rapidly, with his flat-footed feet getting on for right angles to his body, much to the amusement of those looking on.

So, what makes silly walks funny? Clearly such walks are incongruous, not normal walking, however, additionally, according to the theory of Henri Bergson (1859-1941), we laugh when a living being becomes like a thing, an automaton. Bergson states, in capitals, that: 'THE ATTITUDES,GESTURES AND MOVEMENTS OF THE HUMAN BODY ARE LAUGHABLE IN EXACT PROPORTION AS THAT BODY REMINDS US OF A MERE MACHINE.' This is particularly clear with John Cleese's portrayal of a stereotype bureaucrat, stiff-bodied, with arms rigidly by his sides, launching his long legs skywards, in a repetitive fashion.

For Bergson there is a central image, *'something mechanical encrusted upon the living'*, for example, *Baron Munchausen* being turned into a cannonball. For Bergson, anything is comic if it gives, *'...in a single combination, the illusion of life and the distinct impression of a mechanical arrangement.'* Here, he refers to *Punch & Judy* shows, and *The Jack in the Box*.

Core concepts, related to the mechanical, stressed by Bergson, are *rigidity* and *repetition*. He thought that we laugh at, *'anything rigid, readymade, mechanical in gesture, attitude and even facial expression.'*

Bergson's theory of a person becoming a thing being humorous, rather predicted the humour of the subsequent comedic silent cinema, and that is a measure of a good theory, its predictive power. Critchley (2002) points out:

Whether it is the mechanical rigidity of Chaplin's body, the person-become-thing of Keaton's face or the mute perversity of Harpo Marx, humor is here produced by the different ways in which the mechanical or thingly encrusts onto the living.

In slapstick, people fall down a lot, usually onto their backsides. This continual falling is not human behaviour. It is behaviour out of control. No longer are the clowns able to walk like other humans, they are more like animals on all fours. The falling is often due to absent-mindedness, a person without mind.

'In the world of slapstick, people are very nearly never in control—of their decisions, of their social world, or of the material objects in their world, or even of their own bodies.' (Caron, 2006)

So, what else did Bergson add to humour theory, beyond an insight into funny walking, and slapstick

generally? Henri Bergson was a major French philosopher who won the Nobel Prize for Literature in 1927. Of his many works, we are here concerned with his essay, *Laughter: An Essay On The Meaning Of The Comic,* a slim work, which focussed on laughter and its comic cause.

Bergson's consideration of laughter reflects his general philosophy on the nature of man. He despaired at the threatened mechanisation of humanity. He wanted to demonstrate the superiority of intuition over logic (Douglas, 1979).

Bergson does not consider laughter generally, but mainly the ludicrous. Neither does he take a psychological stance, unlike his contemporary Sigmund Freud. He concentrates more on the social function of laughter.

Bergson's essay starts with the question, *'What does laughter mean?'* He then goes on to attempt an answer, admitting that he has set himself rather a baffling task (Bergson, 2008).

Early on, Bergson makes three major points about comedy and laughter:

'...the comic does not exist outside the pale of what is strictly human'; laughter is cerebral-'Its appeal is to intelligence, pure and simple', and, laughter is social-*'Our laughter is always the laughter of a group'.*

As human life needs flexibility, laughter mocks mechanical rigidity in order to try and effect change. Further, where a person falls short of society's rules, laughter functions so as to attempt an improvement.

So, an important function of humour, isolated by Bergson, is its corrective function. Bergson states that, *'In laughter we always find an unavowed intention to humiliate and consequently to correct our neighbour, if not in his will, at least in his deed.'*

Society always holds the threat of ridicule over deviants, hence humour produces conformity. If someone is doing something wrong, acting inappropriately, we may well mock them, in order that they conform. For example, Gunning (2001) found as follows in an American child protection agency:

'Humor served to socialize workers to the beliefs, values, and rules of agency behaviour, and once they had been socialized, it functioned to maintain these norms. Workers who violated these rules of behaviour were subjected to teasing or insulting joking.'

Where workers made simple mistakes, humour was used as a corrective:

'...the same mistake should not be made twice and that is one role played by humor--joking and kidding reminded a worker not to repeat a mistake

There is one type of person who is immune to the threat of humour, and, indeed, may revel at being laughed at – the eccentric. Real eccentrics are comparatively rare. Weeks & James (1995) estimate that 1 in 10,000 people are classic, full-time eccentrics, however, they do point out that eccentricity is a continuum, so a lot of us may have something of the eccentric about us.

It is the absentmindedness of the eccentric that Bergson (2008) would find interesting, as well as the immunity of the eccentric to social pressure. Weeks and James (1995) point out that the funniest eccentrics are those who do things with a straight face, *'...blithely unaware that they leave people convulsed with laughter.'* (Gunning, 2001)

Finally, it is interesting that internet humour is so crude. Funny stuff on the internet is often concerned with, *'...highly explicit sexual humor, jokes about ethnic and sexual minorities, violent and 'sick' humor. '* Kuipers (2006) reckons that this bias is due to, *'...anonymity and lack of social control on the internet and its origins in a culture of young, male computer users...'* There is no-one around to correct them.

Reflection

Henri Bergson isolated both a particular type of incongruity theory, and a superiority/ridicule theory. The incongruity theory concerns the mechanical taking over the living. We laugh at rigid inflexibility. The superiority/ridicule theory is about requiring deviant others to conform. The non-deviant individual conforms because of the on-going dread of potential mockery.

We conform socially because we are scared of people laughing at us and taking the mickey. Not only do we have to cope with the embarrassment, we know that people have long memories and don't easily forget some *faux pas* we have made. Take the following instance, which is oft quoted:

'This Earle of Oxford, making of his low obeisance to Queen Elizabeth, happened to let a Fart, at which he was so abashed and ashamed that he went to Travell, 7 yeares. On his returne the Queen welcomed him home, and sayd, My Lord, I had forgotten the Fart.' (Holt, 2008)

Normally, we take care that our behaviour is not open to mockery. We wear appropriate clothes. We try not to stand out too much. We do what is expected, as Miller (1996) puts it: *'For many of us, a quiet but compelling drive to avoid embarrassment pervades our daily activity.'*

We leave clowning to the buffoons at whom we laugh because of their ludicrous behaviour, thankful that people are not laughing at us. Maybe we avoid joking as this can go wrong, and we end up being mocked for our rubbish humour.

Above all, for Bergson, laughter is social. You may not have laughed much whilst reading this book and the reason is obvious, you are alone. Even if there are people around, they'd think you were a bit barmy if you suddenly started chortling away. They'd give you a look, and none of us like that, *'whose that nutter'* look, except of course, if you're an eccentric.

Activity

1) Your first task is to get hold of a copy of Charlie Chaplin's *Modern Times*, a silent comedy that satirises *Henry Ford* and his production methods. In particular, notice how Chaplin turns himself into a machine, partly by immersing himself in one, and partly by repeating the mechanical movements of work, when not working.

2) Obtain a copy of *David Brent's* dance routine in the *Office* series. Master the routine and demonstrate to others.

3) Count the number of times you laugh in a day when you are on your own and when you are with others.

When Robert Provine (2000) showed individuals humorous videos in the laboratory, all he got was *'a few grudging chuckles'*. However, when he analysed the logbooks of 72 students about their own laughter, he found that they, *'laughed about 30 times more when they were around others than when they were alone…'*

4) Bergson's term *'the mechanical encrusted upon the living,'* is rather quaint, and does seem a bit difficult to grasp, however, it is clearly the basis of *Viagra* jokes:

'I think my Grandad may have taken a couple of Viagra instead of his sleeping tablets last night. This morning it was hard waking him.' (Sickipedia.org)

In these jokes you have all the components for humour. There is sex, of course, and the ridiculous old men with permanent erections. The *Viagra* turns old men into actual Bergsonian sex machines, perpetually able to produce the goods.

There was a cycle of *Viagra* jokes, 1998-2003, at the time when *Viagra* began to penetrate the market (Vares & Braun, 2006). Your task is to produce another *Viagra* joke. Possible themes are: coffin shapes, and the raising of the inanimate.

Embarrassment

'...he (the teacher) turns round with a funny face and he says 'will you two stop fiddling with each other!' I never went so bright red in all my life...and everybody turned round, didn't they...Everybody was scared stiff in that class, everyone just sits there, all quiet' (Woods, 1975).

Blushing is, *'a hallmark of embarrassment.'* The higher the embarrassment, the more pronounced the blushing (Miller & Fahey, 1991).When did you last blush? The younger you are, the more likely you know the answer, as blushing is, typically, an affliction of youth. I can't even vaguely remember when I last blushed.

Although people don't enjoy blushing, the act does have face-saving properties. It is a non-fakeable display that shows someone is truly ashamed. Observers therefore judge blushers more favourably than non-blushing counterparts (Dijk & de Jong, 2009).

That is, the kind observers. The *'nice-guy'* empathises with the victim, and helps him/her deal with the gaffe (Billig, 2001). The extent of the empathy depends on the extent to which the embarrassed is liked (Stocks et al., 2011). Conversely, what we might call the *nasty guy* enjoys the embarrassment of others, exposes it, and laughs at the victim's attempts to regain his/her poise.

The *nasty guy* likes to, as the Americans say, *yank chains*. In Britain, we have that odd phrase, *'getting a rise out of someone.'* Beth Quinn (2000) studied *chain yanking* in a small American company, *Acme*. She found that it was a form of entertainment, whose objective is to get a display of embarrassment or anger.

Sid, worked in maintenance at *Acme*:

'When you go and have poker with the guys, it's just the guys sitting around having a drink and playing cards---You know? We just kinda pull each other's leg a little, pull the chain a little bit to see if we can get a rise out of the guy. Just to see if you can, ah...irritate him a little bit just for the hell of it.'

Quinn reckons that, a successful yank means that, *'You have them, you have control and they don't, and therein lies the pleasure of the act.'* What the *nasty guy* has to do is find the right buttons to push:

Robert, an engineer:

'People have come up and flipped my ear or played childish games on me at work, and I've told them before (that I don't like it). But these guys, that you'd, you just can't (laugh) uh, you just can't tell them anything (laugh). They'll just keep going. Yeah. They just keep doing it just to bug you.'

A particular time when people are deliberately embarrassed can be when they join a new group, usually a group of young males. As part of an initiation process, newcomers can, *'engage in embarrassing, degrading, or dangerous events to prove their loyalty to the group and be admitted into its membership.'* (Howard & EnglandKennedy, 2006)

Howard & EnglandKennedy (2006) recount a case, in an American private school, where the culture supported *Craig*, and his sexual hazing of another boy, *Darren*. The innocent party, *Darren*, eventually left the school.

In the school's locker room, *Craig*, the higher status boy, touched *Darren's* shoulder and cheek with his penis. This act greatly embarrassed *Darren*. *Craig* claimed the incident was just *'joking around.'* Even so, *Craig* was expelled by the headmaster.

Interviews with teachers, students and parents considered *Craig's* behaviour as being a *'practical joke'*. More generally, it was part of the initiation process, common in American schools.

A group of young female teachers supported the expulsion, however, the *'majority of the community'*, saw the behaviour as *"boys being boys"*, that is, *'...an acceptable and excusable form of masculine joking.'*

A year later *Darren*, the victim, had left the school, as he couldn't stand the ridicule. *Craig* was reinstated.

So, what should the embarrassed do? When someone who has been embarrassed doesn't rise to the bait, but makes a joke of the situation, it suggests to others that the matter is trivial. The joke indicates to an audience, that the person is in control, and that he/she wants the situation to be seen as comic, rather than grave. If both sides laugh, then it is likely that the embarrassment will be overcome (Miller, 1996).

For example, Zhukov (2013) found that music students used joking to cover up their embarrassment, *'...their self-deprecating comments often produced smiles from the teachers and deflected criticism.'*

Actually, the victims of embarrassment may not really find their misfortunes all that funny, but still laugh about them to be a good sport, and so as to not be seen as a complainer or whinger (Edwards, 2005).

Embarrassment can cause a loss of self-esteem and social esteem. It is very much a social emotion. We don't tend to get embarrassed in private. The nature of the group observing the embarrassing event is important. The bigger the audience, the more embarrassed we are likely to be (Miller, 1996).

Eller et al. (2011) found that the more an audience consisted of in-group members, the higher was the victim's embarrassment. This is particularly the case where someone identifies strongly with the in-group. People are less concerned where the audience is composed of out-group members, as long as those people are perceived as being of lower-status.

Embarrassment can be experienced even by the very young. It was found in one study that, by the age of 5, the majority of children (57%) were reported by their parents to have blushed (Buss et al., 1979). Billig (2001) argues, in line with Bergson, that the creation of embarrassment is an important role for humour, as embarrassment is essential for social life to function. Children, in particular, according to Billig, need to observe and experience embarrassment in order to learn how to meet social expectations, very Bergsonian.

As we age we are embarrassed by a variety of things. One embarrassment that adolescents are prone to is revelation of their limited knowledge. For example, American teacher, Michael Bobkoff, relates the following, about a normally reticent student, Jon. This lad enjoyed it when others made amistake in class, but got his comeuppance when the class was questioned about the meaning of the word hubris. Bobkoff asked, *'Who remembers the Greek word for excessive pride or arrogance?'* Jon stuck up his hand and said, *'Herpes'*, which reply, *'brought down the house'* (Anon., 1984). No doubt, Jon kept his mouth shut after that.

There is a lot of humour in mistakes. We laugh at the ludicrous nature of failure. We laugh because we feel superior to the mistake maker. We laugh at his/her embarrassment and attempts to regain normality. We also laugh as we are relieved it's not us who've committed the faux pas.

Apart from knowledge failure, other major sources of embarrassment are:

- physical pratfalls-- falling over
- loss of control over the body— burping and farting
- shortcomings in physical appearance-- zips undone , underwear showing
- failure of privacy regulation-- accidentally disturbing someone in the bathroom (Keltner & Buswell, 1996).

A nice example of *'failure of privacy regulation'* is given by John Rae, past head-teacher of *Westminster School*:

'The Australian headmaster has seen it all before and tells me this story: at his school in Adelaide boys are not allowed to take showers during class time, but one boy did, and on hearing voices hid in a cupboard. The headmaster was showing parents round the school's facilities. "Plenty of cupboard space"' the visiting father observed whereupon the headmaster opened the cupboard door only to reveal the naked boy within.' (Rae, 2009)

Tumescence may have added an extra, literal dimension to this particular cock-up story.

All these embarrassing shortcomings are the source material for clowning and farce. Just take Peter Sellers and the *Inspector Clousseau* films. *Clousseau* is constantly falling over, so much so that he says at one stage, *'I see you are familiar with the falling-down-on-the-floor ploy.'* *Clousseau* farts in an elevator. He is attacked in wrong places by his servant *Cato*. He mangles his speech-*'rheum'* for room, and *'meuths'* for moths. He says stuff like *'Roger and goodbye'*. He does things wrong affecting himself and others---he splatters a butler with ink from a pen, he dips his nose into face powder, and he sets himself on fire, via a still-lit cigarette lighter, etc, etc. (Wasson, 2007). (If you've not seen a *Clousseau* film, there are clips on Youtube.)

Jokes that place a person in an embarrassing situation are often quite good:

A lady picked up several items at a discount store. When she finally got to the checkout, she learned that one of her items had no price tag. Imagine her embarrassment when the assistant got on the intercom and boomed out for all the store to hear, 'Price check on Lane 13, Tampax, Supersize.'

That was bad enough, but somebody at the rear of the store apparently misunderstood the word 'Tampax' for TACKS. In a business-like tone, a voice boomed back over the intercom: 'Do you want the kind you push in with your thumb or the kind you pound in with a hammer?' (www.jokes-news.com)

This next one is actually a man walks into a bar joke:

A very shy guy goes into a nightclub and sees a beautiful woman sitting at the bar. After an hour of gathering up his courage, he finally goes over to her and asks, tentatively, 'Um, would you mind if I chatted with you for a while?'

She responds by yelling, at the top of her lungs, 'No, I won't sleep with you tonight!' Everyone in the bar is now staring at them. Naturally, the guy is completely embarrassed and he slinks back to his table.

After a few minutes, the woman walks over to him and says, 'I'm sorry if I embarrassed you. You see, I'm a graduate student in psychology and I'm studying how people respond to embarrassing situations.'

To which he responds, at the top of his lungs, 'Two-hundred pounds? What do you mean £200?'
(http//: jokes4all.net)

You can turn your embarrassing memories into such jokes, or better still, anecdotes. Billig (2001) explains that on the re-telling of an embarrassing story, the humiliated victim can cope with the embarrassment by becoming the unconventional hero/heroine of the tale--a *'revenge against the ridicule of embarrassment.'* They also show that a person is able to laugh at him/herself.

Let me tell you a true story…Once upon a time I was a university lecturer. Part of the job was attending the annual degree awards ceremony, held in the Abbey at St Albans, a historic and venerable site.

At the start of these ceremonies two lines of lecturers, wearing full academic dress, proceed up the main aisle. Trumpets sound, and the assembled parents and graduates stand and stare --the whole event being filmed for posterity.

Well, one year I was the lead lecturer of one of the lines, no doubt selected for my wisdom, indicated by the bald head and glasses. Anyway, I led the line towards the main stage, in the chancel of the Abbey. As I got there, I suddenly became confused, which was the right way to get to the seats for the lecturers? I didn't know. The other line had forked off. Should I go left or right?

Thank God, well yes, I chose right, and everyone got to their seats safely. If I'd chosen left I would have taken the lecturers to the toilets!

I still tremble at the thought. The memory would never have been erased and staff would have taken the mickey for evermore—*'How's it going bog-house'; 'Organised a piss-up in a cathedral'*…..

Reflection

Embarrassment is nature's way of controlling our behaviour so that we conform to the expectations of our social groups. Nature has been so clever to provide us with blushing, as we can signal to the world that we are ashamed, and hence have learned that the behaviour is disallowed.

Embarrassment is about the exposure of something a person doesn't want exposed to others: Their incompetence, their body, the noisy emissions from their body, their gaucheness, etc., etc. The problem is that there is so much that can go wrong in our farcical lives. We can easily: fall, fart, flounder, fail, flash, and falter. We get flustered when we are revealed as the fool in the freak show and signal this with our flushes.

No wonder that embarrassment is the staple diet of the clown. He or she makes a living from embarrassment. How many times have you seen Miranda Hart topple? Her comedy is, for her, '... *a series of embarrassing moments which leave you feeling alone in your confusion and shame.'*...Such fun! (www.goodreads.com)

We don't get embarrassed in private, but in public. The more important the audience is to us, the more embarrassed we get. We are lucky if the observers are *nice guys*, however, the more malicious *nasty guy*, revels in our shame, as he searches for the right buttons to push in future.

The key seems to be not to show you are angry or embarrassed. It only encourages them. It is best to make a joke of the gaffe, laughing it off as if it is of no consequence. This shows you are not damaged and are a good sport. You can console yourself that the embarrassing episode will make a good story for future telling.

Activity

1) Deliberately make yourself the centre of attention

People are often embarrassed when they become the centre of attention. They worry that they may show themselves up, that they will be revealed as incompetent in some way. If you are going to become a humourist, and you have these fears, you must work out how to overcome them. My experience is that you just have to get up, do it, learn from it, and do it again.

It is only experience that makes you realise that you can cope with being the centre of attention. So, grab every opportunity to be in the limelight, wherever that might be. In particular, I found that the students most able to cope with public speaking fears were those who had had acting experience. If you can, join a local amateur dramatics society.

2) Get advice from an established public speaker

The actual fears that people have with regard to public speaking are:

Doing or saying something embarrassing; One's mind going blank; Being unable to continue talking; Saying foolish things or not making sense; Trembling, shaking or showing other signs of anxiety (Stein et al., 1996)

In my time I have observed hundreds of student presentations. It was normal for students to say they thought they'd appeared nervous, when in fact there was very little sign of this. So, even if you are nervous, it may not show too much. The key thing is to prepare what you have to say and practise it. Another little trick is to speak with someone else as a double act. This takes the pressure off you, and both of you can support each other.

Your task is to ask a good public speaker their tricks for appearing cool in the limelight. Here is one of mine: ABC-XYZ = *Always Before Communicating, Xamine Your Zip.*

3) Practice being a nice guy

If you have a job that routinely involves the embarrassment of others, work out ways you can be the *'nice guy'*. Routine embarrassment is probably most likely in the health service, when patients have to talk about difficult things, or display private parts:

A gynaecological oncologist:

'…when I come in the patient is already undressed from at least the way down and in the stirrups with a speculum sticking out of her vagina. And to have someone just walk in at that point can be really embarrassing. So, in introduction, I usually crack a joke about how this is a very awkward way to meet someone for the first time, just trying to ease the situation and make it less embarrassing for her.' (Francis et al., 1999)

4) Talk to someone about embarrassment as an ice-breaker

Today, I was in a cafe with my wife, and I told her all about this embarrassing section. I was hoping she would give me an example from her own experience and she mentioned a friend, who, when she was about 23, had to teach a group of 18 year-old boys. This friend couldn't stop blushing. So, I talked about blushing, well, gave a lecture really (it's a man thing). All of a sudden, a women sitting nearby, interrupted and said, *'that's fascinating.'* She then said, although she was about 70, that she still blushed a lot. She blamed her Catholic upbringing, which still filled her with feelings of guilt.

Well now, it seems quite likely that people are pretty interested in embarrassment. So, talking about such matters could be a great ice-breaker. Try it next time you meet a new person and you're searching for something to say which might be of mutual interest. If you reveal something embarrassing about yourself, you have trusted them with something about you, so they may well reciprocate. Openness begets openness.

If this is too risky you could use the following story, told by Michael Bentine, who was listening to a woman singer, auditioning on stage:

'Her voice was so awful that I turned to the man sitting beside me and remarked upon it. He replied very frostily, "That is my wife." Pink with confusion, I hastily stammered, "I didn't mean her voice was awful, only the song she was singing." To which he replied, "I wrote it." I slunk away.' (Miller, 1996)

This leads into a conversation about embarrassing things you could say to people: When introducing someone: *'And this is….???'* And, a reversal, *'Haven't I seen you somewhere before?'* *'Yes, I work at the V.D. clinic.'*

Group humour

'I don't want to belong to any club that will accept me as a member.'   (Groucho Marx)

Humour doesn't exist in a vacuum. It exists in a world where there are others, and, in particular, to the groups of which we can be members -- Book-clubs, bridge clubs, bowls clubs, Bingo clubs, Boys clubs, bike clubs, and Brownies, and that's just some of the Bs!

Groups may be short-lived or long-established. The humour, important to any group, will vary according to the group's longevity. Basically, a short-lived group will have more tentative and unsuccessful humour, whereas an established group is likely to be more comfortable with humour as routines, roles, and hierarchy have been established.

A humorist really has to understand the dynamics of groups in order that his/her humour is successful. Whereas established groups are fairly easy to cope with, the newly-formed group is much more difficult to master.

Taking newly formed groups first, Terrion & Ashforth (2002) give a fascinating account of the development of humour in a temporary group of Canadian police officers undergoing training. They argue that, *'humour provides a key mechanism for enacting a sense of community for group members.'*

Terrion & Ashforth concentrate on *'putdown humour'-'an attempt to derive amusement at the expense of something or someone.'* Initially, when introducing themselves to the group, individuals may engage in putdown of the self, e.g. *'I'm a goofy Newfie'* (Slang for a native of Newfoundland. *Newfies* are mocked by other Canadians). Such a putdown indicates that the person does not regard himself as superior to the others.

A week after the group had started, the humour turned to putdowns of external groups, e.g. the military. This helped establish a superior group identity. We are an *'us'*. The laughing together gave the *'appearance of unity'*, which became the *'reality of unity.'*

A key moment came fairly early on when the course director put down two group members. This *'signalled the legitimacy of friendly teasing and bantering'*. After this, there were more putdowns about people's backgrounds, traits and motives.

Superiority theory would suggest that the putdowns were intended to raise relative status. In interviews, however, group members claimed they were just *'gently poking fun'*. They were not trying to *'insult or hurt anyone'*.

Putdowns included people in. They indicated that someone was important enough to be teased. Indeed, the putdowns that produced most laughter were the ones aimed at the most popular, well-respected group members. Terrion & Ashforth make a telling point, *'It is ironic that one's inclusion in the group was signalled by acts that ostensibly excluded one.'* It was the less popular people who were less likely to be targets. This lack of attention indicated their lowly status.

Terrion & Ashforth conclude: *'Humor-particularly putdown humor-played a large role in melding* individuals into a group. As group members went through the progressive stages of putdown humor they tested, signalled and reinforced their growing trust and solidarity.'

Robinson & Smith-Lovin (2001) add to our understanding of the humour of the newly formed group. In their study of temporary groups they found that there were humour phases. Initially, there is a 'small flurry', which is relatively unsuccessful, then, a lull, later there is a revival of humorous interaction.

The humour used by group members has various functions according to Robinson & Smith-Lovin. When members jokingly contribute information about themselves, they are 'meaning-making', part of the development of a collective identity. Where members use superiority humour they are establishing a status order for their task activity. Finally, members use cohesion-oriented humour to support an emerging group identity.

Hovelynck & Peeten (2003) considered the humour development in adventure programmes for adults. They agree with Robinson & Smith-Lovin that, at the outset, there is 'a great deal of clowning and joking'. It is suggested that this is a coping mechanism, coping with the uncertainty of the situation.

Hovelynck & Peeten see humour as an indirect form of communication, a safe way to make contact. An unfortunate meaning can be neutralised as being, 'only a joke.' Foot & McCreaddie (2006) explain that this 'social probing' role of humour allows a topic to be introduced in a light hearted way, helping to probe, sensitively, the other's values and attitudes, as well as helping to reveal 'touchy' subjects. The response to the humour also indicates the degree of social acceptance.

As the group matures, Hovelynck and Peeten see the humour as something of a nuisance as its superficiality may interfere with learning, however, they do echo Foot & McCreaddie in that the humour tests the ground for more serious communication. Also, humour can recall previous matters under discussion, 'it reflects the jokers' continual processing and sense making...'

Not all new groups are about fun, but groups with a solemn task may still use humour and laughter to cope as a tension release with regard to the seriousness of their task. Keyton and Beck (2010) managed, legally, to get hold of the transcripts of an American jury, which was deliberating a verdict in a murder trial.

These researchers found that laughter, '...created a sort of buffer that releases the tension about the seriousness of the conversation.' Laughter also enabled this group to have an ambiguous space, allowing them to work out what to do next. It also allowed the jury members to signal shared understanding of the meaning of some information.

If we integrate the work of all these researchers we can sequence humour development in new groups, in a way similar to Bruce Tuckman's famous styling of group development: 'Forming', 'Storming', 'Norming', 'Performing'. I suggest : 'Hails', 'Flails', 'Assails', 'Pales', 'Exhales', 'Tales', 'Wassails', and 'Gales'

To explain, 'Hails' refers to the initial sallies, which may be self-deprecatory. These may 'Fail', just like chat-up lines, as no group culture of experience and trust has been established, but, they may succeed. Participants cannot be sure of the likely effectiveness of their attempts at humour as there is no established trust and mutual understanding. So, instead of *'Fails'*, I suggest *'Flails'*, a rather erratic thrashing about. There may then be conflict as status battles emerge, and humour is used to attack, or *'Assail'* the other. Also, group identity is furthered by attacking external groups.

Next, the task group engages in the work, and group norms develop. The humour here, *'Pales'*, indicating that the group has entered a serious phase, where tension is released via *'Exhales'*. As the group solidifies, jokes are made, ribbing occurs, *'Tales'* are told. In my experience, alcohol is consumed. This leads, invariably, as Freud (1991) pointed out, to *'A cheerful mood'*...'*the grown man once more becomes a child.'* The consequence of the *'Wassails'* and the group cohesion is, *'Gales'* of laughter.

Obviously, this will not be an invariable sequence. There may be a great deal of conflict and little constructive humour. The initial sequence may be more successful than expected. The group may fail at its task, which would be no laughing matter, more *'Wails'* than *'Gales.'* In this case, the sequence might be: *'Hail'*, *'Fail'*, *'Assail'*, *'Impale'*, *'Wail'*, *'Ail'*, *'Curtail'*. Alternatively, the group may fail to achieve its objective because it is having too much fun, and doesn't really enter a necessary serious phase: *'Hails'*, *'Gales'*, *'Gales'*, *'Gales'*, *'Fails'*.

In comparison, established groups do not have to go through the initial difficult stages of group development. Relative status is understood and a joking history established. Fine & De Soucey (2005) argue that a *'joking culture'* is established by each group, which contains a set of humorous references to which members can refer in interactions.

Fine & De Soucey make a very pertinent point that enables a distinction to be made between mature and immature groups. They consider that, a joker in a mature group, has both the *right* to joke and the authority to get *away* with the joke, something which is not necessarily granted to a joker in an immature group.

In a joking culture joking remarks build on each other (Fine & De Soucey, 2005). Holmes (2006) describes this process as jointly constructed or conjoint humour. Here, people are able to build on each other's humour as they understand what is appropriate, adding to the solidarity of the group. In the business world, this group joking may take place throughout a meeting, or, more likely, at the opening and closing sequences, and at points of change during the meeting (Holmes, 2000).

There might be all manner of jokes in a group, but there will be key jokes that are functional for the group in that they: smooth interaction; build cohesion; create norms of action, and set boundaries (Fine & De Soucey, 2005).

For example, the key jokes made by a cohesive group of 18 year-old Greek boys, studied by Archakis & Tsakona (2005), were *all* attacks on two kinds of targets -- those in authority over them, and other members of the group.

The authority figures included: parents, relatives, school teachers, school itself, priests, the Church generally, and the police. The boys also attacked fellow students not in their group, as well as themselves and other group members. The researchers concluded that, *"...the reinforcing-solidarity function of out-group targeting humor is gained via ridiculing the 'others'!"*

Gough and Edwards (1998) found that for a group of young British, working-class men, from

Manchester: *'...the main targets of such 'joking' abuse usually turn out to be absent 'others', notably women and gay men.'*

Here, the *'...most original, outlandish or controversial contributions generally securing the all-important big laughs.'*

Interestingly, although males engage in more other-deprecating humour than do women, the extent of such attacks diminishes with age (Greengross, 2008)

Boxer & Cortes-Conde (1997) analysed the teasing that takes place in established groups. They consider that there is a continuum, *'...that ranges from bonding to nipping to biting.'* A nip is a playful bite.

These researchers found that the maximum bonding occurred where women were talking about men. There was no nip or bite concerned. This teasing confirmed the closeness of the women and re-affirmed friendship.

Whilst all group members may contribute humour, certain individuals tend to set the humour tone of the group. For example, Holmes & Marra (2002) found that in the business meetings they studied, one confident, extroverted individual was responsible for much of the humour.

Duncan & Feisal (1989) studied 25 work groups, in various settings, and observed that a particular type, the *'solid citizen'*, was given special joking privileges. Such a person had power, but did not possess formal authority. He or she was socially close to the ordinary workers. The solid citizen could joke about group members without anyone taking offence, indeed, group members liked to be the target of his or her humour.

Duncan & Feisal reflect that, *'trust, respect,* and *friendship'*, are crucial considerations for where someone is positioned in group joking patterns. They conclude that, *'...joking plays a greater role in reflecting and illustrating an individual's status than it does in determining it.'*

When researching small groups of adults, Goodchilds (1959) found they contained two different polar types of humorists, the *sarcastic wits*, and the *clowning wits*. The sarcastic wits predominantly made biting, ridiculing jokes, whilst the clowns were primarily whimsical and silly.

The sarcastic wits were found to be *'unusually influential'*, but not well liked. Conversely, the clowns lacked influence, but were well liked.

Grotjahn (1981) considers that the wit is sadistic:

'Under the disguise of brilliance, charm and entertainment the wit...is a sadist at heart. He is sharp, quick, alert, cold, aggressive and hostile. He is inclined to murder his victims in thought.'

Although the wit and the clown are important for group humour, it is quite clear that the leader of the group is often more significant for the humorous nature of the group. Some leaders will act officiously and will not generate, or allow humour, *'This is a serious meeting.'* More usually, the leader will use humour for his or her strategic purposes, and subordinates will respond, conjointly, to the leader's humour.

The significance of the leader is confirmed by Graham (2010), who studied 5 leader-led, established work-groups, in a variety of establishments, e.g. a school, and a legal department. Graham analysed why people made humorous comments in these working groups. She found, amongst other things, that, with respect to humour,

'intentions to influence distinguished the leaders and a focus on the boss distinguished the team members…'

Graham agrees with previous studies that have shown that employees with the higher power status produce the most humour. In her case, the strategic purpose of the leader humour was,

'…a strong desire to build cohesion among team members…Leaders also wanted to change and influence their teams.'

A leader's humour could have *'multiple intentions'*. One boss used humour both to show that her committee wasn't too rigid, and to show she was likeable.

Comments made by a boss served as cues for employee humour more often than did comments made by peers. The subordinates would build on what the boss was saying. They would also use humour as a disguise to transmit negative feelings to the boss, such as dissatisfaction or criticism.

In contrast to opposition, politically astute subordinates used humour in an ingratiating way. Once the boss had laid the foundations for something humorous, employees could build on that foundation, cementing, rather than disaggregating.

Graham's major finding was that *'social sensitivity'* plays a much larger role in humour production, in group situations, than is recognised in the literature. People in work groups may well be sensitive to the feelings and thoughts of others, and that affects the type and timing of humour intervention that is made. Graham notes, *'Generally, participants sensed someone else's feelings, internalized them, and reacted accordingly.'* Obviously, this is more easily done in an established group as participants have a fair understanding of the personalities of others.

Schnurr (2009) focused on the humour, particularly the teasing, deployed by bosses in a variety of organisations. She came to the conclusion that leaders use humour differently in different organisations, in ways that are appropriate to the particular organisation.

In a large I.T. company where the owner was the manager, the teasing used was particularly challenging, *'biting'* teasing. Interestingly, the management team, where the teasing was observed, were all male. Schnurr observes that despite the display of power and challenging nature of the teasing, it reinforced in-group solidarity.

Schnurr found a softer style of teasing at a small company where members frequently interacted, and where the boss was female; a *'nipping'* style. This teasing is both collaborative and contestive. It allowed the boss to show herself as both an equal and a superior.

A *'bonding'* teasing style was found to be employed by a male team leader at another company, *Sitcom.* Here the team and leader went in for less challenging, less face-threatening humour, such as self-denigration. The leader presented himself as an equal.

So, clearly, managers can display different types of humour according to the style of management they operate. A manager keen to control is likely to use biting, aggressive humour. A manager who has a democratic ethos will tend to use a bonding, egalitarian humour. A manager who wishes to hide power will use bonding humour, with the back-up of biting teasing where it is thought necessary to show difference.

Finally, established groups vary their membership over time. People leave and people join. The newcomer is faced with a number of problems. He or she has to work out the ways in which the group operates and how to fit in. The humour of the group has to be mastered in order to be accepted. This takes time and a group may well indicate its eventual acceptance by including the newcomer in joking routines. Alternatively, the group may turn against the newcomer, exclude him or her from the joking, and make fun of them.

Spradey and Mann (1975) studied the joking relationships between waitresses and bartenders at an American bar. They found that new waitresses took some time before they got used to the standard offensive and insulting joking routines.

For example, *Denise*, when she first started, found it *'unnerving'* when she made a small mistake to be told, *'You bitches have no brains.'* Eventually, she became like the other waitresses and retorted with *'cutting remarks.'*

Heiss and Carmack (2012) studied the humour surrounding new entrants to a university counselling service in America. They found that humour was used by the veterans to help the newcomers make sense of the rules and expectations of the service.

The boss of the unit said, *'Teasing is a way to say "you're doing something wrong" without just saying it.'…'It's better not to get in someone's face too soon.'* Such joking was less aggressive and *'more socially acceptable.'*

Tracey, one of the veteran counsellors, explained her approach. She recalled that when she had joined she had been told off for wearing a hat and jeans. So, when she saw a newcomer wearing jeans she said:

'…"hey let's get coffee." Then downstairs (at the coffee shop) I joked about how 'professional' we like to think we are up here and had a laugh about how ridiculous my story was. I never said "don't do that!" That way she didn't have to feel like crap, you know? It was not our fault; it's theirs.'

Humorous ability/appreciation can speed the newcomer's transition into the group. Ryan, an intern managed this as follows:

'I will say one-liners. I can sit there and be quiet for twenty minutes then spout out a zinger. Someone said, "I just love being around you because you are so random. I never know what you are going to say." People in the office like me because I'm random.'

Michelle, a temporary receptionist used a funny video to gain acceptance:

'I saw this super funny youtube video. So I said, "come look at this." Then we watched it, and she died laughing. She came back with four other people. There we are. All laughing at the video I had found. Then we all went to lunch together. I think it's because now they think I'm funny or something

because they didn't talk to me before. '

Mallett and Wapshott (2014) give us an example of joking exclusion of a newcomer, and the creation of a butt for the attacks of the group:

'...a new member of staff at FinRec, Paolo, was frequently ridiculed for acting differently from the 'normal' work behaviours that were expected, such as when a colleague recounted a mocking story of her struggle to train him on various company processes. This was later expanded upon to include jokes about his accounting background and the difficulties of working with such 'geeks'. Other members shared their dislike, often failing to respond to Paolo's attempts at humour and making him the victim of humorous pranks such as altering the meticulously positioned settings on his office chair.'

Reflection

Humour is like an electric current for a group. It enlivens the members and supplies the group with power to galvanise its operation.

With a new group the connections have not been fully made, and so the humour can short-circuit. The group, may not, initially, fuse together. The rather frantic humour, often displayed at this stage, can indicate anxieties about the group and the individual's relation to it.

Appropriate humour takes time to establish. Eventually, through trial and error, a joking culture is achieved where roles are understood, teasing is established, and conjoint humour occurs. There is a comedy circuit.

People end up laughing at what the group laughs at. People attend to what in-group members are laughing at and join in. They find the humour of out-groups less funny. (Platow et al., 2005)

Key humorists emerge, including the wit and the clown. However, the focus in a formal group is on the boss who rather sets the tone for the type of humorous interactions which are allowed. The question is, does the boss's humour, bite, unite, or, is it terminal? Remember Ratner?

Activity

1) Work out some self-deprecating humour about yourself to use in a new-group situation.

For example, you can use the following joke by Arnold Brown as a cue joke:

'I enjoy using the comedy technique of self-deprecation, but I'm not very good at it.'

(Carr & Greeves, 2007)

2) Analyse what sort of humour underlies a meeting at work.

In particular, what sort of humour does the boss use? How do people react to the bosses humour? Is there a wit, a clown or a solid citizen? When does the humour take place? What does the boss do when a subordinate's joke is in fact an implied criticism?

3) Get hold of some photos of groups of people at work, and invite captions.

We had this at work once. My effort was in response to a photo of a colleague called Mike, who was greeting a Hungarian female academic at a hotel in Budapest:

Mike, Hotel, Whiskey, Romeo, Tango, Roger, Papa, Bravo.

4) Take a newcomer at your workplace and explain the way humour works round here.

Specify who likes to joke and who doesn't. Indicate what sort of humour is appreciated and what isn't. Tell him or her some key amusing stories from the past. Gauge his or her sense of humour and suggest how that could be used at work.

Youthful Teasing

Barack Obama recalls this incident from when he was 10 years old:

'Coretta's got a boyfriend! Why don't you kiss her, mister boyfriend?' 'I'm not her boyfriend!' I shouted...'Leave me alone!' I shouted again. And suddenly Coretta was running, faster and faster, until she disappeared from sight. Appreciative laughs rose around me.' (Obama, 2007)

This sort of barracking is par for the course for younger children. Both boys and girls, in early adolescence, use teasing to mock someone who mixes with the opposite sex. Thorne & Luria (1986) observe that children, *'...use heterosexual teasing to maintain and police boundaries between "the girls" and "the boys" defined as separate groups.'*

The charge that a boy or a girl *'likes'* someone, is hurled as an insult. In particular, linking someone with someone who has a *'pariah'* status, *'...suggests shared contamination and is an especially vicious tease.'* (Thorne & Luria, 1986)

Teasing, which covers a wide range of behaviours, is part of life. It goes on all the time: within families, when flirting, at work, in schools, and groups everywhere. It is especially important in the life of the young. It is the humour of the young.

The crucial distinction in teasing is whether it is to be regarded as fun or an aggressive act. With regard to fun, the key thing is that there are *markers* which show that the tease is playful. These *markers* include exaggerated facial expressions, hints, understatements, mimicry, etc. It is these *markers* which distinguish teasing from bullying. A direct provocation can escalate into hostility, so the teaser reduces the face-threat by adding the *markers* (Keltner et al., 2001).

Even with the *markers*, there is still an ambiguity about teasing. The target may have difficulty understanding the motives of the teaser. Is the teaser really joking or is he/she actually trying to ridicule? Further, the teaser can always claim that he/she was *'only kidding'*, even if there was actually malicious intent (Kowalski, 2000).

Kruger et al. (2006) studied teaser intent of university students, and the reaction of the students who had been teased. They found that there is indeed a perception mismatch. Whilst the teaser sees the tease as *'innocent and playful'*, the teased target tends to see the tease, *'as considerably more malicious.'* So, whilst teasers act, according to them, with the best of intentions, the teased doesn't necessarily see the tease in that light.

Friendship and trust affect the interpretation of the teaser's intent. For example, Jones and Newman (2005) found, in the American schools they studied, for 13 year old boys and girls, *'teasing by friends was interpreted with a more benevolent frame than that accorded to classmates.'* Indeed, Blatchford (1998) found that English schoolchildren were keen to say, at the ages of 11 and 16 that much teasing was not to be seen as hurtful, more, as everyday banter between friends.

Pichler (2006) studied the teasing within a group of 15-16 year old, British, working class, Bangladeshi girls. She found that teasing was a normal part of conversation, occurring once every 2.1 minutes. The girls used teasing for a variety of purposes: fun & bonding; release of underlying tensions about real issues; constructing toughness, and protection of face.

The teasing assisted the aim of *'having a laugh'* and enjoying a *'good time'*. This was the most important function of the teasing. It also allowed the release of tension, *'...in a relatively non-confrontational way.'* Teasing allowed the girls to show they were *'tough'*, and so claim status within their working class group.

We know more where we are with teasing when the group culture in which it takes place clearly recognises, *taking the piss* as the norm. This colloquial term means, *'...to use jocular abuse to deflate someone else's ego to bring them to the same level as others '*(Plester & Sayers, 2007).

There are other purposes for *taking the piss*. Apart from making a point about something serious, it can be a relief from boredom, and helps define group membership. You know you are an insider when people start insulting you in a jocular way. Established group members demonstrate trust when they can say anything about each other.

So, benevolent teasing is concerned with playfulness and bonding. Its opposite, aggressive teasing, is concerned with criticism, mockery and ostracism; a completely different cup of tease. It is a verbal form of bullying. A 2009 study of adolescent bullies and bullying in America (N=7182) found that, during the previous two months, respondents had been: physically bullied (20.8%); verbally bullied (53.6%); socially bullied (51.4%), and electronically bullied (13.6%). The verbal bullying was defined as, *'name-calling and teasing in a hurtful way.'* (Wang et al., 2009)

Children of all ages acknowledge the *'hurtful nature of teasing'* (Keltner et al., 2001). Scambler et al (1998) point out that childhood teasing is often simply aggressive, without, *'an attempt to soften the blow through humor.'* If any humour is involved it is for the benefit of onlookers. The enjoyment is in watching the embarrassment, and the power of inflicting mental pain on another, together with achieving audience appreciation.

Even if the teasing is painful, it may usefully serve so as to integrate people into a group, and is a necessary learning stage, and enforcement device for group norms to be understood and followed.

For instance, Keltner et al., (1998) studied American university fraternity members, who lived with each other. They found that the students, who had lived in the fraternity house for over two years, teased new arrivals with regard to status differences, and norm violations related to, *'personality, sex, and drugs'*. This teasing provided information to the new members about the group hierarchy and norms.

As Keltner et al.'s study indicates, it is higher status people who are the main teasers. For example, a study by Savin-Williams (1979) found that higher status boys were more likely to tease. Keltner et al. (1998) found that lower status teasers were more likely to refer to more positive attributes when teasing higher status people.

At school, teasing is, *'routinely directed toward the most disliked members of the class, such as those with learning difficulties, physical handicaps, or other differences'* (Lightner et al., 2000).

The type of teasing does vary with age. Scambler et al. (1998) found that for 8-11 year olds (N=113) the top tease topic was *'appearance or clothes'*, followed by, *'weird or age inappropriate behaviors'*, then came, *'Poor school performance'*, followed by teasing retaliation and, finally, *'Clumsiness or poor athletic ability.'*

Blatchford (1998) gives examples of appearance teasing at 11, and clothes teasing at 16:

'They take the micky out of your eyes, the way you speak...take the micky out of your teeth when they have gaps like me and say you have big ears.'

'Mainly what you look like, what you wear. You've got to have fashionable trainers. If you don't have 60 quid trainers then you're a tramp, you live in a doss.'

Wooten (2006) studied the ridicule/teasing surrounding clothes amongst a sample, consisting mainly of African American males (N=43). The respondents were aged 18-23, but were asked to recall the hazing about clothing in their adolescence.

Wooten found that adolescents use ridicule to exclude or admonish others who do not conform to clothing norms. The consequence being that the ridiculed youths disposed of the mocked items, and acquired the required.

When children start school they don't seem to tease too much, and girls and boys play together rather than tease. This mutuality soon collapses, and by the time they are 8 years old, boys distance themselves from girls, looking down on them. The boys teasing of girls, *'becomes a form of ridicule.'* The teasing process reinforces the process of gender homogenous group formation of the pre-teens (Voss, 1997).

Boys at 10/11 years of age, and possibly at other ages as well, may ridicule the scholastic endeavour and success of girls. Renold (2001) gives the example of two boys mocking a girl for reading a very long (400 page) novel, she is *'mad.'* Another boy looks at a girl's work and sneers, *'What is that?— My dog could do better than that...my dog's bum could do better than that.'*

At the age of 16 boys tease girls more than girls tease boys. The boys tease about: physical appearance; clothes; sexist abuse-'cows', 'tarts'; and ability. Girls tease boys about: physical appearance; clothes, and immaturity. Girls tease girls about supposed promiscuity (Blatchford, 1998).

Lees (1986) found that the commonest insult used by both sexes, with regard to girls, is *'slag'*. A problem for the girls with this word is that there is no male equivalent.

Debbie: *'One thing I noticed is that there are not many names you can call a boy. But if you call a girl a name, there's a load of them. You might make a dictionary of names you can call a girl.'*

How then do children cope, in practice, with teasing? Scambler et al (1998) did ask their 8-11 year old respondents to indicate their usual response to teasing. The most popular response was to, *'Ignore it or walk away'* (45%), followed by, *'Tease back'*(23%), then came, *'Tell an adult'* (10%), *'Laugh/turn it into a joke'* (10%) and *'Get upset/pout/cry'* (6%). Whilst younger children find the idea of a humorous response appealing, they find it difficult to produce an appropriate humorous response spontaneously, consequently, Scambler et al. (1998) suggest humour training workshops.

Finally, Feinberg (1996) provides some very useful advice for teasers:

- Save your teasing for people you know well so there is some way to predict their response.
- Try not to poke fun at any serious problems a person may have.
- Don't tease about things that a person cannot or would not want to change. Don't tease someone about their name or their height or weight.
- The safest thing to tease about is behaviour, e.g. hobbies.
- If the teased doesn't like it, stop.
- Unwanted sexual remarks are not teasing.
- People who are obsessive about being in control usually don't like being teased.
- If you must tease, give non-verbal hints that your verbal sting is meant in a playful fashion.
- If you dish it out, people will expect you to take it when your turn comes.
- If you can't take it, don't dish it out.

Reflection

Keltner et al. (1998) described teasing neatly, noting that, *'Teasing is paradoxical. Teasing criticises yet compliments, attacks, yet makes people close, humiliates yet expresses affection.'*

Teasing is either attacking or friendly ridicule that attempts to get others to conform to the requirements of the group or society. It can be an openly aggressive or a more muted message sent to put people in their place.

The humour in teasing resides in the embarrassment caused, and the consequent enjoyment for those looking on. There is also the possible amusing reciprocation to the tease.

People get teased for all sorts of reasons, but mainly because of some sort of difference from the main stream. This could be: appearance, ethnicity, intellectualism, sexual orientation, etc., etc.

Higher status people appropriate the right to tease. They peck at those lower in the order in order to display their position, and to enforce conformity to group norms. The pecked serve their time and repeat the process when they are in the ascendancy.

Activity

1) Classify the teasers in your life

Feinberg (1996) gives an extensive list of 27 different teasing personalities. Where would you classify yourself? Where would you classify important people in your life?

Firstly, there are the teasers who consider themselves superior and/or wish to display superiority. For example, *The Intellectual* tries to turn teasing into a fine art where he/she can demonstrate a gift for words and wit. *The Mocker* feels genuinely superior and uses the tease as a sport to elevate him/herself by putting others down. *The Big Bully* picks on a vulnerable scapegoat as an act of vengeance for being bullied in the past. *The Drill Sergeant* uses the tease to motivate others. *The Peter Pan* takes pride in inventive name-calling, and *The Strategist* allows a tease, and quickly responds in order to demonstrate control.

Then, there are the teasers who are inadequate in some way. *The Bug* is not very clever, and repeats the same unfunny, irritating teases. *The Attention Getter* uses the tease as a way of getting noticed. *The Ham* wants to be the centre of attention and elevates him or herself at the expense of others. *The Rug Puller* is a control freak, who envies the more poised, and tries to unsettle them. *The Mouse* is insecure, scared of the opposite sex, and uses teasing as a way of communicating. The *SideKick* urges the teaser on and criticises the teased. *The Little Guy or Gal* uses the tease to over compensate or overcome physical shortness.

Next, we have the teasers who fall into the Freudian camp. *The Spy* loves uncovering the vulnerabilities of others and exposes them via teasing. *The Sadist* enjoys, maliciously, inflicting pain through teases. *The Sarcazzer* uses sarcasm. *The Sexual Tease* and *The Flirt* use the tease to get sexual attention. *The Flirt* is more about attention whilst *The Sexual Tease* captivates. The *Roaster* hides behind teasing a significant other in order to avoid public displays of sentiment. Similarly, *The Homophobe* avoids emotional displays to another man, communicating by teasing.

Finally, we have the teasers who specialise in incongruity. *The Prankster* enjoys playing tricks on people and teasing them physically. *The Practical Joker* indulges in teasing as, *'a little play.'* *The Mimic* and *The Copycat* do what it says on the tin. *The Copycat* is particularly favoured by school children who enjoy copying others for long periods of time.

Feinberg does isolate two teasers types who fall into the friendly camp. *The Josher*, playfully, makes fun of himself and others. *'He is the funniest kind of tease.'* He/she can, however, be annoying. *The Game Player* is able to apologise and will stop teasing if requested, or if discomfort is observed.

Finally, there is *The Compulsive Tease* who is addicted to any number of the above types, and cannot control his or her teasing.

2) Devise a tease that a child could use where necessary

Georgson et al. (1999) suggest that parents and educators should arm children with one humorous response that could be used as a response in many teasing situations. Children's joke books contain possible responses. How about:

'What's the difference between school custard and the school bully? Well, they're both yellow, but the custard's only thick some of the time.' (Rainsford, 2000).

Or, *'You're just like a little sweet'. 'What?' 'A smallteaser'.*

Work out a general response for someone who teases a child you know. You know you can do better than, *'Sticks and stones will break my bones, but names will never hurt me.'*

Work out a response to someone who habitually teases you. That is, have your repartee prepared beforehand

Foot and McCreaddie (2006) make the following relevant observation about repartee, *'The only satisfactory way of parrying humour of which one is the target may be to retaliate with humour, but, too often, the moment is past and the opportunity lost.'* This is so true. How many times have we all said to ourselves, *'I wish I'd thought of that at the time.'?*

Professional comedians have prepared standard responses to hecklers, which you could use. For example, *'Isn't it a shame when cousins marry?'*; *'I remember my first pint'*; *'Never drink on an empty head.'* (Double, 2005).

Another method is to use ironic praise. How about, *'You're nearly as funny as Jim Davidson'*? Or, *'I've got just the job for you. Writing jokes for The Beano'*. Or, you can venture into the sarcastic…*'Shame you haven't got anything sharp-like a mind.'*

Nicknames

A theological student named Fiddle

Refused to accept his degree

'It is bad enough to be Fiddle,' he said,

'without being Fiddle D.D.' (Watkins, 2002)

There is an obvious connection between schoolchildren's nicknames and teasing. Nicknames are a resource used, to trigger, construct and sustain teasing (Lytra, 2003). Lytra observed pre-adolescent teasing routines where individuals are continually targeted. She found that referring to one's nickname, *'…frequently brought about some kind of game or chase or fighting.'*

Nicknames may be good or bad for the child involved. A study by Crozier & Dimmock (1999) found that primary school children disliked about half the nicknames they were given, with the girls reporting significantly more disliked names. The researchers' classified these nicknames into 6 categories: appearance-*ginger*; psychological attributes-*wally*; ethnic group-*blacky*; sexual-*scrubber*; animal-*cow*; name-*bones* (Jones). The majority of unkind nicknames referred to appearance, e.g. *'rubber nose*, and *'piano teeth.'*

Crozier & Dimmock (1999) did find that nicknames could be liked because they indicated friendship and inclusion. Such names were either abbreviations of names, or cute modification of names, e.g. Ingrid becomes *Ingipoo.*

Most nicknames at primary school age are based on some sort of word play on given names, whilst at senior school, physical appearance, and personal habits become dominant. About 40% of nicknames are transferred, with the children, from junior to senior school (Morgan et al., 1979).

The founder of the Scouting Movement, Robert Baden-Powell, had rather a good, albeit fairly obvious, nickname, based on his name, when he was at *Charterhouse* public school….*Bathing Towell* (Opie & Opie, 1973).

Nicknames, for adults, as Crozier (2002) found, can concentrate on a physical characteristic, like *Barrel* if you're rotund, or *Wiggy* if you wear a toupee, or *Disney* if you have a disfiguring wart. Crozier notes a teacher with a mole in his forehead was called *Malteser*, not a bad tease.

A short name will have a Y added, *Besty, Smithy, Crouchy,* etc. Hopefully you won't have Bull as your surname. If you have a long name, then it is likely to be abbreviated, e.g., *lamps* for Lampard.

Dr. Spooner, of Spoonerism, fame, was nicknamed, *'The Spoo'* (Hayter, 1977). A reversal nickname might have been better in his error prone case, that is, *'Oops'*. Of course, this turns *Spoonerisms* into *Oopserisms*, which is a shaft of wit.

Then, there are the witticisms, Tew becomes *Tulip*, Winter becomes *Frosty*, etc. Two or more stages may be involved in a witty construction, e.g. Underwood to *Underwear* to *Y-Front* (Morgan et al, 1979; Crozier, 2002).

Crozier (2002) argues that the cleverness or wittiness of an insulting nickname is an important contribution to its success, and longevity. Alliteration and rhyme are an aid in the wit, e.g., *Thunder Thighs, Death Breath,* and *Miller the Killer.*

There is a distinct gender dimension to nicknames. Males are more likely to coin nicknames and use them. These names tend to reflect traditional masculine qualities like strength and hardness. Female nicknames are more likely to be affectionate, rather than critical or humorous. They tend to concern traditional feminine qualities like beauty, kindness and goodness. Such female nicknames are more likely to be used within the family, whilst male nicknames are for public display (de Klerk & Bosch, 1996; Phillips, 1990).

Morgan et al. (1979) make sociological sense of the nicknaming process within groups. A nickname marks off a group, e.g. *The Sharks* and *The Jets* in *West Side Story*. Member nicknames denote *'People and non-People'*. If you don't get a nickname you don't count, you are an outsider. Conversely, if no nicknames are the rule, the rejected do get a nickname. Scapegoats are given pejorative nicknames.

The nickname may indicate relative status within the group. Fine (1979) analysed the culture of some American children's baseball teams. He found that lowly status was accorded a dismissive name, whilst, with time, and given a gain in expertise, the original name disappeared, and a status enhancing nickname emerged. So, for example, *Maniac* changed into *Main Eye*. The best players ended up with superlative nicknames, marking their status, such as *Superstar* and *Strike out King*.

Nicknames are part of the subversion process in hierarchies. In schools, student use of nicknames for teachers gives students a sense of superiority, by reducing the teacher's dignity (Woods 1990a). Once a nickname has been devised unlikely activities, often sexual, are imagined for the teacher, making him or her, ludicrous.

Morgan et al. (1979) confirm that most student devised nicknames for teachers are, *'rather nasty.'* They found the following in the two schools they studied: *Bare Bum; Cow Pat; Feeble,* and *Lemonlegs*. Popular teachers were referred to by first name, or by an affectionate nickname. Uninteresting teachers just got called by their surname.

When I was at school, we christened a teacher with the name *Bo Bo*. This stood for two lots of B.O. Which I suppose was better than being called *Puddles*.

In his research, Crozier (2002) found that, *'...the more negatively they (teachers) are viewed, the more hurtful the nickname is thought to be.'* Indeed, one of Crozier's respondents made a telling point, *'He was so horrible and embarrassed students so he needed a nickname.'* The horrible need a label.

Fortado (1998) studied nicknames in work situations and suggests that nicknames for managers, such as *Tweedle Dumb* and *Tweedle Dumber,* are an integral part of the subversion process. A target needs to be named, before being attacked, and indeed, as part of that attack.

Such nicknames can be cruel and even slanderous. Take the nickname of one female manager, *Hal's gal*. This woman had been promoted by *Hal* and was seen as a favourite without merit. The nickname also suggested sexual impropriety, indicating, in this case, the female manager's way of climbing the greasy pole.

Stromberg & Karlsson (2009) found that workers, who packed meat in a Swedish factory, only had abusive nicknames for their bosses. One was called *The Shadow*, because he was never there. Another was called *The Rooster*. This nickname came from a Swedish film, and indicated the manager's inability to control workers, particularly the older females.

And finally, if you choose to be called by your nickname, e.g. Kathy, instead of Katherine, then you will be seen as: cheerful, friendly, playful, with a good sense of humour. If you opt for your official name, then you have a better chance of being seen as intelligent, reliable, trustworthy and successful (Mehrabian & Piercy, 1993). So, nicknames for plebs, full names for celebs.

Reflection

Nicknames can be, affectionate, funny, unpleasant, or non-existent. Once acquired, nicknames can be difficult to shake-off, and follow the possessor down the years. This is particularly the case where the name is witty and apt.

Nicknames are status indicators. They can indicate popularity, increases in popularity, and group inclusion, or, they can demonstrate unpopularity, and ostracism.

For children, a nickname can emphasise that which makes him or her different. Children's nicknames can be painful for their possessors as they are a constituent element of the teasing/bullying process. They rather belie the old adage, *Sticks and stones may break my bones, but names will never hurt me.*

Activity

1) Describe a person

Think about a person and work out a way of describing them in a phrase or sentence. A good one from the world of marketing is from Henry Ford, *'Any customer can have a car painted any colour that he wants so long as it is black.'* This sums up his attitude to customers when cars were scarce.

I've come up with a few of my own:

Isaac Newton—*'Gave gravity its comeuppance.'*

Mrs Thatcher—*'Where there is harmony, let there be discord.'*

Tony Blair—*'A just war or just a war?*

Gordon Brown—*'Bloody Bankers', 'Bloody Blair', 'Bloody Nose'.*

David Dimbleby – *'Like father like son.'*

2) Use a one or two syllable word to describe another person:

John Major—Minor

Lord Sugar—Sour

Brian Blessed—Shout

Lord Archer—Out

Lord Prescott—Nowt

Leslie Ash – Pout (Sorry Leslie, once you get on a roll you just can't stop)

These one word descriptions can give you the essence of the person. With luck, they allow you to move on to a nickname. The best one here is *Lord Sour*, or maybe, *Lord Sweet and Sour.*

3) Make up meld puns on people's names

For example:

Lord Unimpressedscott

Geoff Buffhoon

Simon Cowellnighimpossible

Michael why don't you Gove?

One way to do this is to go to http://thesaurus.com and find relevant synonyms. For example, synonyms for idiot include imbecile, which gives us: *Jimbecile Callaghan; Kimbecile Kardashian; Timbecile Cahill.*

4) Construct puns on politicians' names

For example:

Theresa Mayday

5) Which letter of the alphabet needs to be added to the name *Sid Marx* to produce a pleasing nickname?

K

6) Develop a second order nickname

The nickname of the head of Ofsted, Sir Michael Wilshaw, was *'the sergeant-Major,'* when he was a headmaster (Griffiths, 2014). This is an OK nickname, but it lacks wit. Develop a second order nickname, based on the idea of a stern military officer, which has a mocking ring to it.

For example, Sergeant-Major *'Shut-Up'* Williams was a star of the comedy series, *'It ain't half hot mum.'* Luckily for us, Wilshaw and Williams are very similar names, so, we have Sergeant-Major

Michael *Shut-up* Wilshaw, or just plain *old shut-up*. Of course, *Shut-up* is easily corrupted into a third order nickname.

7) Work out a deflating nickname

The ex-head of the BNP, Nick Griffin, has been called various things, which are usually not complimentary. There is one very good nickname for Nick, and that is *Adolf Brent*. The evil of the first name is cancelled out by the ludicrous nature of the second name, inspired by Ricky Gervaise and *The Office*.

Work out similar nicknames, where the first name evokes negativity, and the second name deflates, or vice versa. Let's do it with football managers, starting with Jose Mourinho. This modest gent actually wants his self-chosen nickname to change from *The Special One* to *The Only One* (Anon, 2012)

My first attempt is *Pretensiosolo*. The Portugese for 'cocky' is *pretensioso*, and we have a meld pun with solo; the cocky one. But, this doesn't quite follow the rules of the game. *'You're solo vain'* came next, then, finally, *The Peacock Roach* – the vain beetle. *The Peacock Eyed* works as well.

Work-place Banter

'As a stay at home mum (for now anyway!) I really miss the staffroom banter of my old school: swearing, sexual innuendo, the odd piece of gossip. The good thing was that everyone joined in and was comfortable with it...even the oldies who had been there for years loved it and we used to have such a giggle.' (community.tes.co.uk)

So, when the school kids rush off to their play-time, their teachers rush off to their play-time, in the staff room. They go and banter.

Banter includes: *'irony, wordplay, argument, cynicism, mock aggression, teasing, and indirectness. It excludes things that make people uncomfortable: 'emotion, soppiness, earnestness and clarity.'* (Fox, 2005).

Banter is a very popular form of interaction for workers everywhere as it helps meet so many people's social needs. There are six main functions of banter:

- making a point
- boredom busting
- socialization
- celebrating differences
- displaying the culture
- high-lighting and defining status   Plester & Sayers (2007)

Plester & Sayers found, in New Zealand I.T. companies, that workers ping-pong banter back and forth in a type of mirth competition. The most common form of banter is jocular abuse--teasing.

Take this interesting case of teasing of a man returning to work after an operation for testicular cancer:

'...a colleague mimicked his new body shape, walking round and round in circles, pretending to be lopsided. This man found this "quite funny," and he said he preferred it if someone "took the mickey" instead of offering sympathy.'

The man pointed out that his, *'...predominantly male colleagues joked about his condition at every opportunity, as a means of having "office fun." '*

Another man with the same condition had this story:

'I have a very nice group of friends, all of whom delight in taking the piss...the cards I was getting...And one stands out...it was just simply entitled on the front, "Sorry for the loss of your loved one." ' (Chapple & Ziebland, 2007)

Chapple & Zieband (2007) consider the importance of banter for these men returning to work after a serious operation. Essentially, jokes reassured the men they were being treated as *'normal'*, that they hadn't been relegated to an outsider role because of their condition.

It seems that banter is employed by equals. Plester & Sayers found that, *'higher status was an inhibiting factor in banter use.'* Higher status people have to be more careful of offending others. Of course, higher status people do banter with each other.

Banter occurs most readily between people who are popular and are, *'fully socialized into the organizational culture.'* However, those who are outside the in-group may find the banter to be, *'painful, exclusionary and even insulting.'* (Plester and Sayers, 2007)

Banter, technically, involves the construction of a *'play frame'*. Here, *'speakers collaborate in the construction of talk in a way that resembles group musical activity, particularly jazz.'* The collaborative talk relies on in-group knowledge and familiarity, particularly obvious where standing jokes are used (Coates, 2007).

Laughter is a cue for a play frame to start. Once the frame is established, laughter signals continued involvement and presence in the playful collaboration. People are present but do not necessarily have to speak all the time.

Let's look at how banter works in practice in various work situations, starting with teacher staff-rooms, which I know well. In practice, the play frame banter extent and quality must vary from staffroom to staffroom. At one extreme is an ideal type of happy collaborative talk, at the other is the unhappy, divided staffroom.

Jarzabkowski (2002) gives an example of a happy banter staffroom, in a primary school in Australia, with about 20 staff, and relatively low turnover. The researcher observed staffroom interaction and noted, *'There were numerous occasions when laughter rang out.'* The staff talked about a wide range of things, including: current affairs, students and their families, and teachers' families.

The school principal made pertinent comments about tension release:

'When the teachers get together, and the staffroom is a bit of an example of this, I think they're more or less inclined to let it go....They're unloading all this stuff that's happened in the classroom and having a laugh, because it's the laughing that diffuses it. Then they can go out again feeling a little bit more refreshed for having had a colleague sit beside them to listen to all these stupid things that have happened in the classroom...' (Jarzabkowski, 2002)

Not all staff rooms are so happy. Paechter (2004) indicates that they tend, in practice, to subdivide into factions based on: gender; age; status, or subject. It seems that science teachers tend to isolate themselves. There is normally an all-female group-*'the knitting circle'*. Male P.E. teachers spend their time talking loudly about sport. Male old timers may indulge in sexist banter and put-downs of women.

There may well be set seating positions based on subject, and hierarchical position. Rogers (2006) recounts the following:

'...when I first started as woodwork teacher, I came into the staff room, my first day, and this senior teacher came over to me—I'd sat down—and she'd said, pointing in a supercilious way, to some chairs in the far corner of the staff room: "The woodwork teachers sit over there."

*'Larger schools may have more than one staffroom. This arrangement acts so as to divide staff, as

particular groups may colonise particular staffrooms, and, in the larger school, this is likely to be by specialist subject area of teaching (Delamont & Galton, 1986).

There may be isolates, new-comers, temporary staff, the disliked, etc. Woods (1979) indicates that there may be a fifth column, which identifies more with the hierarchy, than with the staff. They may not take kindly to some of the humour, particularly where it subverts the organisation.

Just like the school kids the teachers may go too far in their teasing and sexual joking. For example:

'I blush easily and some people seem to like having a laugh at my expense, Do you think that a staff room, which is a shared arena, is an appropriate place for sexually crude banter?, The trouble is I find their humour upsetting,...you learn to bite your lip at the sexual innuendo diverted your way...' (community.tes.co.uk).

Cunnison (1989) found that gender joking was a *'fairly common sport'* in the comprehensive school staffrooms she studied. This joking usually referred to women's appearance and, *'conventional ideas about gender and femininity.'* Cunnison argues that this joking drew attention to female teachers being *women* teachers not just teachers.

Cunnison sees an ulterior purpose in this gender teasing, to imply, *'lesser competence and lesser commitment to the job.'* Acceptance of this viewpoint would assist men in the promotion race within the school. So, the men's put-down jokes suggested that women belonged at home and not at work, *'Women are only fit for breeding.' 'It's all right for you...But I'm in it for life. You can get out at any time.'*

To respond to this male control and subordination women could choose between: silence; playing along with the joke, or deliberately challenging the stereotype. Cunnison considers that in a male dominated staffroom it is difficult for a woman to respond effectively, leaving her with the safer, silence default position. The consequence of this silence being implied consent to the gender joking.

Staffroom teasing may be designed to correct behaviour which is seen as unacceptable. Woods (1979) found, at *Lowfield* school that, the following deviant behaviours were punished: exceeding one's authority; boasting, toadying or *'shopping'*, and professional incompetence.

Teachers may be discussed in their absence. Delamont & Galton (1986) recount the amusement of the staff at *Guy Mannering* school when they were discussing the elderly RE master. This teacher took to wearing plus fours during cold weather, and, when he retired, there was mirth when some pupils refused to contribute to his leaving present.

The staffroom is the place where teachers engage in subversion with regard to senior staff. Woods (1984) observed that, *'...much staffroom humour takes the form of mocking, embarrassment, or compromise of senior personnel, often by subversive ironies.'*

Woods give one example that caused continuing mirth for staff. The head-teacher, in assembly, had directed students as follows, *'When you get to the gym, you must go straight on, you must not fork off to the dining-room.'*

Such *faux pas* give vindictive delight. They also enable a levelling of status. With time they become the stuff of legend, and are regarded with a certain fondness (Woods, 1984).

Some staff rooms are not nice places. Some are, '...*poisoned by rivalry, jealousy and suspicion...*' (Nias, 1989):

'*Working (in that school) was very hard because the atmosphere in the staffroom was so unpleasant. It was fine in the classroom, but you had nowhere to go and unwind.*' (Nias, 1989)

Biott & Easen (1994) found that 16 out of 87 student teachers on placement felt excluded from, or unwelcome in the staffroom (many of the others felt welcomed). These students observed conflicts in the staffroom. The most amusing was: '*There was some fighting about who should put the kettle on. It went on for six weeks.*'

Staff can be abusive towards each other in staff rooms and elsewhere. One of my earliest experiences of this was when relationships between two lecturers got so bad, that they were only allowed to communicate with each other via the college's vice-principal. Ben-Peretz (1991) relates a case in a staff room where a teacher said she was, '...*fed up with working. I'm ready to retire, and help bring up my own grandchildren.*' A school executive, who was present, retorted, '*The students will happily agree with you.*'

Woods (1984a) found that such unfortunate episodes are more likely at times of tension in the school year, notably at around examination time. A tide of misery swamps the staffroom, and the staffroom becomes an unhappy place.

Ben-Peretz et al. give another insight as to why staffrooms may be pleasant or unpleasant places. They studied the '*teachers' lounge*' in 19 Israeli schools, surveying 409 teachers. They suggest that high achievement schools constitute a positive workplace with more social interactions. A low achievement school might have more stressed interactions, and there might be greater teacher burn-out.

In addition, a successful school is likely to be able to attract teachers, and have relatively low staff turnover, leading to longer term trusting relationships. A failing school is likely to have higher staff turnover, with consequent negative implications for relationships and morale.

So, the school staffroom is a very important place for teachers. It provides their main opportunity to interact with other adults, and, particularly, via banter, to let off steam. The humour enables teachers to cope with problems that assail them in the classroom (Woods, 1983). If the staffroom is an unhappy place it doesn't allow the important function of tension release to occur. A staffroom must be a laugh-room. Pollard (1987) indicates that teachers are aware that they need a co-operative atmosphere, so they deliberately avoid contentious topics, such as politics and religion. Instead, they stick to '*innocuous*' topics such as, holidays, family, and television programmes. This assists in-group feeling.

The staff-room is the place where teachers have a chance to get things off their chest. And, from the sound of it, the place where male teachers wish their female colleagues would do just that!

The school staff room is a relatively genteel middle class place, where banter doesn't usually get too raunchy, however, the banter on a factory shop-floor is a different kettle of fish.

In a classic study of joking relationships in a Glasgow printing factory, Sykes (1966) found that:

'The joking relationships between old and young men, and those between old men and old women were very similar. People in these grades exchanged a great deal of obscene banter and, in addition, persons in all these categories did normally talk together seriously on matters concerning the work, trade union activities, etc.'

Sykes considered that the most significant joking relationship was between the young women and the old and the young men. The exchanges between the old men and the young women consisted '...almost entirely of exchanges of obscene banter and equally obscene horseplay...almost anything could be said as a joke without causing offence.'

The conversations between the young men and young women were conducted '...almost entirely in terms of the joking relationship,' in this case no obscenity was permitted. The young men would make suggestive remarks and the young women would pretend to be shocked or not understand.

Sykes made use of the thoughts of Alfred Radcliffe-Brown (1881-1955), a noted anthropologist. Radcliffe-Brown developed the idea of 'joking relationship' amongst kin. In a symmetrical joking relationship both sides are permitted to tease or make fun of the other (in an asymmetrical joking relationship only one person can tease). The joking is not meant to be taken seriously.

The function of the joking relationship is to maintain, 'a stable system of social behaviour'. It is particularly used to stabilise relationships which are potentially dodgy, e.g. mother-in-law and son-in-law (Radcliffe-Brown, 1940).

Collinson (1988) studied the humour used by the male shop-floor workers of a lorry factory in North-West England. He found that the 'spontaneous and cutting creativity of shop-floor banter' was a resistance to the repetitive work and the way the factory was organised. There was a desire to make the best of a bad situation:

'Some days it feels like a fortnight. A few years ago I got into a rut. I had to stop myself getting bored so I increased the number of pranks at work.'

It was important to these workers to 'have a laff.' Indeed, they saw themselves as a 'community of comedians.' Naturally, as part of this system, each worker acquired a nickname. 'Electric Lips' was unable to keep secrets. 'Pot Harry', had, 30 years earlier, dropped and broken all the drinking 'pots,' when he was a tea-boy. 'Silver Sleeve' didn't use a handkerchief. Others had names like: 'Fat Rat; 'Big Lemon' and 'The Snake'. 'Yo-yo' acquired his nickname because of his habit of leaving and returning to the same conversation. His record was fifteen times.

The belief was that, '...only "real men" would be able to laugh at themselves by accepting highly insulting nicknames.' Men had to be able to give and take a joke, '...to laugh at oneself and expect others to respond likewise to cutting remarks.':

'You've got to give it or go under. It's a form of survival, you insult first before you get one back. The more you get embarrassed, the more they do it, so you have to fight back. It can hurt deep down, although you don't show it.'

The men portrayed themselves as powerful and sexually insatiable. By contrast, women were '...dismissed as passive, dependent and only interested in catching a man.'

Collinson describes something of a shop-floor jungle, where workers were waiting to pounce on the weaknesses of others, in order to *'wind them up.'* Practical jokes *'sounded out'* victims to see if they could *'stand'* the attack. For example, an amateur weight lifter was conned into trying to lift someone who was actually fixed to a duckboard, on which they were both standing.

Sometimes victims couldn't cope with the various pranks and verbal assaults, and would *'snap'*. This *'Snapping'* occurred when someone's barriers had been broken down. One guy who couldn't cope was called *'Billy Snap.'*

Young newcomers to the group were particular targets. One apprentice had to sing Christmas carols to the group. Others were sent off for a *'long stand.'* Larks like these are traditional initiation rituals.

There was a control element to the banter. Workers who were thought to not be pulling their weight were subject to *'piss-takes.'* (Interestingly, the classic inter-war study of worker behaviour, at the *Hawthorne* works of the *Western Electric Company* in Chicago, found that workers who worked *too* hard were subject to abuse. The rate busters were given names like *Phar Lap*, a famous race horse. They had pranks played on them, like having metal nuts put in their coffee, and they were subject to minor physical attacks.)

The lorry factory's shop floor working class banter was seen as superior to the politeness of the more middle class offices, as it had, *'...uninhibited swearing, mutual ridicule, displays of sexuality and "pranks." '* :

'You can have a load of fun on the shop-floor, but in the offices they're not the type to have a laff and a joke. You can't say "you fucking twat!" in the offices.'

Management were, obviously, a target of attacks. They were seen as being unable to make decisions, as *'yes men'* and effeminate. There was particular mirth when the three foremen were not informed of a course in communication skills they were supposed to attend.

Male bantering on the shop-floor can obviously be quite a harsh business, full of insult and veiled attack. It contrasts quite strongly with female shop-floor bantering, which appears to be friendlier in nature, as might be predicted. Indeed, in the next example, of female factory workers, there...*'was almost no humour...aimed at testing the ability of workers to take a joke.'*

Marek Korczynski (2011) worked in a West Midlands factory, *MacTells*, which made blinds. This factory employed a mainly female workforce. The jobs were low-skilled and seen as *'monotonous and demeaning.'* : *'For many, the key redeeming factors in their working lives at MacTells were the friendships and community among their co-workers...Banter and having a laugh were key social lubricants underpinning the strong bonds of community.'*

The workers created a bright mood, a *'stayin'* alive culture in order to help them survive. This revolved around the radio music that was played and the need to *'have a laugh.'* To have a laugh, the workers would play with the words and acts of work, routine humour, and then might move that humour into the absurd, routine absurdity.

So, a worker sang a fabric order to the tune of *La Vida Loca*, which was playing on the radio. Two workers, who were carrying barrels, when walking past each other, would pretend to joust. A worker, Angela, made cuckoo sounds every so often. She was pretending to be a cuckoo clock.

There was person-related humour, independent of work. Football is the classic here. At *MacTells*, Katie was a fervent fan of a local team, and when they lost, *'...many colleagues would come up and ask her, with a smile, how her team had done on Saturday. This would often lead to some development of humorous banter.'*

Supervisors and managers were not part of the banter network. Hierarchy was mocked, using irony and mimicry. Sheila says, *'Hey come on, get your 25 an hour.'* A reference to the official output target. This sort of humour was concerned with the ridiculousness of the workplace.

Banter allows workers to cope with their situation. It allows some detachment from the fray. A particular group of workers who use banter to detach and defend themselves, are female prostitutes. Teela Sanders (2004) studied sex workers in a large British city and concluded that:

'...women who sell sex manage their work, in particular their relationships with clients and each other, through joking relations.'

Sanders found that these workers most commonly used humour to ridicule clients. They also sent coded jokes to each other in front of clients. Their stories were full of jest. Overall, their bantering signalled group membership.

The prostitutes ridiculed the *'...clients' physiological features, sexual performance and fantasies...Private jokes are derogatory, offensive in content and aim to ridicule the client behind his back.'*

The male was seen as weak, controlled by basic desires, whilst the female was strong and in control. The men were seen as *'cunning, selfish and perverted.'*

In a group situation, like a sauna, the women would swap jokes with each other that were not understood by the clients. To do this, they would usually use hand signals and facial distortions. The workers would laugh at their clients' antics, and find ways for the other women to observe what was going on:

'On one occasion, the service was delayed while the worker calmed down from laughing after returning to the room to find the man had swapped his suit for a Santa Claus outfit!'

Clearly, this story, together with jokes about Father Christmas coming early, would be part of the anecdote fund that the women would swap. Their stories, according to Sanders, typically focussed on work rather than private life. The anecdotes helped create, *'...solidarity and a mutual sense of community.* Group life in saunas and brothels is not all fun. The women did use humour to attack each other, and to get disliked women to leave the establishment. Those who were not accepted into the group were excluded from the banter.

Overall, the banter helped the women turn their challenging work into something more bearable:

'When you are laughing it doesn't feel like such a daunting job when we have a giggle about the clients.'

It does seem that workers' clients can be seen as an enemy. Joking about them unites the insiders, and makes them superior. Take the clients of an American child protection agency:

'...adult clients more than any other group of people were referred to in a disrespectful manner. They were called "lunatics," "mentally challenged," "horse faced," and "ugly". In general, adult clients were considered inept. This made them prime targets for the subject of joking, teasing and name calling.' (Gunning, 2001)

There is a particular problem for those joining established groups, who are in some sort of minority position. They may not be allowed into the banter, or they may become the subject of banter. Here is how one woman coped with working on a construction site:

'There is so much leg-pulling on site. They (the men) are always larking around, telling jokes and taking the mickey. When I joined the team I think they expected me to be prim and proper but I thought, well, I'll just muck in and be one of them. They soon learned I can tell jokes with the best of them.' (Watts, 2007)

Watts explains that it is important to show that you are a 'good bloke'. So, women, keen to succeed, find they have to fit in to the majority culture, rather than attempt to change it.

These professional women actually got their real comfort from exchanging office gossip with the female secretarial staff in the offices:

'This amusing gossip is not intended to harm or ensnare but rather to create shared identity, is a coping strategy for female engineers and secretarial support staff (almost exclusively female) who are part of the "lower" power order.'

Watts (2007) had another interesting finding and that concerned the difference between office and construction site humour:

'Sarcasm, banter, mocking and irony are the dominant (and, some would argue, more "civilized") humour tools of the office, whereas joke telling (often using crude language), mimicry and comic innuendo are the most common forms on the construction site.'

Plester (2009) studied office banter in four private sector organisations in New Zealand. She found that:

In a law firm, a formal company, the humour was 'cautious and constrained'. As one secretary put it, 'We don't have terribly rude jokes here.' In an I.T. security firm there were, 'few humour boundaries'. The tone was set by the Managing Director, who was 'an enthusiastic joker.' 'The male staff compete to display the most outrageous and potentially offensive forms of humour that they can find.'

In an insurance provider, 'Fun is encouraged.' A male analyst said that, 'People are fairly careful with inappropriate humour...people understand that they don't want to put people out too much so they are reasonably careful.'

In an electricity/gas supplier, 'Humour is careful, appropriate and unlikely to offend others.' The female HR Manager observed, *'We haven't got destructive humour and if we do see destructive humour (such as sarcasm) we point it out and it is not going to be positively received.'*

So, there was a clear difference between the formal organisations and the new informal upstart dot.com company:

'In the careful professional culture of the three more formal companies, few practical jokes or physical humour were recorded. In these three workplaces, shared humour was constrained and very few profane, lewd or racial humour references were observed. At these companies humour forms included mainly mild banter, while fun activities centred on company arranged events such as managers in fairy wings or Friday drinks and pizza sessions.'

At the dot.com company, humour was *'...sexual, racist, and sexist.'* This was in line with the company's rebellious image.

Reflection

Bantering is a key characteristic of working groups. Everybody seems to do it, however the nature of the bantering varies according to a number of factors. Males and females have radically different bantering styles, which reflect their differing senses of humour. Shop floor humour can be pretty crude, but it is not impossible to find offices which are similar. Shop floor humour is a way of coping with boredom, whilst middle class banter may be a form of stress relief. Technology changes the nature of work and this affects interaction and the extent to which banter can take place. Indeed, the computerised office has led to computerised banter.

Banter includes people in, and excludes people out. If you are in a banter network you are an established group member. You are trusted. If you are outside a banter network, you don't count. You may be a new-comer, and people are not sure about you yet. You may have done something to annoy the group, and so you are not rewarded with the bonus of banter. You may be a superior, not really trusted, and definitely not one of us.

Really, work-place bantering is a super skill, involving a collection of skills. These skills have been developed elsewhere in this book. For example: nickname creation; teasing; joking, wind-ups, and practical joking. To be a good banterer you have to be competent at these various skills, and understand when it is appropriate to use them in the group situation.

Activity

A) Just for fun think up some amusing answers to the following bantering problems:

You have been appointed to your first teaching post at an *'outstanding school'*. By happy coincidence, the head-teacher happens to be your uncle.

He has asked you to let him know what is going on in the staff-room. He suggests that you don't mention that you are his niece, and that it may be best not to mention that you got a third in Media Studies from an ex-Poly. He says you can mention that you were *Miss Southend*.

Suggested answers are below.

1) At break on your first day you go into the staffroom and are soon surrounded by male teachers eager to assist. You let slip you are from Essex. They seem to think this is funny. One asks *'What is your favourite teaching position?'* What do you reply?
2) You see two teachers playing darts. The dartboard has a picture of your uncle in the middle. What do you do?
3) One of the male teachers says it's a traditional initiation ritual for new staff to kiss all staff of the opposing gender. What do you say?
4) You discover that your uncle's nickname is *Goebbels* because he has no balls. What do you do?
5) There is a member of the *Socialist Worker's Party* on the staff. He is Scottish. He says something to you, which you cannot understand. It may have been, *'I want you to join the Union'*, or, *'I want to have union'*. What do you do?
6) A female, unmarried member of staff, of a certain age, tells you that you wear too much make-up. She adds that, *'This is a school and not a bordello'*. What do you say?
7) A male member of staff starts telling a particularly dirty joke. He forgets the ending. In fact, you know the ending, which is rather graphic. What do you do?
8) A male member of staff tells you that it is your job to make the tea for the next month. What do you say?
9) There is an on-going joke, whenever your uncle's name is mentioned everyone pretends to be sick. Do you join in?
10) A keen, female member of staff starts talking to you about the theory of learning. What do you do?

The answers are: 1) 'Innuendo' 2) Work out if they are rivals for your promotion, if so, inform on them 3) 'I'm bisexual' 4) Laugh 5) Excuse yourself saying, 'I must rush I have the Trots' 6) 'I'm not used to hearing such tart comments' 7) Smile inwardly 8) 'I'm not your tea-bag-lady' 9) Of course, he is quite repulsive 10) Yawn

B) How would you classify the banter at your workplace? Why is it like it is? Does the banter vary by department/section

Duptrix

(*The Office*. Tim, as a joke, has encased Gareth's stapler inside a wobbly jelly)

Gareth: *'Tim's put my stapler inside a jelly again. That's the third time he's done it. It wasn't even funny the first time.'*

David Brent: *'Why has he done that?'*

Gareth: *'I told him once that I didn't like jelly. I don't trust the way it moves.'*

David Brent: *'Yeah. You showed him a weakness-he pounces. You should know about that.'* (www.imdb.com)

The 'humour' in practical joking is termed *schadenfreude*. This German word has been borrowed by the English to describe, *'the enjoyment obtained from the misfortune of others'* (Titze, 2009). If someone successfully plays a practical joke on us we lose self-esteem and social esteem, and they get to enjoy our misfortune, and laugh germanically.

We obviously enjoy tricking each other and we seem to spend a lot of time doing it, as Frankie Boyle puts it: In Britain, *'...everyone has a Ph. D. in wind-ups.'* (Boyle, 2012)

This section, then, is about the tricks we play on each other in the name of fun. I have invented the word *'duptrix'* to cover all the ways in which we attempt to dupe each other, verbally and non-verbally. *Duptrix* includes: hoaxes, practical jokes, leg-pulls, wind-ups, and tall stories.

Let's start with the hoax: *'Got a phone call today to do a gig at a fire station. Went along and turned out it was a bloody hoax.'* (Adrian Poynton)

That sort of hoax, calling out the emergency services, for no valid reason, isn't funny. Indeed, hoaxes, normally, are not presented as being funny. They are usually deliberate lies, claimed to be true, which are intended to dupe others. Hoaxes tend to be rather complex and large-scale. If the hoax is successful, the victim is unaware of being deceived, at least for some time.

Where hoaxes are amusing it is for the perpetrator's benefit, indicating his or her skill at hoodwinking others. Observers may join in the mirth.

Classic hoaxes include: the discovery, in Sussex, of the *Missing Link* between apes and humans, known as *Piltdown Man*; the photographing of the *Loch Ness* monster, and the creation of *Crop Circles*.

The absolutely classic funny hoax was perpetrated by a celebrated wit, *Theodore Hook*, in 1809. He bet a friend that he could make any house in London the most talked about place in the city. They chose a house in *Berners Street*, owned by a *Mrs Tottenham*. *Hook* went to great lengths to win his bet.

Hook and his friend rented a house opposite *Mrs Tottenham's* and watched an amazing saga unfold. All sorts of things and people began to arrive. There were 13 chimney sweeps, carts of coal and furniture, and a coffin. This was followed by custom made wedding cakes and 2,500 raspberry tarts. A chamber organ and 12 pianos turned up.

Next, more people began to arrive. There were several doctors, lawyers, gardeners, fishmongers, dentists, grocers, priests, carpet makers, wig makers, coach makers, opticians, brewers and shoemakers, etc.

Then, the dignitaries rolled up. *The Governor of the Bank of England, The Archbishop of Canterbury, The Mayor of London, The Lord Chief Justice*, several cabinet ministers and the *Chairman of the East India Company.*

The roads around *Berners Street* became jammed with crowds and people delivering things. *Hook* won his bet, which was for a guinea! (Hiskey, 2011)

The Ban Dihydrogen Monoxide campaign is a nice written hoax, which is unusual in that it uses the truth. Here, this substance, also known as hydric acid, is claimed to be extremely dangerous as it: is a major component of acid rain, causes death by drowning, and corrodes many metals.

Here is one hoax I participated in when I was about 17. Three mates were in the know about a classic rigged game of cards, and the fourth mate wasn't. He hadn't read *Moonraker,* the *Ian Fleming* novel. In *Moonraker, James Bond* manages to win every card in a game of bridge despite the fact that he has a rubbish hand with just one ace and one queen. The villain, *Drax*, has three aces, four kings, two queens and two jacks. *Bond's* victory depended on him being able to trump all the high cards.

We never told Martin that he'd been hoaxed. Indeed, every now and again we would enjoy referring to that amazing bridge hand he'd 'mucked' up so badly! So, Martin, if you're reading this, you now know what happened!! You got dealt the hand of *Drax*. Incidentally, *Ian Fleming* simply used a game of cards known as the *Cumberland hand*, so called because the son of *George 111* had been duped out of £20,000 with the exact same trick (www.bridgehands.com).

The best examples of written hoaxes are to be found in national newspapers on *April Fools' Day*. Actually, I am writing this on April 1st and the press have had their usual fun, for example, *The Independent* had Ronaldo, the footballer, being sold by Portugal to Spain for 160million euros in order to reduce their national debt, and *The Mirror* had the coalition government taxing fresh air.

In the modern era newspaper hoaxing really got going with a type-face spoof by *The Guardian* in 1977, when they published a seven page special report, about *San Seriffe*, a mythical archipelago in the Indian Ocean. *San Seriffe* was described as semi-colon shaped, with a capital city called *Bodoni*. There were two main islands, *Upper and Lower Caisse*. Prior to this gem, the classic media spoof was a *Panorama* item in 1957, about spaghetti farming in Switzerland (Smith, 2009).

Moving on, a practical joke is one where the initiator sets up a playful trick, and, the victim, by his/her embarrassed/confused/angry reaction, provides the punch-line, much to the amusement of the initiator, but not, initially, at least, the victim.

There has to be a victim. So, the following prank, for example, does not qualify as a practical joke. Students, in Portsmouth, painted footsteps from *Queen Victoria's* statue to the nearby public conveniences. As there was no victim to react, this was just street art—funny graffiti.

Unlike a hoax, the practical joke victim finds out that the prank is meant as a joke, and he or she can be pretty sure who set up the joke. A key thing about a practical joke is that it involves physical objects or action. For example:

Buster Keaton, the American silent comedy film star, helped out a friend who had a problem with passers-by, uninvited, using his outside toilet. *Keaton* attached spring hinges to each of the wooden walls. Then, he buried a pipe under the outhouse from which a clothesline emerged. This line went to the kitchen window and was pulled when an intruder was using the toilet. The tug led to the collapse of the four walls, leaving the interloper revealed in all his glory (McPherson, 2004).

The most macabre practical joke I have ever come across is the *'revival of the dead'* joke, carried out at Irish wakes, in the first half of the twentieth century (Harlow, 1997). This joke was achieved by binding the corpse, and then, when an unsuspecting audience was present, the binding was cut. The corpse would spring up, like a jack-in-the-coffin. This must have been a pretty scary apparition, but a neat way to incorporate the corpse into the ritual; a farewell performance.

I have had a go at classifying the various types of practical joke. There are so many possibilities that I do not claim that I have covered every type.

The most popular type of practical joke seems to be *additions.* A simple addition is something like putting confetti in a closed umbrella, filling a room with balloons/newspaper, or covering a toilet with cling film. I particularly like this one, adding black plastic bags, in regular lines, to a White Horse carved out of the British hillside, so as to create a zebra effect. An addition can also be an adulteration like spiking a drink with laxative, putting dye in shampoo, or putting itching powder on toilet paper.

- *Addition and subtraction* – This is a fiendishly clever joke. First, a victim is given something that subsequently increases in size, by the surreptitious regular addition of bigger items. Then, smaller and smaller items are substituted, much to the consternation of the victim. The item could be a plant or animal. It can even be petrol for a victim keen on m.p.g. calculations.
- *Attachment* – Putting glue on a chair, gluing plates to a table.
- *Covering* – Plastering a car with tin-foil, or a desk with post-it notes.
- *Defacing* – Supplying dirty-face soap, or painting someone, who is sleeping, with makeup.
- *Diverting* – Here, people do not end up where they want to be, for example, by the prankster using traffic cones to redirect drivers to where they started.
- *D.I.Y* – Here, the victim triggers some dire effect, when they open a drawer or door or move something. A concealed string attached to the drawer causes glitter or some such to be released from the ceiling. A door can have small balls trapped on it, so that when the door is opened, the victim is showered with the balls. The classic is to perch a bucket of water on top of a door.
- *Double-duping* – Getting someone to help you measure something with some rope. They hold one end, and you give the other end to another dupe around a corner.
- *Embarrassing* – Here, at the simplest level, embarrassing body noises are elicited via whoopee cushions or fart powder. More complicated embarrassments include distributing someone's telephone number as a male or female escort, and ringing *The Jeremy Kyle Show*

and telling them about the victim's incestuous family. Tape a pornographic picture such that a public speaker reveals it at an inopportune moment.

- *Emissions* – Arranging things so that an object emits noises when it shouldn't, for example, by rigging the brakes of a car so that when the victim brakes, music starts playing.
- *Excluding* – Arranging things so that someone cannot access their room, by, for example, making skis fall down internally. A variation is to tie two adjoining doors together, so people cannot get out
- *Explosions* -- Potato on a car exhaust, exploding golf balls.
- *Greed Appeal* – Gluing a coin to the pavement, or tying a £5 note to a string. Leave trashy books around with an inscription, *'Please return to X for a £10 reward.'*
- *Hide and seek* – Needed items, such as bath towels, clothing, and school bags, disappear. A more sophisticated deprivation is where fake bailiffs take away someone's belongings. Ransom notes can be sent in such cases.
- *Idle Threatening* – Promising to carry out a big prank on someone, then doing nothing.
- *Incapacitating* -- Getting someone to balance a full beer glass on each hand, then leaving them. Tape a drunk to a bed. Handcuff someone, usually naked, to a post.
- *Machining* – Adjusting a computer, telephone, or any machine so it doesn't do what it is supposed to do.
- *Manipulating* – Using the power of suggestion to get someone to do something odd, for example, looking interested when a teacher is on the left side of a class-room, and looking bored when he/she is on the right.
- *Out of place* – A car and it seems usually to be a car, but can be animals, is somehow transferred to an unconventional setting, such as an office or onto a building.
- *Prankster Pretence* – Here, someone pretends to be injured or killed, for example by sticking a toe in a vacuum cleaner and putting ketchup on it, or pretending to be electrocuted/stabbed. There is also pretending to be consuming bodily waste, using apple juice, chocolate, or vegetable salad. These are unusual cases in that the prankster appears, initially, to be the victim.
- *Pyrotechnics* – Lighting shoe laces. Pointing a laser at someone's face
- *Removing* – Putting furniture outside, or digging out sand from under a towel on a beach.
- *Revenge* – There is often an escalation with practical jokes, with the victim subsequently becoming the joker. Also, a prankster can get revenge on someone who has treated them unfairly by using a practical joke. For example, a schoolboy filling a satchel with heavy weights which a teacher couldn't move. This was revenge for the teacher throwing his satchel out of the window.
- *Scaring* – Expose the victim to scary items such as fake spiders, mice or snakes. Real animals can be used as well. A man who had cut off a finger was presented with a matchbox inside of which was a finger on a bed of red cotton wool. When he touched it, it moved, as it was the prankster's.
- *Smelling* – Hiding something that will start to produce a bad smell, e.g. fish, cheese, meat.
- *Substituting* -- Putting cheap things in expensive wrappings, for example, by substituting *Marmite* for chocolate or cold gravy for tea, etc. Also, things are changed around, such as the keys on a computer keyboard, times on clocks, or the men/women signs on public toilets.

- *White elephant* – Here, a victim is provided with something that is totally redundant such as a hair brush for bald men, or dead Christmas trees, after Christmas.

That is quite a list, and it's far from complete. Just as there are a great variety of practical jokes, there are many reasons for playing a practical joke on someone. Whilst some pranks are benign, others are more malign in nature.

If we look at school-kids pranks first we find four main motives with regard to playing a joke *on* a teacher: *celebrating; rebelling, misbehaving,* and *atmosphere making.* (Meeus & Mahieu, 2009) *'Celebrating'* is concerned with the last days of term. *'Rebelling'* is about revenge on an over-strict teacher. *'Misbehaving'* is related to classes where the teacher fails to keep order. When *'atmosphere making'*, students think the joke will be fun for both them and the teacher.

When school-children play jokes on *each other* they do so for two contradictory reasons. Firstly, they are played to reinforce friendships, and secondly, to show dislike for certain people.

Sanford & Eder (1984) found that practical jokes between school-children often involve the taking of food or property, and, either hiding it, or destroying it. Between friends it can amount to flattery, as the *'victim'* becomes the centre of attention. However, a disliked butt can be attacked. For example, one student brought an Easter egg for each of her other group members. These eggs were hard-boiled, however poor *Nancy*, the disliked, got an egg, which, when cracked, left raw egg all over her hand.

As with so much humour, the practical joke is two-faced, and the victim has to work out if he/she is the Janus, or the anus of the prank. Is it friendly teasing, or, is he/she the butt of aggressive, exclusionary humour?

Sharkey et al (2001) carried out a major study to discover the reasons why people intentionally embarrassed others, which of course, is the aim of much teasing and practical joking. They found four main reasons: show solidarity/socialisation; negative sanctioning; establish power relations, and self-satisfaction.

- Show solidarity/socialisation

For group fun
For socialisation into a group or organisation
Retaliation
To show solidarity with the group
To look better in the eyes of others
To be one of the crowd
To get a laugh from others
To make the embarrassee the centre of attention
To make a time memorable
To make a person feel important
To honour the person

- Negative sanctioning
To get a person to follow rules
To teach a lesson

To punish

- Establish/maintain power relations

To take control

- Self-satisfaction

The aim here is to cause a reaction in another for the sole purpose of satisfying one's self.

Whatever your motivation, it is important to recognise that practical jokes and hoaxes can go seriously wrong. You need to think carefully beforehand of any major problems, and tailor or curtail the joke accordingly. Here is what you need to avoid, according to advice taken from, Voices.yahoo.com:

- Practical jokes in formal or inappropriate settings

Write *'Help'* on the groom's left shoe and *'Me'* on the bottom of the right shoe. (ahajokes.com)

Pranks that could lead to illness or medical problems:

A man in America called his ex-wife and told her to come over as he had something to show her. When she arrived she found him hanging by a noose from a tree. She contacted the fire brigade who cut him down (he had been supported by a concealed harness.)

The man ended up with a $1,000 fine and a year in jail for falsely reporting an incident.
(www.listverse.com)

- Practical jokes or hoaxes that lead to property damage or legal action

Substantial damages for *'humiliation and mental suffering'* were awarded in an American legal case, *Nickerson v Hodges*. Here, the practical jokers duped their victims into believing there was a pot of gold buried on their land. Digging commenced and went on for some time, but nothing was found. Eventually a 'planted' pot was located. This was opened with much ceremony, in front of a crowd, but all it contained was worthless stones. (Anon., 1920)

It is not very sensible to involve the police in pranks as they may well charge you with wasting their time or worse. Back in 1964 some students were very lucky to get away, without charge, with a mock bank robbery in *Welwyn Garden City*. This was despite the fact that 300 police were called to assist in apprehending the *'thieves'* (Osborough, 1965).

- Jokes that play on people's beliefs or something that they feel strongly about, or, simply, go too far in their cruelty.

A student in a night school class had fallen asleep, so the teacher decided to play a prank on said student. The teacher told the other students to scream loudly at the count of three. He turned off the lights and counted to three. The sleeping student awoke in a panic and the watchers had a *'good'* laugh. Significantly, *'the sleeping student did not attend another class'* (Powers, 2005).

Some people feel strongly about practical jokes, seeing them as childish or cruel. So, only jape those who are likely to accept the joke, which probably means men rather than women:

Samantha H.—'I absolutely detest practical jokes of any kind played on anyone. They're not funny, they're cruel and humiliating and a form of bullying. Even as a young child I wanted to slap some sense into the likes of Jeremy Beadle.' (www.netmums.com)

Be very careful about religious beliefs and dietary restrictions:

'I was making chicken liver pate one day, and a waitress (a vegetarian) came over very excited with a big spoon, asking to try my chocolate mousse. The squeal was ear piercing...' (www.forums.egullet.org)

A work colleague of *Charlotte P.* told her this far too cruel story:

This work colleague had 3 jobs and worked so hard that he got just 4 hours sleep a night. He had to do this as he had built up big debts after his business had folded.

The previous weekend his parents and brothers had given him a lottery ticket. Together they sat down to watch the lottery draw, however they were, in fact, watching a tape of an earlier draw. The lottery ticket he had been given had the winning numbers from that draw. So, it appeared that he had won £3million. *'He said he was screaming, his wife was screaming, and the kids were in tears thinking their problems were over, then the family burst out laughing.'* Hmmm. (www.netmums.com)

- Situations that could lead to injury or worse.

'Six of us went to opposite corners of an intersection after the bars closed. When we saw a car coming we pretended we were playing tug-a-war across the intersection. When the cars slammed on the brakes we ran. It was hilarious. Stupid people should have noticed there was no rope we were all pretending.' (www.forums.plentyof fish.com)

A paramedic persuaded a new employee at a mortuary to get into the body lockers. When he got in the *'corpse'* next to him said, *'bloody cold in here mate'*. The new employee jumped up so fast he broke his nose. (www.netmums.com)

Of course, the joke may eventually be on you if you are a serial practical joker. You can cry wolf too many times, so that when you do need help, people ignore you as they think you are joking. For example, the comic Tommy Cooper collapsed and died on stage and the audience though it was just part of his act.

Tommy Cooper was quite a wind up merchant, pretending he couldn't do magic tricks, but eventually succeeding. We now move on to consider wind ups and leg pulls. These are *verbal* jokes, which are intended to dupe the victim, usually into believing something which is not, in fact, true. Whereas the leg pull is intended for friendly amusement, the wind up is intended to provoke some reaction. The more mild and friendly the joke, the more likely it is to be a leg pull. The more complicated and the more malicious the tease is, the more likely it is to be a wind up.

A wind up merchant (WUM) is someone who consistently engages in wind ups, and *taking the piss*. Indeed, so much so that their constant disruptions can become irritating and annoying. WUM has become internet slang for someone who tries to cause as much disruption as possible by goading others.

One of the most long-lasting leg pulls may be, *'your shoe lace is undone'*. Opie & Opie (1973) consider this simple trick has been played by children since at least 1795, when the call was, *'Sir, if you please, your shoe's unbuckled.'*

Adults go for slightly more sophisticated leg pulls, for example:

Maureen Lipman tells a tale where a friend of hers got *'his sweet old mum'* to read out a list of words as a party game. The list was: *whale, oil, beef and hooked...* (Lipman, 2010)

Richard Whiteley, long-time host of *Countdown*, and lover of bad puns, once left a message for a news programme researcher: *'Please ring Mr C. Lyon, who has an interesting story.'* She did ring the number, which was for Knaresborough Zoo! (Apanowicz, 2006)

The comedian Eddie Grey would stroll down a busy street and suddenly stop in front of a Post Office letter box. He would then listen at the narrow opening of the box. When a sufficient size crowd had gathered, he would say into the slot, *'But how did you get in there in the first place?'* (Nordern, 2008)

New comers to organisations often get their legs pulled in standard ways. They are commonly asked to obtain an impossible item, such as: *elbow grease, a long weight, a sky hook, a bucket of steam, tartan paint*, etc.

The next examples get more complicated to set up, take longer, and/or have a more malicious element, so are closer to being wind ups.

A woman, a budding artist, asked her husband for an easel for her birthday. He came home, 'I've been to the pet shop and ordered the weasel. They are really expensive but dead cute and I'm really excited.' She didn't want to tell him about his 'mistake' for fear of hurting his feelings. He milked it for a fortnight, until her birthday came around...pricing up cages, rearranging furniture, getting a book on breeding. Needless to say, she loved her easel. Eventually. (www.singletrackworld)

The writer, Jack Rosenthal, set up his mother-in-law, Zelma, at a swanky London restaurant, *Elena's Etoile*. In secret, Jack had informed the restaurant owner about Zelma's friends in Hull. So, when Zelma was leaving the restaurant, the owner asked about her friends. Zelma was astounded that the owner knew Miriam Bennett and Jean Abraham. Then the owner mentioned another friend, *'And Dora Green, how is she? Still on the game?'* (Lipman, 2010)

Tommy Cooper would pay taxi drivers by giving the fare and then stuffing a tea bag into the driver's top pocket. He would tell them, *'Have a drink on me.'* (Sykes, 2005) (You could see this one as a leg pull, but a taxi driver does expect a proper tip. Cooper was notoriously tight-fisted, so this was his way of avoiding payment, admittedly in a humorous way.)

Spike Milligan sent the following telegram to his pal Peter Sellars: *'Please ignore first telegram.'* A few hours later Peter Sellars phoned Spike's secretary: *'What was in the first telegram?'* The answer was: *'There wasn't one.'* *'Bastard'*, gasped Sellars. (Farnes, 2004)

Clearly, the dividing line between a leg pull and a wind up is rather vague. A leg pull can morph into a wind-up as a prank unravels.

You should have been there when I teased a new member of staff who had once been a student of mine. We had to agree a mark for a Master's Dissertation. *'So'*, I said, *'What mark have you got?'* She said, *'I think it's a distinction.'* I started to laugh. She looked confused and crestfallen. I said, *'It's a fail.'* She said, *'But, it meets all the criteria.'* I said, *'They've been changed, didn't you know?'* This tease went on for a bit until I finally conceded that it was clearly a distinction. Always after that if we had joint marking to do, she made sure I announced my grading first.

So funny, you had to have been there. We really laughed, well I laughed more than her, quite a lot more in fact. Well, I was teasing her into the group culture. It is the duty of the older, more experienced male to initiate tenderfoots. It was a rite of passage; a mark of initiation.

Something similar happened at a Christmas dinner I went to recently. I found myself sitting next to a woman I did not know. We ended up talking about a lady who was the life and soul of the party. *'She wears a wig.'* I said. *'No she doesn't, does she?'* came the response. The quavering was an entry into the world of wind-up. *'Oh yes, everyone knows that. It's a bit of a joke.'* *'Oh, I didn't, must be a very good wig.'* *'Oh yes, she gets her hair sent from virgins in Croatia.'* *'Really, but I know she goes to the hairdresser to get it cut.'* *'That's an old trick,'* I said. *'She's got two wigs, one long and one short.'* *'Oh.'* At this point the woman I was talking went off to check... I got told off!!

Finally, we need to look at the tall story, which is a massive lie told to deceive and/or to entertain others. This sort of humour has been around for a long time, at least since 1700. In the coffee houses of the day, men used to tell such *'improbabilities.'*:

'One affirmed that he had seen a cabbage so big, that five hundred men on horseback might stand under its shade. And I for my part, says another, have seen a caldron so wide, that three hundred men wrought therein, each distant from the other twenty yards. Then the cabbage-lyer ask'd him. "For what use was that caldron?" Says he, "To boil your cabbage in."' (Loveman, 2008)

The jest books of the day tell us of such lying contests where the aim was, *'...to tell the most extravagant lie without having it rejected by the company.'*

It is more than likely that *Jonathan Swift* got the basic idea for *Gulliver's Travels* from these *'improbabilities.'* Swift used to spend a lot of time in the coffee houses and may well have read or heard this one, which appeared in *Ned Ward's* periodical, *The Weekly Comedy*, 1699:

'...a mysterious land has been discovered off Ireland...the land is populated by a diminutive race of Tom Thumbs and a mighty Gyant.'

Nowadays, it is the Americans who really go in for tall-story telling, although we mustn't forget the BBC TV programme, *Would I Lie to You?*, which is great-great-great grandson of the coffee house jest.

In America they have liars' contests. Each state's stories tend to focus on what is produced there and the exaggeration is a proud boast about that state's abilities. Texas is known as the *Home of the Whopper*. (Neile, undated)

Potatoes grow bigger in Idaho than anywhere else. Once a greenhorn asked me for a hundred pounds of potatoes. I set him straight real fast. I don't believe in cutting into one of my potatoes. 'You buy the whole potato, or you take your business elsewhere,' I told him. (www.americanfolklore.net)

Of course, these tall tales lend themselves to sexual bragging. Here, a New Yorker competes with an Alaskan:

A swimmer loses the race when he sees a beautiful woman on the riverside, and his erection anchors him to the riverbed. 'Why didn't you turn over and float?' he is asked. 'What would I have done when I came to Brooklyn Bridge?'

'You call that big? Why once in Alaska I took out my jock to piss, got thinking of my gal, and couldn't get it back in my pants. It was so cold up there in Alaska I had to rub it with snow to keep it from freezing, and what I couldn't reach with my hands I threw snowballs at!' (Legman, 2006)

Reflection

Duptrix cover the spoken and physical tricks we play on each other.

The hoax, a word derived from the magic words *hocus pocus* can be sinister because it is often a serious attempt to deceive. Hoaxes can be enduring. They are still looking for the *Loch Ness* monster. And, they can be amusing. It is particularly funny when a group gang up to dupe one of its members, especially when the victim doesn't even know he's been fooled.

The thing about practical jokes is that there are so many different types. So much imagination has been devoted to finding ways to trick our nearest and dearest. Despite this, many practical jokes are pretty basic because their simplicity appeals to the young, who are probably the main practical jokers. However, more sophisticated pranks can be found.

Practical jokes can be used to include or exclude. They can make people heroes or zeros. The main aim of the prankster, however, is probably to embarrass, so that the 'superior' joker shames the duped 'inferior.' They are also used to teach people a lesson and as a retribution for a previous prank.

Practical jokes can go wrong. In the worst cases there can be serious injury, property damage or legal action. Jokers can be far too insensitive, lacking respect for someone's core values or precarious mental situation.

Leg pulls and wind ups are like verbal practical jokes. We mostly use leg pulls with children. As mild teasers, we play on their gullibility. Leg pulls are particularly used to initiate new recruits, who feel they have to obey any seemingly legitimate request.

Wind ups are more adult, more complicated and potentially more annoying. *Wind up merchant* is not really such a great title to acquire as people will not trust you completely. They are never quite sure where they are with you.

Finally, the tall story doesn't really feel British, despite *Gulliver's Travels* and all that. Although you can find the tall story in Britain, its real home seems to be the land of the Big, America, for they go in for over-statement, and we go in for under-statement. Some tall tales are clever, but for the most part they are just too big for their 1000 gallon hats.

Activity

1) Produce a tall story

It is best if this relates to your local area, and stresses the quality, strength or size of what is produced there. So, this could be the enormous rhubarb in Yorkshire, the excessively strong cider of Somerset, the magnetising beauty of the women of Nottingham, etc., etc. You might like this one as a cue:

'I caught a fish a while back, a lovely brown trout, down at the lake. I didn't throw it back, or eat it. I kept it as a pet. I called it Brownie and got quite attached. He seemed to recognise me and got quite excited when I got home from work. Anyway, I decided to teach him to walk, which was ok, although he couldn't manage stairs that well. The problem was that Brownie died when I gave him swimming lessons.'   (adapted from Neile, undated)

The secret for getting away with these is to keep a straight face, and show that you really believe in what happened. Do not laugh with the audience. Start with something true, or that could be true, such as *'I have a dog...'* Add in ordinary common place details. Speak in short sentences, with pauses. Go for a major, impossible exaggeration—size, abilities, strength. Make comical comparisons, this includes making animals appear human. (Neile, undated)

2) Play an April Fools' joke

Here is an April Fools' joke, for school teachers to play on their local, rival school. Two teachers are needed for this one, as well as a swanky car. Some bravado is also useful. The joke is that the two teachers pretend to be *Ofsted* inspectors carrying out an unannounced inspection. This is because 'irregularities' have come to light.

The fake inspectors ask to see lessons in progress, and attend three. This allows a useful pre-punch-line tension to build up in the whole school. During the third lesson the imposters sneer, stop the lesson, and ask to see the head-teacher in the school car park, as a matter of great urgency.

As the head-teacher approaches, the imposters shake their heads slowly in a weary fashion. Grim visages, at this stage, add further to the tension. The head is handed a very well-sealed envelope and the imposters make their get-away. A further accomplice is on hand to film the head's reaction when he/she opens the envelope, and out pops, April Fool!

Experience indicates that this prank cannot be repeated the following year, however, an elaboration is to bribe the rival school's administrators to find out the date of the next official *Ofsted* inspection.

On that day, the local police are telephoned and informed as to where the gang, which has been impersonating *Ofsted* inspectors, can be found.

Although the first part of this *Ofsted* jape is original, the second part isn't. It derives from a classic student rag stunt where students told workers, digging up the road, that some students would be coming along, dressed as policeman. They would ask the workers what they were doing. Then, the students telephoned the police and told them that some students, dressed as workers, were digging up the road for a lark.

3) Best man duptrix

Here we have two ideas for any potential *best men* out there. The first one needs care and may not be appropriate for the actual wedding ceremony, but could be modified and fitted into the speech, as a telegram, that the *best man* reads out by 'mistake.'

At the important part of the wedding where the priest asks if *'...anyone knows why these two persons might not be joined together in holy matrimony...*get an actress, who appears to be heavily pregnant, to stand up and say, *'Oh never mind, I'll just call my lawyer.'* (www.ahajokes.com)

At the reception, tell the female guests that, because the groom is now married, they need to return the keys which they have for the groom's house. Previously, you will have given keys to several willing accomplices. Crown the drama with a man coming up with his key, and giving a kiss on the groom's cheek.

This is a pretty good gag, but probably fairly well known. Its style is particularly useful for a nervous *best man* as it takes the pressure off him, and has the added benefit of involving the audience. So, take this as a cue and develop it. For example, audience members could bring up a piece of paper on which is written an embarrassing reminiscence concerning the groom's behaviour. The *best man* reads them out.

4) Create an April Fool's Day hoax

This should be submitted for publication to a newspaper of your choice. It would be best to research the many hoaxes which have already been published, for example, by going to: www.museumofhoaxes.com

Many of these seem to be tall stories such as talking creatures, machines that control the weather, and flying men. There are the impossible like powdered water, and true revelations about the private life of *Sherlock Holmes*. There are amazing events to be held on the day, such as climbing up and down a church in 20 minutes. Here, the aim is to get people to attend. There are the remotely plausible, such as the sale of a national treasure, like the *Eiffel Tower* to *Disneyland*, and a Norwegian wine surplus. These seem to be the best bet as the reader cannot be entirely sure if he or she is being duped. The others are too obvious.

5) Create an addition and subtraction practical joke.

This could involve a present for a loved one. Get three ornaments/dolls/plants/necklaces, etc., which are identical apart from being different sizes. Substitute the smaller for the larger and vice versa. Switching clothing could be particularly effective for someone who has just started a diet.

6) Create a white elephant/substitution practical joke

The victim could be someone who is leaving your workplace. For the white elephant, concentrate on a characteristic like baldness or beardiness. For the substitution, think of something the leaver might really like but cannot afford, like a top of the range smart phone, and present them with a well wrapped toy version.

Part 6: Negative humour

Humour is a double-edged sword. It can uplift and it can cut-down. This final section on negative humour, then, is concerned with the many ways in which negative humour can impale and fail, causing the audience to quail and wail.

We start by looking at superiority humour. The notion that we enjoy feeling superior, by observing and contributing to the misfortunes of others, dates back to the ancient Greeks. It seems that many of us are status-seekers, upgrading ourselves by degrading others; not homo sapiens, but homo mockems.

Next, we turn to cynicism, originally a school of Greek thought, which is a superior attitude towards others, particularly those in power. The cynic regards his or her rulers as being invariably corrupt, incompetent, or self-serving. Cynical humour is aimed at exposing these faults.

Amongst other things, the cynic makes much use of ridicule, exaggeration, irony and sarcasm. All the time the difference between the actual and the expected is revealed.

It is not a big jump to the next subject, which is satire. There is much in common between cynicism and satire. In satire and caricature the big person is made small by ridicule, which is negative for that person.

It may be that satirical subversive humour has little effect and things carry on as before, however it acts as a safety valve and allows ordinary people to have their say in an enjoyable way.

Irony is a major weapon used by the cynical and the satirical. It is very much English humour, lacking in emotion, played deadpan, whilst using word-play in a mocking way.

Irony is the world of the opposite. We deliberately say something that is the opposite of the truth, expecting the other to twig. This is very difficult for outsiders who don't know the rules of the game, so we tend to restrict irony to conversations with friends, and those who get the game.

Sarcasm is a close relative of irony. Some would say an identical twin. However, it is much more aggressive than irony and is used to attack a victim or victims. It is not very subtle, and is justifiably known as the lowest form of wit.

We next change tack and look at the juvenile world of the sick joke. Sick jokes cross taboo lines. The more disgusting the joke is the better, as the intention is to shock. You could miss out this section if you are of a delicate disposition.

This sort of humour is very much the playground of the adolescent male, seeking to display his bravado and toughness. It is macho-mucko humour. Females do not usually find this sort of humour even vaguely entertaining.

Sick humour is followed by gallows humour, which might seem to be related to each other, but gallows humour is much more sophisticated in nature.

Gallows humour, historically, is about reaction to death and execution, and so seems to be pretty dark and negative, however it is also a humour of resistance by the trapped. As such it can be seen as the human spirit defying the world and misfortune.

Next, we make quite a big jump to considering sexist, racist, and disability humour. This sort of humour is about superiority, putting people in an inferior place and mocking the afflicted. Such jokes were once the staple fare of comedians, but they have rather died a death with the development of political correctness.

A major factor restricting the flow of sexist and racist jokes is the law concerning discrimination which can be pretty strict about the telling and sending of such jokes.

We end with a section on the funny peculiar, that is, humour failure which gets a groan and not a laugh. There is quite a lot of failed humour out there. So, a skilled humourist should work hard to reduce the amount of failed humour they produce.

The funny is peculiar because of poor technique or because of insensitivity to the situation or the audience. Technique can be improved by practice. Social insensitivity can improve with maturity, and by recognising that meeting the audience's needs is all important for successful humour.

Superiority and humour

'Why are most midgets good guys?
Because they don't look down on people.' (www.jokes4us.com)

The bad guys, and that's many of us, particularly men, do enjoy looking down on people as we then become superior. We tend to enjoy disparaging others, but not, of course, ourselves. However, this is not a universal rule, *Warwick Davis*, a comic not noted for his verticality, uses self-deprecation as an ice-breaker:

'I do a lot of public speaking and presentations and I'll always start with a self-deprecating joke to make everybody feel comfortable with my size because there can be hang-ups and anxieties.'
(www.Brainyquotes.com)

So, we have a choice. To mock others, mock ourselves, do both, or do none of these. From time immemorial the view has been that we prefer to mock others, indeed, this has been seen as so important to humour that *Superiority Theory* was the first real theory of humour.

The Ancient Greek philosophers were well aware of the relationship between superiority and humour:

Plato—*'When we laugh at what is ridiculous in our friends, we are mixing pleasure this time with malice, mixing that is, our pleasure with pain.'*

Aristotle – *'…since most of us are ambitious, it must be pleasant to disparage our neighbors as well as to have power over them.'* (Perks, 2012)

Interestingly, the first laugh recorded in Western literature is Greek and concerns the lame. It can be found in the *Iliad*, written by *Homer*, 800 BC. *Hephaistos,* the God of fire, had acquired a leg injury when he fell out of heaven. One day, he served the assembled Gods with full cups of wine, which spilt all over him as he shambled along:

At the sight of that ludicrous creature, the gods break out in 'unquenchable laughter' turning Hephaistos into such an object of ridicule that he skulks off and hides, too embarrassed to show his face. (Sanders, 1995)

The importance of superiority and ridicule to humour was later to be observed by Thomas Hobbes (1588-1679). He wrote:

Sudden Glory, is the passion which maketh the Grimaces called LAUGHTER; and is caused either by some sudden act of their own, that pleaseth them; or by the apprehension of some deformed thing in another, by comparison whereof they suddenly applaud themselves.

Indeed, back in the day people used to enjoy publicly laughing at the problems of others:

Eighteenth century Britons-or a high proportion of them-openly delighted in the miseries of others. Women as well as men laughed at cripples and hunchbacks. They tormented lunatics and led blind men into walls. Wife beating was a routine way of maintaining order within marriage-'an honest Englishman hates his wife' went the catchphrase. (Dickie, 2011)

The jest books of the day contained many stories and jokes which mocked the weak and vulnerable:

One Easter Monday, an arch Rogue meeting a blind woman who was crying Puddings and Pies, taking her by the Arm said 'Come along with me Dame, I am going to Moorfields', where this Holliday-time, you may chance to meet with good custome. 'Thank'e kindly, sir' says she. Whereupon he conducted her to Cripplegate Church, and placed her in the middle Isle. Now, says he, you are in Moorfields: which she believing to be true, immediately cried out, 'Hot Puddings and Pies! Hot Puddings and Pies! Come their all Hot!' which caused the whole congregation to burst out in loud laughter... (Dickie, 2003)

Cruel sadistic mockery has rather disappeared in the modern age, but it can still be found. For example, the film director *Alfred Hitchcock* played some really nasty practical jokes on people. One actress, *Elsie Randolph,* told him of her fear of fire, subsequently he got a technician to pump smoke into a telephone box, after the door had been locked. In another prank, he gave *Tippi Hendrix's* six-year old daughter an accurate doll figure of her mother in a miniature coffin.

Hitchcock's nastiest prank was when he persuaded a film technician to spend a whole night in a film studio, chained to a camera. Hitchcock gave the man a big glass of brandy and left him on his own. *'When they arrived on the set next morning, they found the poor man angry, weeping, exhausted, and humiliated. Hitchcock had laced the brandy with the strongest available laxative.'*(Chilton, 2012)

Most people do not go as far as Hitchcock in bringing others down. We usually stick to verbal attack. For example, Gunning (2001) found that, the American workplace she studied was rife with remarks and comments that, *'...support the superiority theories of humour.'* She observed that, *'Ineptness, stupidity, ugliness, and nasty personalities appeared to trigger humorous interplay among people in all hierarchical levels.'*

This joking was primarily at the expense of others, rarely was it self-directed. *'The most vicious humor was aimed at people behind their backs.'* The most common type of humour was *'wisecracks'*. *'Wisecracks were generally putdowns or insults used for expressing the jester's superiority.'*

What makes this particular finding more poignant is the fact that, in focus groups, the employees emphasised the supportive nature of their work place humour. Humour usage as a superiority weapon was denied by the workers.

The attacks don't have to be in the back. Gregory (2009) found that face-to-face banter in the creative departments of advertising agencies, *'...involves attacking colleagues and their work to demonstrate the superiority of the attacker's work...'* That is, the seemingly friendly bantering actually took bites out of rivals. Gregory relates this superiority thrust to the macho *Work hard, Play hard* cultures found in sales and on trading floors.

It does seem that younger men are more likely to use superiority humour. Greengross (2008) found that:

Men report using more other-deprecating humor than women do, and, the use of other-deprecating humor decreases with age for both sexes. The more we dislike the other, *'the more humorous we find jokes or stories in which that person is the butt or victim'* (Foot & McCreaddie, 2006).

Their misfortunes can improve our own self-evaluation. So, for example, a disliked rival failing an exam could please a competitive student, particularly if the student felt threatened, e.g. where they hadn't been doing well on a course (van Dijk et al., 2011).

There is mirth when enemies are belittled, but not when the situation is reversed. As Foot and McCreaddie point out, these latter ideas, *'relate very much to jokes and humour involving social, national, ethnic, and religious groupings with which we personally identify.'*

In the case of nations, other countries are usually considered inferior to one's own. For example, the Danes tell jokes in which *'…the butt, or object, of the jokes is a stupid Norwegian or a Swede whose values differ from those of the Danes.'* (Gundelach, 2000)

The English don't mock the Welsh half as much as they mock the Scots or Irish, however here's one from the 19th century:

An Englishman and a Welshman, disputing in whose country was the best living, said the Welshman 'There is such a noble housekeeping in Wales, that I have known above a dozen cooks employed at one wedding dinner' – 'Ay,' answered the Englishman, 'that was because every man toasted his own cheese.'   (Lemon, 1865)

And an Irish one from the same source:

'The sun is all very well,' said an Irishman, 'but the moon is worth two of it; for the moon affords us light in the night-time, when we want it, whereas the sun's with us in the day-time, when we have no occasion for it.'

We'd better complete the set:

An Englishman was being tried on being drunk and disorderly. The judge asked him where he had purchased the whiskey. 'But, I didn't buy it, your Honour,' said the Englishman, 'A Scotsman gave it to me.' '28 days for perjury,' replied the judge. (www.rainsnow.org)

And what the Scots say about the English:

Why are they putting Englishmen at the bottom of the ocean? They found that deep down, they're not so bad. (www.proudscot.co.uk)

So, what is going on when we mock the Irish for their stupidity and the Scots for their stinginess? It seems that the jokes explain the relative position of the two immigrant groups in English society.

Many Irish people came to England looking for manual work. It was they who helped build our canals, railways and motorways. Jokes about Irish stupidity justify this labourer status.

Scots often do well in business and government, so an explanation is needed for their relative success. The jokes about Scots indicate that they have succeeded illegitimately, by being tight-fisted and crafty.   (Davies, 1982)

This mocking of neighbours and immigrants happens on a world-wide basis. The Americans have Polish jokes. The Canadians have Newfoundland jokes, and the Irish have Kerryman jokes. People at the centre of the society are the superior. Those on the periphery are the marginal, the mocked. (Davies, 1988)

Self-deprecating humour would appear to be the reverse side of the superiority coin, but this is not necessarily the case. It can be a technique used by high status people to deliberately reduce their status so as to bring them closer to the more ordinary people they are with.

Politicians use self-deprecation humour a fair amount. It helps voters connect with them, puts listeners in a good mood, and shows listeners that the speaker, *'does not take him/herself too seriously.'* (Rhea, 2007)

However, self-deprecation is a risky strategy. It can highlight real defects in intelligence, morals, mental health and physical attributes, and so reduce one's status in the eyes of the other. If you say something like, *'I'm hung like Einstein and smart as a horse,'* you just might be believed, or maybe not, as that's quite a clever joke. (Greengross, 2008)

Self-deprecation can easily morph into negative self-denigration and so be non-effective. Take the following comment made by a man to his girlfriend:

 'I like dating you. You are a big step up from the girls I've been dating.'   (forums.plentyof fish.com)

The girl would presumably think that she has made a mistake in dating a man from a lower league, and that she should be with someone higher up the hen-pecking order.

Self-deprecation may be a sensible strategy for newcomers to a group, particularly if they are lower in status. It signals that they recognise their relative status, and do not wish to upturn the social apple cart. They are no threat to the existing order. For example, a new cleaning assistant in a hotel kitchen:

'Don't pay any attention to me. I wouldn't recognise a ratatouille if it ate my cheese.' (Brown and Keegan, 1999)

Actually, those with low power are more dependent on the benevolence of those above them and so they laugh more. They need others to like them. Those in high power positions laugh less, presumably because they don't need people to like them as much. They may also think that their role needs to be displayed with gravitas. (Stillman et al., 2007)

Managers at work do not typically use self-deprecation, but they do use humour: to mask their superiority, to reduce the distance between the managed and the managers, and to be consistent with the culture.

A classic investigation by Coser (1960) found that senior staff made the witty comments even though junior staff did more talking in meetings. Coser argued that humour reduced social distance and that, *'The invitation to decrease social distance is expected to be initiated by the status-superior.'*

Of course, the manager is in the powerful position, and so their humour reflects their position. The workers may well have no choice but to defer to their humour. Ex-England and Chelsea footballer Graeme Le Saux, made the following pertinent comment about the chairman of Chelsea F.C.:

'We see a lot of Ken Bates. He'll always have a laugh and a joke with you. At your expense, obviously.' (Shaw, 2003)

If managers wish to engineer a *'fun'* culture then their requests may be couched in the humorous. Mallett and Wapshott (2014) found that owner managers regarded humour as:

'...something with which to "sugar-coat" instructions in such a way as to maintain the fun, informal working environment and positive working relationships.'

When workers make minor mistakes, managers can use humour to sweeten the reprimand. For example, a head chef admonishing a cooking assistant: *'Rod, give that beef some water wings before it drowns. Less gravy next time.'* (Brown & Keegan, 1999)

High status people do have a problem connecting with ordinary folk. Take Prince Philip, a man famed for his gaffes. Poor man, he is constantly meeting new people, with whom he has little in common. He knows they are nervous, and that for them, meeting him, is one of the most important days in their lives.

So, he is forced to find something to talk about which will reduce the social distance, and put people at their ease. Funny remarks are his solution, which can be non-PC:

He once asked a Scottish driving instructor: *'How do you keep the natives off the booze long enough to get them through the test?'*

In 1994 he asked someone from the Cayman Islands whether he was *'descended from pirates.'*

In 2002, he asked a group of Australian aborigines: *'Do you still throw spears at each other?'* (Molloy, 2013)

Prince Philip sort of gets away with it because, well, he's Prince Philip. He's an old geezer, from a different age, who people find rather endearing for being off message. Boris Johnson is another toff who gets away with being quite outrageous:

'Voting Tory will cause your wife to have bigger breasts and increase your chances of owning a BMW M3.'

'I think I was once given cocaine but I sneezed so it didn't go up my nose. In fact, it may have been icing sugar.'

People probably like Boris because he has a sense of the absurd, and, particularly, because he stands out from the production line of bland politicians churned out from Oxbridge. However, his lack of gravitas may count against him if he seeks higher office. Clowning doesn't usually get you into Downing Street:

'My chances of being Prime Minister are only slightly better than my chances of being decapitated by a frisbee, blinded by a champagne cork, locked in a disused fridge or reincarnated as an olive.' (Gripper, 2012)

Politicians particularly use humorous comments when they are running for election. These comments are mostly in the form of targeting an out group or a competitor for the Presidency. (Stewart, 2011)

Here are some of my favourite political put-downs, which tend to compare a rival to something which lacks strength, or is ludicrous.

'He has the backbone of a chocolate éclair.' (Theodore Roosevelt, 1858-1919, on President William McKinley)

'She behaves with the sensitivity of a sex-starved boa constrictor.' (M.P. Tony Banks, 1942-2006, on Mrs Thatcher)

'The House has noted the Prime Minister's remarkable transformation in the last few weeks from Stalin to Mr Bean.' (Vince Cable M.P. on Gordon Brown)

And, finally, a really beautiful play on an idiom, which was so apt, with regard to George W. Bush:

'He was born with a silver foot in his mouth.'

(Texas Governor, Ann Richards, 1933-2006) www.saidwhat.co.uk

Reflection

People often enjoy laughing at the misfortunes of others as it gives them a sense of being better placed, of being superior. As we are social animals we like to know where we are in the pecking order, so we demonstrate and confirm our position by laughing at others. All the time we prefer to move up, rather than down the scale. Laughing at others bumps us up the ladder, and sends others down the snake.

We laugh at: people's appearance; their mistakes and errors; their clumsiness and their calamities. It is failure we find particularly amusing, maybe sexually, intellectually, or physically. In all of this we forget our defects and set ourselves up as the model to which others should aspire.

We assume our groups are superior to others. We use humour to unify our groups and to demonstrate their strength. Conversely, we mock outside groups for their supposed inferiorities and differences.

People enjoy situations where they can place themselves above others. There is an understanding of a natural order of things. Those who step out of line are ridiculed in order to regain the natural order.

Superiority humour serves to reinforce the status quo, and, so, is conservative in nature. It usually involves the, *'powerful laughing at the powerless'* (Critchley, 2002). As we have seen, society, according to Henri Bergson, uses ridicule and scorn to correct or threaten deviants.

The witty person is a powerful person in groups. Their wisecracks, clever pieces of spontaneity, have a rapier like ability to attack others, and do them down. Their very wittiness reveals their superior intellect, and is a display of it, for others to admire, and maybe fear.

If the wit ends up in control, he or she may decide to mask their skill and turn more to self-deprecation in order to reduce the social distance between them and their audience. This can be overdone, turning into self-denigration, or, as Prince Philip is all too aware, minding the gap, can easily turn into finding a gaffe.

Activity

1) Create a superiority joke based on a viola joke

In the 1990s there was a viola joke cycle among American musicians. The viola is regarded as a second class citizen of the orchestra. This is because viola parts are easier and less important than those of the violins, and viola players are seen as failed violinists. So, viola players are near the bottom of the hierarchy, and the jokes confirm this. (Rahkonen, 2000)

At the outset of the cycle, the jokes were mostly riddles, later they became more narrative in nature.

How is a viola different from an onion?

No one cries when you cut up a viola

(This could become: How is a Jedward cd different from an onion? Etc. A very useful cue joke)

Why isn't a viola like a lawnmower?

Nobody minds if you borrow a viola

(This could become: Why isn't a Marks and Spencer dress like a lawnmower?)

The viola players did fight back:

Why is it that violists do not have haemorrhoids?

Because all the assholes are in the first violins

This could become:

(Why don't Spurs' fans have haemorrhoids?

Because all the assholes support Arsenal)

2) Create a joke attacking a superior, using a conductor joke

Not only are there viola jokes which attack those at the base of the hierarchy, there are also conductor jokes which attack those at the top of the hierarchy. Apparently, musicians hate the conductors who flourish their batons over them.

What's the definition of an assistant conductor?

A mouse trying to become a rat

The punch-line can be moved on. A maggot who wants to become a worm.

To attack a youngster seeking promotion: a cub who wants to be the lion; a kid who wants to be the buck; a pup who wants to put his seal on things

3) Create an insult suggesting that someone is stupid because they are not educated well enough

 to understand the intricacies of the English language.

N. B. This is not meant as an attack on foreigners.

Jonathan Aitken, an ex Tory politician, once made this jibe at Mrs Thatcher's lack of understanding of the Middle East:

'...she probably thinks Sinai is the plural of sinus.' (Hoggart, 2013)

How about: He's so stupid he probably thinks the singular of: adult is adulterous; bone is bonus; sense is census; circle is circus; croak is crocus; cunning is cunnilingus; state is status?

To do these rather good insults, just go to www.morewords.com and find the words ending in us.

Cynicism

'Jack Dee's comedy springs from immaculate sullenness and cynicism. His misanthropic persona is so well established that he can get laughs with the simplest of sentences...His eyebrows raise but his eyelids remain sullen and down-turned. His voice suggests someone making a tiny effort to be polite, while fighting monumental boredom.'   (Double, 2005)

Such cynicism stems from distrust. Distrust of people's competence. Distrust of people's honesty. Distrust of people's benevolence. Too much experience of distrust leads to a world weariness, which can be relieved by mockery. Here is a relevant Jack Dee joke:

'I read in my local newspaper, they had this advert, "Please look after your neighbours in the cold weather," and shall I tell you something about that? I live next door to this 84-year-old woman, do you know, not once has she come round to see if I'm all right. Lazy cow hasn't even taken her milk in for a fortnight.' (www.Thehumorblog)

Of course, it is Jack who has failed to be benevolent. He is not actually accusing the old woman of deceit or incompetence, the two other areas of distrust. If he had, he would have been more of a classic cynic, than a world-weary one. The difference between the two types is indicated by the following quotes made by a pair of witty Irishmen:

George Bernard Shaw –'The power of accurate observation is commonly called cynicism by those who have not got it.'

Oscar Wilde –'I am not at all cynical, I am only experienced—that's pretty much the same thing.' (Chaloupka, 1999)

The George Bernard Shaw quote relates more to the school of philosophy known as Cynicism, which mocks those in authority, as it observes the powerful to be hypocrites. The latter quote, by Oscar Wilde, relates to the more world-weary use of the word cynicism, where an individual is seen as tired, worn-out by negative experiences – Deeism.

The philosophical school of *Cynicism* is the legacy of Diogenes (404-323 B.C.). Diogenes was well known in Athens for, 'criticising conventions, debunking hypocrisy, and refusing to respect undeserved reputations.' The Athenian citizens called him a dog because of his living standards. Diogenes turned this name around, adopting the word for dog, *kyon,* for his philosophy. This became *kynic*, and thence *cynic* (Chaloupka, 1999).

Diogenes and the *Cynics*, '...held society's institutions in very low regard and expressed contempt for them in both words and actions.' Humour was a device they used to attack the privileged and powerful. For example, Diogenes himself was so cynical, he carried a lamp around in daylight in order to help him find, 'one honest man' (Dean & Brandes, 1998).

Some 2000 years have passed since Diogenes passed away, but, surprise, surprise, cynicism hasn't gone away, if anything, it is seen as the prevailing mind set of the post-industrial world. Andersson and Bateman (1997) give a useful modern definition of cynicism:

...a general and specific attitude characterized by frustration and disillusionment as well as negative feelings toward and distrust of a person, group, ideology, social convention, or institution.

Yoos (1985) considers the notion of cynicism in some depth. He thinks that a core notion is that cynics are, *'...disenchanted or disillusioned idealists.'*

For Yoos, there is a close connection between cynicism and irony. Many cynical remarks are ironic. Such remarks allow the cynic to provide the contrast between appearance and reality. The cynic is a moral critic.

Cynicism may be quite common in the population at large judging by American research. Kanter & Mirvis (1987) surveyed 643 people and report that 43% of Americans fit the profile of the cynic, *'...who sees selfishness and fakery at the core of human nature.'* Kanter & Mirvis saw America as sliding into widespread cynicism.

At work, according to Kanter & Mirvis, the cynic mistrusts management. He or she, may disparage other workers, spread rumours, and be resistant to change. Humour is devoted to *'unmasking hypocrisy'*. Ridicule and sarcasm are used, maybe in a satirical way, to demonstrate disbelief in *'the ostensible motive for someone's behaviour'* (Foot & McCreedie, 2006).

For example, one American company had a saying, *'do what's right.'* An employee commented, *'In this group, 'do what's right' means 'make your manager visible.' (Laugh) Aren't all organizations like that?'* (Kunda, 1992)

Often, the hypocrisy of work is the expectation that the employee will produce quality whilst not being provided with the necessary resources. For example, this was found in the case of Norwegian police officers. Where these workers had to cope with *'high job demands'* and *'lack of resources,'* there was a high correlation with cynicism. (Richardsen et al., 2006)

Kunda (1992) studied a high-tech company in America, *'Tech'*, where the motto was *'Working Hard, Having Fun.'* The cynical joke response to the excessively high hours worked, was *'You get to choose which 20 hours to work out of the day.'*

Tech promulgated a strong culture based on its founder, *'Sam Miller'*. The company was seen as a unified family, *'We are One'*. Similarity and unity were emphasised, and power and authority deemphasized. One worker referred to this propaganda as *'Big Brother shit.'*

Workers, such as those at *Tech*, use cynicism as a protective shield to defend their *'private selves'* from incorporation into the employer's values. Here, cynicism acts as a defence, and as a distancing device. So, management initiatives are obeyed, but debunked, enabling the employee to have a sense of dignity and integrity (Fleming, 2005). Cynicism allows workers a space where they can show that they are, *'...not really buying into the dominant ideology.'* (Contu, 2008)

This indicates an alienation from the organisation. Alienation is further developed at work where the work is seen as meaningless, and not meeting the individual's needs for self-fulfilment and growth. This produces disillusioned employees who blame management, via cynical comments, for causing their frustration. (Naus et al., 2007)

Employees can hold negative cynical attitudes, not just to others, but toward the institution that employs them. Organisational cynics may feel contempt for their organisation, and feel shameful when they think about it. Paradoxically, they might secretly enjoy this condition as they may feel superior to the organisation, which has failed their own higher standards.

Consequently, strong criticism of the organisation is inevitable. This may take the form of explicit statements or sarcastic humour. A certain type of body language conveys cynical attitudes,

'This includes knowing looks and rolling eyes, as well as the smirks and sneers by which cynics (and Cynics) have long been known' (Dean & Brandes, 1998).

Reflection

To be called cynical is not necessarily a great compliment. Berk (2009), for example, is particularly critical of cynics in the medical world: *'Simply put, derogatory and cynical humour, as displayed by medical personnel, are forms of verbal abuse, disrespect and the dehumanisation of their patients and themselves.'*

Cynicism comes from experience of the self-serving nature of people and consequent distrust of their benevolence toward others. The employing organisation may act such that the individual feels manipulated, so that the employers' ends can be achieved illegitimately. Consequently, over time, the once enthusiastic person can become worn down and disillusioned, and so sink into cynical despair.

The humorous rider on the wave of cynicism is ridicule, via sarcasm, irony, and mockery.

Activity

Why should I waste my time trying to think of something funny for you to do when you probably haven't laughed at any of the jokes so far? You probably don't get the jokes. I expect you're more the Christmas Cracker sort, probably quite crackers. To keep you happy I'll tell you one I got in a cracker last Christmas.

'What do you get when you cross a teacher and a mother-in-law?'

'Chalk and Talk.'

Alright, don't smile then, suit yourself. See if I care, but a word to the wise, don't cross a mother-in-law.

2) Produce your own piece of cynical writing about the world of education, or your workplace. Here is a cue from Stephen Fry with respect to the Cambridge examination system, The Tripos:

'The tripos weeds out the slow, the honest, the careful, the considered and the excessively truthful— all of whom would be grossly unsuited to public life or high-profile careers.'   (Fry, 2010)

Satire, Parody, and Subversion

The game of choice for unemployed people is basketball.

The game of choice for frontline workers is football.

The game of choice for middle management is tennis.

The game of choice for CEOs and executives is golf.

Conclusion: The higher up on the corporate ladder you are, the smaller your balls are.
(http://unijokes.com)

Ah yes, the old small balls joke. We've seen that before. It just keeps going round and round. Here, the balls of managers are being made to seem ridiculous, in a satirical, subversive way, just like *Hitler, Rommel, Himmler,* and *no balls Goebbels* in times past.

So, what exactly is satire? Satire is *'the use of ridicule, irony or sarcasm to lampoon something or someone.'* (Bal et al, 2009) Satire, as Pollard (1970) observes, *'is always acutely conscious of the difference between what things are and what they ought to be'*. This gap can be either obvious, or, at least, plausible.

The point of satire is usually, to be subversive of the power structure and the status quo, and to be funny when doing it. To do this, satire *'...uses comedic devices such as parody, exaggeration, slapstick, etc. to get its laughs.'* (Coletta, 2009)

When satirising others, people make use of ridicule. The basic technique that is used is reduction, *'the degradation or devaluation of the victim by reducing his stature and dignity'* (Hodgart, 1969). In doing this the satirist may distort and exaggerate.

Indeed, Apter & Desselles (2012) consider satire and parody as being the most obvious examples of distortion humour. They point out that there has to be *'enough similarity'* between the original and the distorted version for the satire to work. The aim of the distortion is to diminish the person, by adding and exaggerating, so as to humiliate, embarrass, trivialise, vulgarise, or dehumanise.

Take for example the satirical thrusts made by the late Simon Hoggart, for a long time a sketch-writer about parliamentary goings-on. For Simon, politicians existed in order to be mocked:

Here, Tony Blair is being humiliated and vulgarised via exaggeration: *'I sat in the front row for Tony Blair's speech. It was like the monsoon in a Somerset Maugham short story. Hot, steamy sweat flew all over the platform. His shirt was so damp you expected him to rip it off in mid-speech and call for horse blankets.'* (Hoggart, 2012)

Here's some more exaggeration, to embarrass and trivialise: *'The local Labour M.P. is Helen Brinton, whom I like personally but whose wide mouth, always slated with scarlet lipstick, makes me long to put a letter in it.'*

And, a final exaggeration, this time of the Eton and Oxford educated, Jacob Rees-Mogg, who had had the temerity to declare himself, *'a man of the people'*: *'He was conceived in privilege, and nine months later born in privilege. No doubt he wore a three-piece romper suit in Harris Tweed, obtained by his parents from Toffs 'R' Us.'*

Hoggart did parody as well. Parody is a sub-type of satire, which relies more on imitation of the satirised. Exaggeration is normal, but this has to be clearly based on some element(s) of the original. To parody a person, you can latch on to some significant, characteristic mannerism, such as word usage, type of body language, etc. Here, Simon Hoggart just uses one phrase from a classic *Churchillian* speech in order to parody *Blairspeak*:

'Hey, you know, never before in the field of human conflict have we owed you guys such a lot, and, well we're really, really, grateful, you know. Right?'

In his regular column in *The Independent* newspaper, the radical comedian, *Mark Steel*, invariably satirises/parodies some one or another, usually using ridicule to the point where his victim becomes absurd. In his *Valentine's Day* column, 2014, he had a go at humiliating and trivialising *Nigel Lawson*, the ex-Chancellor of the Exchequer, by parodying his views on global warning.

In his article, *Steel* demolishes *Lawson's* assertion that: *'There's been no global warming for 15 years and that's a FACT.' Steel* complains that *Lawson* ignores the scientific data by inventing his own FACT. He mockingly suggests that exam candidates should take this approach. For example, in physics exams, students could write: *'Electricity is made up of tiny flames that live in a plug socket and that's a FACT.'*

Nigel Lawson claims that, *'These floods are a wake-up call, to abandon the crazy costly policy of spending untold millions on useless wind turbines and solar panels.'* Steel responds, *'At last someone's had the common sense to say what the rest of us were thinking. Who hasn't watched these floods and thought, "it's those bloody wind turbines and solar panels that have caused all this."*

The solar panels stop the water from draining, as rivers can't get through glass. Then the wind turbines frighten the water so it runs off and hides in living rooms in Somerset.'

Steel's approach is rather selective, but he does reduce the arguments of the other to a puddle of muddle. In his satire he does like to push ridicule to the extreme, a classic approach of the satirist, known as reductio ad absurdium. Here, he pushes the envelope as far as possible with regard to the ever increasing numbers of betting shops on British High Streets:

'Accident and Emergency units will be converted into betting shops, with the heart monitors used to show dog racing from Wimbledon. Cathedrals will be more useful once the racing form is Sellotaped over the stained glass windows. Then we can do the same with crematoriums, airports, schools and high-security prisons...' (Steel, 2014a)

Irony is another tool that the satirist uses. Irony is about opposites. Ironic speech uses words that mean the opposite of what one really means, or, irony is about a situation which is contrary to what one expected. Here Simon Hoggart suggests a surprising result, using an extreme instance, to demonstrate a point:

'Is Alistair Darling the most boring Chancellor ever? Put it this way: he sent Geoffrey Howe to sleep.'

Just as politicians are satirised, so are managers at the workplace. Such subversive humour is one of the few acceptable means, available to the subordinate, to challenge the authority structure.

Subversion unites the lowly and allows them to vent their spleen. Here's a Manchester teacher commenting on this process:

'I indulge in a good gripe with close colleagues as often as possible. This typically takes the form of contrasting the work required of us by managers in a limited time with that required of them in more, and better-paid, time. Pointing up the hypocrisy and incompetence of those 'in charge' is very therapeutic.' (Brown et al., 2002)

You can find satirical, subversive humour within all sorts of organisations: schools; restaurants; call centres; government offices; banks, etc., etc. The targets are those in control, the bosses.

For example, Taylor and Bain (2003) studied two Scottish call centres and found that, *'A group of workers consciously used humour simultaneously to undermine management and to advance trade union organization.'*

Mocking nicknames were invented for the most disliked managers, *'Crafty Christian'* and *'Tricky Dicky'*. Stories were circulated which showed managerial incompetence. This could be via e-mail. Cyber humour, *'... conveyed a subtle, but frequently overt, criticism of supervisory authority.'*

The *'sometimes vicious'* satirical humour helped the workers to form a, *'vigorous counterculture.'* It helped unite an *'outgroup'* of disparate individuals into a collective organisation.

Subversive humour can challenge managers and bring about policy change. Lynch (2010) gives an example of chefs in a hotel kitchen challenging a new ruling, embarrassing the manager concerned, and effecting a change back to the status quo. A new manager ruled that the chefs should only have cheap and cheerful lunches in future, which would be supplied by the hotel and prepared by its chefs. This replaced the better quality food they had been used to having. In retaliation, the chefs delivered a lunch of tomato soup and Welsh rarebit at the next monthly management meeting. The managers smiled ruefully about this, and the new manager wouldn't face the chefs. Over time, the chefs' lunches returned back to the more expensive fare. This joke encouraged the chefs to resist further changes.

In schools the subversion takes place in the staffroom. Woods (1979) notes that, *'...much staffroom humour takes the form of mockery, embarrassment, or compromise of senior personnel, often by 'subversive ironies.'*

It's not just the teachers at the chalk-face who engage in subversive activity, their middle managers can mock organisational policy as well.

Schnurr & Rose (2008) reported a study of the emails of a Head of School, *'Richard'*, in a university in Hong Kong. They found that, about a quarter of the emails that *Richard* sent, were subversive in some way, including those sent to staff about organisational decisions.

Richard's emails challenged and questioned the bureaucracy and its decisions. He would refer to the *'air-conditioning czar'*, and say, *'the university has no head and no heart, only hands.'* The possible merger with another unit was referred to as, *'our new School of Letters & Modular Kitchenware Design.'*

Schnurr and Rose interpret the humour as both challenging the system, and accepting that nothing can be done about a disliked decision, except humorous protest. A middle manager, such as *Richard*, is in a tricky position, when having to implement a policy with which he/she does not agree. The employees have to be kept on side, but the hierarchy has to be obeyed. To distance him or herself from the decision, the person, via humour, emerges, criticising the decision, but still implementing it. What Contu (2008) calls *decaf* resistance--*'all talk and no trousers.'*

Page (2011) studied first tier managers in further education, with regard to their covert and overt acts of resistance. He found that cynicism was a constant when these chalk-face managers discussed senior managers, who were, *'almost unanimously reviled'*, and considered to be, *'...obsessed with money, lacking in strategic vision and authentic leadership, reactive, unorganised and physically, morally and ethically removed from the realities of contemporary teaching.'*

The chalk-face managers didn't just stick to decaf resistance. They also engaged in *'Espresso'* acts, like refusal, and non-compliance, when the actions of senior management threatened student welfare.

Research conducted by Holmes & Marra (2002) indicates that business meetings may well have a subversive element, depending on the nature of the meeting. These researchers studied subversion in 12 meetings in two business organisations in New Zealand, and found that a surprising 40% of the humour in these meetings was subversive in character. The extent of the subversion may well have something to do with the very egalitarian nature of New Zealand society.

The quip was the weapon of choice of the subversives. Holmes & Marra describe quips as follows: *'Quips are short, sometimes witty, and often ironic comments about the on-going action, or the topic under discussion. They often involve exaggeration.'* They see them as *'concise and subtle'* ways of challenging others in the context of a focussed business meeting. The target was, normally, the group leader, or the highest status person.

Business meetings have a distinct ritual quality. Rituals are controlled by a hierarchy. There is an order, which is expected to be followed. There is often predictability as to outcome. Symbols, which are important to the participants, are revered. So, it is not surprising to find much glee when rituals are subverted. To some extent this is what happened at the opening ceremony of the London Olympics, 2012. *Mr Bean* suddenly, and most unexpectedly, appeared, playing the piano in hopeless fashion. *The Queen* supposedly parachuted from a helicopter. All this was a far cry from the order of the previous Beijing Olympic Ceremony.

The successful subversion of a ritual is a distinct victory for the subversive and a decided blow for the hierarchy. It is a brave, or foolhardy person, who arranges such subversion, as you can be pretty sure the consequences are likely to be quite severe. Woods (1990a) gives us a nice example of the ritual of a school assembly being disrupted by the strategic placement of a hymnbook behind a piano's hammers. So, when the music teacher began to play, no music came.

Woods (1984a) observes that teachers mock the pretentiousness of rituals. He relates the case of a school sports day that was marred by rain, much to the delight of teachers who were not keen on the activity, or the increase in status of the P.E staff that it occasioned. Jokes included: *'The shot is sinking!'*; *'Ten to one on the one in the diver's helmet.'*; *'Can we have all runners at the deep end.'*

Rituals, such as Sports day, and school assemblies, are about order. They symbolise harmony within a hierarchy of order. Conversely, jokes are anti-order, and, indeed, Douglas (1968) states that, *'All jokes have this subversive effect on the dominant structure of ideas'*. A joke is potentially subversive since, *'its form consists of a victorious tilting of uncontrol against control, it is an image of the levelling of hierarchy, the triumph of intimacy over formality, of unofficial values over official ones.'*

Hitler was one who was very aware of the belittling power of the joke. He established special anti-Reich 'joke courts' which, amongst other things, punished people who named their dogs and horses, Adolph (Morreall, 1981). Satirical books were banned and political jokes were seen as an attack on the government. Accordingly, people were arrested, imprisoned, and even killed (Collinson, 2002). For example, a Berlin munitions worker, Marianne Elise K. was guillotined by order of the Nazi People's Court for telling this joke:

Hitler and Goering are standing on top of Berlin's radio tower. Hitler says he wants to do something to cheer up the people of Berlin. 'Why don't you jump?' suggests Goering.
(www.spiegel.de/international)

Finally, jokes subvert the usual rules of conversation. These are the understood assumptions as to how a conversation should be conducted. Four of these assumptions are known as *Grice's* maxims (devised by the philosopher, *Paul Grice*), which rest on the presumption that the conversation is cooperative in intent.

- The *maxim of manner* requires speakers to transmit such they are likely to be understood. This indicates an avoidance of ambiguity and wordiness, as well as considering the audience's characteristics.

- The *maxim of relation* requires speakers to make contributions that are relevant to the aims of the conversation.

- The *maxim of quantity* requires that a speaker provides relevant information and avoids redundancy.

- The *maxim of quality* requires that speakers do not lie or say something which lacks evidence. (Shwarz, 1996)

Clearly, jokes and humour can break one or more of these maxims. Irony is a particular subversive force as it may not be signalled as a joke, and is a contradiction, bordering on a lie. Jokes can interrupt the flow of the conversation, and may be a deliberate derailment. Shaggy dog stories are essentially redundant, as they contain far too much unnecessary information. Humour may not be understood as it is beyond the conceptual or linguistic grasp of the listener. A joke is essentially ambiguous, although the punch-line ought to resolve the ambiguity, however, this does not occur with absurdity jokes. An anecdote may be deliberately exaggerated to improve the humorous element. A joker may pretend that something happened to him /her when, in fact, it didn't.

Raskin (1985) argues that when joke-telling takes place, a different cooperative principle from Grice's cooperative communication is operating. He suggests the following maxims for joke-telling:

- The maxim of manner –Tell the joke effectively.

- The maxim of relation—Say only what is relevant to the joke.
- The maxim of quantity—Give exactly as much information as is necessary for the joke.
- The maxim of quality—Say only what is compatible with the world of the joke.

Raskin points out that in this joke-telling cooperative principle, the hearer does not necessarily expect the truth or relevant information. The hearer cooperates by understanding the intention of the joker is to make him or her laugh, and so, suspends disbelief.

Reflection

This section has been about ridicule, the mocking servant of those who wish to undermine the powerful in a satirical way. Mockery reduces the powerful and can therefore be a significant weapon for those who are under the thumb; it's two fingers up, fighting a thumb's down.

The satirist's victim has to be made to appear ridiculous. A mocking name is *de rigeur* in this process. Virtually anything the victim does is then interpreted in the light of their presumed, self-serving nature, incompetence, and/or deceitfulness.

Exaggeration is key to opening up the victim, who, as a result, becomes a laughable caricature of his/her former self. Exaggeration distorts, makes the victim less stable, and assists in demeaning him/her from their exalted level.

Still, it's not funny really that all subversives in organisations can do, most of the time, is to make a joke about some ridiculous decision made by someone, or some group, higher in the hierarchy. Then, it's just ineffectual decaf resistance.

However, subversive humour can serve to unite the oppressed, and may be used, successfully, to attack a change or decision. So, subversive humour can be a potent weapon, and those in power are aware of the anti-order of humour.

Activity

1) Organise a covert *Manager of the Year* competition at your workplace.

Here, your colleagues rate their respective managers using the following dimensions:

arrogance; boringness; carelessness; detachment; equivocation; freakishness; geekiness; hubris; ineptness; joylessness; know-allness; laziness; myopia; negativity; officiousness; partiality; querulousness; reclusiveness; sliminess; tackiness; unoriginality; vituperation; worthlessness; X-ratedness; Yes-man-ness; zealotry.

Present the winning manager with his/her award at the Christmas do. Say he/she is so different from other managers, that there are not enough words in the dictionary to describe him or her. Technically, this is known as *a-zing*.

2) Light bulb jokes

Create a light bulb joke. For example,

'How many bureaucrats does it take to screw in a light bulb?

Two. One to screw it in and one to screw it up.' (www.ahajokes.com)

These jokes are satirical in nature, usually making fun of an occupation, but types, cultures and beliefs can be mocked as well:

'How many men does it take to screw in a lightbulb?

One…a man will screw anything.' (www.lightbulbjokes.com)

'How many Englishmen does it take to screw in a lightbulb?'

'What do you mean change it? It's a perfectly good bloody bulb! We've had it for a thousand years and it has worked just fine.'

'How many Conservatives does it take to screw in a lightbulb?

None, they only screw the poor.' (www.ahajokes.com)

A good way to invent this sort of joke is simply to read the newspaper and see what scandal is currently hitting the headlines. So:

'How many pay day loan companies does it take to change a light bulb?

None, there's not enough interest for them to do it.'

'How many electricity supply companies do you need in order to change a light bulb?

All of them, working together, that's how they generally fix things.'

You can of course, target a group and consider what is generally said about them, or think of an appropriate phrase, based on the work they do:

'How many football referees does it take to change a light bulb?

One, but he'll need his bloody glasses.'

'How many editors does it take to change a light bulb?

One, but he'd need to hold his pages.'

3) Devise a satirical insult for a politician.

Here, the basic satirical notion is that a politician cannot be trusted. Trust is concerned with competence, integrity and benevolence. What we are keen to portray in an insult is the opposite: incompetence, dishonesty and meanness.

Let's start with famous people who were incompetent, dishonest or mean, and compare them to the politician. So, we have: The Honourable Gentleman has the competence of Inspector Clousseau, the integrity of Robert Maxwell, and the generosity of Ebeneezer Scrooge.

That is insulting, but not funny. Wordplay is the next step. The obvious wordplay is on the word integrity and the equivalent word straight. So, we have, using curved comparisons:

He's about as straight as a rainbow

He's about as straight as Piccadilly Circus

He's about as straight as a Baboon's scrotum (bollocks would be better)

Twisted is another word we can play with: *He's as straight as a twisted testicle.*

That's an improvement, and mildly amusing, particularly the last ones with their sexual reference. Idioms are next:

'The honourable gentleman has been so long out in the cold, he is the brass monkey.'

'They say a chain is no stronger than its weakest link. The honourable gentleman is so weak that one is forced to conclude that he must be the missing link.'

'The honourable gentleman does not have an Achilles heel. He has an Achilles body.'

'The honourable gentleman is so out of touch, he probably thinks that Catch-22 is some sort of record cricket score.'

To do these, just work through the idioms at www.usingEnglish.com and make connections. Actually, I think the brass monkey is the best of these because of the castration implication, and the necessity to work out the joke.

4)   Invent an aptly stupid remark for a politician. A you couldn't make it up.

Here is a fantastic example. George W. Bush is quoted as saying:

'September the 11th changed me. I remember the day I was in the---at Ground Zero, on September the 4th, 2001. It's a day I will never forget.' (Erard, 2007)

That is so stupid, it is impossible to parody. Bush has parodied himself better than anyone else could have done. You couldn't make it up.

So, the game is to just change one or two words of a politician's pronouncements to give a more appropriate meaning. There are plenty of politicians' quotes on the internet to choose from:

Mrs Thatcher—*'Where there is harmony, let us bring discord'*

(The one thing the Thatcher years were not famed for was harmony. The Iron Lady was often facing a ruck. The original quote was taken from St Francis of Assissi-*'Where there is discord, may we bring harmony.'*)

Tony Blair—*'The threat from Saddam Hussein and weapons of mass destruction—chemical,* biological, potentially nuclear weapons capability—that threat is surreal.' (www.Brainyquotes.com)

(Blair actually said real, but surreal is so much better, as it is what he should have said.)

Tony Blair—'I didn't come into politics to change the Labour Party. I came into politics to short-change the country.'   (short-change=change)   (www.Brainyquotes.com)

Tony Blair—'What people should understand is that I abhor the Labour Party.' (abhor=adore)

Finally, the most arrogant and stupid statement of the current era, which is beyond parody:

Gordon Brown made the following Canute-like statement, at least 5 times in his Budget speeches, 1999-2007—'Under this government, Britain will not return to the boom and bust of the past.'

I do apologise to Canute for associating him with Brown. At least Canute knew he couldn't hold back the waves. So, Gordon Brown is not quite a Canute.

And, in memoriam, may she Rust in Peace:

'There is no such thing as society'—Margaret Thatcher, 1988

'There is no such thing as Margaret Thatcher'—Society, 2013.   (http://sabotagetimes.com)

Irony and sarcasm

Blackadder: *'Baldrick, have you no idea what "irony" is?'*

Baldrick: *'Yes, it's like "goldy" and "bronzy" only it's made out of iron.'*   (www.imbd.com)

Well, dear old *Baldrick* should have known what irony is because it's one of the main ways for the British to be humorous, as Kate Fox puts it:

What is unique about English humour is the pervasiveness of irony and the importance we attach to it...Only the English do irony with a completely straight face. (Fox, 2005)

In Anglo-Saxon cultures, detachment and self-control are very important virtues. The English prefer to talk about emotion rather than display it. Hence, irony is used in order to hide emotions. As part of this emotion suppression the completely straight face is used. It is a mask that says one thing but means another. (Anolli et al., 2001)

Because irony is pretence it is necessary not to signal its usage, as that would spoil the effect.

All this, of course, can be very confusing, especially for foreigners. Here we have the views of a rather bewildered foreign student, who lived here for six years:

'Firstly, irony and heavy sarcasm are the bedrock of British humour...It is as if it is 'Opposite day' every day in Britain. To make matters even more confusing, the delivery of British humour is almost always deadpan which means that there will be no sign in red neon lights telling you 'This is the joke'.

There is a lot of reading between the lines to be done and so as a result of this, you might find yourself in situations where you just cannot tell if it was harmless banter or a serious conversation that you were having with a British friend.' (Tan, 2013)

So, what is irony? The 'folk' definition is, *'saying the opposite of what you mean'*, but not all forms of irony fit this definition. First of all, there is a basic distinction between verbal irony, and situational irony, which is a state of the world seen as ironical, e.g. the fire station burning down (Attardo, 2000).

Then, there are ironical quotations, *'When a man is tired of London, he's tired of life'*, said whilst sitting in a traffic jam. There are also ironical interjections, *'Ah, Tuscany in May!'* a comment made during a thunderstorm (Partington, 2007).

There is also dramatic irony, where the audience possesses information that the actors do not, so only the audience is aware of the irony. Just like the reader of *Goldilocks and the Three Bears*.

Clearly, there is a range of irony, a continuum from understatement through to sarcasm, some of which meets the folk definition, of saying the opposite, and some of which doesn't.

In its most common form, irony is a positive sentence used to convey a negative meaning. That is, ironic criticism. For example, when someone trips up, and the speaker says, *'You should have been a ballerina!'*

Hatch (1997) reports the ironical comments made by managers at a computer company. This company had a culture where only positive comments were allowed, negativity was taboo. In one case, a senior manager was reporting back significant information about the future of the unit. The unit had been given a very challenging task, which actually implied the eventual end of the unit. The senior manager ended his feedback with the comment, *'Right, other than that, everything went great!'* (Laughter)

A more sarcastic blaming by praise would be this example from a jury discussion:

Juror 2: *'I'm having a hard time deciding here who was the person on trial...'*

Juror 7: *'She is so smart.'* (Laughter)   (Keyton & Beck, 2010)

In its less common form, irony is a negative sentence which conveys a positive meaning. That is, an ironic compliment, praising by blame. For example, when someone does well in an exam, and the speaker says, *'What an idiot!'* (Dews et al., 1996)

Irony is about contrast, and reversal of evaluation. Partington (2011a) notes that:

 '...the principal form of contrast in all types of irony is between good and bad evaluation, between approval and disapproval of the entity or situation in hand.'

There are degrees of irony. Where there is large gap between what is said and what is referred to, then the statement will be seen as more ironic (Giora et al., 2005).

Irony has two main functions. The first is to be humorous, and the second is to mute praise or blame. Irony is supposed to be funny, or, at least, amusing. Ironic usage is a statement of intent to be interesting, at least to some extent, and not to be boring. Ironic statements create a contrast and a critique, which is preferred to a mundane, literal statement. So, instead of saying the factual, *'There is a long queue'*, there is more smileage in saying, *'Oh, fantastic, there is no queue at all'*, or the understated, *'There seems to be a bit of a queue.'*

Irony can bind speaker and hearer when a third party is being criticised. It can be used to tease, and it can be used in a self-deprecating way, self-teasing. (Partington, 2011a)

Take for example, White House Press Secretary, Ari Fleischer, who worked for George W Bush. Fleischer was asked, *'You can fool some of the people all of the time.'* He responded, *'That's why I am here...'* (Laughter). Something bad was transformed into something clever by a witty reversal, in a self-deprecating fashion. (Partington, 2011b)

Humorous muting, via irony, moderates the message, making it less stinging, in the case of blame, and, less laudatory, in the case of praise. Further, the ironic speaker is seen as being less annoyed when criticising ironically, and less praising, when complimenting (Dews et al., 1996), (Dews & Winner, 1995).

The muting function enables the speaker to save the face of the addressee. Indeed, people are less insulted when their behaviour is dealt with in an indirect, humorous way (Creusere, 1999)

For example, an indolent trainee is here admonished by an instructor:

'When Smith presented his group's introduction section to the class he finished by saying, "Two

minutes, that's it. Next!" The class laughed and Hilary (the instructor) said, sarcastically, "For a whole two weeks work Smith, that's very good." He just said, "Yeah" ' (Thomas & Al-Maskati, 2007)

The hearer of irony has four basic reactions. First, he/she can laugh or smile. Eisterhold et al. (2006) found that, in their study, of 395 ironic/sarcastic utterances, that this was the response in 44% of cases. Next, the hearer can make a 'serious' verbal response, that either addresses the literal, or implied meaning. This was the reaction in 28% of cases. Next, the hearer can respond with irony/sarcasm. This occurred in 7% of cases. Finally, the hearer can make no response. This happened in 13% of cases.

Eisterhold et al. (2006) found that laughter was a very common response to the irony displayed by university teachers. They noted a 57% laughter response in the classroom, and a 39% laughter response in face-to-face interactions.

According to Muecke (1969), the ironist always pretends, *'to be innocent of his real meaning or intention.'* As we can see, this is a major problem for those interpreting irony. Without a cue, a listener either has to check the meaning, or, he/she can assume the speaker actually meant what he/she said, or, because they know the speaker so well, they simply assume that he/she is being ironic. It's complicated.

Irony then, is risky. It is easily misinterpreted. As men are generally understood to be greater risk takers than women, it is no surprise to discover that Colston & Lee (2004) found, male and female subjects considered that, men were more likely to use verbal irony.

It is noteworthy that in their study of 395 sarcastic/ironic utterances, Eisterhold et al. (2006) found that the bulk of the utterances were directed at, either, acquaintances (229), or intimates (147). Eisterhold et al. argue that irony is not used with strangers because it is a face threatening act. It seems to be something to be used with people who know each other, as then, less of a cue is needed, and, reactions are fairly predictable (Pexman & Zvaigzne, 2004).

Indeed, Gibbs (2000) found that ironic exchange is fairly standard within an established group, with 8% of conversational turns being classified as ironic. Where there was in-group jocularity, mocking someone, a third of the responses were ironic in nature. Actually, many ironic statements are echoes (reminders) of incorrect statements or predictions made by others (Kreuz & Roberts, 1995).

For example, President George W. Bush was thought to be so annoyed with the French government that it was said he wouldn't even sleep in their country. At a White House press conference his press secretary was asked:

'Is it true that when the President goes to the G8 meeting in France next month, he is going to sleep across the border in Switzerland.'

Mr Fleischer: *'It is not. (Laughter) It is not true.'* (Partington, 2011b)

The lack of cue in irony is in the province of the 'dry wit'. This humorist uses a straight face and ordinary tone to propose, *'some absurd plan of action or defend some outrageous opinion...The response they most appreciate is not a laugh or even a smile but a grave reply in kind...there are some who like best to see their irony go unperceived'* (Muecke, 1969)

One cue that may be available is tone of voice. Anolli et al. (2000) analysed the difference in the acoustic profile between *kind irony* and *sarcastic irony*. They found that *kind irony* is not very high in energy, with a mild voice quality and a moderate pitch. Conversely, *sarcastic irony* has high energy, a tight voice quality, and a high pitch.

The ironical intonation, then, as opposed to the sarcastic, is flat, and this may be a clue in itself, as it may be in contrast to the surrounding speech. This flatness can be reflected in a blank face, which is typical, but, there may be some other cues, such as: raised eyebrows; wide-open eyes; winks, and smiles (Attardo et al., 2003).

Another cue is that a normally truthful person has, out of character, suddenly become untruthful, and this cannot be right. Livnat (2004) argues that, *'Untruthfulness may serve mainly as one of the cues to the presence of irony, rather than an essential ingredient in all its occurrences.'*

Irony could, though, be perceived as a lie, which is defined by Bok (1978) as, *'any intentionally deceptive message which is stated.'* True, irony may deceive those who do not understand it, but the intention of the sender, normally, is not intentionally to deceive. Any deception is an accident, a misunderstanding. The speaker is engaged in a pretence communication which masks the truth (Anolli, 2001). Indeed, the pretence theory of irony argues that the ironist is involved in a game, where the job of the listener is to detect the irony, and thereby the ironist's attitudes on the matter in hand (Clark & Gerrig, 1984).

Even so, if the ironic speaker knows the audience will not understand, but still carries on with irony, then the ironic utterance does rather meet the definition of a lie. Interestingly, ironists, *'in antiquity'*, could be viewed as, *'deceivers, hypocrites, and self-righteous pretenders.'* (Kotthoff, 2003)

Another possible cue is the exaggerated hyperbole of many ironic utterances. For example, if someone says, *'That was simply the most incredible dining experience in my entire life'*, when a meal was mediocre, he or she, is, fairly obviously, being ironic (Kreuz & Roberts, 1995).

Indeed, Partington (2007) found, after an analysis of an extensive amount of newspaper text, that, it was very noticeable, that cases of irony were often accompanied by adverbial intensifiers, such as: *deeply; especially; certainly*, and *supremely.*

If irony is the good cop, its cousin, sarcasm, is the bad cop. Whilst one is witty, the other is far less subtle, and more of an obvious attack:

'Sarcasm is irony without the mystery and the refinement. It is essentially incidental and verbal. It is also cruder than irony, a much blunter instrument. It is lacking in generosity. It has been called, not without justice, the lowest form of wit.' Pollard (1970)

Although some experts consider there is no real distinction between sarcasm and irony, the key difference seems to be that sarcasm tends to focus on a particular victim, whilst irony is much more diffuse (Lee & Katz, 1998). Sarcasm, according to Attardo (2000) is, *'...an overtly aggressive type of irony, with clearer markers/cues and a clear target.'*

With regard to cues, these differ from the blank of verbal irony. Rockwell (2007) found that, *'sarcastic utterances were longer than non-sarcastic utterances and included more sound and fewer pauses.'* The drawing out of the vowel sounds could be *'to mimic or irritate the victim of the sarcastic attack.'*

Sarcasm is dangerous:

'You see, the problem with sarcasm is this: it is just too easy---any of us can be sarcastic at any time we wish. So many of us misjudge its power, or the damage we can do with it.' (Burton, 2009)

Sarcasm can be used strategically, to signal that a change is required, the status quo not being acceptable. Here, E.R. Braithwaite, in his classic novel, *To Sir With Love,* attacks a class, which led to a change in their behaviour:

'Many folk I have met have been disturbed, even distressed at their lack of knowledge; in your case you find such a lack amusing.' I was being sarcastic, deliberately, incisively sarcastic. *'It is therefore very clear to me that we shall have a most delightful time together; you seem to know so very little, and you are so easily amused, that I can look forward to a very happy time.'....'They were not smiling now, but glaring angrily at me. This was much better.'*

It is not always obvious where the humour is to be found in sarcasm. For sure, the victim does not find it amusing. The attacker may enjoy the experience of humiliating another, particularly in front of others. Take this example of Jose Mourinho, the Chelsea manager, who is sarcastically praising a referee who gave a penalty which led to Mourinho losing his 78 match unbeaten record at *Stamford Bridge.* There is no real wit, just an arrogant reversal. The audience knows that this is a case of sour grapes, so the joke is really on Mourinho for being a bad sport:

'I want to congratulate again Mike Dean. His performance was unbelievable and when referees have unbelievable performances it's fair that as managers we give them praise. So fantastic performance. He came here with one objective. To make a fantastic performance. And he did that.' (Northcroft, 2014)

Sarcasm may well be used as a response by a humiliated victim. Here, we have an example from a bank training course where *'Smith'* handed *'Salma'* a presentation sheet:

'...she said jokingly, 'Yes I'll hold it for you.' He then took it and said, 'I've got a better idea, a better spot, your face,' sticking it in her face. She said, without looking at him, 'God you're so funny. I've never met anyone as funny as you are', in a voice that was obviously very upset.

(Thomas & Al-Maskati, 2007)

The sarcastic comment can be witty. For example, *'Your talent is like the Loch Ness monster. Nobody has seen it yet'... 'I know you have an open mind. I can feel the draught from where I'm sitting.'* (Dynel, 2009). Sarcasm can be: *'A wise crack given in a mean fashion.'*

Actually, the victim doesn't have to be present or hear the sarcastic comment for the sarcasm to be funny. Take this example, which occurred after a difficult negotiation:

'Victoria (lawyer) finishes her phone call with another lawyer from a different company. She turns to

Felicity (secretary): "yeah she'd probably just hung up saying 'Thanks for all your help (sarcastically) you cow!' " (They both giggle) (Plester, 2009b)

When you think about it, people do do this sort of thing quite a lot. They end a telephone call and make some sarcastic, insulting comment—*'What a tosser'*. It's a relief device, where they have been forced to be polite for some time, do not agree with the other, and eventually display their superiority by degrading and attacking the other, in their absence.

Given the aggressive nature of sarcasm, it is no surprise to find that, in natural conversations, men are more likely to use sarcastic irony. Females report lower likelihoods of using sarcasm, except where the sarcasm is self-critical (Ivanko et al. (2004).

And, finally, for all those frustrated teachers out there who would like to get some humour out of the tedium that is marking:

Many of you will remember my article in *The Journal of Advanced Markism*, *The Assessment Revolution Begins Here: Working Class Names Should Receive Higher Marks At 'A' Level*. This was well received by *The Guardian*, *'Brave'*, however, *The Daily Mail* was a bit sniffy. In a leading article, *'The Haves and the Chav-Nots'*, they were very critical about my proposal to give more marks to candidates called *Sharon* and *Wayne*, etc., and to deduct marks from candidates called *Boris* and *Peregrine*, etc. I thought it was unfair to call it the *Eastenders'* names compensation benefit scheme.

In my subsequent article I proposed the following recommended approach to marking, which ensured that everyone was a winner. Here are some standardised comments, which can be adapted, for the following, common, student essay writing problems:

1)   A *Wikipedia* based answer: *'I note that Wikipedia has a very similar set of words to yours on the subject of Ohm's law. Coincidences are inevitable. It would be so helpful though, in future, to save any confusion, for you to ensure that at least some of the words were your own.'*

2)   A Minimal answer: *'Well done in reducing 'The Consequences of Colonialism' to one paragraph. By the way, Rhodesia is now called Zimbabwe for some reason, not that it really matters.'*

3)   An off the point answer: *'In discussing Mao's life you might have mentioned: The Long March; The Great Leap Forward, and The Cultural Revolution. Having said that, it was interesting to learn that Mao never cleaned his teeth, and consequently they were a muddy lime colour. I now understand why you entitled your essay The Green Revolution—very clever.'*

4)   An unoriginal answer: *'When I asked you to consider whether 2+2 could ever equal 5, I was rather hoping for a discussion of the concept of synergy, but, as you rightly say, how can the fundamentals of arithmetic be overthrown. I apologise for posing such a lumpen question to someone of your undoubtedly superior intellect.'*

5)   A mistaken answer: *'It was a mistake to mix the potassium pellet with the water, but let's face it, how else do we really learn? Mistakes are vital for the ignorant. I guess you won't do that again, especially as we now don't have a chemistry lab.'*

Reflection

The paradox of irony is that, if people take you literally they will not understand you. The conventions of communication require us to be truthful, but very often when we are being ironic, we are producing an untruth. Irony is really a miscommunication (Anolli et al, 2001).

On top of this, irony may lack a cue, and so can easily be misinterpreted, particularly by strangers. *The Washington Post* has rather a nice word for the gulf between the author of sarcastic wit and the person who doesn't get it--*Sarchasm*

The lack of cue, paradoxically, is the cue. The straight face, the exaggeration, the apparent lie, all point to the fact that someone is joking. Sometimes, of course, we are not sure, and have to check if someone is joking or not. I well remember at a party recently, a guy telling me that Rupert Murdoch had been a force for good in British journalism. I assumed he was joking, but in fact, on checking, I found he was not. End of conversation!

Not surprisingly, irony tends to be used by intimates as they know what is going on. Irony and sarcasm are humours of the in-group. They are too risky to use with outsiders as the stranger might well not understand the un-cued humour, or be offended by the abrupt nature of a sarcastic joke.

Irony is clearly risky and so, is more likely to be displayed by males. This may be especially the case with the more aggressive form, sarcasm.

People use irony for a variety of reasons, but a key reason is to be humorous. Irony is an escape route from tedium. However, irony is not that funny. It has to be said that this section is far from being the funniest in the book. Irony is of the moment, fleeting, funnyish at the time, but often not of great enduring value. Sarcasm is often just rude, involving little wit.

Muting is the other main function of irony. Criticism is difficult to give, and to receive, so ironical praise or criticism makes things easier. The result is more a slap on the wrist than a punch in the face.

Activity

1) Read the classic novel *Catch-22*, by Joseph Heller. This book is full of irony and contradiction. *Catch-22* itself concerns the impossibility of getting out of flying more bombing missions. To do this successfully, a doctor would have to certify a pilot as mad. However, the pilot would have to make an official request to be grounded, in which case he wouldn't be mad.

 'That's some catch, that Catch-22,' he observed. *'It's the best there is,'* Doc Daneeka agreed. (Heller, 1996)

2) Produce an oxymoron and submit it to www.oxymoronlist.com

An oxymoron is a term that contradicts itself, such as *living death*. An indirect oxymoron is similar, but one of the terms is an instance of the contradictory word, such as *sweet sorrow*. Here, the direct oxymoron would be *bitter sweet*, but, in the indirect case, sorrow is just an instance of bitterness. Oxymora are mostly indirect in nature, and involve an adjective-noun combination, like *serious joker*. (Gibbs & Kearney, 1994)

You can find single words which have contradictory meanings, such as *buckle*, which can mean fasten or collapse; *execute*, which can mean to start or to finish, and *downhill* which can mean worsening or getting easier. Such words are known as auto-antonyms. (http://en.wiktionary.org)

A single word can be made up of contradictory elements, such as: *wholesome; weekday; spendthrift; commonwealth.* Whoever decided to use the word *Commonwealth* to describe the remnants of the British Empire must have had a deeply ironic sense of humour. *Commonwealth* has to be the funniest word in the English language.

The pun can provide the humour with what appear to be oxymora: *Anxious patient; press release; divorce court; charm offensive; last initial; civil war.*

Rhetorical oxymora, like *business ethics, bagpipe music, rush hour,* or *married life* are not made up of contradictory words, but an opinion is expressed, usually satirically, that the two words cannot logically go together. (www.oxymoronlist.com)

Rhetorical oxymora are a bit like the things celebrities want to get rid of in *Room 101*. They are your pet hates. So, *Happy Christmas* is one of mine. Another is *Supermarket*.

One way of doing these oxymora is ploughing through the dictionary and seeing what happens. This is a bit random, but you can spot potential and pursue it. For example, *Manageable* led to words ending in *–able*, which led to *notable*, which is close to being an auto-antonym. This then gives a satirical insult: *'Some people say the honourable gentleman is a notable politician, untrue, he is a not-able politician.'*

Another way of doing them is to select a subject you know well, and consider the terms that are used when talking about that subject. So, if we take football we get:

Fair crowd; away supporters; chipped ball; professional foul; match ball; long shorts; flood lights; Manchester United

Other oxymora just sort of happen:

John Updike;

Buy one, get one free.

3) Produce a Sam Goldwynism

Sam Goldwyn was an American film producer who was famed for producing contradictory sentences, such as: *'Let's have some new clichés'; 'Spare no expense to save money on this one'; 'If I could drop dead right now, I'd be the happiest man alive.'* (www.brainyquotes.com)

For some reason, the world of football is prone to Goldwynisms:

'He's such an honest person, it's untrue.' (Brian Little, Aston Villa manager) (Shaw, 2003)

'The lad was sent off for foul and abusive language, but he swears blind he didn't say a word.' (Joe Royle, 1990) (Shaw, 2003)

'I don't make predictions and I never will.' (Paul Gascoigne) (Shaw, 2003)

'We just don't like the males and females playing together. Anyway, it's not natural.' (Ted Croker, FA Chief Executive, 1988) (Shaw, 2003)

We mustn't forget politicians, and first prize goes to John Prescott, Lord Foot-in-the-Mouth:

'The Green Belt is a Labour initiative, and we intend to build on it.' (Powell, 2010)

One way to do these is to go to a list of clichés and see what works. So, using http://clichesite.com:

'This week, I'm going to call it a day.'; 'The twin campanologists are dead ringers.'; 'The artist drew a blank.'; 'She shouted at the satnav "Get Lost" '; 'The teachers in the new academy are old school.'; 'There was some funny business at the undertakers.'; 'The young dentist was long in the tooth.' 'The jury is still out in the Doctor Crippen case.'

Another way to do these is to take a belief and negate it. For example:

'Don't be sexist. Broads hate that.' (Stokes, 2001)

'I don't believe in astrology. I'm a Sagittarius and I'm sceptical' (Dynel, 2009)

So:

'I believe democracy is the best political system. You must agree with me.'

'I pray there is no God.'

'Where on earth is heaven?'

4) Produce a sarcastic insult.

A lot of sarcastic insults indicate that the target is not intellectually blessed, that he or she has a small mind. For example:

'He always finds himself lost in thought; it's unfamiliar territory.'

'That man is cruelly deriving a village somewhere of an idiot.'

'I'm impressed. I've never met such a small mind inside such a big head before.' (www.tensionnot.com)

To do one of these you compare the victim to something or someone who is not blessed with intelligence:

So, *'The big difference between you and an amoeba is that an amoeba has at least got one brain cell.'*

Or, consider absence:

'There's more chance of finding Lord Lucan that there is of discovering an original thought in your head.'

5) Produce a joke with a sarcastic punch-line

A defending attorney was examining a coroner. The attorney asked, 'Before you signed the death certificate had you taken the man' pulse?' the coroner said, 'No.' The attorney then asked, 'Did you listen for a heart-beat?' 'No' 'Did you check for breathing?' 'No.' 'So, when you signed the death certificate you had not taken any steps to make sure the man was dead, had you?' The coroner, now tired of the brow beating said, 'Well, let me put it this way. The man's brain was sitting in a jar on my desk, but for all I know he could be out there practicing law somewhere.'
(www.sarcasmsociety)

Here, it is useful to think of the sorts of things an idiot or an incapable person might do, and use these as the punch-line:

So, *a teacher read out the results of the latest test on student knowledge of the set O level text, Romeo and Juliet. 'Top was Marianne with a score of 75%. Well done Marianne.' After her came Sarah, Martin, John, and so on. The teacher finally got to the bottom of the class, Alan, who'd scored 13%. 'What's your excuse this time?' the teacher asked. 'It's difficult Sir,' came the response. 'It's not difficult,' said the teacher. 'It's just that you've got Binback's disease.' 'What's that sir?' 'Whenever you start reading your lips soon start to hurt.'*

6) Produce a humorous ironic simile

For example, *'His research is about as ground breaking as a foam jackhammer.'*

A simile applies when a topic is said to be similar to, but not identical to, something else. This something else is known as the vehicle. Here, the *foam jackhammer* is the vehicle, and *his research* is the topic. The word, *'about'*, signals that irony is being used. However, using the word *'about'*, does not automatically create a simile. It is the critical notion provided by the vehicle which makes for the irony, together with the contradiction created.

Typically, these ironic similes negate the topic with a clever, ridiculous vehicle. So:

He was about as hairy as a bowling-ball.

Her face was shining like the seat of a bus-driver's trousers (P.G. Wodehouse)

Personalities can be used:

She was about as lost as Paris Hilton in a library. (Veale, 2013)

These are quite difficult to do. I suggest first making a list of qualities you want to mock. For example: *bravery, calmness, communicativeness, kindness, wisdom, sociability.* Then, look up their antonyms: *cowardice, troubled, cruelty, foolishness, isolation.* Then, concentrate on these antonyms.

Lists are very useful here. In particular, lists of things that are less than human. Here, I have looked at vegetables, fruits, and animals.

So, *'He fits in about as much as a clump of dandelions at the Chelsea Flower Show.'*

'He's about as fluent as a mynah bird with dyslexia.'

'He's about as aware as to what is going on as a farmed mushroom in a black-out.'

'He has his ears to the ground about as much as a herd of giraffe on Mount Kilimanjiro.'

'He makes about as much sense as a flying fish in space.'

Sick humour

What was the difference between Princess Di's driver and George Best?

George Best could take corners pissed. (Manuel, 2006)

Essentially, sick humour, which makes fun of *'death, disease, deformity and the handicapped'* (Saroglou & Anciaux, 2004), violates taboos. Its target is those who are normally considered immune from joking. The more disgusting and/or violent the joke is, the better (Simons, 1986).

Death is one thing that can disgust us. Other things which have the potential to disgust are: food, animals, body products, sex, body envelope violations (things like wounds and surgery), and hygiene (Haidt et al., 1993). It is these subjects which are used by the sick-kidder.

Take this one, about food and hygiene, I heard at *Ronnie Scott's Jazz Club* recently:

'For all those who've just finished their meal I should tell you that the chef's just recovering from his rash.' Hmmmmm. Actually, it didn't get that much of a laugh.

That joke is about rudimentary disgust, which is associated with toxicity and disease, and its avoidance. It seems likely that an evolutionary process took place and social and moral violations also became to be seen as disgusting, e.g., incest and bestiality. *'That's disgusting'...'That's sickening'...'That's revolting'* are the usual angry responses to such behaviour. (Chapman & Anderson, 2013)

So, a civilised society shouldn't really joke about the disgusting, as it is too awful, but it does. Indeed, Simons considers that, since the second-world war, there has been a steep rise in sick-joking, with a proliferation of targets. Nothing, any longer, is taboo, *'...the more serious the situation the more likely it will be the target, not just of a joke, but a sick joke...'*

These jokes often appear in cycles. Over time there have been: dead baby jokes; amputee jokes; NASA jokes, Lady Diana jokes, etc. A relatively mild example, after the space-shuttle *Challenger* mid-air explosion, is:

'What does NASA stand for?' 'Need Another Seven Astronauts' (Simons, 1986).

Smyth (1986) analysed the *Challenger* jokes. He found they were quickly circulated and that they tended to be in the relatively simple riddle format, suggesting quick manufacture of the joke. The jokes borrowed the form of past disaster jokes, and updated them.

Smyth cites an example of the same joke being used for three different disasters: the death of film star Natalie Wood at sea; the destruction of Lord Mountbatten's yacht, and the *Challenger* falling into the sea:

'Why didn't they put showers on board the Challenger?'

'Because they knew they would wash up on shore.'

Dundes (1979) found that dead baby jokes were particularly popular with American junior and high school students. The jokes were often used in a *'gross out'*, in which each person tried to outdo the nastiness of the other's joke. For example:

'What do you call a dead baby with no arms and no legs laying on your porch?'

'Matt'   (www.dead-baby-joke.com)

More recently, 9/11 jokes appeared immediately after the attacks:

'Who are the fastest readers in the world?'

'New Yorkers. Some of them go through 110 stories in 5 seconds.'   (www.reddit.com)

These jokes soon went world-wide via the internet. Their rapid dissemination does rather indicate that the common explanation for disaster jokes, that they are coping mechanisms, doesn't really apply. Kuipers (2005) sees the attraction for telling these gruesome jokes is that, as many people don't like them, they are told in order to shock and annoy. There is enjoyment at others' displeasure, as well as pleasure in seeing how far one can go in the process.

Kuipers (2002) explains that these disaster jokes usually employ a *'humorous clash.'* The disaster is related to something innocent or innocuous like *'children, food, advertising or funny tales'*:

'What does Princess Di turn into at midnight?'

'The wall.'

'How did they know the driver had dandruff?'

'They found his head and shoulders in the glove box.'

Brand names and adverts are commonly used in these jokes as well as presenting the joke as information or news:

'Did you know how the Herald of Free Enterprise sank?'

'A Jehovah's Witness put his foot in when the door was closing.'

Kuipers argues that disaster jokes are best seen as a reaction to the collective experience of receiving the news from the media.

The aptly named, Aaron Smuts (2009), points out, that it is the outrageousness of the joke which seems to make it funnier, particularly if it is *'naughty'* as well. He cites the following *'over-the top'* limerick:

There was a young man from Belgrave

Who kept a dead whore in a cave.

He said, 'I admit

I'm a bit of a shit,

But think of the money I save.'

Although that gruesome limerick was probably written by an adult, sick humour is very much the preserve of the young, particularly boys. Stand-up comedians are aware of this, and tailor their material accordingly:

'It's the teenage and university crowd, so we give them lots of sex jokes and gross humor.'
(Keenan Ivory Wayans)

Oppliger & Zillmann (2009) studied the reaction of adolescent males and females to disgusting material. They found that,

'Compared with males, females rated humorous episodes less amusing, the more disgust they involved...males facially expressed more amusement in response to the humorous episodes the more disgust they involved.'

Similarly, Saroglou & Anciaux (2004) found that adult male students appreciated sick humour more than their female counterparts. Saroglou & Anciaux explain that discomfort with sick humour is similar to sensitivity to disgust. Those who are sensitive are more *'agreeable and conscientious.'* Those who are less sensitive to disgust are: more anti-social with a low sense of responsibility, masculine, and liberal.

Even so, adults can laugh at disgusting things, but this does depend on the situation. McGraw and Warren (2010) found that people are able to laugh at what they call a *benign* violation, but they are not able to laugh at a *malign* violation, which causes harm. A malign violation produces strong negative emotions. Conversely, a benign violation, although disgusting, causes no harm. It is not a threat, and people do not see the violation as particularly important.

McGraw and Warren presented a number of disgusting scenarios to samples of American students and recorded their reactions, for example:

'Before he passed away, Keith's father told his son to cremate his body. Then he told Keith to do what he wanted with the remains. Keith decided to snort his father's ashes.'

Here, although the students thought the snorting was wrong, they were more likely to laugh at this scenario than at a scenario where the ashes were buried.

Students who saw the snorting as strictly wrong were far less likely to laugh. For them, despite no one being harmed, the snorting was a malign violation of a moral code that was important to them. It was not as the world *'ought to be.'*

McGraw and Warren concluded that:

'Humor provides a healthy and socially beneficial way to react to hypothetical threats, remote concerns, minor setbacks, social faux pas, cultural misunderstandings, and other benign violations. Laughter and amusement signal to the world that a violation is indeed okay.'

Sick humour is very much about tragedy; the physically and emotionally tragic. A recent tragedy is rarely funny, but, eventually, people find themselves able to laugh about some tragedy from the past. Something tragic that has happened to us personally is rarely funny, but others may find it

hilarious, as Mel Brooks puts it: *'Tragedy is when I cut my finger. Comedy is when you walk into an open sewer and die.'*

Distance is important for dealing with tragedy, humorously. If something is too close for comfort we don't find it amusing. Distance reduces threat so it can be laughed about. Here we have a failed attempt at sick humour which was too close. On September 18th 2001, American comedian, Gilbert Gottfried, told this joke:

'I have to leave for L.A. tonight. I couldn't get a direct flight. They have to make a stop at the Empire State Building.'

Gottfried recalls after these words were said, *'...there was a long gasp in the hall and somebody said: "Too soon." '* (Khitrov, 2012)

The only close tragedies we laugh about are minor tragedies, mishaps. A study by McGraw et al. (2012) asked participants to rate the following scenario:

A young woman discovers that she has unknowingly donated nearly $2000 (tragedy) or $50 (mishap) via text messaging....participants rate their perceptions of these postings twice, once imagining the woman as 'a close friend' and once imagining her as 'someone you don't know.'

The researchers found that where the stranger donated the $2000 it was funnier than the friend doing so, whereas the friend donating $50 was funnier than the stranger doing so. We obviously don't like it when our friends get hurt, but we don't mind it when they get into a minor scrape. We are in the position to take the mickey because of their incompetence or stupidity.

Certain occupations use humour as a way of coping with the tragic nastiness and horror they encounter in their work, even when a malign violation has occurred. For example, workers who deal with child abuse:

Bridgett: This man had sexually molested a girl and one of the ways we found out about it was because he had a picture of himself in bed, naked, with an erection. He wrote at the bottom of the picture the girl's name and "This is for you."

'What we found funny was that he had his socks on and he had a big hole in his sock. It was the strangest thing. I'm sure people would have said, "How can you laugh at that?" ' (Gunning, 2001)

Actually, the secretarial workers at the child abuse agency did not find the 'sick' humour of the front-line workers amusing. They took a moral stance:

Dinah: We all have what other people would consider a warped sense of humour. I also think there are people inside the agency that think we are horrible. So, it makes it difficult sometimes. You do have to make fun of some really serious situations sometimes.

Jokes about the disabled are a distinct sub-type of sick humour. They cover: physical deformity, blindness, deafness, paralysis, speech problems, epilepsy, mental disability and mental health problems (Herzog et al. 2006)

Some professional comedians can get into a lot of trouble in this area. Their general argument is that their job is to make people laugh, so, if people laugh at a joke about the disabled, they have performed their role. They do not see themselves as being limited by taboo, indeed, they see themselves as brave warriors, breaking the ground where others fear to go.

I wonder what they would say to someone, in the same crowded cinema as them, who shouted *'Fire, Fire'*, when there was no fire. *'Good joke mate, you're one of us tabooists'*

Jimmy Carr did this one in 2009:

'Say what you like about servicemen amputees from Iraq and Afghanistan, but we're going to have a fucking good Paralympics team in 2012.'

Although Carr received few complaints from his audiences, there was a furore when the press made a meal of that joke. Families related to wounded soldiers were upset. The Defence Secretary, Liam Fox was *'incandescent.'*

Interestingly, Carr dropped the joke, despite saying, *'I thought my Paralympics joke was totally acceptable.'* Totally, is going a bit too Carr. (Moss, 2009)

Ricky Gervaise is another one who thinks the rules don't apply to him. There was fury when he tweeted this in 2011:

'Two mongs don't make a right.'

Gervaise did eventually apologise after a mother of two disabled daughters was *'reduced to tears.'* The comedian claimed he thought the word referred to a *'div'*, and that he had been *'naïve to use the word without realising that it was still used to insult the disabled.'* (Nathan, 2011)

Ricky Gervaise has explained that he deals in the taboo: *'...I want to take the audience to a place they haven't been before. No harm can come of taboo subjects...I think some people can flinch too soon...I think smart people know what we're trying to do.'* (http://m.imdb.com)

It seems pretty clear that harm can come from dealing with the taboo, that's exactly why some subjects are taboo. TABOO is a keep out sign, even for the very clever people.

That was not the first time Gervaise has been in trouble. He has done *Anne Frank* jokes, and, rather predictably, has angered the Jewish community as a result.

TV viewers in America have threatened to boycott his shows after he joked that, *'Anne Frank's family went into hiding from the Nazis because they did not want to pay rent.'* He has done several others in the same vein: *'She had time to write a novel, mind you, it ends a bit abruptly. No sequel. Lazy.'* (Anon., 2012b, 2012c)

Comedian Frankie Boyle specialises in the controversial. He can go way too far, particularly where he names children in the news, as part of a sick gag:

'Jimmy Saville did an incredible amount of charity work towards the end of his life, just to be sure he could shag Madeline McCann in heaven.' (Anon., 2013c)

The jokes that got Boyle into real trouble were ones about Katie Price's disabled son, Harvey:

'Jordan and Peter Andre are still fighting each other over custody of Harvey—eventually one of them will lose and have to keep him.'

'I have a theory about the reason Jordan married a cage fighter—she needed a man strong enough to stop Harvey from fucking him.'   (Taylor, 2010)

Ofcom criticised Boyle as the jokes appeared to, *'directly target and mock the mental and physical disabilities of a known eight-year-old child who had not himself chosen to be in the public eye.'* (Anon., 2011)

The problem for comedians is that they can come up with what seems to be a clever joke, and they want to tell the world about it. They know they have a bit of taboo leeway, and can get away with stuff that others aren't allowed to say. They take a chance, and sometimes end up regretting their decision. Take Jo Brand with this one, which she admits was ill-judged:

'At a pro-abortion benefit, I made a (made up!) joke about my boyfriend coming to see me, just after I'd had a termination and to cheer me up, bringing a bag of jelly babies.'   (Brand, 2010)

It's not just professional comedians who can get into trouble with sick jokes. Nineteen year old Matthew Woods, posted a joke, modified from *Sickipedia*, about April Jones, a murdered five-year-old child. He was sent to prison for 12 weeks.

Woods had fallen foul of the Communications Act, 2003, which makes it an offence to send a message that is *'grossly offensive or of an indecent, obscene or menacing character'* using a "public electronic communications network." ' (Morris, S. & Sabbagh, D., 2012)

Actually, there was quite a furore about this sentence, and similar ones, as they conflict with the notion of freedom of expression, enshrined in the *Human Rights Act*. The Director of Public Prosecutions published new guidelines about such prosecutions, in recognition of the right to freedom of expression, stating that there should be, *'...a high threshold for prosecution in cases involving communications which may be considered grossly offensive, indecent, obscene or false.'*

The high threshold should apply to the *'grossly offensive'*, that is, when *'...a communication is more than offensive, shocking or disturbing, even if distasteful to those subjected to it...prosecutors should particularly consider whether there is a hate crime element to the communication...'* (www.cps.gov.uk)

Reflection

Sick humour is disgusting. That is the point. People tell sick jokes to disgust others, and get amusement from the negative reactions. The teller displays himself as strong, and the disgusted as weak.

Telling sick jokes is very risky. You cannot be sure of the moral stance of your audience, although you can usually assume that women will not like sick humour. Different people do have different moral views. If someone is seriously committed to a moral principle they will not find situations that violate that principle to be amusing. (Veatch, 1998)

People may laugh at sick jokes if no one is harmed and where the situation is somehow distant from them. If harm is brought into the equation then amusement is unlikely. We run into trouble if we laugh at someone who has harmed themselves and we regard this as a mishap, whilst the other person regards the problem as a tragedy. *'It's not funny!!!!!!!'*

Sick humour is not healthy. It is best to avoid sick humour. It will only get you into trouble and people will regard you as odd and immature. You will get called names like *The Grocer*; *Sick Mick*; *Pukele, Sicky Ricky*, or even worse, *Suppurating Boyle*.

Activity

1)   Barry Humphries used to while away the time on air trips from Australia to England by surreptitiously filling an air-line sick bag with potato salad, then, half through the flight, pretend to be sick into the prepared bag. After 'recovering', Barry would then eat the potato salad. Fruit salad seems to have been a variation on the potato salad. (www.clivejames.com)

Dare a disliked colleague to perform this sick joke at work.

2)   How disgust sensitive are you? Here is a joke from the American sitcom, *Ally McBeal*. A sample of 43 people were asked to rate it on a scale, 1=Good, to 5=Bad. What score would you give it?

A man is walking down a beach. It was a beautiful beach at sunset. The sky is all pretty colours. Nobody is around. Eventually, he spots this girl. No arms, no legs, just a torso, and she's crying. So, he goes up to her and says, 'Why are you crying?' she says, 'I'm twenty-one years old, I have no arms, no legs, and I've never been kissed.' So, he bends down, and gives her the sweetest little kiss. She says. 'thank-you.' He says, 'you're welcome.' And he starts to walk away, when he hears her cry again. He says, 'What's the matter, NOW.' She says 'I'm twenty-one years old, I have no arms, no legs, and I've never been screwed.' So, he heads down, picks her up, throws her into the ocean, and says, 'you're screwed now baby.'

The sample gave that an average score of 3.7, that is, quite bad. (Bubel & Spitz, 2006)

3)   Assess the extent to which you think the following are disgusting/funny:

'When I was growing up we had a petting zoo and, well, we had two sections, a petting zoo and heavy petting zoo, for people who really liked animals a lot.'

(Ellen DeGeneres in Hurley et al., 2011)

After a heavy night of drinking at the local bar, a drunk stumbles into a Catholic Church and slowly makes his way into the confessional booth. There, the priest patiently awaits the man to begin his confession. After a few minutes of silence, the priest politely taps on the window...nothing. The priest taps again and this time clears his throat a bit...still nothing. At this point the priest begins to lose his patience and bangs on the window. Finally the drunk yells out: "Ain't no use knocking, there ain't no paper over here either." '

(Hurley et al., 2011)

This is a true story about a man with testicular cancer:

'Nothing was presented as humorous in this man's account of testicular cancer. He said he received little or no support from family, friends, or medical personnel, and he suffered every humiliation possible, including a time when his false testicle broke through his scrotal skin and rolled down his trouser leg while he was on a London bus.' (Chapple & Ziebland, 2004)

A man in a pub needs to go to the loo, but he's worried that others might steal his drink, so he sticks a note on it, 'I've spat in this pint.' When he comes back, someone has written on the note, 'So, have I.'

Little boy: 'Mummy, mummy, can I lick the bowl clean?

Mother: 'No, just flush it like everyone else.' (Manuel, 2006)

Gallows humour

In 1966, James French, a convicted murderer, was sentenced to die in the electric chair. He is supposed to have shouted the following to the assembled journalists at his execution:

'Hey, fellas. How about this for a headline for tomorrow's paper?' 'French Fries!'(www.listverse.com)

Is that funny? Maybe for people who like sick humour, but for many it crosses the line of what is acceptable. That line is the understood rule as to what can be joked about and what cannot. Death can be laughed at, in the abstract, but an individual's death, in the barbaric clutch of the electric chair, crosses the line. Still, if he did say it, you have to admire his bravado in using such defiant gallows humour.

People do joke about death as a way of dealing with it. For example, Correll (1997) recounts a joke used by a family to remind them of their grandfather, who told the joke:

Do you know why there is a wall around the graveyard?

People are dying to get in.

Pancewicz (2013) studied internet jokes about death. Few of the jokes were sick jokes about death itself, rather they were about funerals, and conversations connected with death. Also, they can be reflections on the life that was led. The action of a story is often in the afterlife when someone meets St Peter at the gates of heaven, or at the other place:

Having been married for nearly sixty years, an eighty-five-year old couple died in a car crash. They had previously been in good health, mainly due to the wife's interest in health food and exercise.

When they had reached the pearly gates, St Peter showed them their spacious living quarters-complete with swimming pool and conservatory-and reminded them that because it was Heaven everything was free. Then he took them around the magnificent golf course and when the husband asked how much it cost to play there, St Peter told them again: 'This is Heaven. Everything is free.'

Next St Peter took them to the restaurant, where a sumptuous buffet was laid out. 'And don't forget it's all free,' he said.

Trying to take in the magnificence of the spread, the husband asked, 'Is there any low-fat and low-cholesterol food here?'

'You don't have to worry about what you eat here,' said St Peter. 'That's the joy of Heaven! You can eat whatever you want.'

'Damn it Jessica!' yelled the husband, stamping his foot in a fit of rage. 'If it weren't for your goddam bran muffins, we could have been here ten years ago!'
(Tibbals, 2009)

The jokes about death are often about incongruous, unsympathetic behaviour displayed by intimates of the dying:

A dying man sees some of his favourite biscuits and reaches out his hand to get one. His wife shouts, 'Back off, they're for the funeral.'

A dying wife tells her husband to remarry and give her clothes to his new wife. He says, 'I can't do that you're a size 16 and she's a size 10.'

There is a real contrast between the sadness of death and the funniness of the punch-line. The death set-up is just a neat way to convey life's dilemmas and entrapments:

A man passed another man in a cemetery, who was wailing and screaming at a grave, 'Why did you have to die', the wailing man shrieks. The passer-by says, 'Pardon me, why are you so upset?' The tearful man replies, 'It's my wife's first husband.'

Here is the classic Jewish joke concerning death bed humour:

Moshe was on his death bed and raised his head gently. 'Mendel are you there?'

'Yes Moshe, I am here.'

A moment later Moshe said, 'Izzi are you there?'

His son, Izzi assured him he was by his side.

'Joshua' said the ailing Moshe, 'Are you there?'

'I'm here poppa,' said Joshua taking his hand. Moshe raised himself on his elbow.

'Then who the hell is minding the shop?'   (www.jewishmag.com)

Gallows humour, also known as black humour, is, well, as the name suggests, associated with execution and death. Freud popularised the term gallows humour, but it has been around in middle Europe for many years:

'A rogue who was being led out to execution on a Monday remarked: 'Well, this week's beginning nicely.' (Freud, 1991)

Gallows humour gets soldiers through wars. For example, in the first world war *'...a robust rejection of victimhood and an emphasis on perseverance, articulately expressed through humour, became the new ideal of courage.'*

'Only humour helped. Humour that made a mock of life and scoffed at our own frailty. Humour that touched everything with ridicule and had taken the bite out of the last thing, death. It was a working philosophy that carried us through the day, a kind of detachment from the "institutionalised pageant of the world."' (Lord Moran in Madigan, 2013)

As Captain Edmund Blackadder put it, *'a war which would be a damn sight simpler if we just stayed in England and shot fifty thousand of our men a week.'*

The notion of gallows humour has expanded over time. Antonin Obrdlik (1942) lived in occupied Czechoslovakia, and observed the humour displayed by the Czechs. He saw their humour of resistance as a form of gallows humour, a humour which, *'arises in connection with a precarious or dangerous situation.'*

The Czech people found a refuge in spreading jokes and anecdotes about their oppressors. For example: *'To find a Czech who is truly loyal to the Germans is no easy task...the Gestapo found one such person at long last. He was an old man walking up and down the street and speaking seriously to himself aloud: "Adolf Hitler is the greatest leader. The Germans are a noble nation. I would rather wish for ten Germans than for one Czech." When the Gestapo agent asked what was his occupation, this Czech admirer of naziism reluctantly confirmed that he was a gravedigger.'*

'In a village the Gestapo men found a hanged hen with the following inscription fastened to her neck: "I'd rather commit suicide than lay eggs for Hitler." '

Obrdlik saw the gallows humour of the Czechs as an *'expression of hope and wishful thinking.'* Not only did it strengthen their morale, it also had a negative effect on the oppressors.

The most oppressed group in the war were the Jews in the concentration camps, and it is amazing to find that, in the words of one inmate, *'...we made a joke out of every situation.'*

Another holocaust survivor observed, *'Look, without humour we would all have committed suicide. We made fun of everything. What I'm actually saying is that that helped us remain human, even under hard conditions.'* (http://web.macam.ac.il)

For example:

In Treblinka, where a day's food was some stale bread and a cup of rotting soup, one prison inmate cautions a fellow inmate against gluttony. 'Hey Moshe, don't overeat. Think of us who will have to carry you.' (http://psychcentral.com)

Another oppressed group, who used gallows humour, were Russian people during the reign of terror in the 1930s, overseen by Stalin:

Stalin goes to a factory incognito and speaks to a worker. 'Who is your father?' he asks the man. 'Stalin,' replies the worker. 'Who is your mother?' is the next question. 'The Soviet Union,' the man replies. 'What would you like to be?' Stalin then asks. 'An orphan,' the worker says. (Thurston, 1991)

'Hoover taught the Americans not to drink,' says a Russian man

'Yes,' replies the other, 'but Stalin taught the Russians not to eat.' (Chamberlain, 1957)

Telling such jokes was a way of testing one's acquaintances. If they laughed, relationships were strengthened. In this way, most of the time, Russian people could work out who to trust. (Thurston, 1991)

Why do people make jokes just prior to execution, in concentration camps, in prisons and other dismal situations? The answer seems to be that the humour is a coping mechanism. Humour allows individuals to distance themselves, and so take things less seriously, *'and thereby to experience them as less distressing or threatening.'* (Foot & McCreaddie, 2006)

A review of the literature about prisoners of war, by Henman (2001), found that prisoners saw humour as *'an effective coping mechanism, a way of fighting back and taking control.'*

Henman reports that the U.S. Navy evaluated the health of Vietnam prisoners of war, twenty years after their release, and found, most surprisingly, that they had the same level of post-traumatic stress disorder as the population generally. Humour, according to Henman, had worked as a coping mechanism. Henman went on to interview 62 ex-Vietnam prisoners of war. She found that they considered humour as *'one of the constructs of their resilience'*. It was *'a tool for building relationships and a weapon for fighting back'*.

The veterans thought humour was so important that, *'they would literally risk torture to tell a joke through the walls to another prisoner who needed to be cheered up'*. In particular, the captives would use ridiculing humour against their guards.

The prisoners lacked power and consequently gained control in whatever ways they could. Henman notes that, *'Anytime the prisoners were able to trick the captors, they gained a sense of control and used the event to generate stories throughout the POW communication system'*.

A prisoner, called Jerry Vananzi, invented an imaginary motor bike which he would ride around the compound, making the necessary noises, and having accidents. He also invented a companion chimpanzee, and, just as with the motorbike, drew the guards into the joke. Vananzi's antics were, *'fodder for many humorous stories'*.

It's not just the controlled who use gallows humour, it's their controllers as well, particularly those who are in control in difficult situations. Sayre (2001) found that medical staff, in an American psychiatric unit, used *'aberrant humour'*, including gallows humour, to deal with *'a series of ultimately unresolvable problems.'*

The medical staff in this case used aberrant humour to cope with the erosion of a sense of professional competence caused by dealing with very ill patients. The jokes the staff used ranged from the whimsical to those which expressed, *'more open hostility towards patients.'* The latter type of jokes could focus on the absurdity of the childlike behaviour of the patients, or be disparaging of the patient's limitations. The gallows humour would be extreme, focussing, for example, on assisting patient suicide. (Sayre, 2001)

Derogatory, cynical and gallows humour does seem to be quite common in the caring professions. Wear et al. (2009) tried to find out why this was the case and asked 70 doctors, in focus groups, about their experiences. They found that the doctors made fun of: alcoholics, drug-abusers; obese people, and *'difficult'* patients. They explained the reasons for their humour as being: to relieve stress, frustration and anger; to make light of difficult work, to distance themselves, and to stay sane. The dodgy humour also was thought to promote camaraderie, and acted as a shorthand form of communication. In all, the humour was very much a coping mechanism to help deal with the stress of dealing with the sick and dying.

Of course, patients themselves may tell jokes about their condition, mocking their affliction. Take this victim of testicular cancer:

'...it was in the hospital somebody asked me what I was in for and I said, 'Oh I can only get it

twice…That's just the way I am I'm afraid, yeah that's the way I deal with life in general. I take the piss out of life because it's the only way to get through it.' (Chapple & Ziebland, 2004)

Sullivan (2000) found that two thirds of the Australian social workers she studied (N=65) used gallows humour, by which she meant a broad philosophical attitude involving the macabre, or bad taste. This humour was used as a method of cathartic stress management. Where it was shared with colleagues it could bolster self-esteem by reaffirming a collegiate relationship, albeit by negatively valuing another.

Sullivan does highlight the unethical nature of gallows humour. She observes that it is the *'very political incorrectness'* which makes gallows humour funny. The stress of constantly acting in a politically correct way, and monitoring such behaviour, may be relieved by using gallows humour.

Gunning (2001) gives a pertinent example of an American social worker's gallows humour:

'One of my foster mothers, Rose Wagner, has a great sense of humor. We were talking about some kid, and she said, "You know, I could just wring his neck." I said "now if you're going to tie him up Rose, you want to put cloth around the wrists first because we don't want to have rope burns.' And we just started laughing. I said, "Geeze, if anybody else hears, they would say, call the police." '

Those who deal with death are inevitably drawn to gallows humour. Roth & Vivona (2010) studied murder scene investigators and found that there were certain rules governing their macabre joking. The victim was always respected and treated with dignity. In the case of children, laughter was never present. It was totally taboo.

The sardonic joking took place during breaks, or briefings/debriefings. An example:

…an intoxicated male subject committed suicide by shooting himself four times…once in the abdomen, once in the left shoulder, once in the chest, and finally once in the head. A comment made by an officer was, 'If at first you don't succeed, try, try, try, again.

Tricia Scott (2007) studied ambulance personnel and their ways of coping with death. She found that it was the situations in which people died that could cause amusement. For example, one man died in his pigeon loft. The paramedics who had attended returned to the ambulance station, covered in feathers and bird droppings, only to be greeted with a pigeon like chorus of *'Hoo-hoo, Hoo-hoo.'*

Clearly, the tragic is a fertile source of humour. Not surprisingly then, the humourist makes much use of gallows humour. The most obvious example is the singing of *Always Look on the Bright Side of Life*, at funerals, football matches, etc. The song was originally sung at the end of the *Python's* film, *The Life of Brian*, by a chorus of men being crucified.

Although gallows humour started out as a way of coping with execution, the concept has moved on, and has broadened its remit considerably. It seems to me that, nowadays, gallows humour is about entrapment, situations from which there is little chance of escape, and people, being what they are, joke about their situation in order to make the best of a bad job.

The most obvious television comedy relating to entrapment is *Porridge*, the 1970s sit com about life behind bars. Here, the hero, Norman Stanley Fletcher, survives by joking with the other inmates and mocking the guards:

Barrowclough (a warder): 'You're writing a book?'

Fletch: 'Yeah—a sort of inside guide to prison life. But don't worry, I've not overlooked you boys in blue—I will be dealing just as much with your issues as those of our fellow felons.'

Barrowclough: 'Oh, good. And what are you going to call this book?'

Fletch: 'Don't let the bastards grind you down.'   (www.imbd.com)

Entrapment is not just about physical restraint. It can be about the restraint of relationships in which people are trapped. For example, the classic comedy, *Steptoe and Son*, was about a young man trapped with an aged father, from whom he couldn't escape:

Harold: 'You are morally, spiritually and physically a festering fly-blown heap of accumulated filth...You dirty old man!'   (www.imbd.com)

Seen in this constrained way, much comedy is gallows humour, just take *Outnumbered*, the sitcom about a couple trying to cope with their three children, and inevitably failing. This is what Hugh Dennis, the actor who plays Pete Brockman, the father, says about the Brockman family:

'Netmums, the online parent community, did an article on the worst father figures and it included Homer Simpson, Peppa Pig's dad and Pete! I thought it was massively unfair because the Brockman family is still together and it's a family where everyone cares for each other. They're just battling through like everyone else. I think every family feels like an Outnumbered family.' (www.whatsontv.co.uk)

Many marriage jokes are about the handcuffs of marriage, and the frustrated desire to escape the relationship and domesticity. Here's one from Michael Winner, interestingly, about a graveyard:

Hymie says to his wife, Becky, 'I'm giving you a very special birthday present. I've reserved the best graveyard plot in Golders Green cemetery, right under that wonderful chestnut tree, just for you.' Becky is not amused.

The next year she gets nothing. She says to Hymie, 'So where's my birthday present?' Hymie replies, 'Why should I give you a birthday present? You never used the one I gave you last year.'

(Winner, 2012)

The world of work can be another prison in which people are trapped. The 1970s sit-com, The Rise and fall of Reginald Perrin, was about a man who hated his work and its routines. He escaped only to return as the boss of a successful alternative organisation, which sold rubbish. Here's how the BBC describes his trapped life:

'It opened each week with a naked Reggie walking out into the sea to end it all before rapidly rethinking the whole idea, and told the story of a man desperate to escape his loving but dull marriage, disappointing offspring and the daily grind of his job.' (www.bbc.co.uk)

A classic study of work as prison was conducted in a Chicago engineering factory, by Donald Roy (1959). His article, *Banana Time*, described the little ways a small group of men enlivened their tedious, long working days. As Roy puts it, *'Patterns of fun and fooling had developed within a matrix* of frustration.'

The horseplay was childish, for example, when *Sammy* left the room, the power to his machine would be turned off. *Ike* would often take a banana from *Sammy's* lunch-box and eat it. *Sammy* never got to eat his banana. *Ike* would startle *Sammy* by dropping a weight behind him, etc., etc. It was as if the men were still at school, with *Ike* being the class clown and *Sammy* the butt. Of course, school is a sort of prison for some (many?) (most?) (all, including the teachers?). Pupils cope with their sentence by *mucking about* and *having a laugh*.

Willis (1977) in his study of working-class schoolboys at *Hammerton* school in the Midlands, saw *the laff* as being extraordinarily important in the counter-school culture. The ability to produce *a laff* was a characteristic of the non-academic lads who used *the laff* to, *'...defeat boredom and fear, to overcome hardship and problems—as a way out of almost anything.'*

It's not just the boys who enjoy having a laugh. Furlong (1977) reports the case of the girls of 4G, in a London secondary school. These girls spent much of their time *'mucking about'*. The best way to do this was to be cheeky to the teacher. The 4G girls blamed the *mucking about* on the teacher and the boredom in the classroom. So, 'almost anything' would be done to reduce, *'...the almost enduring boredom of an irrelevant school life.'*

There is humour in reflecting on escaping from a world from which it seemed there was no escape. Here Lenny Bruce comments on the toughness of his early life:

'I won't say ours was a tough school, but we had our own coroner. We used to write essays like, 'What I'm going to do if I grow up.' (Carr & Greeves, 2007)

The ultimate parody of this type of humour was performed by the *Pythons*, in the *Four Yorkshire men* sketch:

EI: 'We never used to have a cup. We used to drink out of a rolled up newspaper.'

GC: 'The best WE could manage was to suck on a piece of damp cloth.'

TG: But you know, we were happy in those days, though we were poor.' (www.davidpbrown.co.uk)

Reflection

It is quite amazing that people can laugh in the most awful of circumstances. Humour is the last thing a person has with which to declare his or her humanity; that their spirit is indomitable. It cannot be taken away. Gallows humour is a way of attacking an oppressor or coping with an intolerable situation. It proves you are still alive and not crushed by circumstances.

Gallows humour may well be better than the alternative, as Lord Byron put it:

'And if I laugh at any mortal thing

'Tis that I may not weep.'   (http://thinkexist.com)

The concept of gallows humour has become rather elastic over time. It seems to have moved away from being only concerned with death and more towards coping with difficulty and constraint. There

is deep humour in the constraints of the human condition. Such humour relates to everyone and is so poignant, mixing, as it does, the happy and the sad. You should concentrate your efforts here if you are after great affect and effect.

Activity

1) Your task is to design your own gravestone epitaph. Here are some examples:

'Here lies an atheist.

All dressed up

And no place to go!   (Thurmont, Maryland)

'Here lies the body of Jonathan Blake.

He stepped on the gas instead of the brake.'   (Uniontown, Pennsylvania)

'Sir John Strange

Here lies an honest lawyer,

And that is strange!'

(Sir John Strange, 1696-1754, Master of the Rolls, Lowlayton, Essex) (www.pennyparker2.com)

Spinster postmistress, North Carolina:

'Returned—Unopened'

An adulterous husband, Atlanta, Georgia:

'Gone, but not forgiven.'

'Here lies Suzannah Ensign.

Lord she is thin'   (Thin=Thine)   (Cooperstown, New York)   (www.webpan.com)

These epitaphs: are word-plays on people's names; comments on a life lived; reveal cause of death, and consider the hereafter.

My attempts are: Was Spurr, now Hotspurr; Once taught, now taut; Laugh, I really died; Stiff at last.

2) Darsham Singh was Singapore's public executioner for nearly 50 years, 1959-2006. In that time he was responsible for the death of 1,000 people.

Darsham gained satisfaction from his work. He is quoted as saying: 'I am the fastest executioner in the world and I don't ---- about?' (Johnson, 2013)

Supply the missing word (Answer below)

The answer to the first activity is "Hang"

Sexist, racist and disability humour

A blonde is driving down a deserted highway when she gets pulled over. The cop gets out of his car and asks if she has been drinking and she replies 'No.'

His breathalyzer equipment is broken.

So he radios the station and asks what to do.

The cop at the station says, 'Is she a blonde driving a lipstick red Corvette?' and the cop replies 'Yes.'

So the other cop says 'What you do is tell her to get out of the car and pull out your dick and you walk up to her.'

So the cop does exactly what the other cop says.

The blonde gets out of the car and he whips out his dick.

The blonde 'sighs' and says, 'Please not another breathalyzer test!'   (Jokes4us.com)

That American dumb blonde gag basically tells us that women are stupid, and are readily available for the sexual gratification of the dominant, superior male.

Bemiller & Schneider (2010) analysed 153 internet jokes about women and came to the following conclusion, that the jokes:

'…equate women to objects available for men's pleasure, make light of violence against women, denigrate women's personal characteristics, and belittle their social roles.'

Not surprisingly, many women, and indeed, men, are opposed to these jokes as they demean women. They are not politically correct. Consequently, such jokes, and the comedians who tell them, have rather disappeared, particularly from our T.V. screens.

People who are opposed to sexist jokes regard them as offensive. Bergman (1986), for example, argues that: *'Whenever somebody tells or laughs at a sexist joke it is an insult to those people who have been hurt and who will be hurt by sexist beliefs, whether the insult is intended or not.'*

Women are more sensitive to sexist humour as they are usually the victims of it. Sev'er & Ungar (1997) researched Canadian student/staff acceptability of gender based jokes. They found that:

'…female faculty are the most sensitive to the demeaning possibilities of humour, whereas male students seem almost oblivious of these issues.'

When women hear sexist jokes they are more disgusted than amused; they report being angry, hostile, and surprised. They roll their eyes more, possibly in contempt, and touch their faces more, possibly in embarrassment. (La France & Woodzicka, 1998)

The re-telling of sexist (and racist) jokes sustains and normalises sexism (and racism). Ford &

Ferguson (2004) put forward a *prejudiced norm* theory in relation to such disparagement humour. They argue that the humour frame signals the material as non-serious. Therefore, the listener should not be critical. This leads to greater personal tolerance of discrimination and, for the highly prejudiced, there is a perception of a norm of tolerance towards discrimination.

Indeed, Ford et al. (2008) conducted two experiments that supported the hypothesis that showed, for sexist men, *'…exposure to sexist humor can promote the behavioural release of prejudice against women.'*

Men can be hostilely sexist, and hold negative stereotypes and antagonism towards women. These men rate jokes which disparage women as *'more funny and less offensive.'* They are more likely to repeat such jokes than men who are less hostilely sexist. (Thomas & Esses, 2004)

Technically, those totally opposed to sexist and racist humour are adopting a *moralist* position. Here, the view is that, *'…if a joke manifests ethically bad attitudes, it is therefore unfunny, and hence fails as a joke.'*

Those who tell sexist and racist jokes are in the following camps. The immoralist *'…holds that sometimes, but not always, the immorality of a joke enhances its funniness.'*

The *amoralist* detaches him or herself from the content of the joke, *'Amoralism is the idea that when we joke we only entertain ideas and do not actually hold them.'*

Finally, the *ethicist* position is that, *'…the immorality of a joke always counts against its funniness but does not necessarily extinguish it since a joke may be funny in virtue of non-moral qualities, such as inventiveness and the capacity to surprise.'* (Conolly & Haydar, 2005).

If we consider the ethics of sexual banter and jokes at work, there are two sides to the argument. One side argues that this humour creates a *'jovial'* atmosphere and that flirtation can result in love and romance. The other side argue that such humour is not appropriate as it, *'…undermines women's efforts to view themselves, and to be viewed by others, as equal and dignified employees.'* (Berdahl & Aquino, 2009)

Berdahl & Aquino found that, not surprisingly, *'…men tend to view the same sexual behaviors at work as less offensive and harmful than the women.'* Whilst men in 5 North American workplaces (N=800) evaluated sexual behaviour positively (46%), or neutrally (41%), women evaluated it neutrally (47%) or negatively (44%)

Blue jokes at work may have legal consequences in Britain. The law concerning sexual harassment and employment, refers to, *'unwanted conduct of a sexual nature'*. In addition, the conduct, *'…must have the purpose or effect of violating the applicant's dignity, or creating an intimidating, hostile, degrading, humiliating or offensive environment…'* (Lockwood et al., 2011)

Lockwood et al. analysed 317 cases of sexual harassment in Suffolk, 1995-2005. They found that females were 96.5% of the complainants, and that 90% claimed to have experienced verbal sexual harassment. Examples of such harassment were:

'…being sworn at, offensive jokes or remarks, sexually oriented banter, verbal abuse, inappropriate conversation and questions/discussion about a person's sex life.'

Sometimes a tribunal regards sexual remarks as being part of normal staff banter, and do not consider them as being sexual harassment. However, the intention of humour in banter does not *'...constitute a defence against words or actions being interpreted as sexual harassment.'* (Lockwood et al., 2011)

If the applicant *contributed to sexual conduct*, their case may be damaged. So, in some cases where the applicant had indulged in sexual banter, their argument failed. In other, similar, cases, the tribunal held that willingness to discuss sexual matters did not remove the adverse impact of the harassment.

Lockwood et al., suggest that, acting like *'one of the boys'*, and telling inappropriate jokes, *'...might not be the best strategy for a woman who subsequently takes a claim to an Employment Tribunal.'* They observe that tribunals don't seem to recognise that engagement in sexual banter may be a *'coping strategy'*.

The law does seem to be on the side of the blue joke teller, so long as the female victim does not take immediate action. Take the following high profile case, involving Jordan Wimmer, a female city worker, who sued for £4m. in a sex discrimination case. Her boss, an aptly named Mr Lowe, admitted to referring to her as *'decorative'*, and also told her *'dumb blonde'* jokes. He managed to advise her to, *'work more and dress less'*. He sent her, and other female colleagues, *'... innuendo-laden emails containing jokes about topless women, sex and Viagra.'* (Cockcroft, 2011). In his defence Mr Lowe said, *'...he had been guilty only of office "banter" '*

The tribunal rejected Ms Wimmer's claim, observing that she was, *'not a woman who would have suffered in silence.'* They said she should have complained about the jokes, as she did not, *'...We conclude therefore that they were not unwanted.'* (Cockcroft, 2011)

So, the following complainant would probably fail as immediate action was not taken:

A man walks up to a woman in his office each day, stands very close to her, draws in a large breath of air and tells her that her hair smells nice.

After a week of this she can't stand it any longer. The woman goes into her supervisor's office and tells him that she wants to file a sexual harassment suit against the man and explains why. The supervisor is so puzzled by this and says, 'What's wrong with the co-worker telling you your hair smells nice?'

The woman replies, 'He's a midget!' (www.jokes4us.com)

In practice, most women do not take legal action against sexist behaviour at work. Neither do they seem to confront the issue and the jokers directly. What happens is that, *'...so many women maintain a complete silence about harassment.'* (Quinn, 2000)

'...back there (in my department) they, they comment all the time, you know, about my breasts, or whatever. But I know that they're doing it in the context of a joke, and like I say, it rolls off my back...If I thought they really meant it, then maybe it would bother me.' (Quinn, 2000)

(An American policewoman) *'There have been many occasions where male coworkers have made sexually explicit jokes or comments. However, I choose not to take the talk personally. I don't find their behaviour offensive, just childish. I don't put energy into being concerned about what people are joking about...I don't dwell on it.'* (Somvadee & Morash, 2008)

The survival strategy is to deflect the issue by *'not taking it personal.'* The woman has to keep her job and maintain an on-going involvement in her group, so she cannot afford to exclude herself by antagonising the group, complaining about their jokes and banter.

Paradoxically, female co-workers can be in a group, but outside it because of their gender. The males *'...gain power over an individual woman by calling attention to her difference, that is, to her womanliness.'*

It is this calling attention to difference which is one of the problems with racist jokes and banter. Someone who feels they ought to belong is made aware of their difference when racial jokes are made with them as the butt.

Take this piece of banter which led to Sol Campbell, the ex-England footballer, leaving West Ham United, when a schoolboy, never to return:

'Cheer up Sulzeer, you're two-one up,' this coach said to him as he walked to the changing room.

'What do you mean, two-one up?'

'West Indies are beating us in the cricket, two-one.'The test series?'

'Oh yeah, I get it,' the boy replied.   (Walsh, 2014)

The teaser probably doesn't recognise the hurt caused by his exclusionary remarks, whilst it is felt more deeply by the one who wants to belong, but is not allowed through no fault of his own.

Take this example from an American office where *Barry*, an Indian, is teased because of his foreign accent.

'We asked Barry if any of the humor that is used ever made him feel uncomfortable. He replied that it does 'sometimes.' He continued with 'Yeah, because we are foreigners and because of our pronunciation of things.'

One of the teasers made this comment: *'Hey, it's in good fun. We are not racist. We just do it because it is fun, but we never take it too far to hurt someone. I want to show I like you and teasing does that.'*   (Ojha & Holmes, 2010)

Wright (1993) gives an example of a more blatant comment, made in jest, at a Midlands comprehensive school, where, subsequently, there was institutional involvement:

Teacher: *'...I was down at Lower School, I had a black girl in my class, she did something or another. I said to her, if you're not careful I'll send you back to the chocolate factory. She went home and told her parents, her dad came up to school, and decided to take the matter to the Commission for Racial Equality. It was only said in good fun, nothing malicious.'*

These sorts of 'joke' cannot be typical, but the evidence suggests it is not that uncommon. An American survey of 3450 teenage students found that 86% had never heard a teacher make a negative religious remark, 85% had never heard a teacher make a racist remark, 84% of them had never heard a homophobic remark, and 75% had never heard a teacher make a sexist remark (Harris Interactive & GLSEN, 2005). These results do suggest, then, that about one teacher in six is prepared to cross the line at some stage.

One example of line-crossing, recorded by Wanzer et al (2006), is really up there. These researchers asked 284 American university students to recall examples of *'appropriate'* and *'inappropriate'* humour used by their teachers:

The student was of Indian decent (sic) and a practicing Hindu. The teacher mocked her by saying, 'Go worship your cow'

Even people you wouldn't suspect of crossing the line do so on occasion. Take for example, the acclaimed liberal humanist, Professor Laurie Taylor. He got into trouble once at an academic conference organised by the *European Society for the Study of Social Control*. As a key note speaker Taylor started with this opening joke:

'What do you call four sheep tied up to a lamp-post in the middle of Cardiff?'

'A leisure centre.'

The President of the Society had a word with Taylor, and pointed out that the Society had an anti-racist clause in its charter. Therefore, Taylor had to apologise to the conference delegates. It is not clear if he also had to apologise to the Welsh nation, or the sheep come to that.

The Society President went on to ask Taylor from whence he came. Taylor replied *'Liverpool.'* *'Excellent,'* said the President, *'Then you're in an admirable position to answer my next question. What do you call a Scouser in a suit?'....'The accused.'* (Taylor, 1997)

Of course, the main argument against the telling of such racist and ethnic jokes is that they reinforce existing stereotypes and thus help to perpetuate them.

People are aware they shouldn't be telling these sorts of jokes and so reserve them for the times when those who are likely to be offended are not present. For example, a Swedish factory worker made the following pertinent comment:

We have a certain level of morality that keeps us from crossing the line...It's not suitable (to joke) all the time. It's almost like you hold back somehow...It's ok when we (the group members) are alone; we can handle it, but with religious people and others...I don't know.'(Stromberg & Karlsson, 2009)

That is, *'How does every black joke start? With a look over your shoulder.'* (www.ellisjones.co.uk)

Barnes et al. (2001), in their study of conversations in South Africa, found that humour was 'the most commonly used strategy to introduce the topic of race into the conversation.' This strategy allows the speaker to avoid being called racist as an angry response would be '...an inappropriate response to humor.' Even if people just share racist and sexist jokes with confidants at work, they can still get into trouble as many firms have policies that prohibit such behaviour, particularly with regard to transmission via e-mail. For example, thirty BT call centre workers were suspended for sending each other the following, poor, Irish joke:

A man is on top of the Connor Pass in Kerry, watching three of his friends attempting to fly.

The first attaches budgies to each shoulder, jumps from a cliff and falls to his death. The second throws a parrot in the air, jumps off the cliff and attempts to shoot the parrot on the way down, but instead plummets and breaks his spine. The third raises a chicken above his head and also jumps only to fall to serious injury.

The observer says he will never try budgie-jumping, parrotshooting or hengliding. (Nolan, 2009)

You might say suspension was a bit harsh in this case. Maybe it was, but firms are well aware of the legal and financial consequences of condoning a culture where such jokes are commonplace. As long ago as 1994, Irishman Trevor McAuley was awarded £6,000 by an industrial tribunal for taunts at his expense. He was often called a *'typical thick paddy'*:

'I complained to the management about the Irish remarks and taunts day in, and day out, five days a week, and was told not to worry about it. When I made further complaints I was told I had an attitude problem.' (Mackinnon, 1994)

So, it is no wonder that firms can be quite strict about jokes at work. Take another case, this time of a Polish engineer, Adrian Ruda, who was awarded £2,250 by an Employment Tribunal in Leeds, for being *'degraded and humiliated'* by a fellow worker giving him the nickname, *Borat*.

The employment Judge, Jonathan Whittaker ruled that the nickname was direct race discrimination:

'The application of the nickname 'Borat' violated Mr Ruda's dignity in the period in question and created for him a degrading, humiliating and defensive work environment.'

The company, *TEI*, had to pay the fine, and *'substantial'* legal costs as well as having to train the workforce to conform to a harassment and bullying policy. (Doughty & Cooper, 2011)

The Equality Act of 2010 makes matters even more complicated for organisations as it introduced the concept of *'third party harassment.'* What this means is that someone can claim for damages concerning jokes or banter they simply overheard, which were, in fact, aimed at others. (www.informededinburgh.co.uk)

Moving on, is it racist to tell jokes that other races or ethnic groups tell about themselves. That is, for example, can non-Jews tell Jewish jokes? Silberman-Federman (1995), for one, is quite clear that, *'…only Jews may tell Jewish jokes.'* Comedienne, Maureen Lipman, indicates the way Jewish people feel: *'Invariably, I bridle when a non-Jew tells a Jewish joke.'* (Lipman, 1995)

It would be nice if Gentiles could tell Jewish jokes as Jewish humour is a distinctively funny humour, maybe the finest in the world. Indeed, Jimmy Carr claims *"The Jews are widely accepted as the 'jokingest' group of people on earth".* (Carr & Greeves, 2007).

George Mikes (1980) considers that: *"Many people-I am one of them-think that Jewish jokes are the best of all. They are not only funny but are often wise and profound, revealing so much about human nature, the secrets of the human soul…"*

Take this simple one about the long-suffering Jewish mother:

"How many Jewish mothers does it take to screw in a light bulb?

None. It's ok, I'll just sit here in the dark."

(Metcalf, 2009)

Clearly, it is probably best that a Jewish person tells this joke as they may well have had the experience of being the child of such a mother, and so can tell it from the heart. Also, it's probably best told to a Jewish audience as they understand the reference and share the experience. Incidentally, Weinstein (2008) reckons that Jewish mother jokes aren't so funny nowadays, *'because they no longer reflect reality.'* This indicates another problem for the non-Jewish joke-teller, his/her Jewish joke may be out-dated because he/she hasn't realised that change has occurred.

Beyond the level of joke telling effectiveness, can anyone tell jokes about another nationality or ethnic group, or is it only insiders that can joke about themselves? Nilsen & Nilsen (1999) explain that people can tell jokes about their particular group because they are insiders and have rights to criticise, whereas an outsider is more likely to stereotype. Indeed, Freud (1991) did note the particular critical quality of Jewish jokes, *'I do not know whether there are many other instances of a people making fun to such a degree of its own character.'* There are many anti-Jewish Jewish jokes told by Jews.

So, if an outsider tells an authentic Jewish joke that is critical, is he/she mocking or not? The Jewish listener cannot be absolutely sure, which, at the very least, will affect the joke's perceived quality. The reaction will depend on the extent to which a joking relationship has already been established.

Silberman-Federman (1995) points out that the key difference between an anti-Semitic joke and a Jewish joke is that, *'the former emphasizes the faults but never the virtues of the Jew.'* Silberman-Federman alerts non-Jews to be sensitive:

'We (Jews) are all aware of our feelings of resentment and fear at our hearing a non-Jewish colleague or friend relate a joke about Jews. Jewish jokes are only those which are told by Jews to other Jews. Non-Jews tell jokes about Jews.'

The Jews have a history of oppression. As a consequence, they have developed a strong humour as a defence and support. This humour acts as a self-protective fortress (Silberman-Federman, 1995). This is why non-Jews cannot tell Jewish jokes; outsiders shouldn't purloin the Jewish weapons. So, for example, the Jewish fans of Tottenham Hotspur have their humour arsenal.

Similar arguments apply to the telling of jokes about the disabled by the able-bodied. For the disabled, jokes they make together about their condition strengthen group bonds, and make their difficulties a bit easier to bear. However, for the able bodied to find humour in disability, *'... is not politically correct; it is mean spirited and denigrates those with disabilities.'* (Albrecht, 1999)

'What is humorous and accepted by disabled people in their inside world may not be understood by people in the outside world. Also, inside jokes add to disability culture by providing a bond to this minority or marginalised group; hence 'crip humor.' What they accept from their peers, they may not tolerate from others because of the perceived intent of the language or joke.' (Albrecht, 1999)

Interestingly, deaf people tend to strengthen their in-group by attacking out-groups. These groups can be either, people who can hear, or people who are also disabled. The jokes about those who can hear are *'…based on hearing people making idiots of themselves.'* Also, there are *'…many jokes that use three characters of a deaf man, a blind man and a man in a wheelchair.'* (Sutton-Spence & Napoli, 2012)

Finally, it does seem that sexist, racist and disability humour is on the way out. It's just inconceivable that a *Benny Hill* or a *Bernard Manning* would be allowed to broadcast on British television or radio anymore. This is a victory for the forces of political correctness. As Jo Brand puts it:

…the existence of political correctness is a GOOD THING because it protects the vulnerable. (Brand, 2010)

Even the Conservative Party has seen the light. After observing the 'comic' Jim Davidson at a Conservative gala dinner at the *Hilton*, where Davidson mocked the catering staff for being asylum seekers, Parliament's Speaker, John Bercow, said:

People say it's just a bit of fun. We have got to make it clear that bawdy racist and sexist humour is not acceptable. There is nothing funny about it.' (Brogan, 2002)

Of course, not everyone is there yet. Here are some of the jokes made by comedian Paul Eastwood at the UKIP conference gala dinner, 2014:

(About the Olympics) *'Poland did well. They took home bronze, silver, gold, lead, copper-anything they could lay their hands on.'*

'Team Somalia-they did well, didn't they? They had to apologise. Didn't realise sailing and shooting were two different events.' (Glaze & Cookney, 2014)

Perhaps we shouldn't cheer too soon. A 2007 survey found that one in three workers, *'…regularly hears jokes of a racist or sexist nature.'* (Reade, 2007)

Reflection

People have long made jokes about other races, the other sex, and the disabled. It is the more powerful, and the more fortunate, laughing at the less powerful, and the less fortunate. To some extent, with regard to racist humour, such jokes may also express fears about immigration and consequent changes in society and its structures, particularly employment.

These jokes are essentially about superiority. They portray others as weak, ignorant, inferior. They have the function of uniting the in-group, and this is why they are so often used.

For the powerful, usually white men, the jokes are seen as just that, jokes. Something not to be taken seriously, meant in good fashion. For the victims, the jokes are seen as insensitive and hurtful, by confirming their relative position in the system.

The jokes are usually based on stereotypes, which may never have been true, or, if true once, that truth no longer applies. Stereotypes can be very misleading as they are so broad brush, they cannot possibly apply to the whole group which is maligned. There will be much variation within a single large grouping, so it is grossly unfair to tar everyone with the same brush.

Society, and hence the law, has recognised the problem of discriminatory humour. Racist, sexist and disability gags are now taboo, although they continue underground, and even over-ground in some cases.

Activity

1) Change a Jewish joke so that it becomes a non-Jewish joke

In order to do this we need to know what a Jewish joke is. A Jewish joke, *'must express a Jewish sensibility'*, that is, be concerned with, *'subjects and values that receive disproportionate attention among Jews.'* (Telushkin, 1992) Just taking a standard joke and giving the characters Jewish names doesn't make that joke distinctively Jewish. So, for example, this next joke is not really a Jewish joke, although it is dressed up as Jewish:

A student was talking to his rabbi. He asked which personal quality he really needed to become a rabbi. 'Imagination' was the answer from the rabbi, 'You will have to imagine that somebody is paying attention to what you say.' (Spalding, 1979)

You could easily change the word rabbi to lecturer or priest and the joke still works. This is because no real Jewish sensibility is involved in the original joke. It concerns a worldwide problem.

It is a far different story when we get on to real Jewish jokes. Let's take those about Jewish family life. Weinstein (2008) notes that, *'Judaism has always been distinguished by its strong family* life'. *From the very outset, Judaism predicated its survival on family.'* It is no surprise then, that Jewish families have provided much material for the humourist. In particular, Jewish humour looks at the problems where this relationship becomes too intense (Telushkin, 1992).

The Jewish mother stereotype was mater as martyr, *'She is never happier than when she has something to complain about, with the complaint intended to produce feelings of guilt in her children.'* (Dundes, 1985) For example:

A mother gave her son two neck ties as a present. He wore one of the ties when he came to see her. 'The mother took one look at the neck tie and asked anxiously, 'What's the matter? The other one you didn't like? (Spalding, 1979)

Jewish parents may be overambitious, intrusive and nervous (Telushkin, 1992):

Mr. and Mrs. Marvin Rosenbloom are pleased to announce the birth of their son, Dr. Jonathan Rosenbloom.'(Telushkin, 1992*)*

So, can you take those two genuinely Jewish jokes and turn them into jokes with no ethnic connotation? I think not. The following, amended joke just doesn't make sense:

Mr. and Mrs. Martin Smith are pleased to announce the birth of their son, Dr, John Smith.

So, you can only adapt ethnic jokes which are superficially ethnic, but the genuine ethnic joke is best left alone, as its meaning will be lost in translation.

2) Work out your response to non-politically correct humour

Exeter University has published guidelines about what you should do when confronted with discriminatory jokes:

'Simply asking for an explanation may encourage someone to review their behaviour. For example, you might ask: 'Can you explain that to me?' or 'What do you mean?' or 'Can you explain to me what the joke is?' or 'Why is that funny?'

These questions can be confronting. If the joke is stripped away, people are faced with the real implications of what they are saying.' (www.socialsciences.exeter.ac.uk)

3) Determine your moral stance

How would you classify yourself with regard to: a) sexist jokes, b) racist jokes, c) disability jokes?

A moralist stance: *'...if a joke manifests ethically bad attitudes, it is therefore unfunny, and hence fails as a joke.'*

An immoralist stance: *'...holds that sometimes, but not always, the immorality of a joke enhances its funniness.'*

An amoralist stance: *'Amoralism is the idea that when we joke we only entertain ideas and do not actually hold them.'*

An ethicist stance: *'...the immorality of a joke always counts against its funniness but does not necessarily extinguish it since a joke may be funny in virtue of non-moral qualities, such as inventiveness and the capacity to surprise.'*

Are you consistent across a), b) & c)?

I am, of course, a moralist, as two of my favourite stories demonstrate:

A young ventriloquist is touring the clubs, and one night he's doing a show in a small town in Arkansas. With his dummy on his knee, he's going through the usual dumb blonde jokes. When a blonde woman in the fourth row stands on her chair and starts shouting: 'I've had enough of your stupid blonde jokes. What makes you think you can stereotype women this way? What does the color of a person's hair have to do with her worth as a human being? It's guys like you who keep women like me from being respected at work and in the community and from reaching our full potential as a person, because you and your kind continue to perpetuate discrimination against, not only blondes, but women in general...and all in the name of humor!'The young ventriloquist is embarrassed and begins to apologise when the blonde yells, 'You stay out of this mister! I'm talking to that little jerk on your knee.' (Hurley et al., 2011)

Two mathematicians were having dinner in a restaurant, arguing about the average mathematical knowledge of the American public. One mathematician claimed that this average was woefully inadequate, the other maintained it was surprisingly high.

'I'll tell you what.' Said the cynic, 'ask that waitress a simple math question. If she gets it right, I'll pick up dinner. If not, you do.' He then excused himself to visit the men's room, and the other called the waitress over. 'When my friend comes back,' he told her, 'I'm going to ask a question and I want you to respond "one-third x cubed." There's twenty bucks in it for you.' She agreed.

The cynic returned from the bathroom and called the waitress over, 'the food was wonderful, thank you.' And the other mathematician stated: 'Incidentally, do you know what the integral of x squared is?'

The waitress looked pensive, almost pained. She looked around the room, at her feet, made gurgling noises, and finally said, 'Um, one-third x cubed?'

So the cynic paid the check. The waitress wheeled around, walked a few paces away, looked back at the two men, and mumbled under her breath, 'plus a constant.' (Hurley, et al., 2011)

The funny peculiar - Ah Ah!

'How do you describe an elf who refuses to have a shower?'

'Elf-ully smelly.'   (Anon., 2013d)

In this book, hopefully, I have not concentrated on how to produce the funny peculiar, however a skilled humorist needs to know what is un-funny, and how to avoid producing such disasters. One terrible joke can ruin 100 good ones.

The book started with chat-up lines. They are pretty peculiar, with no Ha Ha because they are corny, too sexual, and do not respect the recipient. We moved on to gender humour and saw that men use aggressive humour in a ranking game. When looking at word-play we found that people can blunder in their word choice, and that sound puns can be pretty gruesome. Talking about gruesome, sexual humour can easily offend, especially if it is sexist in nature. When considering the nature of group humour, teasing can be very ambiguous as to whether the tease is aggressive or friendly. Finally, negative humour can humiliate, offend, or disgust.

In all, humour can be pretty ugly. Essentially, this ugliness is due to incompetence with humour production and/or a failure to respect the sensitivities of the other. That is, poor technical skill and/or poor social skill.

Poor technical skill

Looking at poor technical skill first, Berger (2010) claims that many people think the way to be funny is to tell jokes. He argues that this is a *'bad idea'* for three reasons.

- Firstly, the joke may not be funny, which will end up *'mildly'* antagonising the listener.
- Secondly, the joke may be told badly, which won't amuse people.

- Thirdly, the listeners may have already heard the joke, which *'is painful for all concerned.'*

Technically, a joker may not have the ability to recognise that a joke is not funny. For sure, there are plenty of unfunny jokes out there:

Qu.: 'What is as big as a man, but weighs nothing.'

Ans.: 'His shadow.'

That 'joke' was rated, by professional comedians, as a 1.3, on a scale of 1-*'not at all funny'*, to 11-*'very funny'* (Kruyer & Dunning, 1999). Someone, surprisingly, must have given it more than a 1. Really, that joke has no incongruity, no wit, and so, no reason to laugh.

One pretty reliable way to tell something which isn't funny is to tell a, *'You had to have been there.'* This is what Lord Chesterfield, writing nearly 300 years ago, had to say about these second-hand tales:

'Here people very commonly err, and fond of something that has entertained them in one company, and in certain circumstances, repeat it with emphasis in another, where it is either insipid, or, it may be offensive, by being ill-tried or misplaced.' (Lord Chesterfield, c.1750)

Somehow, the *'funny'* thing doesn't seem half as funny when it is just recounted and not actually experienced. Nilsen & Nilsen (1999) give a persuasive explanation of this shortfall. They say that there is surprise and pleasure seeing someone making, *'a quip or a put-down that exactly fits a situation that couldn't have been foreseen.'* This pleasure is lost on the re-telling. There is no surprise.

For example, recently, I went into my local library to pick up a book I had reserved, *The History of Sarcasm*. The librarian picked it up, looked at it, and brought it to me. I saw the book was pretty thin. *'Call that a book'*, I said. We laughed.

That was a funny at the time remark, because it was apt. It suited the situation. It was fairly surprising. Still, it won't go down in the annals of the finest things ever said. It was good enough at the time but not much use subsequently. The aptness goes, and the joke was only relevant to the people in the interaction, not outsiders. That's why it's best not to tell these sorts of stories. They tail off and the teller has to say, rather in despair, *'It was funny at the time, you should have been there,'* somehow, rather blaming the outsider for being absent.

There is at least one time when un-funny jokes are allowed, indeed, expected, and that is Christmas, when we expect awful riddles in our Christmas Crackers. The bad jokes unite the group at their Christmas dinner, as they all cringebo together:

What did Mrs, Christmas say to Father Christmas?

'It looks like rain deer.'

'How does Father Christmas feel when he's stuck in a chimney?

Claus-trophobic.'   (Anon., 2013d)

When people make these sorts of bad puns in conversation, they sort of know they shouldn't do it, but can't help themselves. What they do is tell the pun and share the anguish with the audience. For example a presenter on Countryfile (27.10.13) was explaining sheep IQ testing. To do this, the scientists gradually made things more complicated. The presenter said:

'It's now time to raise the baa (bar).'

He then said, *'I promise that's the last time.'* (He made such puns)

When telling a joke badly the teller may get the timing wrong in two senses. The joke's punch-line may be told too quickly or slowly, or, the joke may be told at the wrong time. There are situations where jokes shouldn't be told at all, and situations, where it may be appropriate to tell a joke, only towards the end of an encounter.

Williams & Clouse (1991) give a pertinent example. An American school principal is explaining how to deal with irate parents. The principal observes that the concerns of the parents have to be taken seriously, so it is important not to be flippant at an early stage, if at all. However, shared humour at the end of such an encounter does signal normalisation of relations and a resolution of the problem, to the satisfaction of both parties.

Another reason why a joke may be un-funny is that the receiver may have already heard the joke.

So, the experienced jokester uses the preface, *'Have you heard the one about...'* before launching into a joke.

An un-funny, boring person may well rely on *'old chestnuts'*, around for donkey's years. For example:

'Knock knock'   *'Who's there?'*   *'Doctor'*   *'Doctor Who'*

Presumably this is not a funny joke as it was first heard in the playground many years ago. The interesting thing is why do we keep telling these old chestnuts to people who have already heard them, maybe several times? According to Gopie & Macleod (2009) this is due to problems with our destination memory, which involves outgoing information. When we transmit information, we focus inwards on the necessary mental processes. This self-focus reduces the attention paid to associating the message with the receiver.

It follows that it is less risky to tell topical jokes as the audience is less likely to have heard them before. The continuing success of the satirical TV programme, *Have I Got News For You* is largely due to the topicality of its material.

Freud (1991) distinguished between topical and perennial jokes. He saw topicality as a *'fertile'* source of pleasure in many jokes. He gives a joke, topical, c.1900:

'The Crown Princess Louise approached the crematorium in Gotha with the question of how much a cremation costs. The management replied: "Five thousand marks normally; but we will only charge you three thousand as you have been durchgebrannt (literally 'been burnt through'—slang for 'eloped') once already.' (The princess left her husband in 1903.)

Freud wrote that that joke, was *'irresistible today'*, but, that, sometime later, *'it will lose its effect entirely'*; so true.

The only thing to do with dated jokes is to discard them or update them. Take this one from the 1930s:

'Where has Mrs Simpson gone?' 'She's gone with the Windsor.'   (Blake, 2007).

The reference to the *Royal House of Windsor* may be easily seen, but the reference to the film *Gone with the Wind* is rather elusive. It is pretty impossible to update that one, so it goes on the discard pile.

People do have old jokes and stories that are tried and tested. They are known to work. So, it is a shock when one of these *'reliables'* is told and it doesn't work. It is tempting to blame the audience, but it may well be that the joke has reached its sell-by-date.

Poor social skill

Humour attempts in group situations can fail, and how. Robinson & Smith-Lovin (2001) found that there were 375 humour attempts in the 29, six-person discussions that they studied, of which, *'almost half'* were successes. This indicates that, on average, a humour attempt in a group situation has a 50:50 chance of success. The failure rate increases, according to these researchers, when a new group forms, when there is no common culture.

Jennifer Hay (1995) gives a useful list of the types of *'failed'* humour she observed amongst groups of New Zealand friends:

- *'Insufficient contextualisation'.*
  SM tells an anecdote about the people who came to see a play he was in. GM then fantasises about taking such people to the bathroom.
  Here, the attempt at humour is not relevant, as it is separate from the situation. It goes unsupported as the flow is elsewhere and the humour is an unwelcome intrusion.

- *"Being too late on reviving 'dead' humour."*
  MM talks about a tape with sound effects on it. The conversation moves on to the fridge, which has beer in it. EM then jokes about sound effects.
  The humour failed because the flow has moved on. It is not easy to return back to the now *'dead'* humour.
  Interestingly, *EM* was conscious his joke had failed. He cleared his throat to cover the silence and cover his embarrassment. Hay considers that throat clearing is a *'relatively common'* strategy for dealing with failed humour.

- *'Assuming too much background knowledge.'*

  About People
  SF tries to joke about a strange couple, Tessa Davies and Tim Dapple. As the audience don't know the couple, the humour fails.
  Unjustified assumptions are made about the knowledge of people. A joke falls flat because the listener has no idea what the joker is talking about.

  About Specialist Knowledge
  AF is a linguist, and no-one else is. She refers to *elision* which is not understood and therefore not seen as funny.

- *'Misjudging the relation between speaker and audience.'*
  JF jokes about her drunkenness and subsequent sickness. SF tries to tease her about it, but appears to have over-stepped the mark and the humour fails.
  Here, someone had assumed they were in a joking relationship, and hence could tease or insult. If this, in fact, is not the case, then the humour will be seen as an affront, and so fail.

- *'Negatively teasing someone present.'*
  BM teases AM that he will be *'killed'* in an upcoming tournament they are both involved in. The audience does not respond.

A negative tease gives the audience a problem. They can either support the tease and so taunt the butt of the tease, or they can support the butt and not laugh at the teaser. If they take the latter view, the joke fails.

- *'Trying to gain membership of exclusive sub-groups*
  DM and *LM* quote from their favourite TV programme, something they often do. *AM* tries to join in. *LM* replies *'yeah,'* and *DM* and *LM* continue with their routine.
  Here, someone has tried to use humour to enter an exclusive sub-group, which has its own joking routines. The humour attempt interferes, and, as a result, it fails.

- *'Disrupting serious conversation'*
  MM needs to know if someone has finished their dissertation. *TM* interrupts with wordplay, *'yeah one way or the other he's finished.'*
  If people are conducting a serious conversation, a humorous interruption may well not be welcomed.

- *'Portraying oneself inappropriately for one's status or gender.'*
  BM, a male is able to joke about drugs whilst *AF*, a female, is not supported when she jokes about the same subject.
  As Hay puts it, *'If we put ourselves across in a way that violates society's expectations or norms then we sometimes will not receive support.'*

These failures are mostly to do with sensitivity failure. Jokers who fail are not sufficiently sensitive to others, their knowledge, their concerns and their feelings; and are insensitive to the situation. Individuals also put their concerns first, and behave inappropriately.

This insensitivity is probably not deliberate. Most of us are not really skilled at knowing when and how to joke and with whom. When people are joking they may well concentrate on the joke and can easily forget the possible impact on others.

Gunning (2001) gives a couple of examples of sensitivity failure:

Vera: There was a training earlier this year. It was grammar, punctuation, that type of thing. And our supervisor was passing around the information wanting to know if people were interested. I thought I would be humorous and on the form I wrote, "Don't need this, no how no way."

Well, another person in the department got it, and she didn't think it was so funny...And I really did feel bad. And, it made me start to think. Sometimes you do have to be careful about what you say or do because somebody might take it the wrong way. I had already taken the training and thought it was a good training. But, sometimes you do just do things without thinking.' (Gunning, 2001)

That is the minor sort of thing that can easily get us all in trouble. Gunning goes on to recount a practical joke, carried out in a child welfare organisation in America, which was much more serious. The person who told Gunning about the prank admitted it was, *'...terribly funny but terribly terrible'*. A worker had, illicitly, got hold of letter headed note paper from a Health Clinic. This paper was used as part of an April's Fool joke. An official letter was sent to a work colleague, telling her she was required to go for testing for HIV/Aids, as her partner had been unfaithful with an HIV carrier.

The victim of this prank was, *'…very, very upset.'*

Such hostile humour seems to be, *'characteristic of an extraverted person with high social self-esteem, but who is neither agreeable nor conscientious.'* (Saroglou & Scariot, 2002). This sort of person is not interested in others. (What we might call the *Bernard Manning* type of extrovert).

The *Bernard Manning* type would probably score high on the *Cavalier Humour Scale* developed by Hodson et al. (2010). This scale measures, *'a lighthearted, less serious, uncritical, and nonchalant approach toward humor that dismisses potential harm to others.'* Hodson et al. found that, those higher in *Cavalier Humour Belief* (CHB) were more extraverted, less agreeable, and less conscientious.

The Cavalier humourists believe that a joke is simply just a joke, so others should not be serious in reading *'non-existent'* meanings into jokes. Hodson et al. point out that this stance enables dominance expression, and the masking of underlying intentions.

People can be insensitive when they use humour to trivialise something which is important to a person making a request or stating an opinion.

Drew (a manager in a Government agency): *'When somebody is coming to you with something pretty serious to talk about and you make light of it; joke about it. Even if you thought it was minor in the scheme of things, to that person it was pretty important. That would be a very inappropriate use of humor.'* (Gunning, 2001)

In the school situation a teacher may be tempted to dismiss a student problem with a joke, in order, literally, *'to laugh it off'*. This may be particularly annoying for the student as, what is an important matter for him/her, has not only not been dealt with properly, but the joke has added insult to injury.

Bauer & Geront (1999) studied humour usage in a nursing home for elderly residents. They found that carers, in the case of sexuality, used jokes, innuendo, and titillating chat:

'Humor as used by caregivers by and large acts as a smokescreen which effectively conceals residents' genuine needs and desires for sexual fulfilment. Joking hides the true face of residents' sexuality and conveys to residents the message that their sexual needs are not to be taken seriously.'

Trivialisation via humour can be a key way that the powerful humiliate the weak. For example, Lindsay (2013) argues that trivialisation was a tactic used to justify the crushing of Native Americans:

'Euro-Americans-mostly white males from the United States-living in California used forms of humor to trivialize Indian humanity, to achieve a state of psychological consonance even while being the perpetrators of and bystanders to a very visible and brutally effective campaign of genocide.'

The trivialising humour fell into five categories: comparison of Native Americans and whites to show their inhumanity; trivialisation of mistreatment; presentation of racist stereotypes; dehumanisation via euphemism, and entertainment and sport at the Native Americans' expense.

One newspaper published this 'joke' in 1864:

A 'big Injun' having strayed from the camp, found himself lost in trying to return to it. After looking about, he drew himself up and exclaimed 'Injun lost!' but recovering himself, and feeling unwilling to acknowledge such shortsightedness, continued, 'No, Injun not lost, wigwam lost' (striking his breast) 'Injun here.'

People also use humour as a defence mechanism to avoid hearing something or discussing something. For example, this is what some hospital patients do:

'Some patients reportedly used jokes to avoid painful topics that needed to be discussed, to distract providers from questions the patients didn't want to answer, or even as a means of denying that they were really sick.' (Francis et al., 1999)

Nurses, if they spend their time joking, may not be doing their job properly:

(Cindy) 'If I'm joking with you I'm interacting with you. We're talking but I don't have to take the time to ask what's bugging you...I'm not really finding out why you're upset...'   (Major, 1998)

Another type of insensitivity is a failure to recognise that foreigners may not have a similar sense of humour. They may define certain situations as not appropriate for joking. Hurn (2007) gives this example, concerning a less than amused German businessman:

'The British, in particular, like to use humour in business presentations, but this is not always appreciated as it may give the wrong impression. A German businessman is quoted as saying when a

British company executive began his formal presentation with a joke: "er ist nicht serios!" '

This inter-cultural problem occurs when native teachers are instructing foreign students. Nahas (1998) found this with regard to cultural differences between a nurse and his/her teacher:

'I did not find my clinical teacher as having a sense of humour, no matter what my peers said. For me, her sense of humour was degrading and belittling and sometimes sexist and culturally inappropriate. In my culture, we take all things seriously, especially when looking after our patients. We never made fun about our patients nor tell jokes.'

There are other reasons why humour fails. Someone may 'get' a joke but not laugh because they disagree with the propositions put forward by the joke. For example, a sexist or racist joke (Smuts, 2010). Again, in this case, the teller has failed to be sensitive to the audiences' possible reaction.

Page (2011) gives a relevant example concerning attitudes towards Liverpudlians. Here, the principal of a further education college contributed an article to a monthly staff newsletter, which was found offensive. The principal observed that it was fortunate that a minibus, used for a field trip to Liverpool, had returned intact, with nothing, like the wheels, for example, stolen. The member of staff responsible for the trip was offended by the negative stereotyping and discrimination. She emailed the principal, and got an apologetic reply, however, there was no formal retraction.

That lecturer made her opinion about the principal's failed humour perfectly clear. It is interesting how e-mail enables criticism to be made, something which is more difficult to do face-to-face, especially with someone in a higher hierarchical position.

Heller (1983) recounts a face-to-face incident where students tried a united protest about the *'ribald'* jokes of a college professor (not him, he hastens to add). The female students agreed a mass walk-out if the professor made an improper remark in his next lecture. The next lecture began with the following observation, *'there is a terrible shortage of prostitutes in Singapore.'* The females got up and started to leave. The professor called after them, *'Don't go now girls. The next plane doesn't leave for Singapore until Thursday.'*

People may not go down the challenge route for fear of losing a battle of wits. They may also fear of being accused of being, *'overly sensitive'*. For example, this is what was found by Davidson (1987) with regard to some black and Mexican American students. They said that many of the jokes told by whites, in their presence, were hurtful, but they, *'felt great pressure not to complain.'*

If he or she is challenged, the aggressor can always say, *'Can't you take a joke?'* This is a very convenient escape route which transfers the blame to the other. This come-back does suggest that everything spoken in jest is permissible, simply because the attack has been clothed in that way.

If challenged further, humour gives people a way of backing down, an escape route. They can say, *'I was only joking'*. So, what started as a confrontation, or where motives can be questioned, can be de-escalated by claiming that the whole thing was a joke all along (Foot & McCreaddie, 2006).

People hearing jokes don't necessarily tell someone that their joke was bad. Bell (2009) studied responses to failed humour and was surprised to find that two responses, *'groaning'* and *'fake laughter'* commonly thought to be standard reactions, *'were among the least frequent reactions.'* The actual reaction depended on the social relationship, with, *'negative reactions more common among intimates and neutral reactions preferred by acquaintances and strangers.'* In fact, the most common response was found to be laughter, which was thought to be an acknowledgement of the humour attempt.

It may be that people are too polite to tell others they are not funny, so, as a result, the un-funny do not modify their behaviour. Further, because they are incompetent at humour, they may well lack the skills to judge their incompetence, and so are unable to change (Kruyer & Dunning, 1999).

Kruyer & Dunning tested students on their judgements as to what was funny. Significantly, they found that, *'those who performed particularly poorly relative to their peers were utterly unaware of the fact.'* As the researchers put it, *'Ignorance is Bliss.'* They suggest that the best way to get someone to recognise their incompetence is to make them competent at the skill. Then, they are in a position to judge their competence.

Finally, it would be useful to confirm the arguments that have been used to oppose humour generally, as explained by Morreall (2010). The anti-humorists have often been clerics, who see religion as a serious affair. Thank God, we in the West have nearly thrown off the miserable clutches of organised religion:

- Humour is insincere. Those who joke around are *'fooling'* and are not to be trusted.
- Humour is idle; *'play'* doesn't accomplish anything.
- Humour diminishes self-control, it *'overcomes'* us.

- Humour is hedonistic. We are not fulfilling our duties/obligations when we use it. It is *'amoral.'*
- Humour fosters *'sexual licence,'* notably as women's laughter excites men.
- Humour is irresponsible as *'vices are to be reformed,'* not laughed at.
- Humour is hostile, as it releases *'violent urges.'*
- Humour fosters anarchy as it *'breaks down social order'*, via, for example, satire.
- Humour is foolish, which is *'irrational.'*

Reflection

Humour can, indeed, be like a lead balloon and fail to work, thus embarrassing both joker and listener. This is particularly likely in new encounters where understandings of acceptability are yet to appear. And, even in established settings, a joker may misread the situation and attempt a joke which turns out to be inappropriate.

Humour failure seems to come down to two main deficiencies: poor technical skill and poor social skill. Technically, people: may not tell jokes well, may tell well-worn jokes, and may not be able to recognise that a joke is in fact not funny for the particular audience concerned.

The paradoxical thing is that someone who is bad at jokes/humour may not recognise that fact, and people may be too polite to tell them. So, the only way for the incompetent to recognise their incompetence is for them to become competent. Good old Catch-22.

Poor social skill concerns a lack of sensitivity to the needs of others, and a desire to promote oneself at other's expense.

The key social skills of empathy and sympathy can be trumped by apathy. Some people, particularly men, are just too cavalier about the jokes they tell and fail to consider the consequences. They end up blaming others who 'can't take a joke.'

Sometimes, humour can appear to be successful but in fact fails because it is a smokescreen. People can use humour as a way of evading the discussion of more important matters.

Cross-cultural humour is a particular nightmare, for whilst all nations joke and laugh, they do so at different things. It is a very clever person who can get under the skin of another nation's humour, and use that humour successfully.

Activity

1) Record failed humour
When you are in a group at work, record the instances of failed humour. See if the failures outnumber the successes.

2) Work on your humour failures

Work out when and where your humour attempts fail. Develop a strategy in order to improve your success rate. This could involve concentrating on those areas in which you are funnier, or practising new types of humour. It would make sense to observe and learn from someone who has a high success rate. Talk to them about their approach.

References

Abrams, J.R. & Bippus, A. (2011) Intergroup Investigation of Disparaging Humor, *Journal of Language & Social Psychology* 30 (2)

Albrecht, G.L. (1999) Disability humor: What's in a joke? *Body and Society* 5(4)

Alden, R.M. (1914) The use of comic material in the tragedy of Shakespeare and his contemporaries *The Journal of English and Germanic Philogy* 13 (2)

Anderson, D. (2008) *Reading is funny!: motivating kids to read with riddles* (American Library Association: Chicago)

Andersson, L.M. & Bateman, T.S. (1997) Cynicism in the workplace: some causes and effects, *Journal of Organizational Behavior* 18 (5)

Anolli, L., Ciceri, R. & Infantino, M.G. (2000) Irony as a Game of Implicitness: Acoustic Profiles of Ironic Communiaction, *Journal of Psycholinguistic Research* 29 (3)

Anolli, L., Infantino, M.G. & Ciceri, R. (2001) 'You're a Real Genius!': Irony as a Miscommunication Design, In: Anolli, L., Ciceri, R. & Riva, G. (eds.) *Say not to Say: new perspectives on miscommunication* (IOS Press: Amsterdam)

Anon. (1883) *English as she is wrote* (Appleton: New York)

Anon. (1920) Torts: Practical jokes damages for humiliation, etc, *Michigan Law Review* 18 (8)

Anon. (1968) *500 best Irish jokes and limericks* (Bell: New York)

Anon. (1984) Our Readers Write: What's the Best Example of Classroom Humor You Can Remember Either Using or Observing, *The English Journal* 73 (8)

Anon. (2008) *Philogelos: The laugh addict*, Yadu.com

Anon. (2011) Frankie Boyle joke about Jordan's son broke TV rules, *The Telegraph* 4th Apr.

Anon. (2011a) Gershon Legman: The Folklorist Nobody Knows, *SCOWAH Chronicle* 4, 20th May

Anon. (2012) Mourinho: I have won too much to be the special one…I deserve to be called the only one, *Mail Online,* 14th Aug.

Anon. (2012b) 'The Office' star's Anne Frank 'jokes' appal TV viewers, *The Jewish Chronicle Online* 19th April

Anon. (2012c) Ricky Gervaise: Why it's kosher to joke about Anne Frank, *The Jewish Chronicle Online* 19th April

Anon. (2013) Monty Python tickets for the O2 still available: how to get them, *The Telegraph* 29.11.13

Anon. (2013b) *Christmas jokes* (Macmillan: Basingstoke)

Anon. (2013c) Frankie Boyle's top 10 controversial jokes: From Katie Price to Madeline McCann, *Metro,* 7th Mar.

Anon. (2013d) *Christmas Jokes* (Macmillan: London)

Anon (2014) Quotes of the week, *The Sunday Times,* 18th May

Apanowicz, K. (2006) *The life of Richard Whiteley* (Virgin: London)

Apter, M.J. & Desselles, M. (2012) Disclosure humor and distortion humor: A reversal theory analysis, *Humor: International Journal of Humor Research* 25 (4)

Archakis, A. & Tsakona, V. (2005) Analyzing conversational data in GTVH terms: A new approach to the issue of identity construction via humor, *Humor: International Journal of Humor Research* 18(1)

Arnott, S. & Haskins, M., 2004) *Man walks into a bar: The ultimate collection of jokes and one-liners* (Ebury: London)

Ash, R. (2010) *It just slipped out* (Headline: London)

Asimov, I. (1972) *Isaac Asimov's treasury of humor* (Valentine Mitchell: London)

Attardo, S. (2000) Irony as relevant inappropriateness, *Journal of Pragmatics* 32 (6)

Attardo, S., Eisterhold, J., Hay, J., & Poggi, I. (2003) Multimodal markers of irony and sarcasm, *Humor: International Journal of Humor Research* 16 (2)

Attardo, S. & Pickering, L. (2011) Timing in the performance of jokes, *Humor: International Journal of Humor Research* 24 (3)

Baddeley, A. (1994) *Your Memory: A User's Guide* (Penguin: London)

Bal, A.S., Pitt, L., Berthon, P. & DesAutels, P. (2009) *Journal of Public Affairs,* 9

Bale, C., Morrison, R. & Caryl, P.G. (2006) Chat-up lines as male sexual displays, *Personality and Individual Differences* 40 (4)

Baring-Gould, W. S. (1974) *The lure of the Limerick* (Hart, Davis, MacGibbon: London)

Barnes, B., Palmary, I., & Durrheim, K. (2001) The denial of racism: The role of humor, personal experience, and self-censorship, *Journal of Language and Social Psychology* 20 (3)

Barreca, R. (1991) *They used to call me Snow White…but I drifted: Women's strategic use of humor* (Penguin: New York)

Bartholome, L. & Snyder, P. (2004) Is it philosophy or pornography? Graffiti at the Dinosaur Bar-B-Que, *The Journal of American Culture* 27 (1)

Bates, J.A. & Martin, M. (1980) The Thematic Content of Graffiti as a Normative Indicator of Male & Female Attitudes, *The Journal of Sex Research* 16 (4)

Batey, M., Furnham, A. & Safiullina, X.) Intelligence, general knowledge and personality as predictors of creativity, *Learning and Individual Differences* 20 (5)

Bauer, M. & Geront, M. (1999) The use of humor in addressing the sexuality of elderly nursing home residents, *Sexuality and Disability* 17 (2)

Baxter, J. (2002) Jokers in the Pack: Why Boys are More Adept than Girls at Speaking in Public Settings, *Language and Education* 16 (2)

Bekinschtein, T.A., Davis, M.H., Rodd, J.M. & M.A. Owen (2011) Why Clowns talk Funny: The Relationship between Humor and Semantic Ambiguity, *The Journal of Neuroscience* 31 (26)

Bell, N.D. (2009) Responses to failed humor, *Journal of Pragmatics* 41 (9)

Bemiller, M.L. & Schneider, R.Z. (2010) It's not just a joke, *Sociological Spectrum* 30 (4)

Benedictus, L. (2012) Where are all the female standups? *The Guardian*, 20th Mar.

Ben-Peretz, M., Schonmann, S. & Kupermintz, H. (1999) The Teachers' Lounge and its Role in Improving Learning Environments in Schools, In: Freiberg, H.J. (ed.) *School Climate: Measuring, Improving and Sustaining Healthy Learning Environments* (Falmer Press: London)

Berdahl, J.L. & Aquino, K. (2009) Sexual Behavior at work, *Journal of Applied Psychology* 94 (1)

Bergen, D. (2009) Gifted children's humor preferences, sense of humor, and comprehension of riddles, *Humor: International Journal of Humor Research 22 (4)*

Berger, A.A. (1998) *An anatomy of humor* (Transaction: New Brunswick)

Berger, A. A. (2010) *Blind men and elephants* (Transaction: New Brunswick)

Berger, A. A. (2010b) What's So Funny About That? *Society* 47 (1)

Berger, A.A. (2011) *The art of comedy writing* (Transaction: New Jersey)

Bergman, M. (1986) How Many Feminists Does It Take to Make a Joke? Sexist Humor and What's Wrong with It, *Hypatia* 1 (1)

Bergson, H. (2008) *Laughter: An essay on the meaning of the comic* (Arc Manor: Rockville)

Berk, R. (2009) Derogatory and cynical humour in clinical teaching and the workplace: the need for professionalism, *Medical Education* 43 (1)

Beynon, J. (1984) 'Sussing out' teachers: pupils as data gatherers, In: Hammersley, M. & Woods, P. *Life in School: The Sociology of Pupil Culture* (O.U. Press: Milton Keynes)

Billig, M. (2001) Humour & Embarrassment: Limits of 'Nice-Guy' Theories of Social Life, *Theory, Culture & Society* 18 (5)

Billig, M. (2005) *Laughter and Ridicule: Towards a Social Criticism of Humour* (Sage: California)

Billington, M. (2005) I sayeth, I sayeth, I sayeth, *The Guardian*, 15th Sep.

Bing, J. (2007) Liberated jokes: Sexual humor in all-female groups, *Humor: International Journal of Humor Research* 20 (4)

Binsted, K. & Ritchie, G. (2001) Towards a model of story puns, *Humor: International Journal of Humor Research* 14 (3)

Biott, C. & Easen, P. (1994) *Collaborative Learning in Staffrooms and Classrooms* (David Fulton: London)

Bird, C. (2008) 'It's Not Very Funny': Heightened performances of Formulaic Jokes in Interaction, *Texas Linguistic Forum*, 52

Bird, C. (2009) 'Women can't tell jokes' – ideology in interaction, Gender & Language Association Conference IGALA

Blake, B. (2007) *Playing with words: Humour in the English language* (Equinox: London)

Blatchford, P. (1998) *Social Life in School* (Falmer Press: London)

Bockenhauer, H.J., Hromkovic, Kralovic, R., Momke, T. & K. Steinhofel (2007) Efficient Algorithms for the Spoonerism Problem, Fun with algorithms: 4th International Conference, Italy.

Bok, S. (1978) *Lying: Moral Choice in Public & Private Life* (Harvester Press: Sussex)

Bolding, J. (1985) *The sexual riddles of the Exeter Book*, M.A. thesis, Simon Fraser University.

Borman, K.M. (1988) Playing on the job in adolescent work settings, *Anthropology and Education* 19 (2)

Bowd, A.D. (2003) Stereotypes of elderly persons in narrative jokes, *Research on Aging* 25 (3)

Boxer, D. & Cortes-Conde, F. (1997) From bonding to biting: Conversational joking and identity display, *Journal of Pragmatics* 27 (1)

Boyle, F. (2012) *Work! Consume! Die!* (Harper: London)

Braithwaite, E.R. (1959) *To Sir with Love* (The Bodley Head: London)

Brand, J. (2009) Comedian Jo Brand on how she copes with pack mentality, *The Guardian*, 7th Sept.

Brand, J. (2010) *Can't stand up for sitting down* (Headline: London)

Breidbart, S. (2011) 13 things a stand-up comedian won't tell you, *Reader's Digest*, Sept.

Brodzinsky, D.M., Barnet, K. & Aiello, J.R. (1981) Sex of Subject & Gender Identity as Factors in Humor Appreciation, *Sex Roles* 7 (5)

Brogan, B. (2002) Anger over Davidson asylum seeker joke, *The Telegraph* 10th October

Brown, R.B. & Keegan, D. (1999) Humor in the hotel kitchen, *Humor: International Journal of Humor Research* 12 (1)

Brown, M., Ralph, S. & Brember, I. (2002) Change-linked work-related stress in British teachers, *Research in Education* 67

Brunvand, J.H. (1963) A Classification for Shaggy Dog Stories, *Journal of American Folklore* 76 (299)

Brunvand, J.H. (1964) Have you heard the elephant (joke?), *Western Folklore* 23 (3)

Bubel, C.M. & Spitz, A. (2006) 'One of the last vestiges of gender bias': The characterization of women through the telling of dirty jokes in Ally McBeal, *Humor: International Journal of Humor Research* 19 (1)

Bucaria, C. (2004) Lexical and syntactic ambiguity as a source of humor and the case of newspaper headlines, *Humor: International Journal of Humor Research* 17 (3)

Buckeridge, A. (1990) *Typically Jennings* (Macmillan: London)

Burton, F. (2009) *A history of sarcasm* (Dog Horn: Leeds)

Buss, A.H. Iscoe, I & Buss, E.H. (1979) The development of embarrassment, *Journal of Psychology: Interdisciplinary and Applied* 103 (2)

Buzan, T. (2006) *Use your memory* (BBC Active: Harlow)

Byrne, E. (2012) Sir Charles Napier's sin, History extra.com

Cameron, E.L., Fox, J.D.. Anderson, M.S., & Cameron, C.A. (2010) Resilient youths use humour to enhance socioemotional functioning during a day in the life, *Journal of Adolescent Research* 25 (5)

Cameron, S. (2013) Margaret Thatcher's double entendre trouble, *The Telegraph*, 18th Apr.

Carnes, P. (1986) Fashion in joke clusters: The life and death of Lucky Pierre, *Western Folklore* 45 (3)

Caron, J.E. (2006) Silent slapstick film in ritualized clowning: The example of Charlie Chaplin, *Studies in American Humor* 3 (14)

Carr, A. (2008) *Look who it is!* (Harper Collins: London)

Carr, J. & Greeves, L. (2007) *The Naked Jape: Uncovering the Hidden World of Jokes* (Penguin: London)

Carroll, N. (2005) Two Comic Plot Structures, *The Monist* 88 (1)

Carson, F. (2009) As BT suspends 30 staff for telling an Irish joke, veteran comedian Frank Carson defends a great comic tradition, *Mail Online*, 24th Feb.

Chaloupka, W. (1999) *Everybody Knows: Cynicism in America*, (University of Minnesota Press: Minneapolis)

Chamberlain, W.H. (1957) The 'Anecdote' & unrationed Soviet humor, *Russia Review* 16 (3)

Chapman, H.A. & Anderson, A.K. (2013) Things rank and gross in nature: A review and synthesis of moral disgust, *Psychological Bulletin* 139 (2)

Chapple, A. & Ziebland, S. (2004) The role of humour for men with testicular cancer, *Qualitative Health Research* 14 (8)

Chesterfield, Lord (undated) Full text of Letters written by Lord Chesterfield to his son www.archive.org

Chilton, M. (2012) Alfred Hitchcock: a sadistic prankster, *The Telegraph*, 13th Aug.

Clark, H.M. & Gerrig, R.J. (1984) On the Pretence Theory of Irony, *Journal of Experimental Psychology* 113 (1)

Coates, J. (2003) *men talk* (Blackwell Oxford)

Coates, J. (2007)Talk in a play frame : More on laughter and intimacy, *Journal of Pragmatics* 39 (1)

Cockcroft, L. (2009) Why bad jokes are easier to remember than the good ones, *The Telegraph*, 22ndMar.

Cockcroft, L. (2011) Jordan Wimmer: female city worker loses sex discrimination case, *The Telegraph* Oct. 15th.

Collinson, D.L. (1988) 'Engineering Humour': Masculinity, joking and conflict in shop floor relations, *Organization Studies* 9 (2)

Collinson, D.L. (2002) Managing Humour, *Journal of Management Studies* 39 (3)

Colletta, L. (2009) Political satire and postmodern irony in the age of Stephen Colbert and Jon Stewart, *The Journal of Popular Culture* 42 (5)

Colston, H.L. & Lee, S.Y. (2004) Gender Differences in Verbal Irony Use, *Metaphor & Symbol* 19 (4)

Conolly, O. & Haydar, B. (2005) The Good, The Bad And The Funny, *The Monist* 88 (1)

Contu, A. (2008) Decaf resistance: On Misbehaviour, Cynicism, and Desire in Liberal Workplaces, *Management Communication Quarterly* 21 (3)

Cooper, M., O'Donnell, D., Caryl, P.G., Morrison, R., & Bale, C. (2007) Chat-up lines as male displays: Effects of content, sex, and personality, *Personality and Individual Differences* 43 (5)

Correll, T.C. (1997) Associative context and joke visualisation, *Western Folklore* 56 (3/4)

Coser, R.L. (1960) Laughter among colleagues: A study of the social functions of humor among the staff of a mental hospital, *Psychiatry* 23

Critchley, S. (2002) *On Humour* (Routledge: London)

Creusere, M. A. (1999) Theories of Adults' Understanding and Use of Irony and Sarcasm: Applications to and Evidence from Research with Children, *Developmental Review* 19 (2)

Cropley, A.J. (2001) *Creativity in Education and Learning: a guide for teachers and educators* (Kogan Page: London)

Cloud, E. (2003) 'Bushisms' from a linguistic view, *Emory Report*, www.emory.edu

Crozier, W.R. & Dimmock, P.S. (1999) Name-calling and nicknames in a sample of primary school children, *British Journal of Educational Psychology* 69 (4)

Crozier, W.R. (2002) Donkeys and Dragons: Recollection of schoolteachers' nicknames, *Educational Studies* 28 (2)

Cunnison, S. (1989) Gender Joking in the Staffroom, In: Acker, S., *Teachers, gender, and careers* (Falmer Press: New York)

Damschen, K. (2014) 10 of Shakespeare's best dirty jokes, http://mentalflosss.com

Daniels, P. I don't get many hecklers now but answering them is an art form in itself, qi.com

Davidson, C. (1987) Ethnic Jokes: An Introduction to Race and Nationality, *Teaching Sociology* 15 (3)

Davies, C. (1982) Ethnic jokes, moral values and social boundaries, *The British Journal of Sociology* 33 (3)

Davies, C. (1988) The Irish joke as a social phenomenon, In: J.Durant & J. Miller (eds.), *Laughing Matters: A serious look at humour* (Longman: Harlow)

Davies, C. (2008) American jokes about lawyers, *Humor: International Journal of Humor Research* 21 (4)

Davies, C. (2012) The English Mother-in-Law joke and its missing relatives, *Israeli Journal of Humor Research* 1 (2)

Davis, S. (2008) Wise fools, foolish virgins and dirty tricksters: Gershon Legman and American folk humor, *Voices* 34

Dean, J.W. (Jr.) & Brandes, P. (1998) Organizational Cynicism, *Academy of Management Review* 23 (2)

De Bono, E. (1990) *Lateral thinking* (Penguin: London)

De Bono, E. (2001) *I am right you are wrong* (Penguin Books: Harmondsworth)

De Bono, E. (2007) *Edward De Bono's thinking course* (BBC Active: Harlow)

De Klerk, V. & Bosch, B. (1996) Nicknames as sex-role stereotypes, *Sex Roles* 35 (9-10)

Delamont, S. & Galton, M. (1986) *Inside the secondary classroom* (Routledge & Kegan Paul: London)

Dennant, P. (2013) The 'barbarous old English jig': The 'Black Joke' in the eighteenth and nineteenth centuries, *Folk Music Journal* 10 (3)

Dewitte, S. Verguts, T. (2001) Being funny: A selectionist account of humour production, *Humor: International Journal of Humor Research* 14 (1)

Dews, S. & Winner, E. (1995) Muting the Meaning: A Social Function of Irony, *Metaphor & Symbolic Activity* 10 (1)

Dews, S., Winner, E., Kaplan, J., Rosenblatt, E., Hunt, M., Lim, K., McGovern, A., Qualter, A., & B. Smarsh (1996) Children's Understanding of the Meaning and Functions of Verbal Irony, *Child Development* 67 (6)

Dickie, S. (2003) Hilarity and pitilessness in the mid-eighteenth century: English jestbook humor, *Eighteenth-Century Studies* 37 (1)

Dickie, S. (2011) *Cruelty and laughter: Forgotten comic literature and the unsentimental eighteenth century* (University of Chicago Press: Chicago)

Dienhart, J.M. (1999) A linguistic look at riddles, *Journal of Pragmatics* 31 (1)

Dijk, C. & de Jong, P.J. (2009) The Remedial Value of Blushing in the Context of Transgression and Mishaps, *Emotion* 9 (2)

Dijksterhuis, A. & Meurs, T. (2006) Where creativity resides. The generative power of unconscious thought, *Consciousness & Cognition* 15 (1)

Dirks, M. (1963) Teen-Age Folklore from Kansas, *Western Folklore* 22 (2)

Double, O. (2005) *Getting the Joke: the Inner Workings of Stand-Up Comedy* (Methuen: London)

Doughty, S. & Cooper, R. (2011) Polish engineer nicknamed Borat by 'racist' colleagues wins £2,250 compensation, *Mail Online*, 24th Aug.

Douglas, M. (1968) The Social Control of Cognition: Some factors in Joke Perception, *Man* 3 (3)

Douglas, M. (1979) *Implicit Meanings: Essays in Anthropology* (Routledge & Kegan Paul: London)

Dubberley, W.S. (1993) Humour as Resistance In: Woods, P. & Hammersley, M. (eds.) *Gender & Ethnicity in Schools: ethnographic accounts* (Routledge: London)

Duncan, W.J. & Feisal, J.P. (1989) No Laughing Matter: Patterns of Humor in The Workplace, *Organizational Dynamics* 17 (4)

Dundes, A. (1979) The Dead Baby Joke Cycle, *Western Folklore* 38 (3)

Dundes, A. & Hauschild, T. (1983) Auschwitz jokes, *Western Folklore* 42 (4)

Dundes, A. (1985) The J.A.P. and the J.A.M. in American jokelore, *Journal of American Folklore* 98 (390)

Dunn, S. Stand-up advice, www.simondunn.me.uk

Dyck, K. & Holtzman, S. (2013) Understanding humor styles and well-being, *Personality and Individual Differences* 55 (1)

Dynel, M. (2009) Beyond a joke: Types of conversational humour, *Language and Linguistics Compass* 3 (5)

Dynel, M. (2012) Garden paths, red lights and crossroads: On finding our way to understanding the cognitive mechanisms underlying jokes, *Israeli Journal of Humor Research* 1 (1)

Easthope, A. (1992) *What a man's gotta do: The masculine myth in popular culture* (Routledge: New York)

Edwards, D. (2005) Moaning, whinging and laughing: the subjective side of complaints, *Discourse Studies* 7 (1)

Eisterhold, J., Attardo, S. & Boxer, D. (2006) Reactions to irony in discourse: evidence for the least disruption principle, *Journal of Pragmatics* 38 (8)

Eller, A., Koschate, M. & Gilson, K-M. (2011) Embarrassment: The ingroup-outgroup audience effect in faux pas situations, *European Journal of Social Psychology* 41 (4)

Erard, M. (2007) *Um—slips, stumbles, and verbal blunders, and what they mean* (Pantheon: New York)

Ewbank, T. & Hildred, S. (2003) *Rod Stewart: The new biography* (Portrait: London)

Exley, H. (1992) *A round of golf jokes* (Exley: Watford)

Eysenck, H.J. (1942) The Appreciation of Humour: An Experimental and Theoretical Study, *British Journal of Psychology* 32 (4)

Eysenck, H. (1985) *Decline and Fall of the Freudian Empire* (Viking: Harmondsworth)

Eysenck, M.W. (1988) Working Memory, In: Cohen, G., Eysenck, M.W., & LeVoi, M.E. *Memory: A Cognitive Approach* (O.U. Press: Milton Keynes)

Farnes, N. (2004) *Spike: An intimate memoir* (Harper Perennial: London)

Feinberg, L.S. (1996) *Teasing: Innocent Fun or Sadistic Malice?* (New Horizon Press: New Jersey)

Field, A., Miles, J. Field, Z. (2012) *Discovering statistics using R* (Sage: London)

Fine, G.A. (1979) The Idioculture of Little League Baseball Teams, *American Sociological Review* 44 (5)

Fine, G.A. & De Soucey, M. (2005) Joking Cultures: Humor theories as social regulation, *Humor: International Journal of Humor Research* 18 (1)

Finnegan, A. & Alford, R. (1981) A holo-cultural study of humor, *Ethos* 9 (2)

Finney, G. (1994) Unity in Difference?: An Introduction, In: Finney, G. (ed.) *Look Who's Laughing: Gender and Comedy* (Gordon & Breach: Penn.)

Fisher, J. (2011) *Tommy Cooper's secret joke files* (Preface: London)

Fleming, P. (2005) Metaphors of Resistance, *Management Communication Quarterly* 19 (1)

Foot, H.C. & Chapman, A.J. (1976) The Social Responsiveness of Young Children to Humorous Situations, In: Chapman, A.J. & Foot, H.C. (eds.) *Humour and laughter: Theory, Research and Applications* (John Wiley and Sons: London)

Foot, H. & McCreaddie, M. (2006) Humour and Laughter, In: Hargie, O. (ed.) *The Handbook of Communication Skills* (3rd ed.) (Routledge: London)

Ford, T.E. & Ferguson, M.A. (2004) Social Consequences of Disparagement Humor: A Prejudiced Norm Theory, *Personality and Social Psychology Review* 8 (1)

Ford, T.E., Boxer, C.F., Armstrong, J. & J.R. Edel (2008) More Than 'Just a Joke': The Prejudice-Releasing Function of Sexist Humor, *Personality and Social Psychology Bulletin* 34 (2)

Fortado, B. (1998) Interpreting Nicknames: A Micropolitical Portal, *Journal of Management Studies* 35 (1)

Fowles, B. & Glanz, M. E. (1977) Competence and talent in verbal riddle comprehension, *Journal of Child Language* 4 (3)

Fox, K. (2005) *Watching the English: The Hidden Rules of English Behaviour* (Hodder: London)

Francis, L., Monahan, K., & Berger, C. (1999) A laughing matter? The uses of humor in medical interactions, *Motivation and Emotion* 23 (2)

Freud, C. (2009) *A feast of Freud* (Bantam Press: London)

Freud, S. (1973) Slips of the Tongue, In: Fromkin, V.A. *Speech Errors As Linguistic Evidence* (Mouton: The Hague)

Freud, S. (1991) *Jokes and their Relation to the Unconscious* (Penguin: London)

Friedman, S. & Kuipers, G. (2013) The divisive power of humour: Comedy, taste and symbolic boundaries, *Cultural Sociology* 7 (2)

Fry, S. (2010) *The Fry chronicles* (Penguin: London)

Fuhr, M. (2001) Some aspects of form and function of humor in adolescence, *Humor: International Journal of Humor Research* 14 (1)

Fuhr, M. (2002) Coping humor in early adolescence, *Humor: International Journal of Humor Research* 15 (3)

Furlong, V. (1977) Anancy Goes to School; A Case Study of Pupils' Knowledge of Their Teacher, In: Woods, P. & Hammersley, M. *School Experience: Explorations in the Sociology of Education* (Croom Helm: London)

Gardener, H.N. (1912) Review of Laughter: An Essay on the Meaning of the Comic, *Psychological Bulletin* 9 (19)

Georgson, J.C., Harris, M.J., Milich, R. & J. Young (1999) "Just Teasing". Personality Effects on Perceptions & Life Narratives of Childhood Teasing, *Personality and Social Psychology Bulletin* 25 (10)

Getzels, J.W. & Jackson, P.W. (1963) *Creativity and Intelligence: Explorations with Gifted Students* (John Wiley & Sons: London)

Gibbs, R.W. & Kearney, L.R. (1994) When parting is such sweet sorrow: The comprehension and appreciation of oxymora, *Journal of Psycholinguistic Research* 23 (1)

Gibbs, R.W. (2000) Irony in Talk Among Friends, *Metaphor & Symbol* 15 (1/2)

Giora, R., Federman, S., Kehat, A. & H. Sabah (2005) Irony aptness, *Humor: International Journal of Humor Research* 18 (1)

Gladstone: Six ways to not suck at stand-up comedy, www.cracked.com

Glaze, B. & Cookney, F. (2014) Inside UKIP's spring conference: Racist jokes, boozed-up delegates and champagne boasts on board £1m yacht, *The Mirror*, 1st Mar.

Goldie, D. (2003) 'Will ye stop yer tickling, Jock?' Modern and postmodern Scottish comedy, *Critical Quarterly*, 42 (4)

Goodchilds, J.D. (1959) Effects of being witty in the social structure of a small group, *Sociometry* 22 (3)

Goodson, I. & Walker R. (1991) Humour in the Classroom, In: Goodson I.F. & Walker, R. *Biography, Identity and Schooling: Episodes in Educational Research* (Falmer Press: London)

Gopie, N. & Macleod, C.M. (2009) Destination memory: Stop me if I've told you this before, *Psychological Science* 20 (12)

Gordon, M. (2010) Learning to Laugh at Ourselves: Humor, Self-Transcendence, and the Cultivation of Moral Virtues, *Educational Theory* 60 (6)

Gough, B. & Edwards, G. (1998) The beer talking: four lads, a carry out and the reproduction of masculinities, *The Sociological Review* 46 (3)

Graham, L.G. (2010) What is it Like To Be Funny? The Spontaneous Humor Producer's Subjective Experience, Unpublished Ph. D thesis, Antioch University

Green, J. (2003) The Writing on the Stall: Gender and Graffiti, *Journal of Language & Social Psychology* 22 (3)

Green, T. A. & Pepicello, W.J. (1979) The Folk Riddle: A Redefinition of Terms, *Western Folklore* 38 (1)

Greengross, G. (2008) Dissing oneself versus dissing rivals: Effects of status, personality, and sex on the short-term and long-term attractiveness of self-deprecating and other-deprecating humor, *Evolutionary Psychology* 6 (3)

Greengross, G. & Miller, G. (2011) Humor ability reveals intelligence, predicts mating success, and is higher in males, *Intelligence* 39 (4)

Gregory, M.R. (2009) Inside the locker room: Male homosociability in the advertising industry, *Gender, Work and Organization* 16 (3)

Griffiths, S. (2014) Schools watchdog 'spitting blood', *The Sunday Times*, 26th Jan.

Gripper, A. (2012) Wiff waff, wet otters and the Geiger counter of Olympomania: Boris Johnson's best quotes and clangers, *The Mirror*, 30th July

Grotjahn, M. (1981) Beyond Laughter: A summing up, In: Corrigan, R.W. *Comedy: Meaning and Sense* (Harper & Row: New York)

Gundelach, P. (2000) Joking Relationships and National Identity in Scandanavia, *Acta Sociologica* 43 (2)

Gunning, B.L. (2001) The Role that Humor Plays in Shaping Organizational Culture, Unpublished Ph.D dissertation, University of Toledo

Haidt, J., McCauley, C., & Rozin, P. (1994) A scale sampling seven domains of disgust elicitators, *Personality and Individual Differences* 16 (5)

Hampes, W.P. (2006) Humor and shyness: The relation between humor styles and shyness, *Humor: International Journal of Humor Research* 19 (2)

Harey, C. (2014) Trigger's best one liners, *The Telegraph*, 16th Jan.

Harlow, I. (1997) Practical Jokes and the Revival of the Dead in Irish tradition, *The Journal of American Folklore* 110 (436)

Harris Interactive & GLSEN (2005) *From Teasing to Torment: School Climate in America* (GLSEN: New York)

Hatch, M.J. (1997) Irony and the social construction of contradiction in the humour of a management team, *Organization Science* 8 (3)

Hay, J. (1995) *Gender & Humour: Beyond a Joke*, Unpublished M.A. thesis, Victoria University of Wellington

Hayter, W. (1977) *Spooner: A Biography* (W.H. Allen: London)

Healy, M. (1995) Were we being served? Homosexual representation in popular British comedy, *Screen* (36)

Heiss, S.N. & Carmack, H.J. (2012) Knock, Knock; Who's There? Making sense of organizational entrance through humor, *Management Communication Quarterly* 26 (1)

Heller, J. (1996) *Catch-22* (Scribner: New York)

Heller, L.G. (1983) Puns, Ironies (Plural), and Other Type-4 Patterns, *Poetics Today* 4 (3)

Hempelmann, C.F. (2004) Script Opposition and logical mechanisms in punning, *Humor: International Journal of Humor Research* 17 (4)

Henman, L.D. (2001) Humor as a coping mechanism: Lessons from POWs, *Humor: International Journal of Humor Research* 14 (1)

Herben, S.J. (1963) A Shakespeare Limerick, *Shakespeare Quarterly* 14 (4)

Herzog, T.R., Harris, A.C., Kropscott, L.S. & Fuller, K.L. (2006) Joke cruelty and joke appreciation revisited, *Humor: International Journal of Humor Research* 19 (2)

Hill, T.P. & Rogers, E. (2012) Gender gaps in science: The creativity factor, *The Mathematical Intelligencer* 34 (2)

Hiskey, D. (2011) One of the great practical jokes of the 19th century, the Berners Street hoax, www.today.foundout.com

Hobbes, T. (1947) *Leviathan* (J.M. Dent: London)

Hodgart, M. (1969) *Satire* (Weidenfeld & Nicolson: London)

Hodgson, C. (2014) Roger Lloyd-Pack: 20 of Trigger's funniest *Only Fools and Horses* jokes, quotes and one-liners, *Mirror TV*, 17th Jan.

Hodson, G., Rush, J. & MacInnis, C.C. (2010) A Joke Is Just a Joke (Except When It Isn't): Cavalier Humor Beliefs Facilitate the Expression of Group Dominance Motives, *Journal of Personality and Social Psychology* 99 (4)

Hoggart, S. (2012) *House of fun: 20 glorious years in parliament* (Guardian Books: London)

Hoggart, S. (2013) The world's most powerful bag lady, *The Guardian*, 19th Oct.

Holloway, S. (2010) *The serious guide to joke writing* (Bookshaker: Great Britain)

Holmes, J. (2000) Politeness, Power and Provocation: How Humour Functions in the Workplace, *Discourse Studies*, 2 (2)

Holmes, J. (2006) Sharing a Laugh: Pragmatic aspects of humor and gender in the workplace, *Journal of Pragmatics* 38 (1)

Holmes, J. & Marra, M. (2002) Having a laugh: how humor contributes to workplace culture, *Journal of Pragmatics* 34 (12)

Holt, J. (2008) *Stop me if you've heard this: A history and philosophy of jokes* (Profile: London)

Hough, A. (2010) James Naughtie: veteran Radio 4 Today presenter in 'Jeremy Hunt' on-air gaffe, *The Telegraph*, 6th Dec.

Howe, N.E. (2002) The origin of humor, *Medical Hypotheses* 59 (3)

Hovelynck, J. & Peeten, L. (2003) Laughter, Smiles & Grins: The Role of Humor in Learning and Facilitating, *Journal of Adventure Education & Outdoor Learning* 3 (2)

Howard, A. & EnglandKennedy, E. (2006) Breaking the silence: Power, Conflict, and contested frames Within an Affluent High School, *Anthropology & Education Quarterly* 37 (4)

Hudson, L. (1966) *Contrary Imaginations: A Psychological Study of the English Schoolboy* (Methuen: London)

Hurley, C. (ed.)(2003) *Could do better : School Reports of the Great and the Good*, (Simon & Schuster : London)

Hurley, M.H., Dennett, D.C. & Adams, R.B. (2011) *Inside Jokes: Using humor to reverse-engineer the mind* (MIT Press: Mass.)

Hurn, B.J. (2007) The influence of culture on international business negotiations, *Industrial and Commercial Training* 39 (7)

Isen, A.M., Daubman, K.A., & Nowicki, G.P. (1987) Positive Affect Facilitates Creative Problem Solving, *Journal of Psychology and Social Psychology* 52 (6)

Ivanko, S.L., Pexman, P.M., & Olineck, K.M. (2004) How Sarcastic are You?: Individual Differences and Verbal Irony, *Journal of Language and Social Psychology* 23 (3)

Jack, A. (2011) *It's a wonderful word: the real origins of our favourite words from anorak to zombie* (Random House: London)

Jarzabkowski, L. M. (2002) The social dimensions of teacher collegiality, *Journal of Educational Enquiry* 3 (2)

Johnson, A.J. & Mistry, K. (2013) The effect of joke-origin-induced expectancy on cognitive humor, *Humor: International Journal of Humor Research* 26 (2)

Johnson, D.T. (2013) The jolly hangman, the jailed journalist, and the decline of Singapore's death penalty, *Asian Criminology* 8

Johnson, L. (2002) *the BIG book of Bloke Jokes* (Carlton, 2002)

Jones, D.C. & Newman, J.B. (2005) A Three-factor Model of Teasing: The Influence of Friendship, Gender, and Topic on Expected Emotional Reactions to Teasing during early Adolescence, *Social Development* 14 (3)

Jones, M. (2009) *Where do comedians go when they die: Journeys of a stand up* (JR Books: London)

Joyce, R.O. (1982) Wall Street ways: Uses of humor in the financial community, *Western Folklore* 41 (4)

Kanter, D.L. & Mirvis, P.M. (1989) *The Cynical Americans: Living and Working in an Age of Discontent and Disillusion* (Jossey-Bass: San Francisco)

Kay, P. (2009) *Saturday night Peter: Memoirs of a stand-up comic* (Century: London)

Kayton, J. & Beck, S.J. (2010) Examining laughter functionality in jury deliberations, *Small Group Research* 41 (4)

Keith-Spiegel, P. (1972) Early Conceptions of Humor: Varieties and issues, In: Goldstein, J.H. & McGhee, P. E. *The Psychology of Humor* (Academic Press: New York)

Kelly, T. (2010) Just too saucy! The bawdy seaside postcards the censor banned 50 years ago, *Mail Online*, 6th Aug.

Keltner, D. & Buswell, B.N. (1996) Evidence for the Distinctiveness of Embarrassment, Shame, and Guilt: A study of Recalled Antecedents and Facial Expression of Emotion, *Cognition and Emotion* 10 (2)

Keltner, D. & Buswell, B.N. (1996) Evidence for the Distinctiveness of Embarrassment, Shame, and Guilt: A study of Recalled Antecedents and Facial Expression of Emotion, *Cognition and Emotion* 10 (2)

Keltner, D., Young, R.C., Heerey, E.A. Oernig, C. & N. D. Monarch (1998) Teasing in Hierarchical and Intimate Relations, *Journal of Personality and Social Psychology* 75 (5)

Keynes, M. (1995) The personality of Isaac Newton, *Notes and records of the Royal Society of London,* 49 (1)

Keyton, J. & Beck, S.J. (2010) Examining laughter functionality in jury deliberations, *Small Group Research* 41 (4)

Khitrov, A. (2012) Irony about tragedy: The Onion's treatment of 9/11, *Topos* 25(2)

Knowles, E. (ed.) (2004) *Oxford Dictionary of Modern Quotations* (Oxford University Press: Oxford)

Koestler, A. (1976) *The Act of Creation* (Hutchinson: London)

Kohn, N., Kellerman, T., Gur, R.C. Schneider, F. & U. Habel (2011) Gender differences in the neural correlate of humor processing: Implications for different processing modes, *Neuropsychologia* 49

Korczynski, M. (2011) The dialectical sense of humour: Routine joking in a Taylorised factory, *Organization Studies* 32 (10)

Kostick, A., Foxgrover, C., Pellowski, M.J. (1998) *3650 jokes, puns, and riddles* (Workman, New York)

Kotthoff, H. (2003) Responding to irony in different contexts: on cognition in conversation *Journal of Pragmatics* 35 (9)

Kotthoff, H. (2006) Gender & humor: The state of the art, *Journal of Pragmatics* 38 (1)

Kounios, J. & Beeman, M. (2009) The Aha! Moment: The cognitive neuroscience of insight, *Current Directions in Psychological Science* 18(4)

Kowalski, R.M. (2000) 'I was only kidding!' Victims' and Perpetrators' Perceptions of Teasing, *Personality and Psychology Bulletin,* 26 (2)

Kozbelt, A. & Nishioka, K. (2010) Humor comprehension, humor production, and insight: An exploratory study, *Humor: International Journal of Humor Research* 23 (3)

Kreuz, R.J. & Roberts, R.M. (1995) Two Cues for Verbal Irony. Hyperbole and the Ironic Tone of Voice, *Metaphor & Symbolic Activity* 10 (1)

Kruger, J., Gordon, C.L., & Kuban, J. (2006) Intentions in Teasing: When 'Just Kidding' Just Isn't Good Enough, *Journal of Personality and Social Psychology* 90 (3)

Kruyer, J. & Dunning, D. (1999) Unskilled & Unaware of It: How difficulties in Recognizing One's Own Incompetence Lead to Inflated Self-Assessments, *Journal of Personality & Social Psychology* 77 (6)

Kudrowitz, B. M. (2010) Ha Ha & Aha! Creativity, Idea Generation, Improvisational Humor, and Product Design, Unpublished Ph. D. dissertation, Massachussets Institute of Technology

Kuhlman, T.L. (1985) A study of salience and motivational theories of humor, *Journal of Personality and Social Psychology* 49 (1)

Kuiper, N.A. & Leite, C. (2010) Personality impressions associated with four distinct humor styles, Scandanavian *Journal of Psychology* 51 (2)

Kuipers, G. (2002) Media culture and internet disaster jokes: bin Laden and the attack on the World Trade Center, *European Journal of Cultural Studies* 5 (4)

Kuipers, G. (2005) "Where was King Kong when we needed him?" Public Discourse, Digital Disaster Jokes, and the Functions of Laughter, *The Journal of American Culture* 28 (1)

Kuipers, G. (2006) The social construction of digital danger, *New Media and Society,* 8 (3)

Kuipers, G. (2006b) *Good humor, bad taste: A sociology of the joke* (Mouton de Gruyter: Berlin)

Kunda, G. (1992) *Engineering culture: Control and commitment in a high-tech corporation* (Temple University: Philadelphia)

La France, M. & Woodzicka, J.A. (1998) No laughing matter: Women's verbal and nonverbal reactions to sexist humor, In: Swim, J.K. (ed.) & Stangor, C. (ed.) *Prejudice: The target's perspective* (Academic Press: San Diego)

Lampert, M.D. & Ervin-Tripp, S.M. (2006) Risky Laughter: Teasing and self-directed joking among male and female friends, *Journal of Pragmatics* 38 (1)

Lavery, J. Sexist heckling a reality for female comedians, www.ihollaback.org

Lederer, R. (1981) A primer of puns, *The English Journal* 70 (6)

Lederer, R. (1991) *Pun and games* (Chicago Review Press: Chicago)

Lederer, R. (2013) *Lederer on language* (Marion Street Press: Portland)

Lee, C.J. & Katz, A.N. (1998) The Differential Role of Ridicule in Sarcasm and Irony, *Metaphor and Symbol* 13 (1)

Lees, S. (1986) *Losing out: Sexuality and adolescent girls* (Hutchinson: London)

Legman, G. (1974) *The Limerick* (Jupiter Books: London)

Legman, G. (2006) *Rationale of the Dirty Joke: An Analysis of Sexual Humor* (Simon & Shuster: New York)

Lemon, M. (1865) *The jest book: The choicest anecdotes and sayings* (Sever & Francis: Cambridge)

Levine, J. & Rakusin, J. (1959) The Sense Of Humor Of College Students And Psychiatric Patients, *The Journal of General Psychology* 60

Lew, R. (1997) Towards a Taxonomy of Linguistic Jokes, *Studia Anglica Posnaniensia* XXXI

Liberman, A.M., Mattingly, I.G. & Turvey, M.T. (1972) Language Codes and Memory Codes, In: Melton, A.W. & Martin, E. (eds.) *Coding Processes in Human Memory* (V.H. Winston & Sons: Washington D.C.)

Lightner, R.M., Bollmer, J.M., Harris, M.J. Milich, R., & D.J. Scambler (2000) What Do You Say to Teasers? *Journal of Applied Developmental Psychology* 21 (4)

Lindsay, B.C. (2013) Humor and dissonance in California's native American genocide, *American Behavioral Scientist* XX (X)

Lipman, M. (1995) *You can read me like a book* (Robson: 1995)

Lipman, M. (2010) *I must collect myself* (Simon & Schuster: London)

Lippman, L.G. & Dunn, M.L. (2000) Contextual Connections Within Puns: Effects on Perceived Humor & Memory, *The Journal of General Psychology* 127 (2)

Livnat, Z. (2004) On verbal irony, meta-linguistic knowledge and echoic interpretation, *Pragmatics & Cognition* 12 (1)

Lloyd, M. (2007) The artful accomplishment of humor in a 'Dick Joke' competition, *Journal of Folklore Research* 44 (2/3)

Lloyd, M. (2011) Miss Grimshaw and the white elephant: Categorisation in a risqué humor competition, *Humor: International Journal of Humor Research* 24 (1)

Lockhart, R.S., Craik, F.I.M., & Jacoby, L. (1976) Depth of processing, recognition and recall, In: Brown, J. (ed.) *Recall and Recognition* (John Wiley & Sons: London)

Lockwood, G., Rosenthal, P. & Budjanovcanin, A. (2011) A quantitative and qualitative analysis of sexual harassment claims 1995-2005, *Industrial Relations Journal* 42 (1)

Lockyer, S. & Pickering, M. (2001) Dear Shit-Shovellers: Humour Censure and the Discourse of Complaint, *Discourse and Society* 12 (5)

Lockyer, S. & Myers, L. (2011) It's about expecting the unexpected: Live stand-up comedy from the audience's perspective, *Participations* 8 (2)

Loomis, C.G. (1963) American Limerick traditions, *Western Folklore* 22 (3)

Loveman, K. (2008) 'Full of Improbable Lies': Gulliver's travels and jest books, *Journal for Eighteenth-century Studies* 26 (1)

Lynch, O.H. (2006) Humorous Communication: Finding a Place for Humor in Communication Research, *Communication Theory* 12 (4)

Lynch, R. (2010) It's funny because we think it's true: laughter is augmented by implicit preferences, *Evolution and Human Behavior* 31 (2)

Lynn, J. (2011) *Comedy rules: From the Cambridge Footlights to Yes Prime Minister* (Faber & Faber: London)

Lytra, V. (2003) Nicknames and teasing: A case study of a linguistically and culturally mixed peer-group, In: Androutsopoulos, J.K. & Georgakopoulou (eds.) *Discourse constructions of youth identities* (John Benjamins: Amsterdam)

Lyvers, M., Cholakians, E., Puorro, M. & S. Sundrum (2009) Beer goggles: blood alcohol concentration in relation to attractiveness ratings for unfamiliar opposite sex faces in naturalistic settings, http://epublications.bond.edu.au/hss_pubs/257

Mackinnon, I. (1994) Irish victim of racist jokes award pounds 6,000: Landmark tribunal ruling over taunts at machinist's expense sends warning to employers over workplace culture, *The Independent* 8th June

Macks, J. (2005) *How to be funny* (Simon & Schuster: New York)

Madigan, E. (2013) 'Sticking to the hateful task': Resilience, Humour, and British understanding of combatant courage, 1914-1918, *War in History* 20 (1)

Major, J.E. (1998) *Critical care nurses use of humor: An exploratory study*, Master of Nursing Thesis, University of Manitoba

Mallett, O. & Wapshott, R. (2014) Informality and employment relationships in small firms: Humour, ambiguity and straight-talking, *British Journal of Management* 25 (1)

Manford, J. (2011) *Brung up proper* (Ebury Press: London)

Manuel, R. (2006) *The bumper b3ta book of sick jokes* (Friday Books: London)

Martin, R.A., Puhlik-Doris, P., Larsen, G. Gray, J. & K. Weir (2003) Individual differences in uses of humor and their relation to psychological well-being: Development of the Humor Style Questionnaire, *Journal of Research in Personality* 37 (1)

Martin, R.A. (2007) Approaches to the sense of humor: A historical review, In: Ruch, W. *The Sense of Humor: Explorations of a Personality Characteristic* (Mouton de Gruyter: Berlin)

McCorkle, D.E., Payan, J.M., Reardon, J., Kling, N.D. (2007) Perceptions in reality: Creativity in the marketing classroom, *Journal of Marketing Education* 29 (3)

McGhee, P.E. (1971) Development of the Humor response: A Review of the Literature, *Psychological Bulletin* 76 (5)

McGhee, P.E. (1974) Development of Children's Ability to Create the Joking Relationship, *Child Development* 45 (2)

McGraw, A.P. & Warren, C. (2010) Benign violations: Making immoral behaviour funny, *Psychological Sciences* 21 (8)

McGraw, A.P., Warren, C., Williams, L.E., & Leonard, B. (2012) Too close for comfort, or too far to care? Finding humor in distant tragedies and close mishaps, *Psychological Science* 23 (10)

McMurty, M. (1990) Reading and writing limericks, *The Reading Teacher* 44 (2)

McPherson, E. (2004) *Buster Keaton* (Faber & Faber: London)

McSmith, A. (2010) *No such thing as society: A history of Britain in the 1980s* (Constable & Robinson: London)

Meeus, W. & Mahieu, P. (2009) You can see the funny side, can't you? Pupil humor with the teacher as target, *Educational Studies* 35 (5)

Mehrabian, A. & Piercy, M. (1993) Differences in positive and negative connotations of nicknames and given names, *The Journal of Social Psychology* 133 (5)

Metcalf, F. (2009) *The Penguin dictionary of Jokes* (Penguin: London)

Mihalcea, R. & Pulman, S. (2007) Characterizing humour: An exploration of features in humorous texts, Proceedings of the Conference on Computational Linguistics and Intelligent Text Processing (CICLing), Mexico City

Mikes, G. (1980) *English Humour for Beginners* (Andre Deutsch: London)

Miller, R.S. & Fahey, D.E. (1991) Blushing as an Appeasement Gesture: Felt, Displayed and Observed Embarrassment, Paper presented at the Annual Convention of the American Psychological Association

Miller, R.S. (1996) *Embarrassment: Poise and Peril in Everyday Life* (Guilford Press: New York)

Miller, K.E.L. (2009) The Unuttered Punch Line: Pragmatic Incongruity and the Parsing of 'What's the Difference' Jokes, www.missourifolkloresociety.truman.edu

Miller, L. L. (1979) A Limerick, *College Composition and Communication* 30 (3)

Mitchell, C. A. (1977) The Sexual Perspective in the Appreciation and Interpretation of Jokes, *Western Foklore* 36 (4)

Mitchell, C. (1978) Hostility and Aggression toward Males in Female Joke Telling, *Frontiers: A Journal of Women's Studies* 3 (3)

Moller, J., Jansma, B.M., Rodriguez-Fornells, A., & T.F. Munte (2007) What the Brain Does before the Tongue Slips, *Cerebral Cortex* 17 (5)

Molloy, M. (2013) Prince Philip quotes: Top 10 gaffes from 'slitty-eyed' students to pirates in the Cayman Islands, *The Metro*, 21st Feb.

Moore, A.E. (2004) The hilarious rump: Our fascination with the arse in early comedic films, *The Journal of Popular Culture* 30 (4)

Morgan, F. (1996) *Wicked: Women's wit and Humour* (Virago: London)

Morgan, J., O'Neill, C., & Harre, R. (1979) *Nicknames: Their Origins and Social Consequences* (Routledge & Kegan Paul: London)

Morreall, J. (1981) Humor and Aesthetic Education, *Journal of Aesthetic Education* 15 (1)

Morreall, J. (2009) *Comic Relief: A Comprehensive Philosophy of Humor* (Wiley-Blackwell: Chichester)

Morreall, J. (2010) Comic vices and comic virtues, *Humor: International Journal of Humor Research* 23 (1)

Morris, S. & Sabbagh, D. (2012) April Jones: Matthew Woods jailed over explicit Facebook comments, *The Guardian*, 8th Sept.

Moss, S. (2009) Jimmy Carr: 'I thought my Paralympics joke was totally acceptable.' *The Guardian*, 11th Nov.

Muecke, D.C. (1969) *The Compass of Irony* (Methuen: London)

Mueller, J.C., Dirks, D., Picca, L.H. (2007) Unmasking racism: Halloween costuming and engagement of the racial other, *Qualitative Sociology* 30 (3)

Murray, L. (2010) *Be a great stand-up* (Hodder Education: London)

Nahas, V.L. (1998) Humour: a phenomenological study within the context of clinical education, *Nurse Education Today* 18 (8)

Nash, W. (1985) *The Language of Humour: Style & technique in comic discourse* (Longman: London)

Nathan, S. (2011) 'I was naïve': Finally Ricky Gervaise apologises for 'mong' comments after mother of two disabled daughters is reduced to tears, *Mail Online*, 21st Oct.

Naus, F., van Iterson, A., & Roe, R. (2007) Extending the exit, voice, loyalty, and neglect model of employees' responses to adverse conditions in the workplace, *Human Relations* 60 (5)

Neile, C. (undated) You must be kidding: Tall tales are a tall order, www.toastmasters.org

Nias, J. (1989) *Primary Teachers talking* (Routledge: London)

Nilsen, A.P. & Nilsen, D.L.F. (1999) The straw man meets his match, Six arguments for studying humor in English classes, *The English Journal* 88 (4)

Nolan, P. (2009) Irish jokes funny? They're laughable, *Daily Mail*, 25th Feb.

Nordern, D. (2008) *Denis Nordern: Clips from a life* (Harper Perennial: London)

Norrick, N.R. (2001) On the conversational performance of narrative jokes: Toward an account of timing, *Humor: International Journal of Humor Research* 14 (3)

Norrick, N.R. (2003) Issues in conversational joking, *Journal of Pragmatics* 35 (9)

Norrick, N.R. (2004) Non-verbal humor and joke performance, *Humor: International Journal of Humor Research* 17 (4)

Northcroft, J. (2014) Chelsea Crack, *The Sunday Times*, 20th Apr.

Obrdlik, A.J. (1942) "Gallows Humor"—A Sociological Phenomenon, *The American Journal of Sociology* 47 (5)

Ohja, A.K. & Holmes, T.L. (2010) Don't tease me, I'm working: Examining humor in a Midwestern organization using ethnography of communication, *The Qualitative Report* 15 (2)

Opie, I & Opie, P. (1973) *The Lore and Language of Schoolchildren* (Oxford University Press: London)

Oppliger, P. A. & Zillmann, D. (2009) Disgust in humor: Its appeal to adolescents, Humor: *International Journal of Humor Research* 10 (4)

Osborough, N. (1965) Police discretion not to prosecute students: A British problem *Journal of Criminal Law and Criminology* 56 (2)

Paechter, C. (2004) Power Relations & Staffroom Spaces, *Forum* 46 (1)

Page, D. (2011) From principled dissent to cognitive escape: managerial resistance and the English further education sector, *Journal of Vocational Education and Training* 63 (1)

Palmore, E. (1971) Attitudes toward ageing as shown by humor, *The Gerontologist*, Autumn

Pancewicz, M. (2013) A matter of joke and death, *Tamara: Journal for Critical Organisation Inquiry* 11 (1)

Oxford Dictionary of Modern Quotations (2004) (Oxford University Press: Oxford)

Park, R. (1977) A study of children's riddles using Piaget-derived definitions, *Journal of Genetic Psychology* 130 (1)

Parry, T. (2011) The best put-downs to silence hecklers, *The Mirror*, 15th Oct.

Partington, A. (2007) Irony and reversal of evaluation, *Journal of Pragmatics* 39 (9)

Partington, A. (2011) Phrasal Irony: Its form, function and explanation, *Journal of Pragmatics* 43 (6)

Partington, A. (2011b) "Double speak" at the White House: A corpus-assisted study of bisociation in conversational laughter-talk, *Humor: International Journal of Humor Research* 24 (4)

Partridge, E. (1954) *The Shaggy Dog Story* (Faber & Faber: London)

Pawlowski, A. (2009) You talking to me? Film quotes stir passion, cnn.com

Pease, A. (2005) *The ultimate book of rude and politically incorrect jokes* (Robson: London)

Pepicello, W.J. (1980) Linguistic Strategies in Riddling, *Western Folklore* 39 (1)

Perks, L.G. (2012) The ancient roots of humor theory, *Humor: International Journal of Humor Research* 25 (2)

Perlmutter, D. D. (2002) Incongruities and inconsistencies: The delicate balance, *Humor: International Journal of Humor Research* 15 (2)

Pexman, P.M. & Zvaigzne, M.T. (2004) Does Irony Go Better With Friends, *Metaphor & Symbol* 19 (2)

Phillips, B. (1990) Nicknames and Sex Role Stereotypes, *Sex Roles* 23 (5-6)

Pichler, P. (2006) Multifunctional Teasing as a resource for identity construction in the talk of British Bangladeshi girls, *Journal of Sociolinguistics* 10 (2)

Platow, M.J., Haslam, S.A., Both, A., Chew, I., Cuddon, M., Gohorpey, N., Mauren, J., Rosini, S., Tsekouras, A., & Grace, D. M. (2005) 'It's not funny if *they're* laughing.': Self-categorisation, social influence, and responses to canned laughter, *Journal of Experimental Social Psychology* 41 (5)

Plester, B. A. & Sayers, J. (2007) "Taking the piss": Functions of banter in the I.T. industry, *Humor: International Journal of Humor Research* 20 (2)

Plester, B. (2009) Crossing the line: boundaries of workplace humour and fun, *Employee Relations* 31 (6)

Plester, B. (2009b) Healthy humour: using humour to cope at work, *Kotuitui: New Zealand Journal of Social Sciences* 4 (1)

Pollard, A. (1970) *Satire* (Methuen: London)

Powell, M. (ed.) (2010) *The mammoth book of great British humour* (Constable & Robinson: London)

Powers, T. (2005) Engaging Students With Humor *APS Observer*, Dec.

Prentice, N.M. & Fathman, R.E. (1975) Joking Riddles: A Developmental Index of Children's Humor, *Developmental Psychology* 11 (2)

Provine, R.R. (2000) *Laughter: A scientific investigation* (Faber & Faber: London)

Purkey, W.W. (2006) *Teaching Class Clowns (And What They Can Teach Us)* (Corwin Press: California)

Quinn, B. (2000) The paradox of complaining: Law, humor, and harassment in the everyday work world, *Law and Social Inquiry* 25 (4)

Quirk, S. (2011) Containing the audience: The 'Room' in stand-up comedy, *Participations* 8 (2)

Radcliffe-Brown, A. (1940) On Joking Relationships, *Africa* 13 (3)

Rae, J. (2009) *The Old Boy's Network: A Headmaster's Diary 1970-1986* (Short books: London)

Rahkonen, C. (2000) No laughing matter: The viola joke cycle as musicians' folklore, *Western Folklore* 59 (1)

Rainsford, S. (2000) *School Jokes* (Macmillan: Basingstoke)

Raskin, V. (1985) *Semantic Mechanisms of Humor* (D. Reidel: Dordrecht)

Reade, D. (2007) Office banter has gone beyond a joke, *Personnel Today* 25th Sept.

Redfern, W. (2000) *Puns: More senses than one* (2nd ed.) (Penguin: London)

Rees, G. (2008) *The mammoth book of limericks* (Constable & Robertson: London)

Rees, N. (1980) *Graffiti 2* (Unwin: London)

Renold, E. (2001) Learning the 'Hard' Way: Boys, Hegemonic Masculinity and the Negotiation of Learner Identification in the Primary School, *British Journal of Sociology of Education* 22 (3)

Rhea, D.M. (2007) Seriously funny: A look at humor in televised presidential debates, Unpublished Ph D thesis, University of Missouri-Columbia

Richardsen, A.M., Burke, R.J. & Martinussen, M. (2006) Work and health outcomes among police officers: The mediating role of police cynicism and engagement, *International Journal of Stress Management* 13 (4)

Richman, J. (1977) The foolishness and wisdom of age: Attitudes toward the elderly as reflected in jokes, *The Gerontologist* 17 (3)

Roberts, R.V. (1962) An unrecorded meaning of 'Joke' (or 'Joak') in England, *American Speech* 37 (2)

Robinson, D.T. & Smith-Lovin, L. (2001) Getting a Laugh: Gender, Status, & Humor in Task Discussions, *Social Forces* 80 (1)

Roche, J. (1999) *Comedy writing* (Hodder and Stoughton: London)

Rockwell, P. (2007) Vocal Features of Conversational Sarcasm: A Comparison of Methods, *Journal of Psycholinguistic Research* 36 (5)

Roediger, H.L (1980) The Effectiveness of Four Mnemonics in Ordering Recall, *Journal of Experimental Psychology Human Learning and Memory* 6 (5)

Rogers, B. (2006) *I get by with a little help...: Colleague Support in Schools* (Paul Chapman: London)

Rot, S. (1983) On the philological essence of Shakespeare's humour, *Modern Language Studies* 13 (8)

Roth, G.L. & Vivona, B. (2010) Mirth and murder: Crime scene investigation as a work context for examining humor applications, *Human Resource Development Review* 9 (4)

Roxas, K. (2011) Tales From the Front Line: Teachers' Responses to Somali Bantu Refugee Students, *Urban Education* 46 (3)

Roy, D.F. (1959) 'Banana Time': Job satisfaction and informal interaction, *Human Organization* 18 (4)

Rozin, P. (2006) Documenting and explaining the common AAB pattern in music and humor: Establishing and breaking expectations, *Emotion* 6 (3)

Rubin, D.C. & Wallace, W.T. (1989) Rhyme and Reason: Analyses of Dual Retrieval Cues, *Journal of Experimental Psychology: Learning, Memory and Cognition* 15 (4)

Rudd, A. (2009) George Bush's 50 worst bloopers and top 10 best moments on video, *Mirror News* 14th Jan.

Rutter, J. (1997) Stand-up as Interaction: Performance and Audience in Comedy Venues, Unpublished Ph. D. thesis, University of Salford

Sackett, S.J. (1968) Another cross-fertilization joke, *Western Folklore* 27 (1)

Salinger, J.D. (2010) *The Catcher in the Rye* (Penguin: London)

Sanders, B. (1995) *Sudden glory: Laughter as Subversive History* (Beacon Press: Oxford)

Sanders, T. (2004) Controllable laughter: Managing sex work through humour, *Sociology* 38 (2)

Sanford, S. & Eder, D. (1984) Adolescent humor during peer interaction, *Social Psychology Quarterly* 47 (3)

Saroglou, V. & Anciaux, L. (2004) Liking sick humor: Coping styles and religion as predictors, *Humor: International Journal of Humor Research,* 17(3)

Saroglou, V. & Scariot, C. (2002) Humor Styles Questionnaire: Personality & Educational Correlation in Belgian High School & College Students, *European Journal of Personality* 16 (1)

Savin-Williams, R. (1979) Dominance hierarchies in groups of early adolescents, *Child Development* 50 (4)

Sayre, J. (2001) The Use Of Aberrant Medical Humor By Psychiatric Unit Staff, *Issues in Mental Health Nursing* 22 (7)

Scambler, D.J., Harris, M.J. & Milich, R. (1998) Sticks and Stones: Evaluations of Responses to Childhood Teasing, *Social Development* 7 (2)

Scarfe, G. (2005) *Scarfe: Drawing blood* (Time Warner: London)

Schermer, J.A., Martin, R.A., Martin, N.G. Lynsky, M. & Vernon, P.A. (2013) The general factor of personality and humor styles, *Personality and Individual Differences* 54 (8)

Schnurr, S. & Rose, C. (2008) The 'Dark Side' of Humor. An Analysis of Subversive Humour in workplace Emails, *Lodz Papers in Pragmatics* 4 (1)

Schnurr, S. (2009) Constructing leader identities through teasing at work, *Journal of Pragmatics* 41 (6)

Scott, T. (2007) Expressions of humour by emergency personnel involved in sudden deathwork, *Mortality* 12 (4)

Sellers, R. & Hogg, J. (2011) *Little Ern!* (Sidgwick & Jackson: London)

Sev'er, A & Ungar, S. (1997) No Laughing Matter: Boundaries of Gender-Based Humour in the Classroom, *The Journal of Higher Education* 68 (1)

Sharkey, W.F., Kim, M-S., Diggs, R.C. (2001) Interactional embarrassment: a look at embarrassors' and targets' perspectives, *Personality and Individual Differences* 31 (8)

Shaughnessy, M.F. (1998) An interview with E. Paul Torrance: About creativity, *Educational Psychology Review* 10 (4)

Shaw, P. (2003) *The book of football quotations* (Ebury: London)

Shifman, L. (2009) Assessing global diffusion with web memetics: The spread and evolution of a popular joke, *Journal of the American Society for Information Science and Technology* 60 (12)

Shultz, T.R. (1974) Development of the Appreciation of Riddles, *Child Development* 45 (1)

Shultz, T.R. (1976) A Cognitive-Development Analysis of Humour, In: Chapman, A.J. & Foot, H.C. (eds.) *Humour and Laughter: Theory, Research and Applications* (John Wiley & Sons: London)

Shurcliff, A. (1968) Judged Humor, Arousal, and the Relief Theory, *Journal of Personality and Social Psychology* 8 (4)

Shuster, S. (2007) Sex, aggression, and humour: responses to unicycling, *British Medical Journal* 335 (7633)

Shwarz, N. (1996) *Cognition and Communication: Judgemental biases, research methods and the logic of communication* (Erlbaum: New Jersey)

Silberman-Federman J. (1995) Jewish humor, self-hatred or anti-semitism: The sociology of Hanukkah cards in America, *Journal of Popular Culture* 28 (4)

Simons, E.R. (1986) The NASA Joke Cycle: The Astronauts and the Teacher, *Western Folklore* 45 (4)

Smith, M. (2009) Arbiters of truth at Play: Media April Fools' Day Hoaxes, *Folklore* 120 (3)

Smith, S. (2004) *The dirty girl's book* (Carlton: London)

Smuts, A. (2009) Do moral flaws enhance amusement?, *American Philosophical Quarterly* 46 (2)

Smuts, A. (2010) The Ethics of Humor: Can Your Sense of Humor be Wrong, *Ethical Theory Moral Practice* 13 (3)

Smyth, W. (1986) Challenger jokes and the humor of disaster, *Western Folklore* 45 (4)

Somvadee, C. & Morash, M. (2008) Dynamics of sexual harassment for policewomen working alongside men, *Policing: An International Journal of Police Strategies and Management* 31 (3)

Spalding, H.D. (ed.) (1969) *Encyclopedia of Jewish humor* (Jonathan David: New York)

Speier, H. (1998) Wit and politics: An essay on power and laughter, *American Journal of Sociology* 103 (5)

Spradey, J.P. & Mann, B.J. (1975) *The Cocktail Waitresses: Women's work in a man's world* (Waveland: Long Grove, Il.)

Stark, J. Binsted, K., & Bergen, B. (2005) Disjunctor selection for one-line jokes, In: *Proceedings of INTETAIN* 2005

Steel, M. (2014) Maybe you're right Nigel. There can't be global warming, because isn't it always colder at night?' *The Independent*, 14th Feb.

Steel, M. (2014) There just aren't enough betting shops on Britain's high streets. Shall we start converting cathedrals and A&E departments too? *The Independent*, 28th Mar.

Steiger, S., Formann, A.K., & Burger, C. (2011) Humor styles and their relationship to explicit and implicit self-esteem, *Personality and Individual Differences* 50 (5)

Stein, M.B., Walker, J.R. & Forde, D.R. (1996) Public-speaking fears in a community sample, impact on functioning, and diagnostic classification, *Arch. Gen. Psychiatry* 53 (2)

Stewart, P.A. (2011) The influence of self- and other-deprecatory humor on presidential candidates during the 2008 US election, *Social Science Information* 50 (2)

Stilmann, T. F., Baumeister, R.F. & DeWall, C.N. (2007) What's so funny about not having money? The effects of power on laughter, *Personality and Social Psychology Bulletin* 33 (11)

Stocks, E.L., Lishner, D.A., Waits, B.L. & E.M. Downum (2011) I'm embarrassed for you: The effect of valuing and perspective taking on empathic embarrassment and empathic concern, *Journal of Applied Social Psychology* 41 (1)

Stokes, J. (ed.) (2001)*The little book of after dinner speeches* (Marks & Spencer: London)

Stokker, K. (2001) Quisling humor in Hitler's Norway: Its wartime function & postwar legacy, *Humor: International Journal of Humor Research* 14 (1)

Stromberg, S. & Karlsson, J.C. (2009) Rituals of fun and mischief: the case of the Swedish meatpackers, *Employee Relations* 31 (6)

Sullivan, E. (2000) Gallows humor in social work practice: an issue for supervision and refelexivity, *Practice* 12 (2)

Suls, J.M. (1972) A Two-Stage Model for the Appreciation of Jokes and Cartoons: An Information-Processing Analysis, In: Goldstein, J.H. & McGhee, P.E. (eds.) *The Psychology of Humor* (Academic Press: New York)

Summerfelt, H., Lippman, L., Hyman, I.E. (2010) The Effect of Humor on Memory: Constrained by the Pun, *The Journal of General Psychology* 137 (4)

Sutton-Spence, R. & Napoli, D.J. (2012) Deaf jokes and sign-language humor, *Humor: International Journal of Humor Research,* 25 (3)

Sykes, A.J.M. (1966) Joking relationships in an industrial setting, *American Anthropologist* 68 (1)

Sykes, E. (2005) *If I don't write it nobody else will* (Fourth Estate: London)

Tan, J. (2013) British humour—six years and I still don't get it, *Huffpost Students*, 1st Oct.

Tartakovsky, J. (2009) Pun for the Ages, *The New York* Times 28th March

Tatum, T. (1999) Cruel and unusual PUNishment (LOW humor is better than NO humor) *The English Journal*, 88 (4)

Taylor, L. (1997) Beware! You can overstep the mark when it comes to establishing rapport with an audience, *New Statesman* 11th July

Taylor, P. & Bain, P. (2003) Subterranean Worksick Blues: Humour as Subversion in Two Call Centres, *Organization Studies* 24 (9)

Taylor, S. (2010) Katie Price hurt by Frankie Boyle's 'despicable' joke, *The Week* 10th Dec.

Telushkin, J. (1992) *Jewish humor: What the best Jewish jokes say about the Jews* (William Morris: New York)

Terban, M. (1992) *Funny You Should Ask: How to Make Up Jokes and Riddles with Wordplay* (Clarion Books: New York)

Terrion, J.L. & Ashforth, B.E. (2002) From 'I' to 'We': The role of putdown humor and identity in the development of a temporary group *Human Relations* 55 (1)

Thomas, A.B. & Al-Maskati, H. (2007) I suppose you think that's funny! The role of humour in corporate learning events, *The International Journal of Human Resource Management* 8 (4)

Thomas, C.A. & Esses, V.M. (2004) Individual differences in reactions to sexist humor, *Group Processes and Intergroup Relations* 7 (1)

Thompson, G. & Lordan, M. (1999) A review of creativity principles applied to engineering design, *Proceedings of the Institute of Mechanical Engineers*, 213

Thorne, B., & Luria, Z. (1986) Sexuality and Gender in Children's Daily Worlds, *Social Problems* 33 (3)

Thurston, R.W. (1991) Social dimensions of Stalinist rule: Humor and terror in the USSR, 1935-41, *Journal of Social History* 24 (3)

Tibbals, G (2009) *The book of senior jokes* (Michael O'Mara: London)

Titze, M. (2009) Schadenfreude and April's Fools: The Prerequisites of Malicious Jokes, *Humor and Health Journal* X111 (4)

Townsend, S. (1992) *Adrian Mole From Minor to Major* (Mandarin: London)

Truss, L. (2003) *Eats shoots, and leaves* (Profile: London)

Tsakona, V. (2003) Jab lines in narrative jokes, *Humor: International Journal of Humor Research* 16 (3)

Vallely, P. (2007) There was a man...The great limerick craze of 1907, *The Independent* 8th.Sept.

Van Dijk, W.W., Ouwerkerk, W.W., Wesseling, Y.M., & G.M. van Koningsbruggen (2011) Towards understanding pleasure at the misfortunes of others: The impact of self-evaluation threat on schadenfreude, *Cognition & Emotion* 25 (2)

Van Munching, P. (1997) *How to remember jokes* (Workman: New York)

Vares, T. & Braun, V. (2006) Spreading the word, but what word is that? Viagra and male sexuality in popular culture, *Sexualities* 9 (3)

Veale, T. (2013) Humorous similes, *Humor: International Journal of Humor Research* 26 (1)

Veatch, T.C. (1998) A theory of humor, *Humor: International Journal of Humor Research* 11 (2)

Vine, T. (2010) *The biggest ever Tim Vine joke book* (Random House: London)

Vinocur, J. (1973) Archivist collects dirty jokes, *Montreal Gazette*, 10th July

Virdis, D.F. (2010) Sexuality, Masculinities and Co. in the Limericks from the Victorian Erotic Magazine The Pearl, *Textus* XXIII

Vitevitch, M.S. (1997) The neighborhood characteristics of Malapropism, *Language and Speech* 40 (3)

Voss, L. S. (1997) Teasing, Disputing, and Playing: Cross-gender Interventions and Space Utilization among First and Third Graders, *Gender and Society* 11 (2)

Walker, N.A. (1988) *A very serious thing: Women's humor and American culture* (Univ. of Minnesota: Minnesota)

Walle, A.H. (1976) Getting Picked up without Being Put Down: Jokes and the Bar Rush, *Journal of the Folklore Institute* 13 (2)

Walliams, D. (2012) *Camp David* (Penguin: London)

Walsh, D. (2014) Pride and prejudice, *Sunday Times Magazine*, 2nd Mar.

Wang, J., Iannotti, R.J. & Nansel, T.R. (2009) School Bullying Among Adolescents in the United States: Physical, Verbal, Relational, & Cyber, *Journal of Adolescent Health* 45 (4)

Wanzer, M.B., Frymier, A.B., Wojtaszczyk, A.M., & T.Smith (2006) Appropriate and Inappropriate Uses of Humor by Teachers, *Communication Education* 55 (2)

Wasson, S. (2007) Splurch in the kisser (Wesleyan University Press: Middletown)

Watkins, P. (2002) *The Soul of Wit* (Canterbury Press: Norwich)

Watts, J. (2007) Can't take a joke? Humour as reactive refuge and exclusion in a highly gendered workplace, *Feminism and Psychology* 17 (2)

Wear, D., Aultman, J.M., Zarconi, J. & Varley, J.D. (2009) Derogatory and cynical humour directed towards patients: views of residents and attending doctors, *Medical Education* 43 (1)

Weaver, J.B., Masland, J.L., Kharazmi, S. & D. Zillmann (1985) Effect of alcoholic intoxication on the appreciation of different types of humor, *Journal of Personality and Social Psychology* 49 (3)

Weeks, D. & James, J. (1995) *Eccentrics* (Phoenix: London)

Weinstein, S. (2008) *Shtick Shift: Jewish Humor in the 21st Century* (Barricade: New Jersey)

Wells, R. (1973) Predicting Slips of the Tongue, In: Fromkin, V.A. *Speech Errors As Linguistic Evidence* (Mouton: The Hague)

Wilbur, C. J. (2011) Humor in romantic contexts: Do men participate and women evaluate? *Personality and Social Psychology Bulletin* 37 (7)

Williams, R.A. & Clouse, R.W. (1991) Humor As a Management Technique: Its Impact on School Culture, ERIC Document ED 337866

Willis, P. (1977) *Learning to Labour* (Saxon House: London)

Willis, P. (1984) Elements of a culture, In: Hammersley, M., & Woods, P. (eds.) *Life in School: The Sociology of Pupil Culture* (O.U. Press: Milton Keynes)

Wilkinson, C.E., Ress, C.E. & Knight, L.V. (2007) "From the Heart of My Bottom": Negotiating Humour in Focus Group Discussions, *Qualitative Health Research* 17 (3)

Winner, M. (2012) *Michael Winner's joke book* (Robson: London)

Winterheld, H.A., Simpson, J.A., & Onna, M.M. (2013) It's in the way that you use it: Attachment and the dyadic nature of humor during conflict negotiations in romantic couples, *Personality and Social Psychology Bulletin* 39 (4)

Wiseman, R. (2006) *Quirkology: The curious science of everyday life* (Pan: London)

Withington, R. (1939) Verbal pungencies, *American Speech* 14 (4)

Woods, P. (1975) 'Showing them up' in Secondary School, In: Chanan, G. & Delamont, S. (eds.) *Frontiers of classroom research* (NFER: Windsor)

Woods, P. (1979) *The Divided School* (Routledge & Kegan Paul: London)

Woods, P. (1983) Coping at School through Humour, *British Journal of Sociology of Education* 4 (2)

Woods, P. (1984) Negotiating the demands of schoolwork, In: Hammersley, M. & Woods, P. (eds.) *Life in School: The Sociology of Pupil Culture* (O.U. Press: Milton Keynes)

Woods, P. (1984a) The Meaning of Staffroom Humour, In: Hargreaves P. & Woods, P. (eds.) *Classrooms and Staffrooms: The Sociology of Teachers and Teaching* (O.U. Press: Milton Keynes)

Woods, P. (1990) *Teacher Skills and Strategies* (Falmer: Basingstoke)

Woods, P. (1990a) *The happiest Days: How pupils Cope with School* (Falmer: Basingstoke)

Wooten, D.B. (2006) From Labeling Possessions to Possessing Labels: Ridicule and Socialization among Adolescents, *Journal of Consumer Research* 33 (2)

Worthen, J.B. & Deschamps, J.D. (2008) Humour mediates the facilitative effect of bizarreness in delayed recall, *British Journal of Psychology* 99 (4)

Wragg, E.C. & Wood, E.K. (1984) Teachers' First Encounters With Their Classes, In: E.C. Wragg (ed.) *Classroom Teaching Skills* (Croom Helm: London)

Wright, C. (1993) School processes-an ethnographic study, In: Woods, P. & Hammersley, M. *Gender & Ethnicity in schools: ethnographic accounts* (Routledge London)

Wuster, T. (2006) The professional comedian: Steve Martin and stand-up history, *Studies in American Humor* 3 (14)

Yalisove, D (1978) The effect of riddle structure on children's comprehension of riddles. *Developmental Psychology* 14 (2)

Yang, W. (2002) Communication slips and their sociocultural implications, *Language and Communication* 22

Yang H., Chattopadhyay, A., Zhang, K., Dahl, D.W. (2012) Unconscious creativity: When can unconscious thought outperform conscious thought? *Journal of Consumer Psychology* 22

Yip, J.A. & Martin, R.A. (2006) Sense of humor, emotional intelligence, and social competence, *Journal of Research in Personality* 40 (6)

Yoos, G.E. (1985) The Rhetoric of Cynicism, *Rhetoric Review* 4 (1)

Young, M.M. (1988) Humor and Social Competence in Middle Childhood, Unpublished Ph. D. dissertation. Texas Tech University

Zajdman, A. (1995) Humorous face-threatening acts: Humor as strategy? *Journal of Pragmatics* 23 (3)

Zhukov, K. (2013) Interpersonal interactions in instrument lessons: Teacher/student verbal and non-verbal behaviours, *Psychology of Music* 41 (4)

Zimmer, B. (2010) 'Refudiate' and other accidental coinages, www.visualthesaurus.com

Zipke, M. (2008) Teaching Metalinguistic Awareness and Reading Comprehension with Riddles, *The Reading Teacher* 62 (2)

Ziv, A. (1976) Facilitating Effects of Humor on Creativity, *Journal of Educational Psychology* 68 (3)
Zwicky, A. M. (1980) *Mistakes* (Advocate: Ohio)

The End

Printed in Great Britain
by Amazon